Time Travel
in Popular Media

Time Travel in Popular Media

Essays on Film, Television, Literature and Video Games

Edited by MATTHEW JONES *and*
JOAN ORMROD

McFarland & Company, Inc., Publishers
Jefferson, North Carolina

ISBN 978-0-7864-7807-1 (softcover : acid free paper) ∞
ISBN 978-1-4766-2008-4 (ebook)

LIBRARY OF CONGRESS CATALOGUING-IN-PUBLICATION DATA

BRITISH LIBRARY CATALOGUING DATA ARE AVAILABLE

On the cover: time fantasy illustration © 2015 iStock/Thinkstock

Printed in the United States of America

*McFarland & Company, Inc., Publishers
Box 611, Jefferson, North Carolina 28640
www.mcfarlandpub.com*

To Rich, who toppled the first domino
—*Matthew Jones*

To my mother
—*Joan Ormrod*

Acknowledgments

There are many people who have supported us in this venture. This is a brief thank you to all of them.

Our thanks go to Rob Weiner for his advice during the preparation of the proposal. For their comments on several of the essays, we are grateful to Ewa Mazierska and Felicity Colman. Thanks also to the delegates of the science fiction symposium at the University of Central Lancashire in Preston, United Kingdom, in June 2014. Their comments on the introduction to this collection and their suggestions for Eastern European films were invaluable, especially those of Malgorzata Bugaj and Pawel Frelik. Paul Booth and Gavin MacDonald generously offered their expertise during the compilation of the list of time travel video games that appears in Appendix 4, while Roger Sabin, David Roach and David Huxley similarly offered excellent advice on our list of comics and graphic novels in Appendix 3. Our thanks also goes to the contributors to this collection for their splendid work.

If we have missed anyone, our apologies.

Finally, special thanks to H.G. Wells, without whose novel this collection would have been a very different book.

Table of Contents

Appendices

Preface

MATTHEW JONES *and*
JOAN ORMROD

This collection was conceived over many caffeine-fueled discussions about our mutual love of science fiction and time travel at a Manchester coffee shop. We were teaching a science fiction unit to undergraduate students of film and media at Manchester Metropolitan University, and had both been struck by the lack of a substantial literature on time travel in the media. Surely it could not be so? Time travel is one of the most popular sub-genres in science fiction, but neither of us could identify one book that dealt with it in detail beyond collections on specific texts, such as *Back to the Future* (1985), *Doctor Who* (1963–6, 1989, 1996, 2005–) and *The Terminator* (1984). We gave ourselves a challenge: find the book that deals with time travel in the media and addresses its narrative diversity. Despite several excellent articles in science fiction collections and journals (Penley 1986, Lewis 1976b, Rascaroli 2001, and so forth), sure enough there was no book wholly dedicated to the range of time travel stories that we had encountered in our media consumption. Why might this be so? Might it be because time travel is a topic that cannot be approached from one overarching grand narrative? It sprawls across and bleeds into several other genres—from science fiction to fantasy, romance to comedy, the western to noir. To borrow Mark Bould's description of science fiction as a genre, it is a "shape-shifting thing" (2012, 2). Like science fiction there are no reliable tropes to define it, so a traveler may travel through time by machine or magic, or even by means never explained to the audience. There are also no specific rules for each narrative. Some time travelers can change the timeline, while others are prevented from causing such temporal aberrations by regulators or the laws of physics. Time travel is also a type of narrative that expects much of its audiences for it plays with media form. Consider the narrative acrobatics of *Back to the Future, The Terminator* and, more experimentally, *Primer* (2004), *Inception* (2010) and *La Jetée* (1962). As a result of these multiple, fluid forms that time travel stories can take, both in terms of narratives and media formats, they have excited curiosity and prompted debate since at least the 19th century.

1

In considering these ideas we brainstormed the main categories that we might use to begin the debate on time travel. We eventually identified four key themes: philosophy and theory, culture and history, narrative and media forms, and tropes, narratives and generic cycles. These ideas inform the structure of the book, which is consequently divided into four parts. The excellence and number of essays we received made it very difficult to choose a core of twenty or so, but our aim was never to cover the topic in totality and instead this collection represents us throwing our hat into the academic ring to invite further debate. Indeed, we have consciously tried to avoid some media texts that might be considered classics and which have consequently already been the subject of sustained scrutiny. For instance, there are several collections dealing with *Doctor Who*, so the good Doctor only makes limited appearances between these covers. That being said, he has crept into a few essays (notably Jørgenson's), but is rarely a primary focus. We also found it difficult to ignore the influence of H.G. Wells' seminal novella, *The Time Machine* (1895). In attempting to move away from such productions, our aim was to introduce less well-known or analyzed texts, particularly video games and digital novels, but there remains much for researchers to add later. In addition to tackling texts that are explicitly concerned with journeys through time, we have also incorporated essays that deal with time in more tangential terms, such as *Inception* or *Pleasantville* (1998), which see temporality in relation to issues of memory and virtual reality. We hope that this helps to underline the fluidity and breadth of the time travel concept.

When attempting such a broad approach to the topic, it would be surprising if there were not omissions. This collection is no exception. For instance, comics and graphic novels are not covered in sufficient depth since we received very few essays in these areas, despite the prevalence of time travel in such media. The collection is also Western-centric and does not deal with manga and anime, or with Eastern European, South American, African and Asian texts. In the hope of going some way toward encouraging others to address our omissions, we include appendices listing media texts from some of these regions that might provide a starting point for future debates.

Since we began putting this collection together, David Wittenberg's monograph, *Time Travel: The Popular Philosophy of Narrative* (2013), was published and we are delighted that a start has been made in debating this fascinating area of popular culture. Wittenberg's book shares our own belief that time travel can serve as a type of narrative laboratory, but our approach, which is laid out in this volume's Introduction, is also informed by a Foucauldian reading of time travel as discursively constructed from the very earliest of times. This, we contend, is the reason that there exists such a variety of approaches to the topic, which is reflected in the diversity of the approaches taken by the authors in this collection. The essays that follow demonstrate the range of potential methodologies writers have used in debating time travel. These are drawn from a breadth of disciplines, such as fashion, film history, museum studies, genre studies, mythology, philosophy, and cultural studies. This broad discussion returns us to the notion of the coffee shop as a place of political and cultural debate, and perhaps more collections and books on this topic in the years yet to come.

Introduction
Contexts and Concepts of
Time in the Mass Media

MATTHEW JONES *and*
JOAN ORMROD

A man steps into an ornate machine and is spirited away to adventure in the far future. In another world, an alarm clock rings and yesterday begins again. In a library, a man meets his future wife for the first time, but she has been visited by him since childhood. Time travel has been a popular trope in the mass media since its early days and in recent years these stories have becoming increasingly prominent in films (*About Time* [2013], *X-Men: Days of Future Past* [2014], *Edge of Tomorrow* [2014]), television series (*Doctor Who* [1963– 1989, 1996 and 2005–present], *Lost* [2004–2010]), comics and graphic novels (*The Return of Bruce Wayne* [2010], *Watchmen* [1986]) and video games (*Mortal Kombat* [2011], *Pac-Man: Adventures in Time* [2000], *The Legend of Zelda: Majora's Mask* [2000]). For, the fact is, we are obsessed with the idea of time travel and the possibilities it offers us to venture into the past, to meet iconic figures and amend mistakes, or to travel to the future to discover our place in history.

However, definitions of time travel as it appears in media texts are difficult to pin down. It has been thought of as a genre, a subgenre, a motif and a narrative device (and indeed the authors represented in this volume take contrasting approaches). It shifts between fantasy[1] and science fiction, magic and technology. Iconography and tropes are disparate and even the presence of a time machine is not always necessary. Some of the various means of transportation through time have been compiled in Table 1 (below) and they impact upon our perception of the genre, for time travel can be facilitated by the supernatural, technology or through unexplained phenomena. However, even when a machine is used in time travel, it may still not be classed as science fiction. For instance, the use of the television remote control in *Pleasantville*

(1998) lacks a scientific rationale and leans instead on something akin to magic, which predisposes the film towards the fantasy mode. Furthermore, time travel frequently makes appearances within other generic traditions as disparate as romance (*Somewhere in Time* [1980], *Portrait of Jennie* [1948]), the western (*Back to the Future Part III* [1990]), comedy (*Bill and Ted's Excellent Adventure* [1989], *Les Visiteurs* [1993]) and the musical (the three musical cinematic versions of *A Connecticut Yankee in King Arthur's Court* [1921, 1931 and 1949], *DuBarry Was a Lady* [1943]).

Theme	Type	Catalyst	Examples
Biological	Heredity	Genes	*About Time, The Time Traveler's Wife*
Biological	Mutation	Genes	*X-Men: Days of Future Past*
Biological	Time loop	Alien blood	*Edge of Tomorrow*
Enigmatic	Karma	Poor behavior	*Groundhog Day*
Enigmatic	Love	Mailbox	*The Lake House,*
Enigmatic	Unexplained	Unexplained	*Sliding Doors, Midnight in Paris*
Mind	Meditation	Hypnosis	*Somewhere in Time*
Mind	Memory	Diaries	*The Butterfly Effect*
Mind/ Technology	Memory	Experimental device	*La Jetée*
Natural world	Rip in space-time	Aurora borealis	*The Langoliers*
Natural world	Weather	Storm	*The Final Countdown*
Supernatural	Magic	Dagger/Sands of time	*Prince of Persia: The Sands of Time*
Supernatural	Magic	Spell	*Les Visiteurs, Once Upon a Time*
Supernatural	Music	Magical instrument	*The Legend of Zelda: Ocarina of Time*
Supernatural	Paranormal	Ghosts	*Portrait of Jennie, The Incredible Mr. Blunden, Tom's Midnight Garden*
Technology	Invention	Time machine	*The Time Machine, Command and Conquer: Red Alert*
Technology	Leisure	Hot tub	*Hot Tub Time Machine*
Technology	Media	Television remote	*Pleasantville, Click*
Technology	Telecommunications	Radio	*Frequency*
Technology	Telecommunications	Telephone box	*Doctor Who, Bill and Ted's Excellent Adventure*
Technology	Time loop	Experimental device	*Source Code*
Technology	Transport	Alien time machine	*Doctor Who*
Technology	Transport	Car	*Back to the Future*
Technology	Transport	Sled	*The Time Machine* (1960)
Technology	Transport	Starship	*Star Trek*

(Theme)	*(Type)*	*(Catalyst)*	*(Examples)*
Technology	Transport	Train	*Back to the Future Part 3*
Technology	Virtual reality	Simulated worlds	*Thirteenth Floor*
Technology	Virtual identity	Interface with the computer	*Lucy*

Table 1. Some of the various means of time travel in media texts.

Of course, these problems are not specific to time travel as genre itself is a notoriously fluid concept. Many media products blend genres and, in some cases, texts may be marketed through a particular genre for reasons that have little to do with their content (Altman 1999). Many early films, such as *Metropolis* (1927), were reclassified in both industrial discourses and the public imagination as science fiction when the genre became better established. As David Blanke's essay on the films of Cecil B. DeMille in this volume highlights, this process is ongoing and there remain many media texts that may yet be reclassified as time travel narratives. As such, while time travel is not unique in its ability to slip between and merge with different genre classifications, it is perhaps best for us not to attempt to solidify it through a totalizing definition. Instead, this collection leaves the question open to further investigation and offers multiple perspectives on the issue through its various essays. Each of the authors whose work appears here handles the question of time travel's generic status in a manner that suits their own line of enquiry. Sometimes this is done explicitly, sometimes implicitly. We invite readers to sample the range of approaches that are on offer here in the hope that they shed light on the various means of addressing time travel that are available to media scholars.

Of course, the questions raised by time travel go beyond narrative and genre. The plasticity of time and its relationship with storytelling has proven to be fruitful territory for media producers, but media forms themselves can also be thought of in relation to time travel. We could, for example, ask how the act of turning a page, clicking a mouse, fast forwarding and scrolling back engages a media user with the flow of time. These various means of manipulating texts highlight the specificity of the relationship between different media forms and issues of temporality. So, for instance, Doane (2002) shows how time in early cinema emerged as a symptom of modernity and Stewart (2002) deconstructs changes in the ways temporality is represented in analogue and digital cinematic time.

Apart from Matthew Freeman's essay, which deals with the transmedia storytelling in *Planet of the Apes* franchise, comics do not feature in this collection.[2] However, developed in parallel with cinema, comics used similar editing devices to articulate time, including montage, flashbacks and cuts (Eisner

2008; McCloud 1994). Despite this, each of these media expresses time differently; cinema relies on the illusions of movement and duration produced through the display of 24 frames per second (although even this seemingly rigid rule of the cinematic apparatus' temporality is malleable), whereas in comics time is expressed in the juxtaposition of panels and through the braiding of themes through the page and meta panel (Groensteen 2007; McCloud 1994; Eisner 2008). The arrival of recording and digital technology transformed television's relationship to time, as noted by Sky in their promotion of the Skybox S12 with the invitation to "Turn your television into a time machine." Video games, too, manipulate time, enabling their audiences to relive and replay a narrative until they achieve perfection, much like the protagonist in *Groundhog Day* (1993). In this sense, both the gamer and the game develop different but equally complex relationships to time—a phenomenon noted in several of the contributions to this volume. Media forms are thus interlaced with issues of the representation and experience of time, but each format gives voice to these concerns in different ways.

With this dual focus on media texts and forms in mind, our aim in producing this collection is to prompt wide-ranging debate on a topic that, despite its popularity, has garnered little sustained research and academic comment. There have been edited collections devoted to individual franchises, such as *Doctor Who* (Lewis and Smithka 2010; Butler 2007; Hansen 2010; Layton 2012; Decker 2013; Newman 2005), *Back to the Future* (Cooke 1999; Ní Fhlainn 2010; Shail and Stoate 2010), *La Jetée* (Harbord 2009) and *The Terminator* (French 1996). There have also been occasional chapters or sections devoted to time travel in edited collections (Redmond 2004; Rickman 2004; Kuhn 1990; Lewis 1976) and chapters in monographs (Schneider 2009; Penley 1991; Sobchack 1987). Much of this existing literature revolves around a relatively narrow range of concerns, such as the narrative paradoxes of time travel (Rickman 2004; Rascaroli 2001; Penley 2004; Lewis 1976), feminism (Grosz 2005), connections between the time traveler's present crisis and the resolution of the journey (Gordon 2004; Penley 2004), the traveler as tourist (Bignell 2004) and the carnivalesque (Dimitrakaki 2002). However, the only work to address the full breadth of time travel as a cross-media phenomenon in a sustained manner is Wittenberg's *Time Travel: The Popular Philosophy of Narrative* (2013).

Wittenberg argues that time travel narratives are a response to epistemic shifts in scientific thought and can be divided into three phases. The first phase (1880 to 1905) is organized through Darwinian evolutionary discourses and Isaac Newton's notion of the mechanical universe. This is a period in which it is believed that Grand Narratives can explain the meaning of life and writers respond through their predictions of possible utopian futures. The second phase (1920s to 1950s) is influenced by Einstein's theory of relativity, which aligned space with time. It sees the development of more complexity in time travel and the embracement of temporal phenomena such as paradoxes, time loops and varying notions of causality. The third phase (1950s to present) is affected by quantum physics, string theory and notions of the multiverse. It features the "ongoing *visualization* of parallel and multiplied lines of narrative" (82). Developments in this phase include the use of time travel as a framing device for future histories (*Cloud Atlas* [2012]), existential/ethical themes (*Primer* [2004]), repetitious time (*Triangle* [2009], *Last Year in Marienbad* [1961], *Save the Date* [2013]), nostalgia (*Back to the Future* [1984], *Virtual Nightmare* [2000]), subplots (*Lost* [2004–2010]) and parody (*Red Dwarf* [1988–1999, 2009 and 2012–present] and *Futurama* [1999–2003 and 2008–2013]).

While we broadly agree with Wittenberg's framework, our intention is to extend and develop the analysis of time travel in a few new directions. Two of these are perhaps particularly worth highlighting here. First, Wittenberg supposes that time travel can only be explored through narrative but, as the essays in this collection show, time travel can also be fruitfully analyzed through other analytical frameworks. Booth, Furby and Remesal, for example, demonstrate that ludology is an especially pertinent concept for understanding time in video games and new media. Second, while Wittenberg's history of time travel begins in 1880, we would argue that it could also be traced back much further than this. The following section takes up this issue and offers what might be termed a prehistory of time travel, identifying its precursors in antiquity and describing the ways it emerged through changing cultural practices of spectatorship, time and technology. In doing so, we seek to explore how time travel narratives appeared in different national and regional cultures and their relationship to these contexts. This introduction then concludes by tracing the themes and tropes identified within this discursive analysis of time and time travel in the essays of this collection, where they are developed further.

Precursors of Time Travel: Re-creation, Re-enactment, Dislodgement and Projection

Many authors writing about the cultural and religious aspects of time draw a distinction between cyclical time in ancient and rural cultures and linear time. Cyclical notions of time, as described by Eliade (1971), are expressed though the rituals of religion and their relationship to myth. For Eliade, rituals serve not only as a means of recreating, invoking or performing religious or mythic time, but also of transporting participants back to the sacred time. For example, in Catholic doctrine, the bread and wine used in the sacrament of the Eucharist are not simply representations of the body and blood of Jesus, but become, through transubstantiation, his *actual* body and blood. Such rituals allow time to be imagined as circuitous and looping, bringing people back to sacred times through the rituals of the present.

Of course, there other ways in which time can be understood and Rayment-Pickard (2002), for example, has identified four different types of time in biblical discourse: catastrophic, apocalyptic, kairic and prophetic. Catastrophic time refers to the ways in which time affects the body through age, decay and the destructive end of time (42). Apocalyptic time is a time of waiting for the moment of revelation (65). Kairic time is the concept "of history as a series of moments each potentially complete in itself" (87). Kairic time enables us to make sense of history through iconic moments—the death of a particular figure, a battle, an epoch—and is significant in drama from the Renaissance onwards, as noted below. Prophetic time is spent "questing for higher goals, greater achievements, new discoveries" (110) and is consequently aspirational, often seeing a hero attempting to mold time to create, rather than wait for, the future. Rayment-Pickard's ideas, while rooted in a Christian tradition of temporality, mark a starting point for our own analysis of the development of time travel in oral storytelling, rural cultures and modern mass media. They sit alongside notions of ritual and cyclical time as indicators of complex notions of temporality at play prior to the formal emergence of time travel literature, which is often dated to the publication of H. G. Wells' *The Time Machine* in 1895. As such, it is perhaps unsurprising that time travel texts tend to slip between fantasy and science fiction, since elements of these mythic and religious understandings of time underpinned the development of this narrative tradition and recur in many modern stories.

If time travel as a narrative device is often seen as an invention of the late 19th century, but is prefigured by a long history of temporal play in storytelling, it is perhaps useful at this stage to offer a suggestion of the different ways in which people represented their experience of time from antiquity to the end of the Classical period through folklore, myth and performance. This can be broken down into four categories: re-creation, re-enactment, dislodgement and projection. The first two, re-creation and re-enactment, can be considered as forms of repetitive time, based as they are on the notion of resurrecting past moments in the present. However, the former is predicated upon myth and the latter on secular representations and contexts. Re-creation, which we have encountered above in cyclical time, brings the present into the past through ritual, while re-enactment returns the past to the present through dramatization. Projection, on the other hand, offers a line of sight through time, for example where a prophecy, an auger or an oracle foretells the future or elucidates a problem of the past. Prophecy offered one means of discussing the future in biblical and Medieval times, but it has also been accused of preventing the development of other ways of reflecting on the future that were to emerge in the late 17th century (Alkon 1987). These three concepts are often constructed through religious and spiritual discourses, but perhaps much more familiar in modern storytelling is dislodgement, where an individual steps outside of time, where two different time zones coexist, or where an individual moves into a different time state from the rest of the narrative world. This is certainly evident in contemporary popular culture, for example in films where virtual reality allows the user to experience one time zone through technology that simultaneously signals their presence in another. However, dislodgement is not exclusively a modern phenomenon and also has a long history that can be traced via the depiction of limbo and Heaven as places where time runs differently than it does on Earth.

Re-enactment has been particularly significant in the development of time travel stories due to its reliance on narrative, which brings tales of and from the past into the present through its two key traditions, oral storytelling/folktales and drama. While both narrative forms thus often represent a journey into the past for their audiences, many fairytales and legends of the oral storytelling tradition also present time as a fluid concept. This is commonly seen through an encounter with the supernatural that results in characters becoming dislodged in time. Thus Sleeping Beauty experiences 100 years of slumber, while the monk listening to the song of a magical bird and the traveler foolish enough to accompany the fairies under the hill might be there for one hour and emerge 100 years later. This fluid construction of time in folklore is not confined to the West. In Japanese folklore of the eighth century, a fisherman travels to the palace of the Dragon God beneath the sea and returns to find centuries have elapsed. Such disparities of time also appear in religious texts in the Hindu and Islamic traditions. In these tales the dream or altered state is a significant element in a character's ability to manipulate time. For instance, in the *Mahabharata*, King Revaita meets the creator in Heaven and, upon his return, discovers many ages have passed. Muhammad ascends into Heaven and Jerusalem on his *Buraq*[3] and returns on the same night. The development of theatrical retellings of religious stories enabled a different type of experience of earlier times, in which the re-creation of the sacred gave way to the re-enactment of kairic time. Consequently, the concept of individual historic moments became significant. The Renaissance saw performances of certain events in classical or recent history, such as Julius Caesar's assassination or, in Britain, the Wars of the Roses. These re-enactments, which represented a form of drama and often propaganda, enabled audiences to connect the political and cultural concerns of the present with the past.

Re-enactment prefigures the ideological functions of time travel in contemporary narratives for, as suggested above, sedimented traces of precursive practices in culture and storytelling influence contemporary time travel narratives. Indeed, all four types of antique time can be seen in time travel media texts. Re-creation has been discussed at length in relation to films such as *Twelve Monkeys* (1995), *La Jetée* (1962) and *Groundhog Day*. In these films the time loop, which sees a specific period of time repeating over and over again, functions to re-create cyclical time and the mythic moment of creation and devastation. Time travel stories have also shown a clear tendency towards re-enactment through the (often deliberately inaccurate) reconstruction of historical moments on film. For example, *Doctor Who* has seen the Doctor visiting the siege of Troy ("The Myth Makers" [1965]) and the destruction of Pompeii ("The Fires of Pompeii" [2008]), while *Bill and Ted's Excellent Adventure* sees the titular time travelers meeting Billy the Kid, Socrates and Sigmund Freud, among others. These productions serve to make historical moments available to the time travelers, but also to re-create them for their audiences. While projection is evident in its traditional form through prophecy in many recent media texts, such as *Minority Report* (2002), it is also perhaps one way of understanding flashbacks, which have been used in cinema since at least D. W. Griffith's *Intolerance* in 1916. As noted above, dislodgement is particularly common in modern time travel texts, since transporting characters between different eras is itself essentially an act of dislodgement, but it is also evident in time loop films such as *Source Code, Edge of Tomorrow* and *Groundhog Day*. As such, time travel is a narrative trope that can trace its roots much further back than Wells' *The Time Machine* and which draws on storytelling traditions from antiquity, biblical discourse, rituals and myth.

Time, Space and Knowledge from the 16th Century to the Modern Age

While contemporary time travel media texts clearly draw on historical conceptualizations of temporality, they also make use of narrative tropes and discourses of modernity that first emerged in earlier eras. Alkon (1987) documents a wide range of literatures from the late 17th century, beginning with

Jacques Guttin's *Epigone: Histoire du Siècle Futur* (1659), that tell stories of times yet to come. Félix Bodin's *Le Roman de l'Avenir* (1834), Samuel Maddon's *Memoirs of the Twentieth Century* (1733), Louis Sébastien Mercier's *The Year 2440* (1770) and Mary Shelley's *The Last Man* (1826) all projected ideas about what the future might hold. While this in itself does not necessarily constitute time travel, Mercier's novel does see people and diplomatic papers transported between time zones, though this is not the key concern of the book. In some senses these texts belong to a prehistory of time travel literature, toying with the same ideas but not yet realizing them fully.

Alkon suggests that these proto-science fiction texts are the product of a time when the technologies and philosophies that would lead to science fiction, and hence time travel as it most commonly appears today, had not yet emerged. This was to come in the late 19th century, when technology, travel and shifting ideas about the nature of work encouraged people in industrialized societies to conceive of time as a segmented, measured phenomenon. Jameson (2002) has suggested that notions of cyclical time based on ritual and myth diminished to some extent after the Enlightenment, when they were undermined by the more mundane rigors of timetables, schedules and factory shifts. As such, time was instead imagined as being compartmentalized, or divided into a series of discrete segments (seconds, minutes, hours and so forth) that are experienced in a linear manner. Clocks and accurate time devices were developed, as was the notion of a fixed spatial point (Greenwich) in the late 18th century as the basis for measuring time. Railway timetables demanded that disparate communities conformed to a national timetable, doing away with the slight variations that had previously existed in local records of the time of day. Urbanization and the requisite decline of seasonal, agricultural employment necessitated a demarcation between work time and private time. These shifts produced an image of time as a segmented, fixed and linear phenomenon.

In turn, this change produced new modes of spectatorship that would prove crucial to the development of time travel texts in later years. In tandem with the rise of the concept of work time, leisure or free time emerged in the late 18th century as a space in which one was free to follow one's interests, improve oneself and, in some cases, travel or go on holiday. From the mid–18th century, rich folk traveled on the Grand Tour to become more educated, while the democratization of travel developed during the 19th century, when middle- and working-class people visited spas or foreign destinations (Inglis 2000). This was facilitated by better transport systems and the founding of companies like Thomas Cook in 1871, which organized trips to foreign and exotic destinations. Historical sites such as Pompeii and Knossos were excavated and tourists were able to step back into the past lives of cultures thought long dead. Meanwhile, when back at home in the cities and urban environments of Western Europe, some people were able to use leisure time to watch the world go by. In Paris, this led to the development of the concept of the *flâneur*, an individual, usually male, who could observe the life of the city's inhabitants but who was himself simply one of the crowd and, consequently, all but invisible.

With these notions of passive spectatorship, tourism and rapid development in place, the conditions were ripe for the emergence of time travel literature, which often proposed the traveler as one who used new technologies to take trips to and witness other societies in the far future or the past. As tourists in places of historical significance (be they sites of our own history or of imagined societies that are yet to come), time travelers are points of confluence in these emerging discourses. In this sense, it is possible to think of H. G. Wells' nameless wanderer as the arch *flâneur*. While the historical precursors of modern time travel narratives can be found among ancient rituals, myths and modes of storytelling, these discourses of temporality were shaped into the modern concept of time travel amid the changing perceptions of time produced through the processes of industrialization that characterized the 19th century. The next section shows how the themes discussed above, along with scientific philosophy and technological advances, were brought together to produce the narrative fascinations of time travel in 20th- and 21st-century media texts.

Modernity, Spectatorship, Science

As these new perspectives on temporality, spectatorship and modernity took hold and conceptualizations of time based on myth and ritual declined, time travel stories began to emerge that marked a shift away from magic and towards technology as the means of temporal transportation. At the end of the 19th century, Dickens' *A Christmas Carol* (1843) and Mark Twain's *A Connecticut Yankee in the Court of King Arthur* (1889) both relied on the supernatural to facilitate their journeys through time, but there were also contemporary texts, such as Edward Page Mitchell's "The Clock that Went Backward" (1881), that preferred to locate time travel within a technological sphere. This short story is one of the earliest examples of time travel's move towards science fiction and away from fantasy, but it was virtually ignored on its initial release and remains little-known today. However, by way of contrast, Edward Bellamy's *Looking Backward: 2000–1887* (1888) was a publishing phenomenon that became the third bestselling novel of the year.

As noted above, time travel narratives are now most widely thought to have come of age with H. G. Wells' *The Time Machine*, which was published fourteen years after Mitchell's story. Wells' novel not only established the technological time machine as the defining element of time travel science fiction, but it also borrowed from and critiqued the technological, entertainment and spectatorship discourses of the late 19th century discussed above. *The Time Machine* bore the influences of early cinematic discourse through cinemacity, the Victorian tendency "to conceptualize and represent the world in terms of moving photographic images that culminated in the [Lumière Brothers'] *cinématographe* apparatus in 1893" (Williams 2009, 347). From the mid–19th-century, technology enabled the development of different types of entertainment, such as projector shows, traveling fairs, early forms of cinema and dioramas. The diorama, among other proto-cinematic devices, was of great significance to the development of time travel narratives, for it set in place a new type of spectatorship, which in turn drew on those popularized through emergent forms of tourism, based on the mediation of perception in what Friedberg describes as a "mobilized virtual gaze" (1993, 2). For Friedberg, "the virtual gaze is not a direct perception but a received perception mediated through representation ... a gaze that travels in an imaginary *flânerie* through an image elsewhere and an image elsewhen" (Friedberg 1993, 2–3). The virtual mobilized gaze was shared by both cinema and the time machine, which emerged within two years of each other.

Cinema's manipulation of time and the gaze through techniques such as flashbacks and jump cuts signals to some writers its similarity to a time machine (Coates 1987; Rascaroli 2001). While this connection is tantalizing in relation to George Pal's adaptation of Wells' book to film in 1960, the novel itself displays a fascination with the same Victorian concepts of spectatorship that connect cinema, travel and the *flâneur*. The *flâneur,* as noted above, looks but does not act. The cosmopolitan visits places as a tourist, but does not ultimately have any emotional engagement with the indigenes they meet. Similarly, the time traveler frequently does not engage with the indigenes, not from disinterest, but out of necessity. The grandfather paradox, proposed in *Le Voyageur Imprudent* (Barjavel 1943) and discussed in a number of the essays in this collection, notably Nikk Effingham's, is a popular means of justifying and sometimes critiquing a protagonist's disengagement with the societies visited in time travel texts. It asks what would happen if a traveler to the past were to accidentally kill their own grandfather, causing the protagonist never to have been born and, therefore, the grandfather to still be alive, which in turn would result in the birth of the protagonist who would go on to slay his relative once again in a never-ending and nonsensical loop. As such, issues of regulation enter into time travel discourse and are present in franchises such as *Back to the Future*, leading to a situation where the travelers are often forced into a situation akin to that of the *flâneur* or the cosmopolitan tourist, who are unwilling to engage with the environments they pass through. As such, Wells' protagonist hero observes, ponders and theorizes the division of the human race into the brutish Morlocks and the dispassionate Eloi, but does little to challenge the exploitative social structure of this future world, embedded as he is within a time travel story that displays the hallmarks of the Victorian understanding of spectatorship, travel, visuality, technology and time.

The Collection

The brief explanation of the development of time travel fiction presented above is, of course, only one way in which one might understand such texts, and the essays of this collection trace their own approaches through a range of theoretical and empirical traditions. As such, we intend that this volume serves not as a definitive guide to the genre (or sub-genre, motif or trope) but as a starting point for debates about the issues it raises. We have only been able to sketch some general outlines of the key areas of discussion, but the essays in this collection expand upon much of this material in more detail. They have consequently been grouped thematically. The first group focuses on philosophical and theoretical approaches to time travel, the second on its place in different national and historical contexts, the third on its relationship to media formats and narrative, and the fourth on its key tropes and their relationship to the generic cycles in which time travel has played a significant role. These parts are followed by a number of detailed case studies of significant time travel media texts. Finally, the appendices include a range of material that, we hope, will prove useful to readers who are interested in following up on the ideas encountered here through further research.

The parts into which this collection has been divided indicate some of the key themes that emerge in the essays that follow, but this is by no means definitive. There are other themes interwoven throughout the collection that equally deserve to be highlighted as potential strands for further investigation. For example, notions of play and ludic time appear in several of the essays, notably in Paul Booth's analysis of the video game *Eternal Darkness: Sanity's Requiem* (2002), Charles Burnetts' exploration of the virtual spaces of *Inception* (2010), Jacqueline Furby's concept of "play time," and Victor Navarro-Remesal and Shaila García-Catalán's examination of the time loop as a space free from consequences. These essays frame time as a rule that governs our existence, but highlight how the malleability of time within various narratives and media formats opens up new ways of playing.

As suggested above, cinema has been closely associated with time travel through its apparatus and narrative play. It is worth noting the highly influential philosophical ideas of Gilles Deleuze on cinema. Deleuze discusses cinema's representation of time as time-movement (1983) and time-image (1985). Broadly, Deleuze argues that time in cinema prior to World War II is driven by causation in the actions of the characters, with one action leading to another. He describes this as time-movement. After World War II, Deleuze argues that images in cinema became infused with time and narrative became concerned with temporal experimentation, especially in art house films such as *Last Year in Marienbad*. This crude explanation is developed in much more depth later in this collection in essays by David Deamer, Michael Starr, Matthew Kimberley and Jason N. Dittmer. For instance, in his analysis of Sokurov's *Russian Ark* (2002), Deamer explores how cinematic time is "a radical confrontation with our understanding of temporality" and our understanding of the past, present and future using Deleuze's idea on the time-image.

The relationship between media form and time is taken up by several contributors, such as Matthew Freeman, who analyzes *Planet of the Apes* as a franchise whose looping and leaping in time is mirrored by its own ability to cross between different media formats. Pete Falconer, too, is interested in media form and locates the American West as a space that, through its generic traditions, cinema has imagined as a temporal, rather than simply a geographical, phenomenon. Giacomo Boitani also turns his attention to genre in his discussion of Italian comedy cinema and its interaction with time travel, while David Blanke points towards silent cinema, and specifically the films of Cecil B. DeMille, as an area in which time travel is evident, but which has often been ignored. As such, these essays underline that different media forms and their genres are integral components of a text's relationship to time.

Alongside these themes, a number of time travel's key tropes and motifs also emerge in this collection. For example, Dolly Jørgensen, Elissa Nelson, Charles Burnetts, and Travis L. Martin and Owen R. Horton draw attention to the prominent place occupied by memory, nostalgia and dreams in stories about time travel. Jørgensen is also concerned with the ways in which museums operate within such texts, an idea that reappears in Byard's essay. Notions of cyclical time and the time loop are the focus of Navarro-Remesal and García-Catalán's essay, but also recur in Freeman's, while Starr observes the existence of a constellation of texts that all feature H. G. Wells as a fictionalized character. As such, while the essays of this collection have been grouped by theme, there are numerous other strands of connective tissue that link them together and which suggest potential frameworks through which time travel can be understood. There also remains much scope for further research into this neglected popular cultural narrative, notably in relation to comics, and the national traditions found in Eastern Europe, Latin America, Asia and Scandanavia.

Notes

1. Our concept of the fantastic is informed by Todorov's definition: "In a world which is indeed our world ... a world without devils, sylphides, or vampires, there occurs an event which cannot be explained by the laws of this same familiar world. The person who experiences the event must opt for one of two possible solutions: either he is a victim of an illusion of the senses ... and the laws of the world then remain what they are; or else the event has indeed taken place, it is an integral part of reality—but then this reality is controlled by laws unknown to us... The fantastic occupies the duration of this uncertainty. For once we choose one answer or the other, we leave the fantastic for a neighboring genre, the uncanny or the marvelous. The fantastic is that hesitation experienced by a person who knows only the laws of nature, confronting an apparently supernatural event" (1973, 25).

2. To address this we list some texts that might be of interest to scholars who wish to research or explore the rich diversity of comics, manga and graphic novels dealing with time travel in Appendix 3.

3. A horse.

Philosophy and Theory

Contemporary Philosophy

Nikk Effingham

Time travel has seen some discussion within analytic philosophy; this essay surveys some of that debate. The first section discusses whether or not time travel is logically possible; the second section discusses further issues arising from considerations of time travel.

Physics, Philosophy and Logical Impossibility

It is important to distinguish two types of possibility: logical possibility and physical possibility. Physically possible situations are those permitted by the laws of nature: it is physically possible for me to walk up the stairs, but not walk to the moon; it is physically possible to travel faster than the speed of sound, but not faster than the speed of light; it is physically possible (though unlikely) for a planet made of gold to exist, but not a planet made of uranium (as it'd explode). Logical possibility outstrips this, comprising all situations that are consistent with the laws of logic: it is logically possible that I walk to the moon, travel faster than 300,000 kms⁻¹, or have a planet made of uranium. None of those things is inconsistent—they do not engender a contradiction. Only contradictory things, like there being round squares or the square root of 4 being 6, are logically impossible. This distinction is important for while both philosophers and physicists are interested in the possibility of time travel, philosophers tend to focus on the logical possibility of time travel, leaving its physical possibility to the physicists.

You might wonder whether philosophers have a legitimate role to play: why should we care about the logical possibility of things, rather than just focus on what is physically possible? One reason is that if it's logically impossible—that traveling in time is on a par with making the square root of 4 equal 6—then it will not be physically possible either. So, just as no scientist need conduct an experiment to see if there are round squares, the scientific community would not have to entertain physical theories that permit time travel if time travel were logically impossible.

The Grandfather Paradox

One reason, much discussed in the philosophical literature, for why time travel is logically impossible is the Grandfather Paradox (with examples and variations of it replete in film and literature). The argument proceeds as follows:

(1) If time travel was possible I could go back in time and kill my own grandfather before my father was conceived.

(2) If I killed my own grandfather (before my father is conceived), a contradiction would result.

(3) If a contradiction could come about given the possibility of time travel, time travel is impossible.

(1), (2) and (3) entail that time travel is impossible, so those philosophers who believe time travel is possible must deny one of them. Before examining the details of such denials, first examine the *prima facie* case for each one.

(1) seems straightforward enough to motivate. In 1930, before the conception of my father, my paternal grandfather—call him "Pappy"—was alive. If time travel was possible and we could travel back to a million BC, or a thousand BC, or AD 1500 etc., what's to stop me traveling to 1929? And once there, what's to stop me using my high-powered sniper rifle from the 21st century to shoot Pappy dead? (Who knows why I would do such a thing, of course!)[1] It seems that I can kill Pappy in 1929, which would mean he will not be alive in 1930. So (1) seems defensible.

The defense of (2) is also straightforward. In the thought experiment, Pappy is alive in 1930, i.e., the following proposition is true:

In 1930, Pappy is alive.

If I go back in time and shoot Pappy dead in 1929, the following proposition must then be true:

It's not the case that in 1930, Pappy is alive.

Often expositions of the Grandfather Paradox argue that if my grandfather were dead I would no longer be born in order to go back in time and kill him, therefore I could not be there to shoot him so he should be alive, but if he lives then I would be born and go back in time and shoot him (and so on *ad infinitum*). But the crux of the paradox is far simpler than this convoluted regress: if both of the above propositions were true, we would have a contradiction. Just as it cannot be the case that, at any given time, an object is both a square and not a square, or 2 + 2 both equals 4 and does not equal 4, it is a contradiction—a *logical* impossibility—that it's the case and it's not the case that in 1930 Pappy is dead. Thus (2) seems defensible as well.

Finally, consider (3). Little defense of this premise is needed. An assumption leading to contradiction is almost universally taken to be a reason to think the assumption is false. For instance, in mathematics we might assume the truth of some principle (e.g., $0 \div 0 = 1$), demonstrate some contradiction results (e.g., that $2 = 1)^2$ and use this to conclude that the assumed principle is false. (This line of reasoning is called "reductio ad absurdum.") Or imagine a murder case wherein the accused argues that his line of defense—e.g., that he was at home when the murder happened—is not false even though it has been proven that some contradictory fact is the case—e.g., that he was definitely present at the scene of the crime. Only a deranged juror would think this was a sensible line of argument!

So that is the *prima facie* motivation of the Grandfather Paradox. Obviously, more can be said against the above premises (otherwise this would be a very short chapter!), to which we turn to in the following sub-sections.

The Ludovician Response to the Grandfather Paradox

Name a famous philosopher and I'm sure you'll find Nietzsche, Aristotle, or Plato bandied about. In current professional philosophical circles you'll hear an extra name: David Lewis. Working on just about every area (from philosophy of religion to philosophy of language, from metaphysics to logic) his influence on contemporary analytic philosophy has been undeniably extensive. When it comes to time travel it is his "Ludovician" response to the grandfather paradox that is often brought to bear (the same line of response was also developed by Paul Horwich, although it is usually Lewis's exposition that is focused on).[3]

The Ludovician response comes in two parts. The first part is to deny that (1) is true. Imagine a blacksmith. The blacksmith can take a block of iron and smelt it into a certain shape. The blacksmith can make the iron into a cube—that's possible. The blacksmith can make the iron into a sphere—that's possible. But the blacksmith cannot make it into a spherical cube—that's (obviously!) impossible. Lewis thinks time travel is a bit like this. I can shoot a man dead with a high-powered sniper rifle—that's possible. I can go back in time and meet Pappy—that's possible. But that does not mean I can go back in time, meet Pappy, and shoot him dead with a high-powered sniper rifle—that's impossible! Lewis thinks we are confused when we believe (1) is true, just as someone would be confused if they thought blacksmiths could shape impossible objects like those from the works of Escher.

But what, then, would happen if I went back in time to shoot my grandfather? What would *explain* my failure to be able to shoot him with a high-powered sniper rifle? Why can I have a cup of tea with him, but not murder him? The Ludovician says something would stop me. The possibilities are endless: in a case of mistaken identity I shoot someone who looks like Pappy instead; my gun jams; I meet the girl of my dreams seconds before the attempted assassination and give up on killing poor Pappy; I die of a heart attack just before firing; I, while aiming, slip on a banana peel that causes me to miss, etc. In the literature, these options for what event might intercede in my assassination attempt are called "banana peels" (as a nod to the last example) even if they involve strokes, mistaken identity, or the girl of my dreams rather than the skin of a piece of fruit. (The idea that we cannot change the past, and always end up with logically consistent situations, has been explored in many media representations, e.g., Bradbury's "A Sound of Thunder" [1952], Moorcocks' *Behold the Man* [1969], various episodes of *Quantum Leap* [1989–93] and *Star Trek* [1966–present]—at least when the plot finds it convenient!—and Terry Gilliam's *Twelve Monkeys* [1995].)

You might think it's strange that banana peels always get in the way. Is it not weird, you might think, that such things always crop up? Is there some force of nature—or some collection of individuals, like a cosmic protection agency—that act to prevent paradoxes coming about and keeping time travelers in line? Is it not simply true that I *can* shoot dead Pappy with my high-powered rifle? It certainly seems it!

The second part of the Ludovician theory, then, is to explain away this problem—and explain the apparent correctness of saying that you can shoot Pappy—by paying careful attention to our "modal language" (i.e., to sentences concerning what is, or is not, possible). Lewis points out that modal sentences are context-dependent, and whether they are true or false does not depend just on what words make up the sentence, but also the context they are to be evaluated in. That the evaluation of sentences is context dependent is clear enough. For instance, in one context it might be true to say "Jim is tall" if, say, Jim is 5'10" and trying to get on a roller coaster ride with a minimum height of 5'7" (for he is, after all, tall *enough*), but that same sentence—that same concatenation of words—is false if we are picking tall people to play in a basketball team and Jim is surrounded by men 6'2" and taller. The sentence "Jim is tall" means different things, and varies over whether it is true or false, in different contexts. Lewis thinks the same thinking applies to modal sentences. For instance, the sentence "I could not communicate with Spaniards in their native tongue" will be true or false in different contexts. In one context it is true for I *cannot* speak Spanish and, if I was in Spain right now, I would be unable to communicate in their native tongue. But in another context, it is false. If we are looking for someone to undergo intensive training and learn Spanish, and the candidates are me and an ape, then it's true to say I *could* communicate in Spanish—the ape, on the other hand, clearly could not. Clearly different contexts lead to us evaluating the truth of modal sentences differently. Lewis cashes this out thus: to say X is possible (or impossible) is to say X is consistent (or inconsistent) with certain facts, where the facts in question are determined by context. So to determine whether "I could not communicate with Spaniards in their native tongue" is true or not, we try and figure out whether the proposition

I am talking Spanish with native Spaniards

is consistent with certain other facts. In the first context, those facts are, e.g., "I lack the ability to speak Spanish right now" and "I am talking to the Spaniards right now." Clearly those two things are incompatible with the above proposition. In the second context, we are to instead ask whether the proposition is consistent with facts like, e.g., "I have a year to learn Spanish," "I will receive intensive training in Spanish during that year," "The point at which I am talking Spanish with native Spaniards is a year from now," etc. And those things *are* consistent.

Lewis then turns his attention to sentences like "I could kill Pappy with my high-powered sniper rifle." That sentence is true or false depending upon what context we are in. If I did not travel in time, it would be true—there is no (non-moral) problem with me killing my grandfather in that situation. If I travel in time, it becomes trickier. In one context it's true—my shooting the man I aim the gun at (who happens to be Pappy) is consistent with the wind conditions, consistent with my aim, consistent with the aerodynamics of bullets and the facts about what fast moving lead does to soft tissue and vital organs. In that context—considering *those* facts—I *could* kill Pappy and the sentence is true. However, in another context I cannot, for in another context—a context where we recognize that the man before me is my grandfather before my father's conception—my shooting of Pappy is not consistent with *that* fact. These facts about context dependence explain why we so readily believe we could, even in time travel scenarios, shoot Pappy (you can! in a certain context!), even though you cannot shoot Pappy (you cannot! in a certain other context!).

Or here is another way of thinking about it: *something* will stop the blacksmith making the spherical cube—no matter how hard he tries to shape it, it just will not work! But is there anything mysterious or weird about his inability to do this? Should we posit a mysterious force of nature that affects blocks of iron and blacksmiths? Or posit some mysterious agency of people who intervene to stop all blacksmiths from making round cubes? Certainly not! Rather, the sentence "The blacksmith could make the iron into a cube" is true in some contexts—say the context we are in *before* the blacksmith has shaped the metal into a sphere. But when the blacksmith has shaped it into a sphere we are now in a different context, and when we ask whether it could be shaped into a cube the context we are in means we have to assume that one of the facts that the iron being a cube is to be consistent with is that it is, in fact, a sphere—and it clearly is not consistent with that! So, in that second context, it is false to say it could be a cube. That is, the context you are in makes it that the sentence expresses something closer to "The blacksmith can make the iron into a cube *given he shaped it into the shape of a sphere.*" And that is clearly contradictory! Similarly, then, that I can kill Pappy is true, but that I can kill Pappy *given he is my grandfather and we are at a point in time before my father's conception* is false. (And there is nothing special about me, either—during 1930 it was true of *anyone* that they could kill Pappy, but false of *everyone* that they could kill Pappy given that Nikk Effingham would be born in 1979, Pappy was my paternal grandfather, and my father had not yet been conceived. We do not need time travelers for the latter sentence to be false!) So it is true and it is false that I can kill Pappy; but this is not a contradiction once we see that those statements are uttered in different contexts. Compare: it's not a contradiction to say "All the beer is in the fridge" having come home from the supermarket and put the beer in the fridge, even though I recognize that not *all* the beer— not every can and bottle from anywhere in the world—is now inside my fridge. There is no contradiction as the true sentences "All the beer is in the fridge" and "All the beer is not in the fridge" are from different contexts.

Ludovicians and Changing the Past

So Lewis thinks that time travel is possible, although he also thinks there are limits on what can be done: if X is the case in the past, then you can never bring it about that X is not the case. Does that mean the Ludovician says that we cannot *change* the past? It depends what you mean by "change." If X was the case in the past, you cannot change it so that X is no longer the case; but that, says Lewis, is different from banning a time traveler from *causally affecting* the past. I can, for instance, go back in time and shoot some random person in 10,000 BC with no fear of paradox—it is just that such a person will not be an ancestor of mine or, indeed, anyone else for it was *always* the case that I went back and shot them. This is not a case of *changing* the past—it is not that, at one point, the man was alive in 10,000 BC and lived a full and happy life, never once laying eyes on a rabid rifle wielding time traveler, but that, after I use my time machine, it is now the case that he dies instead at my hands, with no full and happy life. No: if Lewis is right, it was *always* the case that, in 10,000 BC, I turned up and shot him. I causally interact in the past, and in one sense change it (for I changed a live man to being a dead man), but in another sense of changing the past (of making what once was no longer ever having been) I cannot.

We can sharpen the difference by introducing some (very basic) symbols. Use letters ("A," "B," "C" etc.) to represent arbitrary propositions (e.g., using "A" to stand for "Pappy is alive"). To say a proposition is true at a given time, t, use the prefix "At t": (so to say Pappy was alive in 1930 we would write "At 1930: A," which is itself a—larger, more complex—proposition). To say some proposition is not the case stick a "~" before it. So, to say that a proposition is true at a time we say:

(4) At t: A

At a later time, t^*, A is false (e.g., in 2014 when Pappy has died):

(5) At t^*: ~A

When Lewis says that we can change the past he means it in the innocuous sense that we can make it the case that

(6) [At t: A] and [At t^*: ~A]

We can do things like that quite regardless of time travel! But no-one—not even God—can, if at some time (4) is true, do the impossible and make it the case that

(7) ~ At t: A

That is to say that no-one can bring it about that

(8) [At t: A] and [~ At t: A]

Notice the difference between (6) and (8)—the latter, but not the former, is contradictory.

The Multiverse Theory

Whatever the merits of this Ludovician approach, not everyone is convinced. Some people think that time travel can, and should, permit us to, e.g., go back in time and kill Pappy. (Certainly lots of time travel stories involve such events!) So, as an alternative to the Ludovician view, we may deny a different premise of the Paradox, e.g.:

(2) If I killed my own grandfather (before my father is conceived), a contradiction would result.

Such philosophers deny that a logical contradiction arises from killing Pappy. One example of a theory denying (2) is the "multiverse theory" according to which time travel takes me to another universe.[4] That universe has exactly the same past as the one I left, up until the point that I arrive at (at which point I kill Pappy, and history diverges from how it originally was). In the initial universe, Pappy remains alive and well: he never gets visited by a murderer in 1929, he conceives my father (who conceives me, etc.) and in 2014 I step into a time machine, intent on murdering Pappy, and ... vanish. It is in the other universe where the macabre grand patricide takes place. In that universe, Pappy is shot by me back in 1929, my father does not exist and I am never born (although I do not vanish from existence—while, as I will never be born, my younger self never exists in that universe, my time traveling self from the other universe still "hangs around" after Pappy's death presumably trying to avoid the police of the early 20th century). Now there is no contradiction (and [2] is false) for in the same way that a proposition can be true in one place and not another (for instance, "It is raining" can be true in one place and not another) "Pappy is alive in 1930" is now true in one universe (the one I left) and not in the other (the one I arrive at). Contradiction averted! (Stephen Baxter's *The Time Ships* [1995] utilizes just such a theory, as does David Gerrold's *The Man Who Folded Himself* [1973]; and films explicitly buying into this understanding include Richard Kelly's *Donnie Darko* [2001] and Shane Carruth's *Primer* [2004]—it also features in *Back to the Future Part II* [1989] and the *Star Trek* series, although sometimes this theory is conveniently ignored as the plot demands.)

This theory gets a lot of backing from philosophy's equivalent of scripture: contemporary science. David Deutsch (1991) has argued that quantum mechanics demands that exactly this story should be told about time travel, and that a Ludovician style tale is in conflict with various scientific principles (Deutsch and Lockwood 1994; although see Sider 1997). As a discussion of this errs more on the territory of science than that of vanilla philosophy, I will set aside the details (although it bears noting that Deutsch's interpretation of the laws of physics are readily contestable).

Qua philosophy, the multiverse theory is not without problems. It has been argued, for instance, that the upshot of this theory is that were any extended object to try and travel through time, it'd be "chopped up" into an infinite number of slices.[5] The details of that argument are lengthy, so I neglect them in favor of a more popularized problem: the doppelgänger objection.[6] The fear is that I do not genuinely go back in time, and instead only get the chance to kill Pappy's doppelgänger. If correct, the "past" I arrive at is more like a brilliantly staged mock-up of the past—exactly the same in every way, such that I'd never notice the difference. Nevertheless it is *not* the past, and it not really being the past makes a difference! If I was hell-bent on seeking revenge on my grandfather, I will not be sated if I, say, killed his identical twin. Killing someone *a lot like* Pappy just does not cut it—I want Pappy himself! So the objection goes, this is the situation time travelers end up in.

So the multiverse theorist needs some sort of response to this doppelgänger problem. One response is to think of time travel as being a lot like a "fission case." A fission case is where an object "splits" into two, for example when an amoeba divides. When this happens, which of the resulting cells is identical to the original amoeba? Both? Neither? One but not the other? We can also imagine a fission scenario involving people where a woman steps into a duplicate-making machine and two versions of her step out, or where a man somehow divides—amoeba-like—into two. If the woman who stepped into the machine (or the pre-fissioning man) was the one you sought vengeance on, who should you kill on the way out? While there is a lot of room for saying otherwise, many philosophers think that it's correct to say that they are *both* the person who stepped in (and both the person who existed pre-fissioning).[7] If that's right, then killing either of them will suffice for vengeance! Similarly, we can say that universes fission at the point at which a time traveler arrives. When my time machine takes me to 1930, the entire universe—and all of its contents—fission into two, leaving me in one of those universes with a fissioned version of Pappy—a version who will satisfy my death lust just as much as the one I left behind...

Variations on the Multiverse Theory

An alternative solution is to drop multiverses in favor of "hypertimes."[8] For instance, we might think that, just as there are three dimensions of space, there are two dimensions of time—our ordinary dimension of time and a "hypertemporal" dimension. For every moment of time that elapses, a moment of hypertime elapses as well e.g., if 15 billion years of time have elapsed since the start of the universe, 15 billion years of hypertime have elapsed. Imagine that, in 2014, no-one has time traveled before and I return to 1930; time "rolls back" to 1930 but hypertime keeps on going. Think of it in terms of clocks, where we have two clocks—one measuring what time it is and one measuring what hypertime it is. Imagine I travel at one minute past midnight on New Year's Day 2014 to the early hours of a day in March 1930. The clocks would progress thus:

Clock One (Measures time)	Clock Two (Measures hypertime)
2359, 31 December 2013	2359, 31 December 2013
0000, 31 December 2013	0000, 31 December 2013
0500, 8 March 1930	0001, 1 January 2014
0501, 8 March 1930	0002, 1 January 2014
0502, 8 March 1930	0003, 1 January 2014
...	...

Similarly, if I waited from 1930 to 2014 all over again (and became a very old man!) I could go back in time to 1930 again. In that case the hypertemporal year would be 2098 but the year would be 1930 (for the third time).

You might prefer this theory because it better serves to solve the doppelgänger objection for, in the same way that Pappy at one time is the same person as Pappy at another time (and there is no mystery about that, even if very different things are true of Pappy at those different times), Pappy at one hypertime will be the same person as Pappy at another hypertime (and there is no mystery about that, even if very different things are true of them at those different hypertimes e.g., being alive at one and dead at another).

This theory is also like the multiverse theory in that (2) is false. Just as it is unproblematic having a proposition like "Bob is alive" being true at one time and not another, you can have a proposition of the form "At some time *t*: A" be true at one hypertime but false at another hypertime. So I can go back in time and kill Pappy by making it the case that at one hypertime it is true that in 1930 Pappy is alive, but at a later hypertime it is true that in 1930 he is dead. There are, though, some differences and this theory leaves open some frightening possibilities. Imagine a cosmic terrorist deploys a time traveling device that forever travels back in time one second with the instruction to send itself back in time again: now hypertime will keep on rolling, but every time the terrorist's device goes back in time, time rolls back with it! We will, forever in hypertime, be caught in the same looping second, with the future never playing out in front of us. Scary stuff. But the resolution as to why (2) is false is substantially the same: they introduce some extra element—either a universe or a hypertime—and hold that the allegedly contradictory events play out according to different elements (either in different universes or at different hypertimes).

Once we note that similarity, we might imagine that different elements could play a similar role; that is, we could relativize temporal events to something other than hypertimes or universes. One suggestion has been to use *time itself* as such an element. This gets a little tricky (and the daunted may wish to skip this subsection) but if we go slowly it should make sense. The multiverse theorist says of Pappy's being dead and alive:

(9) [At universe α it's the case that in 1930 Pappy is alive] and [At universe β it's not the case that in 1930 Pappy is alive]

The hypertemporal theorist says:

(10) [At the hypertemporal year 1930, it is the case that in 1930 Pappy is alive] and [At the hypertemporal year 2014 it is not the case that in 1930 Pappy is alive]

More generically, saying something of the following form avoids a contradiction:

(11) [At element X, it is the case that in 1930 Pappy is alive] and [At element Y it is not the case that in 1930 Pappy is alive]

Jack Meiland (1974) proposes a theory in which the elements are simply "times" (Goff [2010] argues likewise). So in 1930, and all of the years leading up to 2014 (at which point I hop into the time machine and go back and kill him), it is the case that, in 1930, Pappy is alive. But when, in 2014, I travel back, I make it the case that from 2014 onwards, Pappy is *not* alive back in 1930. So it follows that we get a proposition of a form like (11):

(12) [In 1930 it is the case that in 1930 Pappy is alive] and [In 2014 it is not the case that in 1930 Pappy is alive]

Such a theory seems attractive for two reasons: first, we can again get around the doppelgänger objection in exactly the same way as the hypertemporal theory; second, we can do so without postulating weird notions like hypertime (or, indeed, postulating lots and lots of universes!). But here is a major problem for this theory: what is true of a time is no longer *always* true of it. Many will baulk at this—while facts about things might change over time (e.g., facts about me might change, such as my going from thin to fat, or short to tall) *facts about what the past is like* should not change like this! If Pappy was alive in 1930, the thinking is that this will be true *even later on*; the past is not like me—it never changes. Call this the Principle of Eternal Past Truth.

It is not inconceivable to see how we might deny this Principle. Peter Geach, in a work disconnected from time travel and instead on the philosophy of religion, argued exactly that.[9] Imagine I am in a car, careering towards the edge of a cliff. I bash the brakes and they do not work, before I hit upon leaping out of the vehicle. Hurling myself out of the door, I save myself from death. As I brush myself off I say "I was going to die right up until the point that I realized I could dive out of the door." Geach says this is clearly a true statement, but taken literally it shows that what is true of a time changes. Take three moments in time: t_1 is when I am jabbing at the brakes; t_2 is when I realize I need to leap out of the vehicle instead; t_3 is the time at which I am brushing myself off, and is also a time I would be dead at had I still been in the vehicle when it went over the cliff. I seem to say that something is true at t_1—me being dead at t_3—that is not then true at t_2. That is, I assert

(13) [At t_1 it is the case that at t_3 I am dead] and [At t_2 it is not the case that at t_3 I am dead]

I leave it to you to think whether or not this Geachian objection to the Principle of Eternal Past Truth is a good one or not—most philosophers, I dare say, will say "not."

Dialetheitic Time Travel

We have covered two broad families of theories concerning time travel: the Ludovician theories that deny (1), and the theories that deny (2) by "relativizing" truth to different "elements" (either universes, hypertimes, or times). But we might think there is a way to deny the final premise of the Paradox:

(3) If a contradiction could come about given the possibility of time travel, time travel is impossible.

It has rarely been suggested in the philosophical literature on time travel that this could be false (although presumably every film that opts neither for a Ludovician explanation nor a multiverse explanation of time travel is depicting exactly that![10]). It is an interesting omission, for in other areas of philosophy it *is* the case that a premise like (3) is denied; in those cases the truth of a contradiction is not taken to necessarily indicate that something has gone wrong—it just turns out there are some true contradictions! Such philosophers are called dialetheists (as true contradictions are known as "dialetheia").[11]

Dialetheism is meant to be attractive because it's the upshot of various problematic, paradoxical situations, the most famous of which is the *Liar Paradox*. Consider:

(14) This sentence is false.

Is (14) true or false? If it's true, then—as it says it is false—it must be false. If it is false, then the sentence—which says that it is false—must be true. So it is both true and false—a dialetheia! Thus, says the dialetheist, we can see that there are at least *some* true contradictions. Before returning to time travel, note two things. First, the dialetheist does not think just any old sentences can be contradictory (for instance, returning to the defense of (3) given all the way back at the start, they do not think mathematics is now bust, and dialetheists can serve on a jury just like anyone else). They have developed complex theories to deal with the presence of contradictions—theories that are meant to avoid the madness of thinking any old sentence might be contradictory. Secondly, there are alternative responses to the Liar Paradox—dialetheism is one option among many (for instance, we might say [14] is meaningless, or [14] is neither true nor false, or that [14] is a contradiction and so, like all contradictions, is false—indeed, more options besides these exist). I do not mean to suggest that dialetheism is uncontentious—the truth is that it is far from being popular, even among philosophers. But it might be that it turns out to be true, so it's worth considering.

If dialetheism were true, then we might think that Pappy being both dead and alive is just one example of a dialetheia. It is not clear to me what would be wrong with such a claim if we were to buy into there being dialetheia elsewhere. You might care little for this theory—perhaps you find it too bizarre or, perhaps, too uninteresting (after all, if it were true, there'd be little of interest to be said about the Grandfather Paradox). But there is one thing to be said in defense of considering it seriously: we said at the top that the philosophy of time travel was important even if it only considered the logical possibility of time travel rather than its physical possibility. But now we see that this might not be true, for if we thought this dialetheitic version of time travel was plausible and coherent—a "live option" as it were—then even if the scientist was convinced that the Ludovicians and the multiverse theorists (etc.) were wrong, it would still be worth pursuing theories that permitted time travel. After all, if it turned out to be possible, we would have an empirical proof of dialetheism.

Beyond Possibility

A lot of ink has been spilt concerning whether time travel is logically possible, but there are more interesting issues besides. This last section briefly looks at some.

PROBABILITY

Even if time travel is *possible* that still leaves awkward questions concerning how *probable* it is. Imagine two situations. In one I do not have a time machine and am trying to complete a particularly difficult crossword puzzle, such that I have only a 20 percent chance of success. In the second, the situation is the same except I *do* have a time machine and so, every now and again, my time traveling future self turns up to help me out with the crossword. Presumably this means my chance of completing the crossword in the second sit-uation increases above 20 percent—but by how much? Or imagine that some-one goes back in time to kill their grandfather: how likely is it that they'll slip on a banana peel versus having a stroke? Does it end up becoming likely that we just do not discover time travel in the first place (as in Paul Levinson's short story "The Chronology Protection Case" [1995])? And, if it does, is the best explanation for why we do not discover time travel in the first place—the biggest and best banana peel of all—that the entire human race is wiped out before such a discovery is made? These questions still need a prolonged treat-ment and, as the last one indicates, even if time machines have not been invented yet, the answers to these questions might be of vital and immediate interest to us.

TIME MACHINES

Just because time travel is possible does not mean that every mode of time travel is also possible. We might imagine a time machine to be a lot like a TARDIS, where we turn it on and it magically teleports to another point in time and space. But what if a time machine was more like the vehicle from H.G. Wells's famous story (1895)? When it travels in time, it does not travel in space but stays exactly where it is—were you to witness it then you'd see in front of you a time machine piloted by a man acting in reverse as he traveled into the past (as in Watson's "The Very Slow Time Machine" [1978]). But, the philosophical worry is, if this is true, then as soon as it started time trav-eling would not it collide with its past self?[12] (Or consider Silverberg's *The Masks of Time* [1968] where matter traveling back in time acts like anti-matter—a scientifically plausible view—so strikes itself and immediately anni-hilates.) So even if the possibility of time travel is settled, the exact methods of time travel that are logically possible remain open for debate.

Conclusion

Films, TV, comics, etc., which feature time travel have generally focused on the possibility of time travel (and weird scenarios involving causal loops, etc.). Correspondingly, as we've seen, contemporary analytic philosophy has been dominated by discussion of those issues (is time travel possible? how do we resolve the Grandfather paradox? etc.). Time travel's possibility (or impos-sibility) is of interest to more than a niche of philosophers and the ramifica-tions, if it were possible, are noteworthy.

Notes

1. For discussion of why one might want to do such a thing see Smith (2005).

2. If $2 \times 0 = 1 \times 0$, then $2 \times (0 \div 0) = 1 \times (0 \div 0)$. Given $0 \div 0 = 1$, $2 \times 1 = 1 \times 1$, which it to say $2 = 1$.

3. See Horwich 1975 and Lewis 1976. For a general survey of the work of David Lewis, see Weatherson 2009.

4. See Abbruzzesse 2001, Deutsch 1991, and Deutsch and Lockwood 1994.

5. See Effingham 2012.

6. See Hewett 1994 and Richmond 2003, 303–4.

7. For an introduction to these issues, see Noonan 2005.

8. See van Inwagen 2010, with a similar theory from Goddu 2003 (see also Goff 2010, although he believes he does not require hypertime to make his theory work). Responses, including variations on these schemes whereby hypertime works differently, include Forrest 2010 and Hudson & Wasserman 2010.

9. See Geach 1977 and Todd 2011, where they discuss the—fairly closely related—problem in philosophy of religion of divine foreknowledge (see Zagzebski 2011 for more on that). Nor is this the only crossover between the philosophy of religion and time travel. Explicit connection is made with the Trinity (Leftow 2004, Effingham MS).

10. Consider *Back to the Future* (1985) where Marty McFly starts to fade from existence (similar things happen in *Looper* [2012], Gregory Hoblit's *Frequency* [2000] and *Austin Powers in Goldmember* [2002], among others), or Christopher Smith's *Triangle* (2009). In these films, time definitely changes (so Ludovicianism is false) but the changes do not seem to merely take place in some alternate universe where the time traveler can continue on unabashed concerning the changes they've made to the timeline. All seem to involve internal, inconsistent, narratives. Anecdotally it's worth mentioning that many analytic philosophers find this inconsistency to be an aesthetic flaw (I, however, am not one of them!).

11. For an introduction to dialetheism see Priest and Berto 2013.

12. See Le Poidevin 2005 for more on this problem.

Time Travel and Temporal Paradox

Deleuze, the Time-Image and Russian Ark

David Deamer

Never present but always yet to come and already passed (Deleuze 2004: 116).

Time and Temporal Paradox

Alexander Sokurov's *Russian Ark / Russkiy Kovcheg* (2002) has everything to excite an aficionado of time travel movies: a spectacular temporal enfolding; a vast array of characters, fictional, fictionalized and real; strange situations and baroque settings, both historical and imaginary; ravishing beauty and permeating unease; mystery and revelation; self-reflexivity, intertextuality, and an inventive filmic process at once spontaneous and rigorous. An unnamed 21st-century Russian filmmaker—(Sokurov himself?)—arrives in the past from our present. Hooking-up with a fellow traveler in time, the 19th-century French aristocrat Marquis de Custine, together they wander the St. Petersburg's Hermitage—Winter Palace of the Czars, grand museum of Mother Russia. Leaping this-way and that-way in time, the Unnamed and the Marquis encounter a cascade of moments spanning some 300 years of Russian history: the founding St. Petersburg; the (renamed) city under threat of destruction during the Second World War; Nicholas II, Anastasia and family on the morning of revolution. *Russian Ark* abounds in many such cinematic pleasures. Yet the film not only celebrates the possibilities of time travel in the movies; it also disrupts the genre through an ungrounding.

The general principle of time travel concerns an immediate encounter

with temporal paradox. No longer is time merely chronological: a past begetting the present begetting a future. No longer is time simply homogenous:
a chain of presents—the present a now preceded by a now that has passed,
to be superseded by a now to come. Rather, the present interfolds with
pasts and futures; pasts and futures interfold with the present. A traveler
jumps from one time to another (from a present to the past or the future;
from the past or the future to a present) disturbing homogenous chronological
time with non-chronological relations, generating temporal paradox. In
this way, the as-it-was or yet-to-come are reconfigured or revealed, in turn
transforming the as-it-is. Time travel, in other words, creates or averts a
temporal crisis—sometimes even averting the very crisis it created. Thus the
tendency of the narration: to mend time, put time back together as it was or
reconstitute it as it should be. To re-impose order upon the chaos that has
arisen.

Yet *Russian Ark* neither creates nor averts a crisis. The travelers are witnesses, seers—sometimes of a relative past, sometimes of a relative future.
They do not intervene and what they witness will not transform their relative
presents. We encounter here a fascinating reversal. *Russian Ark* does not disturb
chronological time with non-chronological relations. The film rather considers
time as fundamentally non-chronological. Temporal paradox is not introduced
into the narration through time travel, but is exposed as being the condition
of time. An always there; and being so, irresolvable. Chronological time is a
ruse, mere appearance, a chimera.

Thus the intention of this chapter, to explore the time travel narration
of *Russian Ark* as exemplar of, and thereby argue for, such a non-chronological
image of temporality. To do so the film-philosophy of Gilles Deleuze will
prove essential. Deleuze invents what he calls time-images, cinematic concepts
that can be used to encounter the narration of a film and discover the co-
ordinates of non-chronological temporal relations. Such an engagement with
Russian Ark through Deleuze will require, by way of explication, an unearthing
of the philosophy and film theories that inspire and can elucidate this time-
image: Henri Bergson and his philosophy of matter and memory; theories of
cinema from Jean Mitry, André Bazin and Brian Henderson. What will be
discovered in *Russian Ark* is not only an honoring of the time travel genre,
but a simultaneous ungrounding of the discipline by way of the visual and
sound elements composing the images. *Russian Ark*, after such a Deleuzian
adventure, will be revealed as a radical confrontation with our understanding
of temporality, not only as we live it in the present, but also of how we
encounter history and the future.

Deleuze After Bergson: Matter and Memory, Movement and Time

Gilles Deleuze wrote two books of film-philosophy: *Cinema 1* (1983) and *Cinema 2* (1985). These books draw upon critical moments of film history to crystallize two different cinematic conceptual frameworks. *Cinema 1* describes movement-images. The movement-image expresses cinematic creations concerned with depicting a determined and determinate world—a world corresponding to common-sense mappings of space and time, a rational mise-en-scène providing the co-ordinates of a milieu which characters will traverse. No matter if the movie is populated with ugh-ughing cave people, wise-mouth gangsters and whores or a silent alien horde; no matter if set in the contemporary scene, the historic moment or some future state; no matter if the tone is comedic or tragic—what we see is a cinema organized around bodies which can perceive and are affected by the world, which react to and transform the world.

Deleuze's movement-image is inspired by a reading of Henri Bergson's *Matter and Memory* (1896). For Bergson the body and its brain (which are the same thing) operate within a sensory-motor process: the world as an encompasser of the body, the body as a moment within the world. First—the body perceives the world external to it (seeing, hearing, touch and so on). Second—the body is affected by its perceptions, is crisscrossed with internal intensities (biological, chemical, physical) redistributing affects throughout the body. Third—the body reacts, converts affect into externalized actions that occur in the world. Thus the images (as Bergson describes matter) of the sensory-motor trajectory: perception → affect → action. Matter interacts. Images of the external world give movement to the body; and the body gives back movement to external images. Crucial to this formula is affect, the internal intensities of the body at the center (the matter, or image, between perception and action). Organic images—such as humans—have complex nervous systems: accordingly, external perceptions generate internal intensities which traverse the body in a multitude of ways, giving rise to any number of different possible actions. The body is thus selective; it selects an actual action from virtual infinity. Correspondingly, the body is bombarded by boundless perceptions at every moment, yet only selects what interests it. The body is selective in that it actualizes perceptions from virtual infinity. In other words, the sensory-motor process is grounded in memory—conscious or unconscious, or rather some enfolding of the latter into the former. Bergson names this memory a memory-image: an image of habitual recognition and an image of habitual response. Thus the organic sensory-motor process in full: memory-image [perception → affect → action].

Deleuze's movement-image follows Bergson's sensory-motor process—and is decomposed into perception-images, affection-images, action-images and mental-images. Perception-images describe the matter of the world and create the matter of the body in respect to them. Images of a subjective human perceiving objective images of the universe. Affection-images are expressions of internal intensities upon this body at the center. Images of the face: faces expressing wonder; faces expressing emotion. Action-images capture the body giving movement back to the world: the body fighting or fucking, the body transforming the world. Mental-images interfold with affection-images—a perception generates an affect triggering a flashback-memory (then affects and action); (perception and affect lie dormant) and a dream-image prophesizes that which must be enacted. In this way narration is created from linking movement-images. A character as a center of the film sees the world, feels, remembers and imagines, then acts. For Deleuze every movement-image film is composed of such moments: these images are edited together and create the logical and rational flow of the film. Such moments are temporal in that they are chronological: see → feel → act. While mental-images may appear to disrupt chronological movement (a flashback to the past, an imagining of the future), they rather bring past and future into the present. Mental-images enfold with affects, they are images actualizing memories and imaginations in the present, constituting a strengthening of the co-ordinates of chronological time: a past present caused the present of the now which in turn will cause the future present to arrive.

Are all films movement-images? Not according to Deleuze. There is another kind of cinema, a cinema that not only resists linking perception-images, affection-images, mental-images and action-images in logical, rational and chronological sequence, but also ungrounds their very constitution. *Cinema 2* describes such time-images, which are—once again—inspired by Bergson. For Bergson, the body and its brain may operate within a sensory-motor process and be grounded upon memory-images, yet there is another kind of memory, a more fundamental process: pure, spontaneous thought. This is the anarchic flow of thought, disruptive of, yet captured in habitual recognition (which says this thing is the same as that thing) and habitual reactions (which says that thing requires this same act). Pure memory is not a memory-image, although it is generative of such. It is rather the virtual, the not-actual. It is potential, in the sense of increases and decreases in neuronal activity, a relation of forces. This spontaneous memory may (or may not) become actualized, become memory-images and then affects resonating with perceptions and actions. The body, for Bergson, is thus not ultimately determined by, nor determinate of, the external world: the human is not at the center of the universe but with the universe; and if the body and its brain is a center, it is a center of indetermination. This is freedom. Indeterminacy as a freedom from the bounds of sensory-motor determinacy: pure memory ↔ memory-image (perception → affect → action).

Deleuze's time-image is conceived as a cinematic echoing of Bergson's pure memory. Time-images depict an undetermined and indeterminate world—a world resisting the common-sense mappings of space and time; a disruptive mise-en-scène destroying the co-ordinates of any given milieu and problematizing the formation of characters. Broken, blank and banal landscapes are populated by people who are seers. They wander as witnesses, they disappear, they never existed, they fragment—appear as ciphers, shadows, whispers. Pasts, presents and futures intermix, remain undefined, undergo repetitions. Comedy is tragedy; tragedy is comedy. This is a cinema where bodies are not perceived as a purely subjective presence in relation to a purely objective world. This is a cinema where affects and memories are incongruous, absent or uncertain; where acts are stymied, where transforming the world becomes a question mark. Filmmakers create what Deleuze calls pure optical and sound situations, crystal-images where the actual moments on screen do not flow from one image to another, but are instead like a hall of mirrors, actual images giving on to the virtual. The time-image in this way creates the opportunity of thought for the spectator. The film is not only seen (as with movement-images), but must undergo interpretation. For Deleuze, the time-image echoes Bergsonian pure memory: spontaneous, inchoate, riven with forgettings, resonances. At the heart of this is a reconceived temporality, time-image narration, non-chronological time. No longer is time a linking of homogenous moments of the now (a past now, a present now, a future now), but past, present and future fracture, each has its own multitudinous qualities. Different parallel presents coexist with each other; moments of the past interweave in patterns effacing cause and effect; the future is empty, null, void, radically unforeseeable. Deleuze calls these temporal organizations chronosigns: peaks of the present, sheets of the past and powers of the false. And these "three time-images," writes Deleuze, "interpenetrate" and thus "shatter the empirical continuation of time" (Deleuze 2001, 155).

From Narration and Time to Time Travel Narration

Can it be said this film is a movement-image; that film is a time-image? Absolutely. However, for Bergson the sensory-motor process and pure memory interweave—neither exists without the other. It is thus better to say all films are composed of movement-images and time-images: all films are composed of perception-, affection-, mental-, and action-images which link actual image to actual image effacing virtual relations; and all films are decomposed through peaks of the present, sheets of the past, and powers of the false which reveal virtual relations. Yet, any film is dominated by either movement-images or time-images. There are at least three aspects to this domination. First—in one sense time-images are fundamental, coming before (the virtual or actualized) movement-images. If time-images are chaotic, dispersive, perplexing, it is the movement-image function of cinema that will cut and link, select and organize (edit) these moments, give them a determined situation and a central character who can see, feel, think, and act. However, second—time-images come after movement-images (are invented in the wake of movement-images). Time-images are a radical response to films that believe in a governed milieu, that people can understand and know the world, others, themselves, and that the chaos of the universe can be tamed and resolved. Making and discovering time-images takes an act of will that ungrounds the movement-image function which wants to assert itself at every moment: the time-image is both fundamental and difficult to reconstitute. Finally—such befores and afters are nominal: movement-image and time-image films occur in cinema history in parallel. Accordingly—"there is no value-judgment here," writes Deleuze, both movement-images and time-images can shape "masterpieces to which no hierarchy of value applies" (Deleuze 2002, x). All that can be said is that movement-images and time-images conceive narration differently.

The essential difference is between their conceptions of temporality: chronological time and non-chronological time. Chronological time allows the organic structures of the movement-image to triumph: determined milieus, characters as centers, the revealing of truths, acts resolving situations. The time-image will unground such co-ordinates through non-chronological temporal organizations.

The time travel genre—as a discipline of narrative exploitation—can thus be seen as an explicit surfacing of the temporal philosophy underpinning movement-image and time-image narration. Time travel films confront chronological time and non-chronological relations. The domination of one over the other—in the way in which the film plays out—constitutes a self-reflexivity: the triumph of movement-images over time-images; or alternatively, the ungrounding of movement-images by time-images. The triumph of movement-images is a reconstituting of order from chaos, putting time back together as it was or remaking it as it should be. More often than not, of course, it is just such a function that triumphs: *Cinema Demands Re-established Order!* *Russian Ark* is thus the rarest of rare things, a time-image time travel movie.

A film that ungrounds movement-images, posits chronological time as a fragile surface, a deception, phantasm. As will be seen, Sokurov achieves this through a re-evaluation of cinematic techniques that create an interweaving of the diverse qualities of the non-chronological present, past and future as—what Deleuze has called—peaks of the present, sheets of the past and powers of the false. Accordingly, the film can be explored from the perspective of each of these chronosigns through film theories—articulated here by Jean Mitry, André Bazin and Brian Henderson—describing the function of the camera (and framing), the shot (and mise-en-scène) and editing (or montage-collage); theories which allow collaborations with and are extended by Deleuze's Bergsonian film-philosophy.

Peaks of the Present

Peaks of the present describe parallel moments of the present. These moments are "never a succession of passing presents," writes Deleuze, "but a simultaneity" (Deleuze 2001, 101). The time-image, in this way, captures different dimensions of presentness, all of which are conceivable and all together impossible. It is this that makes "time frightening and inexplicable" (Deleuze 2001, 101). How do these different presents occur? One formation would be where "narration will consist of the distribution of different presents to different characters, so that each forms a combination that is plausible and possible in itself, but where all of them together are "incompossible," and where the inexplicable is thereby maintained and created" (Deleuze 2001, 101). There is just such a distribution of presents to characters in *Russian Ark*, an exemplary propagation that arises as one consequence of the technical procedures used to generate the time travel narration. In order to fully appreciate these coordinates we can do no better than approach by way of Jean Mitry's theory of camera position.

For Mitry "camera position provides ... a more or less pronounced feeling of objectivity or subjectivity" through "four distinct types of image" (Mitry 1998, 218). In the first instance the objective, where the camera surveys characters traversing the set, where the camera is "impersonal," neutral, non-aligned (Mitry 1998, 218). The second instance is the exact opposite, the subjective, where the camera "takes the place of the characters" (Mitry 1998, 218). Here the camera becomes aligned with the character's senses of sight and sound, it sees and hears as if it is the character. The third instance is the "symbolic," or "filmmaker's point-of-view," shots composed to create meaning, "particular relationships which bring out, underline, or contradict the meaning implied" by subjective and objective procedures (Mitry 1998, 218). In other words, fore-grounding style. Finally—the fourth and most familiar case—the semisubjective. Here the image "adopts the viewpoint of a particular character who, objectively described, occupies a special position in the frame... The camera follows him wherever he goes, acts like him, sees with him and at the same time" (Mitry 1998, 218). These four procedures of camera positioning relate through editing and are ultimately arranged around the semisubjective, a character as center who perceives, feels, thinks and acts. This formula of framing can be said to describe the movement-image.

In *Russian Ark*, however, there is a radical transformation of Mitry's formula. It is no longer the semisubjective that organizes subjective, objective and symbolic images; rather style dominates. In the first place, this concerns the long-take. *Russian Ark* is famously composed of one shot lasting nearly 90 minutes. Such a procedure—one film, one take—foregrounds style, but more importantly nullifies the necessity of editing together different shots, thus problematizing the creation and distribution of subjective, semisubjective and objective framing. Yet, in the second place, these other types of image occur simultaneously by being given to different time travelers: the 21st century unnamed Russian filmmaker; the 19th century French aristocrat Marquis de Custine; and the people from different times across the 300-year historical backdrop. Unnamed is captured purely in the subjective: the camera becomes his eyes and his voice is disembodied. The spectator never sees him, and he is curiously invisible to and unheard by all except the Marquis. Custine is captured in the semisubjective: the camera discovers him, follows him, loses and finds him as he explores the Hermitage complex. The people are captured in the objective, seen at a distance: Peter the Great who seized the Baltic coastline upon which St. Petersburg was founded, Empress Catherine II who transformed the Hermitage from palace to museum, guests at the last Great Royal Ball of 1913 and modern visitors to the galleries haunted by the music of Mikhail Glinka, halls and hallways displaying the sculptures of Antonio Canova and paintings by El Greco, Van Dyck and Rembrandt.

The camera captures images composed of three strata as a simultaneity of presents. The long-take is in-itself a continuity of the present that would become a foundation for chronological time if it were not radically decomposed through the time travel situation. This situation is that of a concurrence of parallel presents that simultaneously capture different times: the present of the present, the present of the past and the present of the future—the Unnamed, the background characters and the Marquis. Unnamed is the presentness of the present, a subjective absence that positions the spectator in the context of the moment in which the film is constituted (our now). The presentness of the past is the people who momentarily appear then disappear, objective encounters that create the destiny of Russia. Custine is the presentness of the future, a semisubjective caesura in the flow of time—on the one hand, his 19th century life coming before the yet-to-come of some moments; on the other hand, his life a yet-to-come occurring after some events have taken place. The time travelers of *Russian Ark* constitute a paradoxical simultaneity of peaks of the present. Everyone is traveling in time, but all are in their own present.

Sheets of the Past

Time-image narration will also appear as sheets of the past. "Between the past as a pre-existence in general and the present as infinitively contracted past," writes Deleuze, there are "all the circles of the past" (Deleuze 2001, 99). In this way, temporality is captured from the perspective of pure pastness (rather than the past being a function of the present as in the movement-image). With the time-image the now is effaced and pasts appear as moments of coexistent singularity arranged non-chronologically. There is no cause and effect, just events that resonate with each other, backwards and forwards. These sheets of the past are seen in exemplary fashion in *Russian Ark*, the film creating an extraordinary encounter for the time travelers with historical events as mise-en-scène. It was André Bazin who first apprehended such a function of mise-en-scène in the cinema.

Approaching Bazin requires us to acknowledge a theoretical position dependent upon an "evolution" of filmmaking, one both technical and artistic, arising from two intertwined propositions and two reciprocal consequences (Bazin 1997, 23). First proposition: resist montage. It is only after we have discovered the function of montage to concretize associations (after Kuleshov and Eisenstein) that we can turn away from it. We thus encounter a "refusal to break up the action" and rediscover the long-take (the sequence-shot, as Bazin names it) allowing us to "analyze the dramatic field in time" (Bazin 1997, 34). Second proposition: deep focus becomes depth-of-field. Deep focus can be used to create (after Renoir and Welles/Toland) a "composition in depth" by way of introducing planes of coexistent action (Bazin 1997, 34). "One shot sequences in depth," writes Bazin, will thus give "new meaning" to the image (Bazin 1997, 36). First consequence: "a sense of the ambiguity of reality" (Bazin 1997, 36). Hollywoodesque realism is undermined by uncertainty—and is so aligned with the neo-realist project (after Visconti and Rossellini). Second consequence: the "theatricalization of cinema" ("the exact opposite of a passive

recording of theatre ") (Bazin 1997, 69). Cinema must (after Dreyer and Hitchcock) reveal the illusion of reality as the reality of illusions—thus allowing the
audience the role of judgment in respect to filmic events. These consequences
are "bound up with the very essence of the mise-en-scène" captured through
the long-take and depth-of-field (Bazin 1997, 102).

Such a conception of mise-en-scène is immediately apparent in *Russian
Ark*. The long-take and moving camera form a sequence-shot that provides the
foundation upon which everything occurs in-depth through multiple planes,
which generate theatricalization and ambiguity. Early on in *Russian Ark*,
Unnamed and Custine encounter a window into the chambers of Peter the
Great and his entourage. Voices are heard, actions performed by those inside,
but these occur at a distance, movements and sounds obscured by dark glass and
old stone in the mid-ground while the camera snakes around attempting to
achieve a better visual and sound apprehension (though it never succeeds). Why
is the Czar angry? Is he always angry? We never really know: this realism propagates opacity, indeterminacy and ambiguity. Custine and Unnamed climb a
dark and tortuous spiral staircase. They emerge into a vast space divided into
discrete sections which the camera will pass one-by-one along a lateral track,
right to left: men turning wooden wheels and working a massive concertina system; Roman soldiers in plate armor, a throne of gold with a woman in robes;
dancers dancing; an orchestra playing in the pit; then out into a sumptuous theatre, an audience of nobles and Catherine the Great. The camera now re-
orientates through 90° revealing a stage, partitions now planes of an exposed
composition-in-depth, lead characters, secondary players and mechanical scenery
in motion. Such a movement through space in time is pedagogy, a signaling of
the theatricalization of the entire film. "Has all this been staged for me?" asks
Unnamed at the very beginning of the movie, "What kind of play is this?"

Yet seeing these events as a reciprocity of realist ambiguity and theatrical
illusion goes only so far. A film composed with long-takes, for Bazin, should
"not exclude the use of montage"—this would result in "primitive babbling"
(Bazin 1997, 35). Montage must bring a secret order to ambiguity and illusion.
Depth-of-field remains in the service of "continuity," in "the specific effects
that can be derived from unity of image in space and time" (Bazin 1997, 34;
35). In *Russian Ark* the long-take babbles and depth-of-field propagates a
baroque cascade of elements that overwhelm the screen. People are everywhere
and everything happens at once. Accordingly, Deleuze writes that "neither a
function of theatricality nor one of reality seems to exhaust this complicated
problem" (Deleuze 2001, 109). Rather, "sequence shot" and "depth of field
create ... a certain type of direct time-image that can be defined by [pure]
memory" (Deleuze 2001, 107; 109): sheets of the past.

Appearing between the past in general and the immediate present as the edge of the past, these sheets are manifold: from the moment of the Unnamed and Custine as focal point to a receding limit—the Winter Palace and Hermitage from 1732 giving way to St Petersburg from 1700; the art collected from Europe created in preceding periods giving way to—as will be seen—mythical time. Between such limits and the focal point appear all the sheets of the past. Each sheet will have "its own characteristics, its 'tones,' its 'aspects,' its 'singularities,' its 'shining points' and its dominant themes" (Deleuze 2001, 99). These sheets will be arranged in "non-chronological time," moments between which the narration will "jump" (Deleuze 2001, 99). Finally, these sheets create coexistence, they are "inextricable" happenings—there is no cause and effect; sheets of the past rather reveal the conditions for and disrupt cause and effect through selection, resonance and a multiplicity of connections (Deleuze 2001, 99). The time travelers traverse these sheets of the past, one after another, from arrival in the early 1800s to the encounter with Peter the Great in the early 1700s to Catherine the Great directing her theatrical production in the 1760s. They jump back and forth between sheets: on to the 21st century; then the German blockade of Stalingrad; the Persian Ambassador presented to the court of Nicholas I. Catherine again (this time as an old lady with her grandchildren); Nicholas II and family at breakfast with whispers of the coming revolution. There is no chronological continuum here, and thus no actions to be performed—the travelers are seers jumping between moments of the past—but never depicted as coming from or returning to their relative presents. They are adrift in pure memory. In the final moment of the film the Unnamed finds the Neva has flooded, the Hermitage is an Ark preserving concurrent pasts afloat on the waters of time—the myth of Noah experienced anew. Resonances, reverberations, echoes: *Russian Ark* produces a coexistence of sheets of the past.

Powers of the False

The third chronosign is the power of the false. It can be said that this time-image constitutes narration from the perspective of the future, the fundamentally impenetrable, unknown and unknowable. Accordingly the future acts as an eternal ungrounding of temporality giving to time multiplicity, disorder, forgetting, anarchy and chance: "becoming as potentialization" (Deleuze 2001, 275). And "everything," writes Deleuze "is changed in the perspective of time as becoming" (Deleuze 2001, 146). Becoming is that which brings the future into the present and "carries the living being to creation"; it is that which brings the future into the past, a creative reminiscence where we can "oppose becoming to history" (Deleuze 2001, 142). Two questions immediately appear. First, why does Deleuze see the future as the power of the false? Because the future ungrounds temporality by disrupting the succession of the arrow of time and breaking open the circles of the past: the next event does not necessarily follow from the present moment; and the next event can never necessarily be foretold in reference of the past. In this way, proclaims Deleuze, time "is fundamentally liberated, becomes power of the false" (Deleuze 2001, 143). To put this another way, "truth is not to be achieved, formed, or reproduced; it has to be created" and appear as a creation (Deleuze 2001, 147). Time-image cinema is no longer concerned with cinema as a pretense to truth, but instead with exposing this pretense: the falsity of unitary and total truth. Second question: how are powers of the false created in cinema? If peaks of the present and sheets of the past "concerned the *order of time*, that is, the coexistence of relations or the simultaneity of the elements internal to time," for Deleuze, the power of the false "concerns the *series of time*, which brings together the before and the after in a becoming" (Deleuze 2001, 155). This is the serial form. One way to approach the serial form—and explore how it inspires the images of the time travel narration of *Russian Ark*—is through Brian Henderson's concept of collage.

Collage concerns editing. For Henderson montage composes camera images capturing the mise-en-scène "in order to reconstitute it in highly organized, synthetic emotional and intellectual patterns" (Henderson 2004, 58). "Collage does not do this," rather "it collects or sticks its fragments together in a way that does not entirely overcome their fragmentation. It seeks to recover its fragments as *fragments*" (Henderson 2004, 58). Immediately, of course, there may appear to be a problem: there is no editing in *Russian Ark*. Yet understanding editing as purely the cutting and linking of shots is reductive. Cinema is always a nexus of camera, mise-en-scène and montage; of framing, the shot and the edit. Framing is a type of montage through the creation of the infield and the out-of-field; the shot creates montage through the movement of a camera and its reframings, as well as through the movement of elements within the mise-en-scène. There is also sound design: voice, music, effects—and silence. How is montage constituted in *Russian Ark*? There is the in- and out-of-field, reframings; the movement of elements and the sound design; there is the composition of planes of depth-of-field. Furthermore, editing occurs through post-production visual manipulations, some 3,000 digital events (Rodowick 2007, 75). As Deleuze puts it, filmmakers will always "'insert' montage into the shot" (Deleuze 2002: 29).

The crucial point is that in the movement-image editing (in its widest sense) has methods "obliged to conceal themselves" and has to become "imperceptible" (Deleuze 2002, 25). All movement is "still attached to people or things" and so becomes invisible giving the image and narration "unity" (Deleuze 2002, 25; 27). Collage, in comparison, would foreground fragmentation over unity, create aberrant movement and make connections perceivable. In *Russian Ark* such moments permeate the film. Consider the creation of the time travelers, one subjective, the other semi-subjective; one invisible to all except Custine, the Marquis visible to all. While describing a simultaneity of the present these positions also fragment a unity (sameness) of character creation. The time travel function of the film fragments temporality: there are always different presents at any one moment ripping time asunder. An exemplary scene: different Hermitage directors appear together at once—Iosif Orbeli (1934–1951), Boris Piotrovsky (1964–1990) and Mikhail Borisovich Pyotrovski (the latter played by the real and current director of the Hermitage, the others played by actors). At the end of the film all the characters from all times flow down the Hermitage's fabulous Jordan staircase; thousands of people across 300 years of history, making their way out into the world. Concomitantly, consider the historical events: there is not just an encounter with the coexistence of sheets of the past but a collage of moments that do not link, that foreground a fragmentation of historical chronology. The camera turns away from a soldier making coffins during the battle of Stalingrad to chase Catherine the Great through a freezing courtyard to then enter into the grand reception of the embassy of Persia with Nicholas I before entering the 21st century with puffa-coated tourists viewing paintings hung upon walls. In short, if peaks of the present and sheets of the past concerned the order of time through a simultaneity of presents and the coexistence of pasts; with powers of the false there is a fundamental and genetic fragmentation where coexistence and simultaneity fail to fully cohere—this is the serial form. Fragments of the world: fragmentation made perceptible.

But this is only one side of the series of time: the other—and the one that increases its power—is the gap. These fragments are fragments because of the interstice opened up between elements: chasms of darkness that obscure the past; that makes the present a break—an instant—between the past and the future; that take the future as fundamentally unknowable. It is the obscure and opaque nature of the future that enters and ungrounds present and past alike, destroys the idea of the presentation of truth—this is the true power of the false. And *Russian Ark* creates an exemplary interstice. Something is missing. Everyone knows of the role the Winter Palace and the Hermitage had in the Russian Revolution. Everyone has seen *October / Oktyabr* (1927) and *The End of St. Petersburg / Konets Sankt-Peterburga* (1927). *Russian Ark* appears to be missing an image of revolutionaries, a tumult, ascending the Jordan Staircase. Such a forgetting disrupts the historicity—the historical integrity—of the entire film. How could Sokurov not incorporate this event? Why did Sokurov not incorporate this event?

The Revolution Is Never Present, Always Past and Always to Come

Take the insightful, beautifully researched, in-depth analyzes of writers Dragan Kujundzic—"The 'Arkive' Fever of Alexander Sokurov" (2003)— and Kriss Ravetto-Biagioli—"Floating on the Borders of Europe" (2005). These theorists focus on *Russian Ark* as a cinematic artwork reconstituting historical events. Yet, due to the interstice of the revolutionaries on the Jordan staircase, both see the film as effacing the Soviet era and, furthermore, as a reactionary 21st century nationalist nostalgia for pre-revolutionary Imperial Russia. Such claims may appear unassailable. Except—curiously—neither writer explores the film as a time travel movie. It seems to me, however, interpreting *Russian Ark* as a time travel narrative allows for a radical revaluation of the film.

The problem seems to originate in an unwillingness to consider (what is seen as) a serious cinematic artwork within the co-ordinates of a genre. For instance, Brown (2013) takes *Russian Ark* as one touchstone of the new digital screen and sees the film, after Deleuze, as an exemplary time-image. Yet despite a number of engagements with *Russian Ark*, it is named a time travel movie only once (103). Is this telling? Must a film of the time-image necessarily escape the co-ordinates of mere genre? Is genre—seen as being populated with stock characters and repeating typical events—necessarily a movement-image? Martin-Jones (2011) seems to affirm such a position. By way of an exploration of three South Korean time travel movies, his claim is that the genre is either an enfolding of movement-images with time-images or time-images with movement-images, and that this "effectively amount[s] to the same thing" (107). Thus the conclusion, with the time travel genre "the message is that the past can be revisited, and that it is an archive ... from which lessons can be learned" (123). In other words, time travel films allow for "new histories and new chronologies" (107). Such an inference, effectively, believes this genre as always re-establishing homogenous chronological time—always the triumph of the movement-image function.

Herzog (2012) challenges such assumptions "we must take care ... not to dismiss genre as merely the static 'bad object'"—both movement-images and time-images, for Herzog, can engage with a "typology" but in so doing have different "functionality" (142). Accordingly, while all time travel films are explicit about confronting chronological time with non-chronological relations (enfolding movement-images and time-images), the crucial aspect is that either organization can dominate. This domination constitutes a self-reflexivity—the triumph of movement-images over time-images; or the ungrounding of movement-images by time-images. *Russian Ark* is a time-image, time travel movie, a film that ungrounds movement-images, reveals chronological time as a fragile surface and façade. A time travel film dominated by movement-images may well be concerned with giving a new version of chronological time; but the domination of time-images is concerned with something far different. This is the essential point: the time-image does not give or reconstitute empirical content, but rather makes empirical content indeterminate, discordant, dissonant; problematizes an image of history, of truth; foregrounds failures of memory and forgettings of history; disrupts temporal succession. Rodowick (1997) captures this exactly. In his introduction to the book he uses a time travel film—*La Jetée* (1962)—as exemplary of time-images. In "*La Jetée*, the image of time is no longer reduced to the thread of chronology where present, past, and future are aligned on a continuum," instead "chronology is pulverized, time is fragmented like so many facets of a shattered crystal" (4). Such crystal-images are a hall of mirrors, and as such create the opportunity of thought for the spectator. Such images with their virtual links engendered through interstices must be interpreted. As Herzog puts it, such images become a "provocation [that] must be taken up by the viewer: how will the gesture register?" (152). Will the spectator turn towards time-images? Or will the spectator attempt to understand such images within the framework of the movement-image? Deleuze (with collaborator Félix Guattari) in *Anti-Oedipus* (1972): "to be sure, one can always establish or re-establish some sort of links ... organic links" in a radical text (2003, 324). The viewer can always turn away from an encounter with the time-image.

Yet seeing—or rather, reading—*Russian Ark* as a time-image time travel film can radically transform our understanding of temporality, not only of how we live it in the present, but also of how we encounter both history and the future. Historical cause and effect can never be fully constituted—and if this is the marker of success in a film, it will always be doomed to failure, even if what is forgotten goes unnoticed. There is no "as-it-was" that can fully explain the present. The present is, in-itself, unknowable—we are never in the present, but an absent infinitesimal point between past and future. And the future is open, our becoming. All foretellings are stargazing, tealeaves in teacups, palm readings. It is this image of time—through peaks of the present, sheets of the past and powers of the false—that *Russian Ark* foregrounds. The revolution appears neither as a glorious triumph over Czarist evil nor as Soviet malevolence and devastating tragedy. The revolution is missing. It remains unfound by Unnamed and Custine, searching for it—without ever knowing (this is) their task—from the before and the after. The revolution is missing in the past: thus the problem, what happened, how did it happen and what—if anything—changed? And the revolution is missing in the future, in the sense that its forms, causes and effects can never be anticipated. The revolution is never present, always past and always to come. Forever.

"I flung myself into futurity"

H.G. Wells' Deleuzian Time Machine

Michael Starr

H.G. Wells' 1895 novel *The Time Machine* is generally acknowledged to be the first appearance in popular culture of a time travel vehicle that moves selectively through time at the behest of its human controller, and this device has subsequently become ubiquitous in science fiction. As a powerful intellectual influence and self-confessed "uninvited adventurer who has felt himself free to criticize established things without restraint" (Wells 1984, 823), Wells saw his work as a vehicle for the diffusion of advanced ideas, the notion of time travel arguably being the most enduring in regards to his fictional output. To this end, Wells has become synonymous with his own chronoclastic creation, as can be witnessed via his recurrent appearances as a fictionalized character in science fiction film, television and literature. This chapter explores the nature of such corporeal representations, initially by placing the novel in its critical and cultural context, in the process demonstrating its convergence with a succession of contemporary media, before then performing a poststructural reading using the philosophical concepts of Gilles Deleuze.

An increasingly powerful force in cultural theory, Deleuzian thought (presented via such texts as the two volumes of *Capitalism and Schizophrenia; Anti-Oedipus* (1972) and *A Thousand Plateaus* (1980), both co-written with Félix Guattari) offers a challenging set of conceptual tools to rethink existing texts and critical paradigms, providing unprecedented ways to map the human mind, body and world, and to re-evaluate literature, film and other fields. Deleuzian theory embraces a sense of the constructive; each reading of a philosopher, an artist or writer should be undertaken in order to provide an impetus for creating new concepts that do not already exist. Works examined from such a perspective therefore serve not only as inspiration, but also as a resource from which concepts can be gathered, along with the force to develop new, non-pre-existing concepts. In this regard, in an immanent philosophy, with immanence defined by Deleuze as the absolute background of life expressed only in the intersection of form, subject and function, concepts and representations may no longer be considered vacuous forms awaiting content but become active productions in themselves. In this way, an immanent life carries with it "the events or singularities that are actualized in subjects and objects" (Deleuze 2001, 29). Ultimately, through this reading strategy, Deleuze strove to produce something recognizably new, distinctively "his." He provocatively stated that he saw his philosophical approach as a form of immaculate conception: "I saw myself as taking an author from behind, and giving him a child that would be his own offspring, yet monstrous" (Deleuze 1995, 6). These monstrous "offspring" of Wells are the focus of this essay, as Deleuzian theory is used to conceptualize the philosophical implications of manifestations of Wells as fictional character in a variety of texts.

The significance of and impact upon popular cultural of Wells' time traveler who "flung [him]self into futurity" (Wells 2001, 17–18) cannot be overstated. Indeed, Wells has become so synonymous with notions of time travel, that he often embodies a time traveling figure in fiction. Fictional representations of significant authorial figures are, of course, common, but are generally viewed in terms of tribute or homage, and hence are rarely conceptualized in philosophical terms. However, academic studies do on occasion move beyond this remit, interpreting such representations in more sophisticated terms; one such study that provides a prescient bridge into the approach taken in this essay is Orr's "Hitch as Matrix Figure: Hitchcock and Twentieth Century Cinema" (2009). In order to emphasize the titular film director's vast influence, Orr positions him in terms of a "Matrix-Figure" who is "at the centre of a product [cinema] that he nurtured into existence on all levels" (10). As the lattice of cinema as an art form both precedes and follows him, Hitchcock thus functions as "a form of fate that ties in through echo and repetition down the years" (8). Significantly Orr cites Deleuze's interpretation of Hume (2001), stating that for the latter communication of concepts inevitably takes place by way of "external relations and ... the mediation of objects" (32). In this way, through the figure of Hitchcock and the enduring power of his narratives, themes and images, meaning and identity are not individual truths of being where the real person is revealed, but instead changing forms of transaction between subjects and characters that are always mediated by object and situation, that have an external fate (32–33).

In terms of his influence upon the science fiction genre (and more specifically in regards to this essay, the time travel device), Wells can undoubtedly be positioned as a matrix figure, both as the locus of science fiction time travel and, as such, a figure who is infinitely adapted and replicated. However, such conceptualizations can be further extrapolated; whereas Orr positions Hitchcock as a central figure through which contemporary cinema passes, this essay espouses a more esoteric notion, positioning Wells not as a central "Matrix-figure," but instead as an element of an infinitely expandable "rhizome." The rhizome is a term which derives from Deleuze's description of the standard epistemology of Western thought as functioning on the principle of an arboreal structure in which a trunk grows vertically and produces branches which subdivide into smaller and lesser categories, hence an insistence upon linear, hierarchic and totalizing principles. To challenge this, the image of the rhizome is utilized, in which the stem of a plant sends out interconnecting roots and shoots as it spreads underground, to describe the way in which ideas should be conceived as multiple, interconnected and self-replicating. Hence it is advocated that we must "make rhizomes, not roots, never plant! Do not sow, grow offshoots"! (Deleuze 2004b, 27). In other words, adopt a mode of knowledge that allows for multiple, non-hierarchical entry and exit points in interpretation, in opposition to an arborescent conception of knowledge which works with dualist categories and binary choices. Within a linear chain only imitation remains possible, but within a rhizome the possibilities for different associations and links become endless, because "ideas do not die... Their application and status, even their form and content, may change; yet they retain something essential throughout the process, across the displacement, in the distribution of a new domain" (2004b, 259).

In accordance to this theoretical remit, *The Time Machine* is initially investigated as a genesis for time travel fiction, leading to a conceptualization of Wells himself as a manifestation of both his time travel device and the resultant science fictional concept. To this end, Wells is positioned in the theoretical terms of a Deleuzian "conceptual persona."

Wells' Virtual Time Machine

Since its initial appearance, Wells' novella has never been out of print. Indeed, *The Time Machine* has been the subject of reams of critical analysis since its publication, exploring variously its position as social commentary, its function as an exposition of Darwinian theory and, in terms of more recent criticism, its stance in the light of the development of psychoanalytic, postmodern and poststructuralist theories. *The Time Machine* is arguably the best known and most influential work of Wells' entire oeuvre and, although by no means the first piece of fiction to explore the concept of traveling through time, its significance lies in its pseudoscientific explanation of how time travel could possibly occur. It is thus credited with the universal popularization of the concept of time travel using a vehicle that allows an operator to travel purposefully and selectively. Wells' work remains an inexhaustible rhizome for intelligent and visually self-aware science fiction on film and television (Williams 2007, 130), and time travel as a fictional genre, with its paradoxes, ruptures, alterations and juxtapositions of past, present and future. Indeed, time travel is "perhaps the hardiest form of science fiction" and has "not passed with any modernist vogue, nor succumbed to postmodernist temptations for closure" (Slusser 1995, 181). This is possibly due to time travel's inherent premise of asking intriguing questions about causality, identity, cognition and even ethics.

Following *The Time Machine*'s popularization of the concept of vehicular-controlled time travel, a multitude of other time travel narratives in literature, cinema and other media have consequently used the same archetype. Although these subsequent narratives may feature a more complex structure, including time-loops and paradoxes not featured in Wells' novel, time travel has become an intrinsic ingredient in popular culture. Correspondingly there is also a vast amount of literature documenting reactions to time travel narratives; whether such ideas are coherent, whether they are consistent with the understandings of modern physics, and what it would mean to be in the position of a time traveler.

Significantly, such questioning as to the credibility of time travel as a narrative device, which has remained a constant in the critical appraisal of such science fiction stories, is pre-empted within the narrative of *The Time Machine* itself. For example, though he returns to the time and place where his journey began, Wells' time traveler does not have a happy homecoming. His audience (a representative ensemble of professionals from the author's time) to whom he recounts his adventures in the far future do not believe his story. Only one member of the gathering, the unnamed primary narrator, makes an effort to suspend his disbelief, and even he remains strictly a man of his time, hoping that if the traveler were to go to the future again would choose "one of the nearer ages, where men are still men" (82), while his epilogue contains trite platitudes about the human race enduring in "gratitude and mutual tenderness" (82). Indeed, against all the evidence that the time traveler has presented to him in his account of his future experiences, he maintains that "it remains for us to live as if it were not so" (82). The reaction of the fictional audience corresponds with the initial skeptical critical response to the novel. Wells' Victorian peers believed time travel, even as a literary device, to be an outrageous conceit, with magazine reviews in the *Spectator* and *Daily Chronicle* referring to the novel as "hocus-pocus ... a fanciful and lively dream" and "bizarre" respectively. Such reactions perpetuated for decades (Nahin 1999, 22). However, in the intervening century since its publication, *The Time Machine* has been critically reclaimed from these early dismissals and is now lauded as a vital work. In discussing this shift of audience response over time, Slusser suggests:

> [Wells] was writing, it seems, for a virtual audience, for the audience that would exist in the twentieth century and beyond, an audience that would grapple with such "wonders" as the fourth dimension, temporary displacement, time machines. All disciplines, scientific or literary, that were represented among the traveler's audience of professionals remained closed to the message of the future. For Wells' virtual audience, however—the readers we have become—these same disciplines have become dialogue partners, wrestling with the multiple complexities of the author's visionary work [Slusser 2001, xii].

Obviously Slusser does not intend his use of the term "virtual" to equate with a philosophical understanding of the term, but his claim does indeed resonate with a statement from Deleuze and Guattari's *What is Philosophy?*: "The creation of concepts in itself calls for a future form, for a new earth and people that do not yet exist" (1994, 108). It is these "future" incarnations of Wells (i.e., those synonymous to the contemporary audience) that shall now be positioned as conceptual manifestations of his visionary work.

Wells as Fictional Character

This notion of a "future form" can be applied verbatim to the science fiction genre, whose inherent purpose is to "write the future" (Pinsky 2003, 13). Deleuze himself proclaimed that philosophy itself must be a kind of science fiction, in that the strange rhetoric and "monstrous" slang of science fiction estrange one from the historical inertia of the "now" and allow a leap into "untimely" futures with singular self-consistency (Deleuze 2004, xix–xx). As Fancy (2010) states: "It is clear that science fiction, with its core concerns around future assemblages of technologies, humans, other planets and species, is a series of assemblages that can provide the "lines of flight" Deleuze felt would be necessary to help undo the various stratifications he saw gathering" (105). Simply put, such "lines of flight" are the processes that lead out of the midst of the struggle produced by a power relation, to another place, to another territory. In the terms discussed by Fancy, this constitutes an intellectual trajectory, and hence the pursuit of such lines enables us to "be able finally to think otherwise" (Deleuze 1988, 119). For example, literature can function in this manner, in that "characters are concepts, and the settings, the landscapes, are space-times. One is always writing to give life to something, to liberate life where it's imprisoned, in order to trace lines of flight" (Deleuze 1995, 41). Hence, vital to Deleuze is the sheer fact of conceptual invention: the creation of new concepts (and hence the undoing of established stratifications) means that we see the world in a new way, one that was not available to us before: "a perception as it was before men (or after) ... released from human coordinates" (Deleuze 1986, 122). Via a Deleuzian conception, we can imbue the text of *The Time Machine* with a more radical reading, in this case, in its approaches to time, and the significance of the time traveler himself as a manifestation of concepts.

In a 1988 interview, Deleuze states (in reference to his own writings, but this is rhizomatically expandable to any other aspect of the critical process):

> In the act of writing there is an attempt to make life something more than personal, to free life from what imprisons it.... It's organisms that die, not life. Any work of art points a way through life, finds a way through the cracks [Deleuze 1995, 143].

The aim in a Deleuzian reading is therefore to "give back to the author a little bit of the joy, the energy, the love of life and politics that he knew how to give and invent" (Deleuze & Parnet 2007, 119.) Wells, of course, died in 1946, but his visionary, creative and analytical treatises on humanity's future are still unfurling; or, as Deleuze puts it, they persist in their ability to "find a way through the cracks" (Deleuze 1995, 143). This can be witnessed in the manner that Wells' concepts and source texts are subject to constant rhizomatic reinvention and adaptation through the medium of literary criticism, countless references to his work in popular culture, cinematic and literary adaptations and remakes, board and video games, the intersection of fan culture with the Wells canon, *ad infinitum*. However, though Wells' writings and legacy have had an enormous impact upon popular consciousness, there is also another significant notion that his literature has spawned: the concept of H. G. Wells himself as a character in time travel texts. Using Deleuze's notion of "deterritorialization": a process that decontextualizes a set of relations, preparing them for other actualizations, I wish to explore Wells as fictional character.

The reasons for Wells-as-character would initially appear to be self-explanatory. The fact that the protagonist of *The Time Machine* is unnamed and narrated from the first person led to subsequent adaptations placing Wells himself in this role. In addition to acting as homage, such characterization may function as a form of critique, or "surmised lampooning" as Kenneth Bailey describes Wells' appearance in C. S. Lewis's novel *That Hideous Strength* (1990, 226). Similarly, the appearance of a "Dr Wells" in *Brave New World*, "openly avowed [Huxley's] aim to expose the horror of the Wellsian Utopia" (Firchow 1976, 260).

In more contemporaneous terms, there are many such examples of Wells as time traveler appearing in a wide variety of fictions. To cite but a few: as a clichéd Victorian gentleman in the film *Time After Time* (1979), as (ironically) a skeptic towards the possibility of time travel in Michael Moorcock's *Dancers at the End of Time* (1972) novels, and as Helena Wells, a female mad-scientist cum evil genius in the science fiction television series *Warehouse 13* (2009–present). In the *Doctor Who* episode "Timelash" (1985), the Doctor encounters a pre-published Wells, taking him on an adventure that inspires him to write *The Time Machine*. An episode of *Lois & Clark: The New Adventures of Superman*, titled "Tempus Fugitive" (1995), features a plot closely resembling *Time After Time*, in which Wells has accidentally unleashed a criminal from his past upon the present. A 2010 episode of the satirical science fiction cartoon series *Futurama* features Wells' head in a jar in the 31st-century "Head Museum," a showcase of history's most important people. Animations and internet series have also produced their own appropriations; web serials *Cataclysmo and the Battle for Earth* (2008) and *Solar Pons's War of the Worlds* (2008) both feature Wells as a protagonist. It is also worthy of note that Wells is featured on the sleeve of The Beatles' "Sgt. Pepper's Lonely Hearts Club Band" (1967), his appearance on this iconoclastic and epoch-shattering album befitting of a man who "knew the future was not going to be what respectable people imagined" (Orwell 1970, 171). It is also worthy of note that along with these multifarious contemporary citations, Wells also consciously referenced himself within his own fiction. For example, the narrator of *The War of the Worlds* (1898) refers implicitly to Wells' own journal article "The Man of the Year Million," describing the author, possibly somewhat self-effacingly, as "a certain speculative writer of quasi-scientific repute" (2006, 101). Clearly, Wells himself was not averse to contributing to his own mythicization. The principal point being demonstrated here is that the "real" figure of Wells has become just as "constructed" as one of his characters.

However, the role of Wells as time traveler can be positioned in Deleuzian terms. Deleuze stated that literary characters struck him with the same force as philosophical concepts, as both possess their own autonomy and style. Compounding this, there are also stylistic concerns that are comparable in both philosophy and literature. Deleuze suggests that great literary characters are also great thinkers: just as a philosopher creates concepts, within literature a concept adopts the form of a character, and as a result the character takes on the various dimensions of the concept that was their genesis (2007, 113–115). Hence, a literary character is not a self-contained and unified subject within itself or within the novel in which it appears, but instead is an amalgamation of different relations and forces, these forces extending beyond the novel containing the character and into the social sphere. Therefore, Wells' time traveler is not unified or self-contained, but becomes "a functioning of a polyvalent assemblage of which the solitary individual is only a part" (Deleuze 2004a, 42). In accordance, through the time traveler we can witness these individual forces and their function, both inside and outside the text. Hence, Wells himself is reconceptualized in a variety of unique ways; these depictions are obviously not "true" representations of the man himself (even if such a thing could exist), being an assemblage of biographical details, attributes of his nameless fictional characters, and personifications (or indeed, celebrations) of his prophecies, politics, ideas and fictional inventions. A machinic hybrid of the "real" character of Wells (subject of numerous biographies) and his fictional creations (that many readers and critics take to be personifications of him), he has himself become a source of myth. Each Wells is different, each arising independently as a unique "solution" to a common disparity or problem, a concept that needs exploration.

In the context of this essay, it is the occurrence of these "mutations" of Wells that is significant, as opposed to what each manifestation individually does, but to give just one example, the character of Helena Wells from *Warehouse 13* is a utilization of the Wells concept that serves to debate issues of gender equality. Obviously this in itself can hardly be said to be unique in the realms of science fiction, a genre renowned for its feminist concerns, but via the concept of Wells himself and the use of the time travel device with which he is intrinsically associated, varying attitudes towards gender in different historical eras (in this case, Victorian and present day) can be directly confronted, without the chronological transition between them that the actual progression of linear time insists upon. *Warehouse 13* may not do this in a particularly sophisticated way; Wells is depicted primarily as a misandrist due to her subjugation by patriarchal Victorian society (indeed, she specifically states that the Wells known to history was actually her brother, who took all the credit for her work). However, in its unique way of extrapolating into a modern environment a variation of Wells' own (and for his time, fairly radical) stance towards gender equality, the virtual potential of Wells as concept is demonstrated.

Conversely, Wells' appearance in *Time After Time*, in which he uses his time machine to pursue Jack the Ripper into the 20th century, serves as a critique of both contemporary society and idealistic notions of socialism. As with Wells' original novel, this film uses the time machine to carry its characters to a new temporal position, where their conflict points to a flaw in our current society and suggests a need for reform (Renzi 2004, 27). To this end *Time After Time* portrays Wells as deeply shocked by the chaos, crime and lack of morality he finds in contemporary San Francisco, which he perceives to be entirely at odds to the enlightened socialist utopia future he anticipated. Hence, in *Time After Time*'s portrayal of Wells, the sexually liberated present of the film's making topically recasts the novel's Morlockian depredation and themes of changing mores and gender roles (Williams 2007, 135). In broader terms, although the appearance of Wells as a character in fiction is not unique to the science fiction genre, the flexible machinations of science fiction narratives with which he is inherently associated (specifically in this case, Wells' time travel device) allow him to "legitimately" make appearances, thus reinforcing the fact that science fiction is a genre of ideas to which Wells is still contributing.

Wells as Deleuzian Conceptual Persona

Deleuze allows us to view Wells' characterizations in different terms. In his appearance in these fictional roles, Wells becomes more than a mere archetypal tribute, character, or characterization. What is significant about the various examples previously presented is that Wells' persona is not that of a character in the traditional sense. Rather, he is a figure that accompanies concepts, "a figure through whom thought moves" (Deleuze & Guattari 1994, 63), which Deleuze refers to as a "conceptual persona." It is these personas that have been previously exemplified via *Warehouse 13* and *Time After Time*.

Deleuze states that the role of a conceptual persona is "to show thought's territories ... conceptual personae are thinkers ... and their personalized features are closely linked to ... the intensive features of concepts... A particular conceptual persona thinks in us" (1994, 69). In other words, the identity of a concept itself is conveyed through something referential, allowing the concept to be understood, reasoned with and questioned. Conceptual personae are hence "subjective presuppositions" (1994, 62), not identical to an author, philosopher, artist or self, but rather testifying to a third person: "we do not do something by saying it but produce movement by thinking it, through the intermediary of a conceptual person" (1994, 64). Consequently, conceptual personae are figures of thought that give concepts their specific force, their raison d'être, and through them the concepts are given body. Deleuze and Guattari argue that conceptual personae, while often only implicit in philosophy, are decisive for understanding the significance of concepts.

The conceptual persona is one of Deleuze's more esoteric constructs, particularly in regards to how a "fictional" character can possess their own autonomy. Although it makes sense to say that a novelist can "bring a character to life," even when such a character is purely fictional, to insist that such characters are alive in the sense that they may free themselves from the manipulation of their creators is a substantially bolder claim. However, regardless of their status as free agents in themselves, Deleuze and Guattari suggest that conceptual personae plays an important structural or intermediary role in philosophy, facilitating the creation of new concepts by drawing ideas together for the philosopher to use. This can be equated to the manner in which Wells can be seen as a Deleuzian "mutation" subject to an eclectic variety of new identities via contemporary media depictions, as demonstrated through his appearance as a female in *Warehouse 13*, to give but one example. Nevertheless, conceptual personae are "not the author[s] of a concept, but the figure presupposed by the concept" (Colebrook 2004, 74). These personae are not "signatures," that is, claimants whose ownership of a concept cannot be disputed; they are more like "friends ... internal to the conditions of philosophy" (Deleuze 2004, 4) who cultivate concepts rather than attach their signatures to them. Instead, via the medium of various fictional extrapolations, Wells himself can be transformed into one of a myriad of "fluctuating figures who express the presuppositions or ethos of their philosophy and through their existence, no matter how inchoate or unstable, give life to concepts on a new plane of immanence" (Rodowick 2000, n. p.). Importantly, these figures are not allegorical as they do not specifically "stand for" some idea, concept or thought, but figure in the search for still unformed thoughts. Colebrook highlights Romanticism as a specific example, stating that we could not have this movement without the figure of the Byronic individual, who is not the historical Byron but a broad-brushed character (Colebrook 2002, 74).

Deleuze provides examples in Socrates (who provided the conceptual persona for Platonism) and Homer (who provided the conceptual persona for the *Iliad* narratives). It is not necessary for these individuals to have actually existed, but it is necessary for them to have existed as vessels that contain a body of ideas. In *What is Philosophy?*, Deleuze names several fictional characters he regards as conceptual personae such as Don Juan, Herman Melville's Captain Ahab, and Nietzsche's Zarathustra, stating that "the conceptual persona is not the philosopher's representative... Conceptual personae are the philosopher's 'heteronyms,' and the philosopher's name is the simple pseudonym of his personae" (Deleuze & Guattari 1994, 54).

In this manner, as a "heteronym," Wells is the figure through which the concept of time travel is given force. He remains conceptual in that he has no consistent identity; his many depictions take on a variety of names, labels and even physicalities. For example, in the 1960 film adaptation of *The Time Machine*, the time traveler is named as George, an obvious reference to his literary creator. Even more explicitly, "H. George Wells" can be seen inscribed on a plaque on the time machine itself. Similarly, C. S. Lewis's novel *That Hideous Strength* features the character of Horace Jules, a pseudo-scientific journalist and caricature of Wells.

Rather than all being conceptual personae in their own right, the one constant in all of these "mutations" is, of course, that they invoke Wells in some form or other, regardless of the actual nature of the depiction. However, they are not functioning merely as Wells' representative. In conceptual terms they are the "fictional characters of philosophy" that Deleuze advocates; these are not aesthetic figures, but "powers of concepts" (Colebrook 2002, 65). There are many different variations of Wells, which is in keeping with the manner in which the multitude of conceptual personae burgeon; "each persona has several features that may give rise to other personae, on the same or a different plane: conceptual personae proliferate" (76). In these processes, the conceptual persona, in deterritorializing thought, assists in making concepts available that would otherwise remain stagnant on their plane. Through these processes, the concepts of Wells endure, mutating into an abundance of new forms in the process.

Obviously, in their wide variety of manifestations, not all these "conceptual Wells" are "accurate" depictions of his original ideologies, but are indeed Deleuze's "monstrous" mutations. So, more than a "reading" or "interpretation," we face a Deleuzian "production" of Wells, connected in a new philosophical space: a new and entirely Deleuzian plane of immanence. However, Deleuze would argue that Wells would still recognize himself in the medium of his conceptual persona; "I am no longer myself but thought's aptitude for finding itself and spreading across a plane that passes through me at several places" (Deleuze & Guattari 1994, 54). Indeed, it is the destiny of the "philosopher" to become his conceptual persona or personae, and "become something other than they are historically, mythologically, or commonly" (Deleuze & Guattari 1994, 64). Such is Wells' legacy; ultimately, as a thinker, philosopher, prophet, and father of modern science fiction, through endless proliferations he has become something other, and as conceptual persona he continues in the production of a legacy of "an infinite and plastic ambiguity" (Borges 2000, 87). In these terms, Warren Wagar poetically surmises that Wells was "like the ambiguous hero of his first novel, an intrepid time traveler, a man whose mind traversed time from its beginnings in the inferno of Earth's creation to the broad spectrum of futures imaginably awaiting our species and our globe" (2004, 2). Correspondingly, Deleuze and Guattari state that the task of art in all its forms is to "capture," "summon," and make visible these otherwise imperceptible forces (1994, 181–182). If the purpose of science fiction is to "write the future" (Pinsky 2003, 13) then Wells fulfills this remit, proving himself to be an inexhaustible rhizome, to which the application of Deleuzian theory can only assist in the understanding.

Indeed, as one of the most significant minds at work in our times, and one of the few whose worldview remains fresh and imperative today, the answers Wells supplied to the most pressing issues of the human condition have lost none of their relevance. The Deleuzian concept of the conceptual personae allows us to read Wells as more than just a great mind occupying a specific era of history, or as a central locus of concepts as per Orr's notion of a Matrix figure. As Buchanan states, "If it is well conceived, the conceptual persona remains fresh and new, alive, no matter how many long years pass between the moment of conception and reception" (2000, 49). Through the medium of Deleuze and the conceptual persona we are indeed witness to the eternal and untimely power of Wells' literature and ideas, incarnated via the medium of the time travel concept.

To Boldly Go Where ~~No~~ Man Has Gone Before

Complexity Science and the Star Trek Reboot

Matthew Kimberley *and* Jason N. Dittmer

Introduction

From its first broadcast as a television series in 1966 until its recent reboot with *Star Trek* (2009) and *Star Trek into Darkness* (2012), the *Star Trek* franchise has amassed a total of five distinct television shows and twelve films (six with the original cast, four with that of *Star Trek: The Next Generation*, two with that of the reboot), not to mention a host of transmedia texts; novels, computer games, comics, audio books and so on. It is not unsurprisingly regarded as "the mother of all television franchises ... [which has gained] a multinational fanbase devoted to its utopian ethos" (Geraghty 2010, 131). Set in the twenty-third and twenty-fourth centuries, the franchise is renowned for its use of science fiction to explore themes of social, cultural and political importance. It also endeavors to couch its fiction and "technobabble" in real science.[1] One science fiction plot device found frequently throughout the history of the show and integral to its reboot is time travel. Sometimes used to reflect on the tragedies of history, sometimes to highlight the dangers of altering past contingencies, it has often been an essential tool for social comment and reinforcing the "utopian ethos" the franchise espouses.

In spite of its longevity and dedicated following, poor box office figures for the later films and the premature cancellation of the fifth televisual incarnation, *Enterprise*, prompted Paramount to seek to reboot this lucrative franchise. This took the form of the 2009 film helmed by J.J. Abrams, a dominant figure in American science fiction film and television. Together with regular production and writing collaborators Roberto Orci and Alex Kurtzman,

Abrams gave *Star Trek*'s continuity a radical overhaul, using a time travel narrative to rewrite this "history of the future" and open it up to new possibilities (and, of course, audiences).

In this essay, we cast a skeptical eye on the claim, frequently made, that time travel science fiction offers the opportunity for politically progressive tales to filter into our consciousness and for our present to be denaturalized and set aside to make way for more utopian imaginings (Freedman 2000; Warf 2002). Certainly this is possible, but it seems rarer in practice than in theory. Our second goal is to show how the recent *Star Trek* films provide us with resources to rethink the way in which time is considered in time travel narratives, trying to shift away from a "timeline" perspective with an efficient mode of causation, to a more complex understanding of time and causation in which various virtual pasts and futures shape the lines of flight emerging from the present. In order to achieve these goals, we begin with a literature review of various philosophical approaches to time, emphasizing those that connect with the notion of "becoming" found in complexity and assemblage theory. We then examine the recent *Star Trek* reboot, which is premised on a "new timeline," but which features both this more complex form of causation and also a fairly conservative (in that it closely parallels the "original" timeline) outcome. In our conclusion we extend our arguments regarding the conservative nature of much time travel in science fiction to show the implications of our understanding of time for genre theory.

Linear Time and Time Travel in Star Trek

The nature of time in science fiction has often been imagined, not surprisingly, in terms that owe a great debt to Albert Einstein. In the late nineteenth and early twentieth centuries, physics began to utilize the language of geometry in order to formalize time. Through this process of visualization, physical processes came to be imagined as occurring in space rather than time. Time came to be understood through its spatial manifestations—in the movement of a star across the sky, in the development of wrinkles in a face, in the passage of sand through an hourglass. Time began to be measured extensively, that is to say in the spatial difference between point 1 (the sun rising) and point 2 (the sun now overhead). Indeed, even the idea of *measuring* time at all implies its specialization. What was lost was a sense of time as *intensive*, or as experienced by a subject. While it is possible to mathematically manipulate extensive time (e.g., to go back to the midpoint of a process we can divide the length of the process by two), it is impossible to do so with intensive time because it is entirely qualitative. Intensive time can no more be divided in two than you can divide the color yellow in two. It is incommensurate with measurement and is rather a fundamentally unidirectional process whereby the world is constantly becoming.

This rendering of time via space, drawing on geometry, enabled time to be linearized; it was just one dimension of spacetime, the proverbial "fourth dimension." This linearization meshes with not only the serialized nature of much (but certainly not all) popular science fiction, but also not coincidentally the temporal imagination of time travel often found in this science fiction. Considering that the long-lasting serial narratives of science fiction have tended to be world- or universe-building endeavors, fandom and the producers of such popular science fiction have tended to focus on the concept of continuity—the formation of a canonical history within the universe in question (see Reynolds 1992; Hills 2002; Johnson 2005). A linear history of this sort—embodied in timelines, chronologies and other metatexts produced to accompany science fiction—emphasizes relatively simple linear relations of cause and effect. That which came before produced that which came after.[2]

Within this context, time travel is itself an envisioning of time as space; one can go backwards or forwards, just as one can go east or west. Given the simplistic notion of causation found in this linear image of time, if one goes back in time key events can be changed, enabling new futures to unfold. In fact, there are many science fiction texts that are precisely concerned with this phenomenon—*Terminator* (1984), *Back to the Future* (1985) and *Star Trek IV: The Voyage Home* (1986). Another variation is the concern over time paradoxes—killing your own grandfather and so on—which can be found, for example, in many episodes of *Star Trek* (such as the original series' "The City on the Edge of Forever" [1967] or *Deep Space 9*'s "Trials and Tribble-ations" [1996]). All of this is to say that the deployment of linear notions of time in science fiction has been used as an opportunity to play with historical continuity, to envision new possibilities beyond what has been actualized in "our" history. Warf (2002, 25) argues that such imagined worlds can be politically emancipatory, a point he makes with regard to counterfactual histories: "Successful stories, such as the USA, generally snuff out consideration of paths not taken; after all, once they have become wealthy and powerful, it is inconceivable for the past to have unfolded in any other way."[3] While time travel science fiction offers the chance to explore these alternative possibilities, even a quick survey of the genre shows that despite this radical potential, most time travel narratives culminate in the restoration of "our" timeline in one way or another. For instance, in the three films cited above the protagonists all struggle to maintain worlds/universes that are familiar to "ours." This is what is so interesting about the *Star Trek* reboot; here we see the creators explicitly moving forward with a new universe, shorn free of the trappings of past continuity. However, despite several significant changes, the *Star Trek* universe emerges in a startlingly similar form.

The two critical points of deviation from the original continuity, or timeline, which occur in the reboot are at the beginning of the film and later with the destruction of the planet Vulcan. Their emancipatory effect on continuity is counterbalanced by Spock, who physically moves from one timeline to another and vies to steer events towards a recreation of the original narrative universe. While exploring deep space, the *USS Kelvin* (identifiable to fans from the original 1960s series) encounters a "lightning storm in space" from which emerges an advanced ship crewed by Romulans, a classic adversary. The Romulans cripple the *Kelvin* and demand that it surrender and that its captain be transported to their ship. As he is leaving, the *Kelvin*'s captain hands command to one Lieutenant George Kirk, the father of James Tiberius Kirk, the captain of the *Enterprise* in the original series. The Romulans, it transpires, are looking for "Ambassador Spock" and, when the *Kelvin*'s captain does not co-operate, they kill him and attack the *Kelvin*. George Kirk saves his crew, including his pregnant wife, by evacuating them while he steers the ship into the Romulan vessel. Just before he dies, he has a conversation with his wife, Winona, and they agree to call their son James Tiberius.

This opening plays with established continuity and audience expectation in a number of ways. To the fan, there are numerous indications that the timeline deviates from established fact: James Kirk makes references to having known his father in the original series ("Where No Man Has Gone Before" [1966], "Operation—Annihilate!" [1967]), so his death is incongruous with canon; the Romulans are seeking "Ambassador Spock," a title the equally famed character of the original series does not acquire until much later (first referenced in *Star Trek: The Next Generation* "Unification I" [1991]), indicating that they are from the future; the *Kelvin* is destroyed though it should not have been. We know, therefore, that we are about to embark upon a time travel narrative in which the past is altered at a significant juncture. What is not known is how these alterations will be resolved.

Though the opening sets the scene for all subsequent changes, the crux of the story is the destruction of Vulcan, Spock's home planet. Indeed, the destruction of Vulcan is the primary motivation for the Romulans' time travel in the first place: Ambassador Spock of the original timeline was on a mission to save the Romulan homeworld, but he failed to arrive in time. Driven to madness by the loss of his planet, the Romulan commander Nero decides to exact revenge by traveling back to the past and destroying Spock's homeworld.

The significance of the act for *Star Trek*'s timeline is that Vulcan is one of the founding and foremost civilizations of the Federation, and plays an integral role in many of the stories that are told throughout the franchise's history. Furthermore, in Abrams and his production crew's reboot, there is no restoration of the original timeline: Vulcan is destroyed and remains so with the film's conclusion. In this respect, the film conforms to the politically emancipatory potential of time travel (or counterfactual history) narratives described by Warf. It is, however, in the finer details of the film's plot that the drive toward conservatism manifests itself, nowhere more so than in the actions of Ambassador Spock.

As Vulcan is destroyed, this new timeline's younger Commander Spock attempts to rescue the elders of Vulcan's High Council, including his parents. However, his mother does not survive, a loss that Ambassador Spock never suffered in this way. With his mother's death and his planet destroyed, Commander Spock becomes emotionally volatile. Provoked by the young James Kirk, Spock loses his temper and has Kirk ejected from the ship. It is this act that brings Kirk, in the jettisoned escape pod, to be marooned on a planet where he encounters Ambassador Spock. Older Spock explains to Kirk the events leading up to the present, which brings in an essential element of the time travel narrative. Up to this point, the revisionism of the reboot is perceptible only to the audience: none of the main characters are any the wiser to changes in the past since this is the story of their timeline. But through an interaction between the Kirk from this timeline and the Spock from the original continuity, the ability to consciously alter the course of change is introduced. It is Ambassador Spock's actions that lead to the changes in the first place and, as the only character with knowledge of both the original timeline and its new iteration, he has a greater degree of influence over how radical or conservative the new timeline will be relative to the previous one. Tellingly, he makes a conservative choice. He emphasizes the importance of returning Kirk to the *Enterprise* and even tells him what he must do to psychologically destabilize his alternate self in order that Kirk can take his "rightful" place as captain. There is no inherent necessity to this beyond Ambassador Spock's conviction that things *should*, as best as possible, reflect his own timeline.

Ambassador Spock's prioritization of reestablishing the rank and file of the *Enterprise* is also revealed through an encounter with another key character on the planet, Chief Engineer Montgomery "Scotty" Scott. In order to get Kirk back to the ship, Spock decides to reveal to Scotty a means of transporting someone to a distant ship traveling at warp speed, years in advance of when this technological capability is achieved by the original timeline's Scotty. It is an act of significant alteration to the development of the timeline, but Spock clearly feels the decision is offset by the far greater importance of reuniting the original *Enterprise* crew. The decision reflects the greater prioritization of recreating the original crew's composition (and ranking) than of the technological development of the new timeline. The reboot's political conservatism manifests itself via the production of hierarchies within multiplicity; some possibilities for the unfolding of time are privileged over others.

Complex Emergence, Multiplicity and Basins of Attraction

How can we understand this conservatism? To answer this we turn to work inspired by Henri Bergson (1910). Bergson disputed Einstein's spatialization of time, or at least argued that this was not the only form of time that should be considered. Bergson argued for a more subjective understanding of time, called duration, which was tied to materiality and the unfolding of processes, both human and nonhuman. In this consideration of time, the present cannot be understood as the "dot" on a timeline that signifies "now." Rather, the present must be understood as elastic, capable of expanding itself to include what from the past and immediate future it requires to remain in continuity with itself, to complete its present action. It has no measurable length, for it takes as long as it takes to perform a continuous action; the present may be nearly instantaneous for a quick action (the blink of an eye), or it may stretch itself to include minutes, hours, days, and even longer. When, for example, we talk of geological or evolutionary duration, we may define the present in terms of centuries or millennia (Grosz 2004, 177).

Causation, therefore, is not as simple as a present overdetermined by the past. Rather, the present should be understood as a range of temporalities, "force fields," which interact with one another in entirely unpredictable ways, producing events (Connolly 2010, 5). These events are not predictable in their specificity from what came before. The materializations of the past are manifested in the present, for instance, in forms as varied as evolutionary holdovers such as the appendix, reminders of past architectural thought in still-standing buildings, and as neurological structures such as habits or memories. All of these shape the present's actualization in particular outcomes. The branch of science that has become concerned with this form of "emergent causality" in the last several decades is known as complexity science.

Complex systems are unpredictable but it is possible to understand their tendencies (DeLanda 2006). Take, for example, the birth of James Kirk. His parents could produce a near-infinite multiplicity of individual children, even though they bring the same DNA to the "event." This is because of the near infinite possible interactions between individual sperm and eggs, and also because of contextual issues—things like vitamin levels in the mother's body, levels of outer space radiation in their reproductive systems at the moment of conception and so on. Therefore, Captain Kirk's sex, his phenotype, his genetic mutations and so forth cannot be predicted in advance of his actual development. Having said that, it is possible to sketch out the statistical probabilities for "James Kirk" given his two specific parents (George and Winona). This distribution of probabilities is called a possibility space and individual iterations (e.g., babies) can be mapped in that space. The possibility space can have as many dimensions as there are variables. Statistically, for any two parents the babies will cluster around certain attractors in that space—for instance, two blue-eyed parents are likely to produce a blue-eyed baby. However, that cannot be guaranteed.

Another feature of possibility spaces is that they take the form of basins of attraction. It might be fruitful to imagine a possibility space that looks like a galaxy, where individual stars equal (continuing our earlier example) possible "James Kirks" given the DNA of his parents. Just like stars cluster in particular patterns because of gravitational fields, "Kirks" will cluster in this possibility space because of the interaction of the past (parental DNA) with elements of the Bergsonian present (Winona's age and health habits, or the random selection of George's sperm at conception) around certain attractors. The further away from those attractors you move, the fewer "babies" can be found until we leave the basin of attraction and cross over into another one. In our example, that would be to cross the grim line of human viability. Less morbidly, we can imagine a possibility space for water. Water can be heated or cooled and remain seemingly unchanged (clustered around a single attractor); however if it crosses 0° or 100° Celsius, it leaps from one basin of attraction to another and becomes ice or steam.

In these examples, unlike the linear causation found in most science fiction, the past is here only a series of resources that can be drawn on in the unfolding of the present. There is nothing determinative in the past. For instance, computers have been able to simulate the emergence of life from non-life (DeLanda 2011), giving us a hint of how such an event might have transpired at some point far in our past via an unexpected confluence of "force fields" and material elements that changed the dynamics of our "system" ever since, but one that need not have happened at all. However, to highlight the emergence of the new and unexpected is to overemphasize one half of Deleuze's formulation: "difference and repetition" (1994). Deleuze was referencing the fact that everything exists as a multiplicity. To speak of this in terms of *Star Trek*, the James Kirk of the "original" continuity is as equally "Kirk" as the "new" one. They are both possible iterations of the Kirk multiplicity within a possibility space; fundamentally similar (a repetition) while also distinctive (a difference). While every individuation is unique, it is also a repetition within a possibility space. An emphasis on novelty is politically useful (for instance, the utopian possibility of time travel in science fiction), but is statistically minor within a complex system. Most of the James Kirks that can be actualized will be clustered around the attractors of his possibility space, or else he ceases to be "Kirk" at all. From this discussion of time and causation associated with complexity science, it is evident that we need to reconsider how academic accounts of time travel in science fiction approach the subject. To illuminate this point, we return to the recent "reboot" of the *Star Trek* franchise, which provides powerful evidence of emergent causality.

Assembling the Federation's Finest

What are the force fields, attractors and possibility spaces at work in this reboot? Where do we see difference and repetition? One of the core attractors to the identity of the original series and first six films is the configuration of the key crew members around whom the stories center: Captain James T. Kirk, Commander Spock, Chief Medical Officer Dr. Leonard "Bones" McCoy, Chief Engineer Montgomery "Scotty" Scott, Helmsman Hikaru Sulu, Communications Officer Nyota Uhura and Navigator Pavel Chekov. The first film of the reboot deals primarily with how these individuals are drawn together both *in spite of* and as a *consequence of* the change to the timeline shown in the opening scene. In short, it articulates an alternate concatenation of events that produce the bridge of the *Enterprise* as something fundamentally similar to that found in the original continuity. These are alternate paths to the (almost) same point; nevertheless, the path taken matters.

The new convergence of the *Enterprise*'s crew begins with a young adult Kirk encountering Cadet Uhura in a bar and culminates in the arrival of Scotty and soon-to-be Acting Captain Kirk on the ship much later. The bar fight Kirk gets into over his attempts to seduce Uhura is what brings him into contact with Captain Christopher Pike who, having revealed that the actions of George Kirk aboard the *Kelvin* were the subject of his dissertation, eventually persuades Kirk to enroll in Starfleet. This in turn brings him into contact with another fresh, albeit older, recruit in the form of Leonard McCoy with whom a friendship is formed. The narrative skips forward in time to their later days as Starfleet cadets and the reception of a distress signal from Vulcan. Although

Kirk is on suspension, it is this friendship with McCoy that surreptitiously secures him passage aboard the *Enterprise*. We also learn here that Uhura is in a relationship with Commander Spock. Through a combination of self-advocacy in her talent and personal influence over Spock, she is also able to get herself transferred to the *Enterprise*, where he is serving as Pike's First Officer. By the time the action has delivered all these characters to the ship, it hardly comes as a surprise to any fan that Sulu is at the helm and Chekov at navigation.

We should take pause to consider how all the differences have amassed to create an essentially repetitive iteration: the failure of Ambassador Spock to save Romulus leads to him being marooned in the past. His very appearance in the past changes the circumstances of Kirk's birth and early life, which is in a sense "corrected" by his chance encounter with Uhura and McCoy in a bar and recruitment to Starfleet Academy. Together with Spock, Sulu and Chekov, they end up aboard the *Enterprise* because, although only cadets (with the exception of Spock), an emergency has arisen which requires "all hands on deck," that emergency being the attack on Vulcan. For all the incalculable differences that the original change to the timeline could and should have had, what Abrams *et al.* deliver is a very familiar configuration born of a rather different path.

While in terms of the crew's composition, the *Enterprise* appears as a literal attractor in space, playing host to those elements (personnel) that give *Star Trek* its identity, it is also notable that the "original" *Enterprise* functions as a virtual element in this complex temporal system. When all other ships mounting the Vulcan rescue effort are destroyed upon their arrival, the *Enterprise* is spared because Nero, the Romulan who is transported back in time at the start of the film, remembers the ship's name, which is a materialized structure in his brain and thus crossed through the temporal rift with him. The ship in his timeline is famous as one on which Kirk (and more importantly Spock) served and therefore affords him the chance to punish all "Spocks." Nero uses his knowledge of the alternate timeline to shape how this one unfolds. While small but important differences in the lives of Kirk, Spock, McCoy, Uhura, Sulu and Chekov have changed the paths leading to their service on board the *Enterprise*, it is precisely those differences which create the sequence of events through which they arrive there and subsequently prevent catastrophe. The elements that are the well-established command crew of the original *Enterprise* and the attractor that is the ship itself thus bring radical differences in character history iterations back to an essentially conservative repetition of the continuity's established order. Nevertheless, this iteration of the *Star Trek* possibility space is not understandable without reference to the

virtual past that Nero (and Spock) brought with them from the "first" iteration. The present—in *Star Trek* and in our lives—is composed of the intersection of various virtual pasts and futures in the lived present.

An important dialogue, coming at the final moments of the film after
Earth has been saved and prior to the crew all being promoted from the Academy into their canonically established ranks and roles on the *Enterprise*, takes
place between the two Spocks:

> COMMANDER SPOCK: Why then did you send Kirk aboard when you alone could
> have explained the truth?
> AMBASSADOR SPOCK: Because you needed each other. I could not deprive you
> of the revelation of all that you could accomplish together, of a friendship that
> will define you both in ways you cannot yet realize.

As shown already by his willingness to reveal future technologies to ensure
Kirk and Scotty get aboard the *Enterprise*, the dialogue here emphasizes that,
though the most expedient solution to the Romulan threat would have been
for the older Spock to reveal himself and influence the course of action taken
by the young crew, he regarded it as more important to this future that they
forge a bond through the common experience of unidirectional time, in the
way Bergson describes as a force that changes us. While he had persuaded Kirk
that he could not encounter his younger self for risk of inducing a "universe
ending paradox" of the kind often associated with time travel narratives,[4]
what he endeavors to achieve through this ruse is to ensure that the alternate
reality steers towards his own. It is not enough that Kirk and Spock should
serve on the same ship; they must feel the intensive effects of time on their
relationship such that the new iteration of the possibility space remains firmly
in the *Star Trek* basin of attraction.

Starfleet: "A peacekeeping and humanitarian armada"

Integral to the philosophy and identity of the *Star Trek* universe as envisioned by creator Gene Roddenberry is its humanist utopianism (Jindra 1999;
Hark 2008; Short 2011). The narratives present the United Federation of
Planets as a democratic coalition of worlds committed to space exploration,
diplomacy and the care and support of its interplanetary citizenry. This inter-
stellar geopolitical mandate constitutes another attractor around which the
future history coalesces and forms the basis for how the new timeline evolves
in the sequel, *Star Trek into Darkness*. With the command crew established
aboard the *Enterprise*, the film picks up a little further in the future while they
are exploring space. The opening set piece involves them saving a pre-industrial

species from destruction through natural disaster. This act, and the fact that in saving them they also reveal themselves and their advanced technology to a species far from achieving such things themselves, violates Starfleet's "Prime Directive": to in no way interfere in the normal social, cultural and technological development of sentient species less advanced than the constituent members of the United Federation of Planets. Though this directive is held to be the highest code of the Federation, to the extent that a commander should sacrifice their ship and crew rather than violate it, an audience familiar with the episodes and films of the canon will be well aware that it has been routinely broken by the various crews of the *Enterprise* in the course of their adventures. To the inducted audience therefore, this beginning to the film is a self-aware acknowledgement that this crew is not so different in behavior from the one familiar from original continuity. However, the Prime Directive itself privileges a linear, developmentalist notion of history, one we have already seen endorsed by the original Spock in his efforts to get the crew to follow their "normal" path despite the changing events of history in this iteration.

The second film centers on the character of Khan Noonien Singh, an adversary first brought into the original series in the episode "Space Seed" (1967) and again in the second film, *Star Trek II: The Wrath of Khan* (1982). In the original continuity, Khan is a genetically engineered human who was involved in the eugenics wars of the 1990s. When their dreams of conquest dashed, he and seventy-two of his followers leave Earth in suspended animation aboard an early star ship. In the original series, the *Enterprise* crew come across this ship in deep space, resuscitate its inhabitant and a struggle ensues as Khan attempts to wrest control of the *Enterprise*. After defeating him, Kirk deposits Khan and his people on an unpopulated planet where they can establish their own preferred authoritarian social order. The film finds them many years later, greatly reduced in number after the natural destruction of one planet in the system shifted the orbital plane of their own world rendering it virtually uninhabitable. Khan and the survivors escape, seeking revenge against Kirk, and are ultimately killed when Kirk cedes control of the *Enterprise* to them, having evacuated his crew, and self-destructs the Enterprise with Khan and his followers on board.

With a new iteration of the timeline now in place, Abrams and his production collaborators created a new way to bring this popular character back into the *Star Trek* universe, this time combining features of the original episode and film with the new geopolitical situation facing the Federation. It is revealed that after the destruction of Vulcan, Starfleet begins pushing farther and faster out into deep space in order to find a new home for the displaced surviving Vulcans. They discover Khan's vessel and bring him to

Earth prematurely. Over the course of the film it is revealed that one particular senior Starfleet figure, Admiral Marcus, believes that the only way for the Federation to be able to cope with increasing new threats, such as the advanced Romulan ship of the first film, is to militaries Starfleet. He uses Khan as a collaborator to this end, but inevitably Khan has plans of his own and this drives the film's plot. From the point of view of how differences and repetitions emerge in this iteration, what is noteworthy about the most recent film is that it creates a scenario in which the geopolitical order (the extension of the Federation in space and its subsequent relationships with its neighbors) and orientation (exploratory and diplomatic versus colonizing and militaristic) are challenged. As with the first film, however, we see that the potentially revolutionary changes in the timeline in fact actualize within the possibility space as something much closer to the political and moral values of the original iteration.

One of the final sequences to the film involves a battle in which the *Enterprise* is critically damaged and Kirk must sacrifice himself to save the ship. This is a direct homage to events at the end of *The Wrath of Khan* (in which Spock saves the ship, giving his own life). The scenario is replicated exactly, with some of the same dialogue between Spock and Kirk, but with their roles inverted. However, the meaning of the scene is quite different, embedded as it is in a new context. Whereas Spock's death scene in the older film highlighted his commitment to Benthamite logic even if it meant sacrificing his life ("the good of the many outweighs the good of the few"), as well as his personal friendship with Kirk, in the new film Kirk's death scene illustrates his character's development from the brash, selfish officer resultant from his father's early death into a more humble, thoughtful leader (a change presaged by other moments in this film where his relationship with Spock matures into mutual respect). This too illustrates the conservatism of this iteration of the *Star Trek* universe, as Kirk now more closely resembles the Kirk from the more developed continuity. This is a repetition with difference, however, as the more emotional Spock of this timeline, forged through the trauma of his planet's destruction and death of his mother, sets off to avenge Kirk's death on Khan with bloodthirsty abandon. Some things have definitively changed, but the "world" produced is recognizable to the *Star Trek* fan.

Conclusions

The *Star Trek* reboot has been fairly exceptional in its approach when compared to other rebooted texts of recent years and it offers a unique insight into the relationship between time travel and science fiction. Reboots have tended to focus on simply remaking films with some modernization (*Carrie* and *Evil Dead*, both 2013), taking advantage of advancements in special effects (*War of the Worlds* [2005], *The Day the Earth Stood Still* [2008], *Robocop* [2014]) or expanding but not really altering existing narrative worlds with prequels and sequels (*Terminator Salvation* [2009] and *Prometheus* [2012]). The superhero genre has seen a number of reboots of previous film franchises, notably Nolan's *The Dark Knight* trilogy for Batman (2005, 2008, 2012), Snyder's *Man of Steel* (2013) for Superman and Webb's *The Amazing Spider-Man* (2012). Even so, the role of the origin story in superhero narratives has always been somewhat more complex, with many iterations occurring in the continuities over the decades (Wandtke 2007; Brooker 2012). However, what Abrams has done with *Star Trek* is to reiterate the narrative universe as a multiplicity, albeit one that rather conservatively values the original narrative as a model for the new. This conservatism limits the political potential of time travel narratives within science fiction, maintaining worlds that appear similar to our own even if slightly different. In this case, the ship and crew seem ineluctably drawn together, not only through the conscious machinations of Spock but also through the random workings of the universe. Seemingly all turbolifts lead to the bridge of the *Enterprise*. Of course, there is no reason to think that no good can come from these narratives; indeed the anti-militarism running strongly through *Into Darkness* feels positively refreshing (itself a throwback to the Roddenberry vision for the original *Star Trek*), but it indicates the limits of difference within a broader repetition.

Of course, it would be easy to criticize this chapter's linkage of the events in *Star Trek* with complexity theory for overloading a pop culture phenomenon with scientific jargon. However, complexity theory, with its sophisticated understanding of temporal relations within systems, offers some insights into genre theory as well. If we think of genres (like science fiction) as a basin of attraction, in which a virtual Platonic science fiction text occupies the position of attractor, we can imagine individual texts as instantiations within that possibility space, approaching that attractor in some dimensions (generic conventions) while perhaps remaining distant in others. If a text is distant enough in all dimensions it may tip into another basin of attraction and be labeled something else (e.g., detective story or fantasy). Further, genres are temporally-specific and over time they evolve, both "forgetting" past texts and appropriating others as the entire system evolves both internally and in relation to other genres. This constant reterritorialization of a genre accounts for both the seemingly solid tangibility of genres and also their tendency to evaporate into a multiplicity of loosely related texts when examined closely. Altman (1999,

69–70) describes this using similarly geographic language in his discussion of the changes in form and distribution of genres:

> We usually represent slapstick, romantic and burlesque comedy on the same map, within the very same space, that holds, say, epic, lyric and dramatic poetry or tragic, tragicomic and comic theatre ... [t]he map looked one way when musical comedy, musical drama and the musical Western were cycles within the genres of comedy, drama and the Western, and quite another way when the musical was established as a stand-alone genre. We would surely benefit from careful description of successive generic maps, yet most critics remain unaware that generic cartography involves multiple superimposed maps of differing ages and extents—even though many of them use the same place names.

Complexity science may offer a useful tool for addressing the issue of generic cartography. Genres emerge in the present as a set of relations instantiated among past media texts to shape future texts. This phenomenon can be witnessed in microcosm within the *Star Trek* universe. Just as the elderly Spock and Nero drew from the "original" timeline to shape their present and future, Abrams poached the parts of continuity he wanted and left the rest, imagining a future of narrative yet to be written. The generic present reaches not just into the past and future, as per Bergson's notion of duration, but also laterally into parallel universes and timelines.

Notes

1. See for example *The Physics of Star Trek* (Krauss 1995) and *Life Signs: The Biology of Star Trek* (Jenkins and Jenkins 1998).

2. Ample examples of this can be found in the paratextual material surrounding *Star Trek*, including *The Star Trek Encyclopedia: A Reference Guide to the Future* (Okuda, Okuda and Mirek 2011), *Star Trek Chronology: The History of the Future* (Okuda and Okuda 1993), and *Star Trek Federation: The First 150 Years* (Goodman 2013).

3. As mentioned, the very rebooting of *Star Trek* is itself a consequence of the decline of the franchise's wealth and power, prompting the studio to embark on a "counterfactual history of the future."

4. For instance, this is the subject of the final episode of *Star Trek: The Next Generation* ("All Good Things... Parts I and II" [1994]). It is likewise found scattered throughout episodes of *Doctor Who* including "The Big Bang" (2010) "The Wedding of River Song" (2011) and "The Angels Take Manhattan" (2012).

Control Dramas and Play Time

Tales of Redemption and the Temporal Fantasist

Jacqueline Furby

This essay considers the ways in which film narrative becomes a temporal playground, a kind of "play time," in texts about time travel into the past. Play time is opposed to "real time," which can be thought of as time in the real world. This time is the same as clock time, passing at a uniform rate of one second per second. It only runs in one direction. This differs from our subjective experience of time, which is more malleable. Our thoughts can move easily and quickly from an appreciation of the present moment to a memory of the distant past or an anticipated point in the future. In fact, there is no limit to where (or when) we might travel to in time in our thoughts and dreams. As such, internal, subjective time is a playground where we might freely roam. Cinema is also a site where we can find time in the world behaving like subjective time, and this "play time " enables us to experience time in ways that are not normally available in our daily waking lives. Nearly all cinematic narratives involve a kind of time travel as they reshuffle and reorder time, stretch and shrink duration, and alter the frequency of events. In addition to this idea of time travel *of* narrative there is the idea of time travel *in* narrative: films whose *stories* involve temporal manipulation. Through these stories we encounter a malleable play time and are given a chance to fantasize a different relationship with time that is not necessarily based on the familiar, linear, unidirectional model.

This essay considers a particular sub-class of time travel narrative, the Orphic rescue fantasy, named after the character of Orpheus, who is famed for his (failed) attempt to cheat death by rescuing his bride, Eurydice, from the underworld (Ovid 1955, 234–237). Orpheus was unable to redeem Eurydice from death's realm and heal the pain of his loss, but versions of the redemptive fantasy continue to play with the possibility of recovering something or someone otherwise gone forever; something or someone lost in time. Film narratives modeled on the Orphic rescue include *Back to the Future* (1985), *Frequency* (2000), *La Jetée* (1962), *Timescape* (1991), *Twelve Monkeys* (1995) and *Vertigo* (1958). Such narratives offer the fantasy of a different relationship with time, one that allows us to go back and change the past.

Raising the Dead

Mulvey (2000, 142) writes that "when rays of light inscribe an object's image onto photosensitive paper at a particular moment, they record the object's presence but they also inscribe that moment of time, henceforth suspended." Therefore, as a character from Clark and Baxter's novel, *The Light of Other Days*, comments, "every time you watch a movie you're looking into the past" (2000, 139). Watching a movie involves not only the reanimation of the past, but also the tantalizing possibility of a return to it. The viewer is lifted from their present and resituated in an alternative present, one that has already taken place, but which often feels as if it is happening again for the first time because the film's tense is the continuous present. Time travel rescue fantasies add the element of redemption and involve a cyclical movement of return and change. If movies are slices of the past reanimated, or visions of alternative worlds, into which the time traveling spectator is drawn, then they represent the perfect medium for the exploration of nostalgic return rescue narratives. In this type of film the past is explicitly revisited and, importantly, reactivated in order to make an alteration, which in the most extreme examples involves bringing individuals back from the dead. This, as mentioned above, is an old story, and Orpheus is perhaps one of the earliest time travel fantasists. Ovid tells us that when Orpheus goes into the underworld to rescue his wife Eurydice from among the dead he fails because his success is conditional upon him not looking back as he leads her from the underworld. However, he does and she is lost forever. Following Orpheus, the type of rescue narrative I am concerned with demands a movement into the past with the intention of restoring one or more characters, or initiating a redemptive change. Actions, and actors, in the present are seen to affect the realm of the past. Things that are feared to be lost in the past are renewed and brought back and so the present and future are changed for the better.

The loss, recuperation and closure that is the subject of this kind of story has been read as a point of interconnection between narrative and psychoanalysis, because psychoanalytic theory posits that the edifice of human selfhood is founded upon a sense of loss, or lack, and the resultant desire for restoration (Mulvey 1975; Penley 1990; White 1991; Berman 2001, 29–62; McGowan 2011). The stories of resurrection, redemption or reanimation of the past indirectly address this sense of loss or lack through the fantasy of return. This is a recuperative temporal movement commonly found in film and may address the *spectator's* latent desires (for the purpose of emotional resolution) to revisit or change the past as much as it apparently addresses the *character's* manifest desires. However, reanimation of the past does not always serve the pleasure principle. Equally often the return of the past is figured as an unwelcome return of the repressed, or simply as an unpleasant memory prompted by a particular stimulus. An example of the first is seen in Gilliam's *The Fisher King* (1991), where Perry is pursued by the imaginary Red Knight, a manifestation of his repressed memories of his wife's death (Furby 2013, 79–91). An example of the latter is seen in *The Terminator* (1984), where Kyle Reese (Michael Biehn) hot-wires a car located next to a building site. The heavy machinery operating on the site prompts Reese to remember a traumatic episode from his past, when he was pitched in battle against machines whose remit is to destroy humanity. By means of this and other similar insights into the future post-apocalyptic world, the viewer is made aware of the high stakes involved if Reese fails in his redemptive mission to locate John Connor's mother and safeguard the future leader of the victorious resistance movement.

Many traditional psychoanalytic readings, drawing on the work of Freud (1991), contribute to a view of cinema as an arena for addressing related desires, argued to be latent in the (normally male) subject, which circulate around the Oedipal loss of the mother. Other, connected, readings (Mulvey 1975, 6–18; Metz 1983) use Lacan's theories of the Imaginary, the Symbolic and the Real, particularly the first two, to describe a relationship between the spectator and the text in which the spectator is returned to a time when they experienced a sense of transcendence through identification with an idealized self during the mirror phase (1977). Baudry (1986, 313) argues that one pleasure obtained through the relationship between the spectator and the cinema is a form of regression to an even earlier "archaic moment of fusion" between the subject and the maternal body, which exists prior to the mirror phase. However, Metz (1983, 7) reminds us that any reparation or satisfaction of unconscious desires thus experienced is only imaginary and temporary. The sense of lack begins to seep back once the lights in the auditorium are raised. This argument might lead us to the conclusion that the spectator is left with a fresh, intensified, sense of loss brought about through comparisons between the filmic world, where wishes are temporarily fulfilled, and the world outside, where wishes are newly unsatisfied. However, perhaps there is satisfaction in the idea that cinema is a place to which we may return at will, where everyday rules about time, including what (or who) may or may not be lost to the past (or even the future), do not necessarily apply. This place is not just in our imagination, but is a place with a foothold in the external realm. We may go there to *see* (and so in a sense to recover, if only temporarily) sights that are otherwise lost in time. Krämer (2005) offers an example of how cinema might enable a redemptive experience for the viewer in his study of the top grossing movies in North America since 1977, which identifies the following story common to the majority of the most popular films during this period:

> Loved ones ... have been, or are being lost, and this loss influences the protagonists' outlook on the world; their wishes and anxieties gradually—or occasionally very abruptly—take shape in their reality, often magically so; they achieve an emotional resolution in the end.... And always the power of cinema itself to bring fantastic scenes to life, to translate an individual's wishes and anxieties, dreams and nightmares into a shared reality, to make up—albeit only temporarily and imaginarily—for all our losses ... is being foregrounded and celebrated [130].

Krämer's description suggests a spectatorial relationship in which a loss is addressed by indirect means and the cinema itself features in bringing about a sense of restoration and closure.

The element of human authority over, or freedom within, time is important in the rescue narrative because it addresses another characteristic lack of temporal autonomy in everyday life. Our usual relationship with time in the external world might be summarized as a lack of a sense of control. It alters us; we cannot alter it. We cannot influence the *speed* of clock time. We can move through space at different rates and we can even remain stationary, but no similar options seem to exist with regard to time. We cannot slow time down, stop time's passage or speed time up. Nor can we change the direction of time or our position in it. We are unable to visit, or revisit, particular moments in the past except within the realms of our memory and imagination. The desire for control over where we are in time *can* be fulfilled however, through filmic play time. Backwards movement may be motivated by a desire to change the past, as in *Timescape*, a quest for knowledge, as in *Twelve Monkeys*, or a need for psychological redemption as in *The Fisher King*. All these examples speak of a need to gain a form of temporal control.

Modern rescue fantasies have something in common with Orpheus, but importantly they usually add an element of success lacking in the original tale. However, the demands of narrative complexity, anticipation, suspense and catharsis mean that any route to success is not without its obstacles and there is often a tariff to be levied for the backwards glance. Examples of films that employ time travel as a way of redeeming the past include Simon Wells' adaptation (2002) of his great-grandfather H.G. Wells' novel *The Time Machine* (1895). Simon Wells' version, in common with George Pal's 1960 adaptation, has the time traveler hurtling eight hundred millennia into the future, but this film has a redemptive twist not found in previous versions. His time traveler is motivated to build his time machine in order to attempt to rescue a loved one, Emma, in his present, rather than by curiosity about the future. *Time After Time* (1979) is also loosely based on Wells' novel. In this film Jack the Ripper escapes Victorian London by means of Wells' time machine. H.G. Wells follows him to 1979 (the film's present) and succeeds in banishing the Ripper from all time periods by projecting him into limbo. An action theoretically occurring later in chronological time has an effect in an earlier period (Wells deals with the Ripper in modern San Francisco, but the effects of the Ripper's absence are felt in Victorian England).

The central structuring motif that drives the plots of the *Back to the Future* series is that events throughout time can be tweaked to ensure a successful life for time traveler Marty McFly and his family, but as in *Time After Time* there is often a price to be paid. The first film introduces the idea that returning to the past can result in both positive and negative changes to the timeline. When Marty first arrives in 1955 from 1985 he inadvertently alters past events, the result of which is a temporal paradox: he prevents his mother and father from meeting and thus jeopardizes his own chances of being born. This threat to his existence is signaled in the film via a photograph he possesses of himself and his two siblings in which the three of them progressively fade as the chances of his parents falling in love with one another diminish. In this way a paradox arises; if he does not exist in the future of this new timeline, then he cannot travel back in time to meddle in his own destiny. In order to resolve the paradox he must make things happen as they did in the original timeline so that he can be born. In resolving the paradox, an action that makes up the major part of the film, Marty is in effect saving his own life. Similar life-saving, redemptive stories are found in *Back to the Future Part II* (1989) and *Part III* (1990). In the former, Marty's interference in the future results in his father's murder, which he then has to undo, and in the latter he returns to 1885 to prevent the murder of Doc Brown, the scientist who devised the means of time travel that he uses. The kind of redemptive operation conducted in these examples is a common trope in time travel stories. It makes use of the opportunities offered by the idea that a flexible timeline means that cause and effect relations can work in any direction and also that spacetime events, which are simply "out then," can be accessed, re-accessed and altered.

The Trouble with Time Travel

The tariff levied for the backwards glance demonstrates the frightening legacy of change that is experienced in the present and future as a result of perhaps only very minor changes initiated in the past through interactive time travel. This follows Lorenz's notion of chaos theory, popularly known as "the Butterfly effect" (Prigogine and Stengers 1984; Gleick 1988). The change made to the past ripples outwards, increasing in magnitude, and can have unforeseen consequences for the present and the future lives of the perpetrators. Films that envision past-directed time travel, such as *Back to the Future* and *Frequency* (discussed below), almost always build their plots around the positive and negative consequences of *interactive* past-directed time travel. Interactive past-directed time travel, which results in effects taking place chronologically earlier than their causes, violates the laws of causation. Under normal circumstances the direction of cause and effect and the direction of time agree: they both run from the past to the future. The present that we know has emerged from one particular past state. If that past state (cause) is changed by contamination from interaction with a time traveler then the course that led up to our present (effect) may be rendered invalid, and therefore the present would have to be different in order to comply with the laws of cause and effect. Changing the past retrospectively reverses the direction of cause and effect (reverse causation).

Naturally, this is problematic. Grey (1999) summarizes the problem as follows:

> We know quite generally that once an effect has occurred then its cause must have occurred. But if the cause were later than the effect, then once the effect has occurred then its cause would have to be unstoppable. However we also believe, in general, that we are able to intervene in the world to bring about or to prevent contingent happenings. If the cause of some event is located in the future then such interventions are subject to clear constraints, and in some cases will turn out to be impossible [63–4].

In addition, past- and future-directed time travel is only conceivable in a universe where past, present, and future times are real and stable (i.e., the time exists so that it might be traveled to). The idea, therefore, of being able to affect change in the past is incompatible with the idea of a real and stable timescape (55–70). Such difficulties suggest that certain physical laws that have yet to be discovered (perhaps a system of chronology protection or censorship as suggested by Stephen Hawking) would intervene and prevent successful interactive past-directed time travel (Hawking 1990, 89; Harwich 1987,

91–145). Deutsch (1997) is less pessimistic about the possibility of past-directed time travel. He argues that this kind of time travel would open up different versions of the past, within the framework of a multiverse, and so would not create paradoxes. Instead, to paraphrase Doc Brown in *Back to the Future Part II*, the time continuum would be disrupted and would create a "new temporal event sequence resulting in [an] alternate reality." Therefore if we changed the past we would not necessarily be able to return to the original starting point in the present. Despite his disagreement with refutations of the possibility of past-directed time travel on the basis of the creation of paradoxes, Deutsch does agree that it is likely that the fundamental laws of physics will be found to prohibit it (313; see also Hawking 2001, 131–154). In addition, Deutsch argues that it is not possible to travel back to a period before the invention of a time traveling method, which proves a limitation for contemporary time tourists (289–320). Even if such obstacles can be surmounted and a method of past-directed time travel proved possible, successful time travel may always necessitate the existence of a preventative barrier against any interaction between the tourist and the time visited.

Chaos theory and its quantum mechanical counterpart, quantum indeterminacy, suggest that the mere physical presence of matter profoundly affects the world around it in unpredictable ways. This implies that the preventative barrier might even disallow actual physical presence, which means the time traveler is only permitted to exist in the past in spirit rather than in body. Therefore the barrier that some physicists posit must exist between the time traveler and the time visited, may not be very different from the barrier extant between a film and the viewer—a barrier of non-contamination.

Although Einstein's theories of relativity led to the renaming of the three dimensions of space and the one dimension of time as four-dimensional, fixed spacetime, in which events in time are laid out all at once and where "the distinction between the past, the present and the future is only an illusion," we cannot yet imagine how it would be possible to overcome the difficulties inherent in past-directed time travel (Einstein in Coveney and Highfield 1991, 42). Einstein's work revealed previously unknown aspects of reality, such as the way space and time are curved in the presence of gravitational forces and how speed effects the relative passage of time, making external time/time in the world seem to behave much like subjective time (where we can travel anywhere in time through memories of the past and anticipation of the future). However, in spite of Einstein's relativistic time we are no closer to doing in reality what we can do in our imaginations, fantasies and dreams, and what we have been encouraged to do since the beginning of film's playtime.

The Infective, Persistent Past

Even in films that imagine successful backwards-directed time travel to be possible there are usually difficulties to be overcome, often relating to "the Butterfly effect." An example is seen in *Frequency,* where freak atmospheric conditions give John Sullivan the opportunity to use a ham radio set to talk to his father, Frank, across a thirty-year gap. In John's present reality (1999) his father died thirty years before, leaving John with a legacy of nostalgic melancholy, but by means of his dialogue with the past, John is able to prevent his father's premature death. He then also prevents his mother, Jules, from being murdered. In the process he repairs his own unhappy personal life and secures a happier present and future for his family. In the real everyday world cause and effect run from past to future, but in *Frequency* John influences his father (in the past) to behave differently, thus reversing the normal direction of time, disrupting linear cause and effect.

John's father Frank follows John's advice and survives. Interference with the past changes the present for both good and bad. However, a direct consequence of Frank's survival is that a serial killer, Jack Shepard, does not die in this new reality and continues to kill women, including John's mother. The tariff levied for the regretful backwards glance is renewed loss and further threat to the individual in the present. The reactivated past works fresh destruction in the present, signaled by John's mother's death and an attempt made on John's own life. John and his father work together across time to trace the killer. The killer attacks the six-year-old John and his family in 1969, while simultaneously attacking the adult John in 1999. John and Frank eventually defeat the killer by exploiting the opportunities offered by the temporal anomaly and all ends happily. Films such as this, then, offer us a fantasy, a play time, where time behaves differently. The past is normally closed to us, in that we cannot normally change events that occurred in the past; we can only change how we think about them. Conversely, we assume we have some degree of control over the future because we are free to make choices about our future actions. Redemption narratives can be thought of as stories that deal with the fantasy of reopening the past to us, or stories that force the past to behave as if it were the future.

Venturing into the past, though, is not without its complications. This idea of there being fresh perils awaiting us in the past reflects our ambivalent attitude to it. One can set the nostalgic fear that the past has been lost forever against the "fear that it is not lost enough." Middleton and Woods (2000, 43) suggest that "both the fear of loss and the fear that it is not lost enough are structures of fantasy which offer ideological energy to everyone trying to locate a past for the future of their bewildering present." The danger of becom-ing too involved with the past, of becoming nostalgically obsessed, jeopardizes one's relationship with both present and future.

In *Twelve Monkeys*, for example, James Cole's obsession with the past sets up the conditions for his death. The present is the year 2035, an Orwellian dystopia where the world's population has been devastated by a virus, forcing the survivors to live underground. Cole, who has been imprisoned for crimes against authority, is haunted by a childhood memory of a man being shot to death in an airport. Cole is "volunteered" by a panel of scientists to go back to 1996, before the virus was released, in order to trace a sample of the "pure" virus before it mutates, so that the population of 2035 might find a cure. While in 1990 he is arrested, diagnosed as schizophrenic and hospitalized in a mental institution under the supervision of psychiatrist Kathryn Railly, with whom he eventually falls in love. She returns his affection and they begin to plan a life together, but are thwarted by the future scientists who arrange things so that Cole is shot and killed in an airport. The death he witnessed as a child was his own.

Cole does not have the vision to predict the outcome of his actions. His attempts at redemptive time travel result in the repetition of the past, but not in the way he expected. Far from being malleable, the past is seen to be an infective agent—analogous with Freud's repressed, always threatening a return and revivification, or Bergson's notion of the past "continually pressing for-wards, so as to insert the largest part of itself into the present action" (Bergson 1991, 168). Once released from temporal confines, the past's influence spreads, mutates and invades the body of the present. This idea of an infective, per-sistent past is literalized in *Twelve Monkeys* through the viral plague that dev-astates the global population.

A theme common to all of the films discussed here is the persistent past, where, as is the case with the human psyche, the past continues to exert a pres-sure and an influence on the present. This is often complicated in film, as in life, by the acquisition of fresh knowledge, which changes our perspective on past events and reactivates or alters their effect. The film spectator must review, in light of this new knowledge, all that has gone before. In *Twelve Monkeys* this process must be carried out continuously as the film reveals more and more information. Thus the spectator is implicated in a perpetual dance of reading and rereading in the quest for (retrospective) understanding (Furby 2014).

The idea of the persistent past is also the central agent in *La Jetée*, a film that is, aside from one fleeting moment of movement, made up entirely of still images and which influenced *Twelve Monkeys*. The film's present is the aftermath of World War 3. The protagonist, who is haunted by memories of a child, a woman's face and a man dying, is held captive and experimented on by scientists seeking a means of survival through time travel—to rescue the present by recourse to the past (and the future). The protagonist is chosen because he has a strong link to the past through the image of the woman's face. He is subjected to a strange process that involves tapping into his mind. He yearns for the girl and is somehow able to re-enter the past and meet her.

The scientists continue to send him back and he builds a relationship with the woman, imagining that there may be a way that he can remain in the past. However, the scientists then send him into the future. He travels forwards and encounters people who reluctantly provide him with means to aid the people in his present. Back in the camp he waits for execution, but he gets a message from the people of the future who say that he can go to live there. He prefers to go back into the past, where his death is witnessed by the child from his memories: himself. In both this film and *Twelve Monkeys* the end takes us back to the beginning. As in the tale of Orpheus, we have a woman as the lost object who is linked with a yearning for a lost way of life, and a desire to return to the past. *La Jetée* is set in a world ruined by war, while *Twelve Monkeys* is set in a world devastated by a viral plague. The dynamic which drives the time-technologists to send their "volunteers" back is nostalgia for the pre-apocalyptic world. Both time travelers search for a lost time of unity and innocence and this search for the lost love-object resonates with homesickness for the pre–Oedipal.

In *The Interpretation of Dreams* Freud theorizes that the infant who cries in vain for food resorts to fantasy to satisfy a hunger (or need) that cannot otherwise be satisfied (1991, 718–720). In Lacanian terms, when the infant's need for food is satisfied by the parent, the need for parental love is also met. The need for the parental presence soon becomes a separate need from that for simple nourishment. Lacan says of desire that it "is neither the appetite for satisfaction, nor the demand for love, but the difference that results from the subtraction of the first from the second" (1977, 287). Desire is thus what remains after biological satisfaction. We apparently need to stage our desires and fears and to set them within narratives. Cowie (1984, 79) suggests that what "fantasy involves, is characterized by, not the achievement of desired objects, but the arranging of, a setting out of, desire; a veritable *mise-en-scène* of desire." A fascination with time travel is one way of narrating a nostalgic desire for that part of a formative experience that is lost in the past.

The idea of a past that has not been lost forever beyond the reach of the present is, then, both seductive and comforting, but also disquieting. Clearly our relationship with the past may be tinged with yearning, but also with the anxiety that repressed memories will return to unsettle the present. Perhaps the time travel film can function as a protective "screen memory" positioned between the dangerous past, which might threaten the present, and the spectator desirous to gaze, to glance back, but not too closely nor too directly. Time travel narratives add an extra layer of pleasure and anxiety as they explore more clearly this notion of an eternally available past that has not been lost but which can be revisited or reactivated. The fantasy of a persistent past is explored in *Twelve Monkeys,* where the favored temporal scheme is one in which the past is not pliable and is only subject to review through reinterpretation. *Twelve* Monkeys and *La Jetée* enact an obsession with the past and with loss, and they embody the layering of past and present. Death is at the heart of the sense of loss.

There is a moment in *Twelve Monkeys* when, watching a cinema's program of Hitchcock films, Cole remarks that "It's just like what's happening with us. Like the past, the movie never changes, it cannot change, but every time you see it it's different, because you're different." This may be taken as a comment on one view of time travel. In some films it *is* possible to go into the past and effect changes, or to bring something back from the past (*Timescape, Back to the Future, Frequency*), but in *Twelve Monkeys* and *La Jetée* it is not. Early in *Twelve Monkeys* Cole says, "How can I save you, this already happened? I cannot save you, nobody can.... 1990 is the past, this already happened." His rescue attempt is aimed not at the five billion people doomed to die from the plague, because within the logic of time travel presented by this film the past cannot be changed because it has already happened. The target for his rescue mission is the population of the future, who could return to the surface of the Earth if they were to be offered a cure. His rescue attempt is also not aimed at saving himself from death, because he does not know that the man who dies in his memory fragment is himself. He does, however, look to bring about the conditions whereby he can remain in the past with the woman he loves. There is no possibility of a time loop paradox in this film and no hope of rescue. As in *La Jetée,* a rereading of the past merely leads to a fresh sense of loss. Yet there is some sense in which the film itself performs the rescue that cannot take place within the story. The boy–Cole is alive at the end of the film. He has been born, as it were, as the man–Cole in embryo, and will live through the plague and beyond into the future—until 2035. Time travel preserves the possibility of Cole's life; his lifeline is apparently reforged into a recurring lifecycle.

Having discussed a number of films that are centrally and explicitly concerned with the notion of time travel, I shall conclude this chapter with a discussion of a film that is superficially innocent of time travel, but which does

possess a strong element of nostalgic rescue. *Moulin Rouge* (2001) deals with
the idea that narrative functions redemptively. Indeed, watching the screen
past being invoked by film's redemptive re-narration is similarly a low-risk,
cathartic route into the past for the spectator who identifies with on-screen
characters but retains a distancing sense of themselves as spectator. The fleeting, temporary play time that film offers can be read as a homeopathic remedy
for nostalgia or fear of the past caused by repressed trauma, disappointment,
bereavement or guilt. Homeopathy seeks to strengthen the body's immune
defenses against a damaging agent by the administration of a dramatically
diluted, and therefore safe, solution, whereupon the body recognizes the harm-
ful substance and is able to fortify itself without risk. Onscreen events are
similar, but different enough (sufficiently diluted) to achieve a therapeutic
combination of familiarity and strangeness. A cinematic image can be read as
a same but different version of the original "real" person or event. Watching
a film is like watching the past. In this way loss is addressed and the cinema
itself features in bringing about a sense of restoration and closure.

Moulin Rouge is a film about storytelling that makes the resurrecting
power of cinema the emotionally uplifting factor that transforms the final
scenes from tragedy into hope. The chief protagonist, Christian, is an Orphean
character: a singer, lyricist and storyteller. He goes into the Bohemian underworld of Paris, finds his Eurydice, Satine, and attempts to take her from the
underworld. He fails as she is fatally ill with consumption. As Satine dies she
says "Tell our story Christian. Promise me. Promise me. That way I'll always
be with you." The tale Christian tells becomes the film, which he describes in
the final frames as "above all things, a story about love; a love that will live forever." As Bergson says, at the moment that the past is invoked it ceases "to be
a memory and pass[es] into the state of a present thing, something actually
lived" (1991, 139). Being alive on film stands in for being alive, whereas Neale
argues that "a photograph embalms the ghosts of the past; film brings them
back to life" (8). At the start we know that Satine is dead, that the film is a
story told in the past tense. It unfolds as Christian writes the story. Christian
looks back, as Orpheus did, but this time his backwards glance is instrumental
in her survival. His narration resurrects Satine and there is no difference, for
the spectator, between Satine alive in the filmic present and Satine alive on
film. *Moulin Rouge* is a closed loop of spacetime in which Satine is always alive
and she and Christian are always together.

The representation of human life as fleeting might be thought of as a
simple way for film to be seen as rescuer. In telling stories about the tragedy
of human mortality, film is able to make a contrast with its own powers of
durability and resurrection. The films discussed in this chapter not only talk

of rescue, but also of the necessity of seeing and understanding the past, and having a sense of authority over time. Cole (*Twelve Monkeys*) is blind to the past and consequently cannot function properly in the present. Nostalgia overwhelms the protagonist in *La Jetée*. In *Frequency*, John deals successfully with the past. Christian (*Moulin Rouge*) uses story to redeem his loss. All of these tales suggest that the temporal fantasist wants to feel in control of time, to play with it rather than be its plaything. Being in control means the capacity to move freely in the fourth dimension. Temporal freedom means that any discomfiture with the past has been worked through to remove any residual fear that the past may threaten the integrity of the present. If movies offer us a means with which to explore our fantasies and fears safely in "play time" without actually moving from the safety of the present, then the real object of rescue is the spectator. Human beings outside of the world of film are doomed to be bound by time and mortality; human beings inside the world of film, including the spectator, may share in film's particular relationship with time and become, albeit temporarily (paradoxically), immortal, heroic, time travelers.

Culture and History

Experiments in Time

The Silent Films of Cecil B. DeMille

David Blanke

Expecting to find a stable and consistent narrative genre in early silent film, particularly one as complex as time travel, appears at first glance to be a wholly unreasonable prospect. Driven by a host of conflicting forces, both internal and beyond the flimsy walls of their production studios, early commercial filmmakers had their hands full with the development of editing techniques and experimenting with cinematic grammar. Successful directors, including D. W. Griffith, Thomas Ince, and Cecil B. DeMille, had to entertain their patrons, enrich their investors and engage with audiences pre-conditioned by their experiences with vaudeville, live theater, the novel, and other pleasurable pastimes. These customers harbored stubborn attitudes about the *meaning* of popular entertainment and the *legitimacy* of new cultural forms, which required successful commercial producers to both sustain and surpass these expectations. Scholars examining this period have long noted how Hollywood quickly turned to familiar cinematic genres (such as the melodrama) and consistent narrative techniques (montage, cross-cuts, and continuity editing) to bridge this divide between the past and present. By examining Cecil B. DeMille's experimental work with time travel in his silent films, this essay examines one of the ways that this compromise was achieved. With no exemplar of the mature time travel genre to come, DeMille's films do in fact display a consistent pattern. Through his use of framing, flashbacks, and a sentimental reliance on older, "legitimate" thematic tropes, these works offer an intriguing early look at how one successful Hollywood director helped his audience to receive and take meaning from this unfamiliar narrative style.

While DeMille's interest in time travel and temporal experimentation was neither trivial nor expedient, his work was not, strictly speaking, a precursor of the formal genre. As Altman (1984) notes, cinematic genre exists largely as on-going and didactical interplay between an audiences' expected observations—that is, their recognition of familiar semantic elements (cowboys and Indians in a western)—and a producer's ideological intent—the purpose or syntax to which these elements are used within a film (for example, the western as metaphor for social order). Acknowledging the indeterminacy of this process and that "genres are driven by an amazing variety of forces, often working at cross purposes," Altman provides a useful historical model to identify and track these elements (Barnett 2003, 68). Early silent films, such as those by DeMille, are tailor-made to examine this process. While DeMille made little use of the (now) conventional qualities of time travel narration, his films exhibit, in the words of Ludwig Wittgenstein (1953), a strong "family resemblance" (cited in Rieder 2010, 192) to the semantic structure of the genre to come. Significantly, the director did not use these building blocks to assemble an equally robust syntax. Indeed, DeMille's decision to abandon time travel, once synchronized sound allowed him to more succinctly explain the ideological context of his work, suggests that he always considered time travel as an innovative yet expendable modifier of traditional narrative topics.

As a case study, DeMille provides a wide sample set. In spite of critical, popular, and corporate objections, the director used variations of time travel in eleven of the fourteen films he released between 1916 and 1925. These experiments included extended allegorical flashbacks, the reincarnation of major dramatic characters, chronological comparisons between characters (usually played by a single actor) across time, and subtle framing devices intended to contrast modern society and its mores with those of the distant past (including pre-historical, pagan, early Judeo-Christian, and medieval eras).

Moreover, in the spirit of Altman's warning, DeMille's personal and professional motivations during these years evidenced "an amazing variety of forces" that included his family history, his commercial incentives, and production methods that "often work[ed] at cross purposes" (Barnett 2003, 68). Born to a family steeped in the "legitimate theater," DeMille's directing, writing, and managerial style displayed a heavy hand that clashed with the needs of the rapidly maturing studio and star systems. Central to the formation of one of Hollywood's leading commercial studios, Paramount Pictures, the director used his films as aggressive corporate stratagems intended to boost his creative and commercial control. His resistance to the star system, for example, justified DeMille's assemblage of a core stock company of actors who often appeared and then re-appeared in his flashback sequences. Visually and narratively, time travel also abetted the director's desire to follow his theatrical instincts. He featured lavish and spectacular sets that only accentuated the recurring appearance of stock characters and that, by the force of their relative anonymity, helped bring his parallel chronological narratives to the fore. In sum, DeMille's use of time travel served multiple, often contradictory masters. Clearly lacking anything resembling a formal genre, these tactics allowed DeMille to follow his unique artistic and cultural instincts while remaining faithful to the commercial demands of his employers.

These subjective factors are most obvious in how DeMille and his staff imagined time travel. While the director never hesitated to employ unconventional narrative twists or inject modern scientific discoveries into the plots of his early work, there were limits to the ways he conceptualized time travel. These typically took three forms: reincarnation, parallel flashbacks, and New Age mysticism where objects, not people, served as the critical dramatic linkage between eras. In keeping with what scholars today generally assume about generic syntax, this tradition drew from a wide range of existing and commercially successful fantasy literature, including H. G. Wells' *The Time Machine* (1895), Edward Bellamy's *Looking Backward* (1888), and Mark Twain's *A Connecticut Yankee in King Arthur's Court* (1889). Lacking common semantic elements, these works did contain a consistent message about time. Much like the Progressive history emerging at this time, these novels rested on the assumption that the past and present remain in a constant state of dialog and that contemporaries could fashion a new "usable past" through a more critical engagement with the contingencies of time (Novick 1988, 92–97). In this way early feature film, which simultaneously developed montage and crosscut editing techniques to surmount the narrative challenges posed by time, proved well suited to take up these dramatic possibilities.

DeMille's *Joan the Woman* (1917) is his initial venture into time travel as well as a model for what was to follow. While the main plot of the film focuses on the life, faith, and passion of Joan D'Arc, DeMille injected an intriguing time travel twist at the very start of the picture. After a brief introductory scene showing a humbled Joan accepting the spirit of God, her enraptured body tracing both the sign of the cross and (via double exposure) the *Fleur-de-Lis*, the film shifts to the front lines of World War I. There a modern English soldier, Eric Trent, is asked by his commander to accept a suicide mission to sabotage a strategic German installation. Considering his fate, Trent returns to his dugout quarters only to discover the long-buried sword of Joan herself. He is then visited by the Saint, who demands that "the time has come for thee to expiate thy sin against me," seemingly a generic call for Allied sacrifice during the Great War and an implicit censure of America's neutrality. We soon learn that DeMille and his co-author, Jeanie Macpherson, intended to use time travel to inject a much deeper temporal linkage between these two principles. Not only are the English obliged to "expiate" their past transgressions, but so too is Trent's very soul. Trent's consciousness is returned to the body of a medieval English officer who both loved and then betrayed the Maid of Orleans.

Modified time travel narratives such as this offered DeMille a way to follow his artistic and cultural instincts while remaining faithful to the commercial demands of his employers. Reincarnation and flashbacks allowed for a sentimental defense of what Hollywood perceived to be "timeless truths" (most couched in Late Victorian assumptions about innate character that were criticized during the modern era). Using powerful framing devices and familiar cultural references, DeMille's work proved popular with his audience and supported a competing corporate vision to that championed by his studio bosses, Jesse Lasky and Adolph Zukor. While cynics might argue that profits alone drove DeMille's cinematic choices, the stability and persistence of these narrative devices support the argument that the success of his silent films was, in part, fueled by the development of a recognizable film genre, although one that was significantly different from the later work to come. By examining three of his films in greater detail—*Joan the Woman*, *The Ten Commandments* (1923), and *The Road to Yesterday* (1925)—the semantics and syntax of these early experiments in time travel narration become clear.

Framing Devices and the Semantics of Early Time Travel

DeMille used time travel as a narrative framing device in his early silent films. The central goal of any framing method is to direct the audience towards an easy appreciation of the dominant themes and dramatic trajectory of a picture. In *Joan*, for example, DeMille's chronological jumps during the initial few minutes of the film establish the two main perspectives of the larger work. The first, underscored in its title, was to humanize Joan "the woman." Introduced by a relatively static and traditional domestic image of the maid spinning wool—one of many such visual quotes that DeMille took from popular artwork and lithography, as discussed below—an intertitle informs us that Joan's sex, not merely her faith, will shape the dramatic arc. Unlike male heroes, she was "the Girl Patriot, who fought with men, was loved by man, and killed by men." We know immediately that a love story will factor into the film's dramatic resolution. Following a slow dissolve, as the cruciform Joan receives the grace of God, DeMille then jarringly introduces the energetic insanity of trench warfare and the world of men: violent, organized, technical. A second intertitle links the two, reassuring us that Joan's spiritual struggle "is not dead.

She can never die—and in the war-torn land she loved so well, her Spirit fights today."

The nature of this film, an epic retelling of a dramatic moment in Western history, granted DeMille the freedom to keep the two chronologies clearly separated throughout the main body of the picture. By concisely framing both themes at the outset he avoided the all-too-subtle and often misleading allusions created by the repeated time displacements found in a film like D.W. Griffith's *Intolerance* (1916). These editorial choices, between a clear initial framing of dramatic time shifts and the less predictable, intermittent staging of the same, are intriguing for what they suggest about the effect that early time travel narratives had on the grammar of silent film. Chronological flashbacks, particularly within epics that highlighted spectacle and *mise-en-scène* editing, seemed to work much better when segregated into the "extended flashback" (Birchard 2004, 39). While montage editing certainly provided directors with the means to more precisely guide an audience through complex dramatic narration, time travel threatened to unnecessarily burden a film when these cuts crossed significant chronological thresholds.

Given the critical and popular response to both *Joan* and *Intolerance*, it seemed that DeMille had happened upon a valuable lesson. Rather than disperse his historical allusions throughout a work, DeMille selected critical moments when he would sweep his audience into the past. For *Joan* this occurred at the film's beginning and end. In *The Devil-Stone* (1917), where he had access to only a fraction of the budget he enjoyed for *Joan*, he injected a significant yet condensed historical flashback within the body of the picture. In this case, the time shift returns modern characters to the court of a pious Norse queen. Her betrayal by superstitious rivals curses the titular jewel and underscores the film's central theme of the timeless battle between superstition and faith. Two years later, in *For Better, For Worse* (1919), DeMille again situates his extended flashback within the main body of the film. In this case, a woman's struggles at the home front of World War I are contextualized and given significance by those experienced by women during Viking times, at the mythical court of King Arthur, and during the American Revolution. As a framing tool, DeMille clearly intended his time travel segments to accentuate *modern* problems rather than explore the complexities of the past as an end to itself. By segregating these passages, he canonized history as the "truth revealed" while simultaneously investing the present with significance as an ongoing test of ethics. In this sense time travel narratives worked like testimonials; ancient knowledge waiting to be revealed, heeded, and then absorbed by the wisest students.

Nowhere was this more evident than in the 1923 release of *The Ten Com-*

mandments. DeMille proposed the idea of dramatizing the Decalogue amid a period when studios green-lighted numerous big-budget pictures like *The Hunchback of Notre Dame* (1923) and *The Covered Wagon* (1923) seemingly on faith alone. Typical of their approach, DeMille and Macpherson, once again his co-writer, intended to contrast contemporary mores against those that they believed served as the bedrock of Western society. Searching for an encapsulating theme, the pair adopted the notion that humans could not break the Commandments without facing the costs of their transgression; in a phrase, "You cannot break the Ten Commandments, they will break you" (DeMille Archives, Box 242, Folder 8). The film's modern narrative was a conventional morality tale set between two brothers: one who respected the ancient edicts (although, notably, without religious dogma and updated to suit the times) and another who rejected the idea that universal ethical codes either exist or carry any meaning into the modern world. By the end of the film the prodigal brother lay ruined, contracting leprosy and killing his mother in the process, while the other had won the girl through his defense of these timeless decrees.

The framing flashback of the Exodus served these ends, of course, but it was the manner in which DeMille presented his time travel testimonial that offers the most intriguing case study. Temporarily freed from budget constraints, the director abandoned the short historical vignettes that he had regularly employed following *Joan.* At half the length of the 100-minute film, the historical prologue featured no dramatic character development, little dialog (aside from intertitles cleaved from the King James Bible), and no dual-role acting. Part of this can be explained by the subject matter. Dramatizing secular history is one thing, but modifying the Bible in 1923 was another entirely. Still, it is clear that DeMille saw the introductory frames as his greatest opportunity to ground his modern times into these truths. It was this idea of a universal and timeless code of ethics, not one individual's past or present sins, which held the picture together.

Under these conditions the dominance of the visual spectacle and *mise-en-scène* editing used to establish this chronological link was not accidental. With thousands of extras driving thousands of animals, massive Egyptian sets, state-of-the-art special effects (including colorized passages, double-exposures, and novel studio production units), the prologue follows the fleeing slaves past an authentic replica of the 107-foot Per Rameses gate, through a parted Red Sea, amid carnal celebrations at the base of Mt. Sinai, and to their fateful reckoning as a Chosen People where God/DeMille wrote the commandments using volcanic fury and swallowed both idol and idolaters into a chasm ripped through the earth's surface. While similar breath-taking spectacles dotted the modern half of the film, including a collapsed cathedral and dramatic shipwreck, the director framed the "timeless truths" of the Commandments through the visceral experiences of a people witnessing God's *direct* instruction. The effect was so profound that the subsequent modern half feels drained of its drama. The only modern character who appears to retain any dramatic volition was the Bible-thumping mother of the two brothers. In spite of her love for the boys, her spiritual inflexibility—that is, her inability to travel time and *adapt* the ancient wisdom to her modern circumstances—sealed her fate. Regardless, the raw visual power of the film sustained DeMille's cinematic time travel.

In addition to the powerful framing devices displayed in his overtly historical films, like *Joan the Woman* and *The Ten Commandments*, DeMille began to use more subtle historical cues and cultural reminiscences to invoke a familiar, almost nostalgic quality to his more modern tales. DeMille employed a rare subtlety to quietly inject time shifts within his dramas. Often, as in *Joan* or *The Devil-Stone*, messages from the past appeared through talismans or other physical objects from previous epochs, such as Joan's sword or the Norse queen's gemstone. In *Male and Female* (1919), the modern male protagonist kills and wears the skin of a leopard while stranded on a desert island. Later, we see this same visual construction in the characters set amid ancient Babylon. In addition to talismans, climactic dramatic episodes also cued audiences towards a meaningful temporal shift. DeMille relied on trials by ordeal—most typically through fire, but also via lingering physical ailments or the disfigurement of his main characters—as a means to visibly link events of the past to those in the present. Most famously, and discussed more fully below, in *The Road to Yesterday* (1925) a husband suffers from a mysterious partial paralysis in his arm which stokes an irrational fear in his newlywed bride. After a horrific train wreck, in which his wife is trapped amid wreckage and faces a fiery death, they are transported back to the past. There the husband realizes that he suffered his mysterious injury in the process of burning his future wife at the stake. Thus, without understanding the importance of their previous lives these characters can never fully comprehend their contemporary problems.

Such triggers were not always linked to fantasy, mysticism and magic. DeMille also imparted chronological meaning by subtly quoting memorable artwork and popular lithography. Part of this, no doubt, was his Victorian artistic affectation, seen almost immediately by his effort to promote his film's chiaroscuro cinematography as a form of "Rembrandt lighting" (Birchard 2004, 148). More explicitly, the director leaned upon prominent poems— such as Henry Wadsworth Longfellow's "The Village Blacksmith" in *Some-*

thing to Think About (1920) or William Ernest Henley's "Or Ever the Knightly Years" in *Male and Female*—works of art—such as Jean-François Millet 1863 painting, *Shepherdess with her Flock* for *Joan*—and even popular engravings and illustrations—such as Maxfield Parrish's 1910 print, *Young King of the Black Isles*, used to model Raymond Hatton's surly "King Charles" in *Joan*, or several selections from Gustav Dore's illustrated Bible used throughout the prologue of *The Ten Commandments*—to give his modern sequences a sense of cultural depth and déjà vu familiarity. The most famous instance remains the scene depicting Gloria Swanson lying prostrate beneath a mature male lion in the Babylonian flashback of *Male and Female*, framed to model Gabriel von Max's 1908 painting, *The Lion's Bride*. Swanson herself recalled as a child seeing the print hanging in her grandmother's parlor. DeMille's consistent and intelligent use of these and other cues strengthened his audience's innate appreciation for the chronological parallels between past and present.

Far more common, however, were explicit and even prescriptive meanings that DeMille took from the past to enhance his modern themes. For example, amidst a growing national indignation in the United States over the teaching of Charles Darwin's theory of evolution in public schools, DeMille released *Adam's Rib* (1923). Its main story stands as a seemingly straightforward defense of the modern flapper—one who, in this case, proved willing to deny her love for a young paleontologist in order to protect her parents' marriage. However, the narrative relies on an extended flashback featuring prehistoric cavemen slouching through ancient redwood forests to show how the power of modern woman had long been held captive by the ruthless demands of men.

DeMille's recurring use of extended flashbacks, his focus on character development across epochs, and his effort to inject recognizable cultural references that stirred his audiences' historical imagination and heightened the effect of his films' temporal displacement all support an argument that his work evinced the "common traits, attitudes, [and] characters" of an emerging genre (Altman 1984, 10). This was not to be and raises the question of why. DeMille's decision to abandon time as a meaningful plot device was not justified by box office receipts. His films from 1916 to 1925 remain some of the most profitable of his long career. Nor was the director opposed to exploring paradoxical or unfamiliar concepts. As late as 1956, he hoped to film an extended sequence featuring evolution through natural selection as part of a reworked *The Ten Commandments*. The most reasonable conclusion is that DeMille and his staff consciously decided not to marshal the recurring "family resemblance" of his time travel narration into an equally coherent and predictable ideological framework. In other words, while the semantics of his silent films offered DeMille the *possibility* for further exploration of time, the purposes to which he set these qualities worked counter to the needs of generic syntax.

Thematic Tropes and the Failed Syntax of Early Time Travel

While DeMille's use of time as a dramatic narrative device failed to provide a stable syntax, his methods remained both purposeful and ideological. As noted above, *Joan* served as his first significant experiment with time travel narration. By the film's end, a modern English infantryman has literally seen history's shining path (in the form of a shining cross) and is infused with a divine passion to right past wrongs. Moreover, through time travel DeMille expressly challenged his audiences to reconsider additional aspects of their own era: the nature of gender, of modern faith and organized religion, and even America's obligations during the time of the Great War.

Joan's portrayal follows from DeMille and Macpherson's loose adaptation of Mark Twain's 1896 novel, *The Personal Recollections of Joan of Arc*. An odd book, the pair clearly were attracted to the idea of humanizing such a prominent historical figure. In DeMille's own words, he wanted to capture "an absorbing personal story against a background of great historical events." The "iron clad saint had been depicted many times," he later recalled, "but the tender woman had not been reached until Mark Twain wrote his work.... And I followed that line" (Pratt 1989, 137–138). Casting the 34-year-old Metropolitan Opera star Geraldine Farrar in the title role served his studio's contractual obligations, but Farrar also represented something of the "New Woman" to many Americans.

More than a little of this intertextuality made it onto the screen. While Farrar's performance was restrained, her historic role embodied all the qualities of the modern woman in 1917: independence, purity of spirit, steely determination, and self-sacrifice. Farrar's Joan easily commanded the respect of her male army *and* the love of a seemingly honorable man. When brought before the effete French king and his court, Joan stands ramrod in support of her countrymen and their cause. The French clergy, led by the lecherous L'Oiseleur and treasonous Bishop Cauchon, were portrayed in white-hooded robes that called to mind both the genocidal atrocities of the Ku Klux Klan as well as *The Birth of a Nation* (1915), which sought to absolve them. The clerics appeared to take an almost sexual satisfaction from seeing Joan the woman finally bound before them and burned at the stake in the film's climactic and visually stunning scenes.

Significantly, DeMille *directed* his audiences to draw these parallels. The film's framing device, which was later cut for foreign distribution, forced his audience to adopt the director's conception of cinematic time travel through Trent's historical epiphany. Like Trent, patrons were compelled to see Joan's suffering through the lens of modern gender norms and the Great War, not just those of the 15th century. Later, the director sought to distance himself from the "hint of reincarnation" in *Joan* (hints such as the Saint's *direct* ultimatum to the modern Trent that he "expiate thy sin against me" or the use of Reid to play both roles), arguing instead that it "appealed particularly to Jeanie Macpherson" (Hayne 1959, 171). However, the fact remains that throughout the 1910s and well into the 1920s DeMille regularly turned to reincarnation and contemporary spirituality to show *why* the past must be reborn in the present. In 1920, he admitted his own interest in the "great wave of mysticism ... sweeping across the world." DeMille acknowledged that all the "table rapping" and unorthodox "religious movements ... may be superficial to a degree," but held that his films exposed the "tremendous truth" within these quirky doctrines that was "struggling for expression" in his audience (Louvish 2007, 184).

Moreover, DeMille understood how his treatment of an intrepid and *canonized* woman would send shock waves through more religiously orthodox audience members. Writing to forestall his studio from censoring the picture's American release, DeMille suggested selective edits so that targeted audiences could be spared the modern inferences he made via the past. "In the strong Catholic communities," he wrote, "those scenes relating to [poor behavior of] the Catholic Church might be best [cut]; while in the Protestant portions of the country, it might be desirable to retain such scenes." He concluded, "I would most urgently suggest that the two modern incidents, at the beginning and close of the picture, be retained" (DeMille Archives, Box 238, Folder 16). In other words, DeMille used time travel as a tool to highlight specific ideological goals and not necessarily to explore how the narrative method constructed meaning.

This shift became particularly evident as he neared the end of his "flashback" period. Here, DeMille increasingly tasked his films to explore spiritual themes without actually exploring the meaning of time travel itself. This decision was wholly a product of his times. As noted above, questions of faith and "legitimate" religious expression blazed across the United States during the 1920s. In addition to a rise in fundamental Christianity and charismatic revivalism, a variety of new spiritual doctrines—including somnambulism, hypnotism, Darwinian materialism, Asiatic philosophies, and a revival of Arthur Schopenhauer's writings—were popularized. DeMille's own struggle for personal revelation was equally complex. Raised Episcopalian, his modern faith trended towards Theosophy and the tenets of Mary Baker Eddy's Christian Scientism, which was sweeping Hollywood and had found converts in many of Cecil's closest friends and colleagues. Preparing for *Something to Think About*, the first of his films to bring doctrines of faith directly into the lives of his modern characters, DeMille told Jesse Lasky "I have worked on the Christian Science theme of 'right thinking' into [the picture] very strongly. In fact, it is almost a Christian Science play without, of course calling it that" (DeMille Archives, Box 241, Folder 5).

While retaining the semantics of time travel, including flashbacks, cultural triggers, and other visible reminders, the director increasingly avoided any exploration of its syntax. The 1924 production of *Feet of Clay* (1924), for example, shifted his use of reincarnation from the intriguing and open-ended comparisons offered in *Joan the Woman* to stricter, less imaginative purposes. The drama revolves around two lovers who commit suicide rather than face public scandal. In the film's ultimate scene, as their souls cross the "Bridge Between the Worlds," the two must "discard everything they have ever had," including their love for each other, before passing on to their salvation. Unwilling to foreswear their love, they will themselves back into the world of the living. Unlike DeMille's earlier expressions of magic, mysticism, and reincarnation, however, here the focus is not on the broader tale of past meanings and modern contingencies but rather the more personal and idiosyncratic spiritual journey of these characters. Audiences and critics alike, who once praised the director for his intriguing reconsideration of past and present (a central ideological component of the mature time travel genre), found *Feet of Clay* full of "wild and weird ideas" (DeMille Archives, Box 249, Folder 6). *The New York Times* (1924) correctly concluded that DeMille was now merely "indulging himself in making this production."

This trend returns in *The Road to Yesterday*, the last film where DeMille employed extended flashbacks, reincarnation, or any other hint at temporal experimentation. As with his other works, *Road* included numerous time travel triggers and explicit references to contemporary events. The story follows two couples, a wealthy pair of newlyweds unable to consummate their union because of the wife's sudden disgust for her husband's (Joseph Schildkraut) paralyzed arm, and a hedonistic flapper (Vera Reynolds) whose love for a poor yet virile minister is unrequited. Both Schildkraut's and Reynolds' characters are professed Atheists yet, as the story progresses, we discover that their lack of faith stems from their inability to grasp and understand true spirituality (the former out of bitterness and the latter, who DeMille describes as an "ultra-modern," out of self-indulgence). In his preparatory notes, DeMille compared the treatment to that of *"The Ten Commandments* [and] the expression of a great theme, namely—that we are apt to blame God for the results of our own acts." "The purpose of this story," he continued, "is to show [modern audiences] that the individual, himself [in a previous life] put into motion the thing that strikes him now" (DeMille Archives, Box 261 Folder 2). Violently thrown into their past by a horrific train crash and trial by fire, the foursome discover that their contemporary problems stem not from God's wrath but rather the spiritual choices they once made yet still do not comprehend.

As in *Joan the Woman* and *The Ten Commandments*, DeMille again positions his audience to make a direct connection between distinct chronological periods. Through these couples and their reincarnation, the director establishes a temporal link that is active, ongoing, and designed to signify that a new "usable past" is available to his audience. DeMille inserts an introductory intertitle that reads: "Everyone in this audience has felt an unaccountable fear either of the dark or of the unseen; of great height or of great depths.... How do you account for this phenomena? How deep is the cause hidden, and why?" (DeMille Archives, Box 261, Folder 2 & Box 264, Folders 2–3). Rather than explore these intriguing questions and their unpredictable links through time, DeMille uses the semantics of time travel to further a conventional plot device: faith overcoming the problems of a modern age. In the end, following their painful forays into medieval Europe, the characters in *The Road to Yesterday* save their marriage but take nothing of lasting importance from their experiences with time.

Conclusion

As a distinct case study, DeMille's silent films show that early commercial filmmakers did indeed experiment with the outward appearance of time travel narration. Through both familiar and novel means, including New Age ideas about reincarnation, magical talismans, and prophetic injuries or disasters, DeMille offered a consistent pattern—indeed, a cinematic "Bridge Between the Worlds"—that required patrons to see time as a meaningful plot device. His commercial preference for recurring stock company actors over the latest studio star reinforced these methods visually and provided audience members with a stable perspective from within each tale. Just as clearly, however, DeMille failed to establish a discreet syntactical meaning for time travel as a subject unto itself. Time travel served merely as a dramatic adjective, typically as a way to demonstrate the time*less*ness of passions such as love, patriotism, or faith, and never a noun. While DeMille quickly fades from scholarly interest

on this subject, his failure does serve as a meaningful reminder to the importance of generic syntax. As Altman concludes, the genres that prove to be "the
most durable are precisely those that have established the most coherent syntax
... [and] those that disappear the quickest depend entirely on recurring semantic elements" (Altman 1984, 16).

Ironically, DeMille's slippery professional circumstances denied him the
time he needed to develop such a syntax. Struggling as an independent producer with falling box office revenues, he learned that narrative experimentation could alienate as many loyal patrons as it attracted. His commitment to
his stock company and, in particular, cinematic spectacle was a costly luxury.
Having fought the studio system and lost, DeMille returned, hat-in-hand, to
the majors in 1927 (first to MGM and then, desperately, back to Paramount)
where he vowed to faithfully follow their commercial imperatives. By 1934,
the now fifty-three-year-old director admitted to the *Los Angeles Times* that
this new yet conventional style of storytelling boiled down simply to a "question of employment" (Louvish 2007, 323–324).

Other practical considerations also helped to delegitimize his earlier
experiments in time travel. The onset of the Great Depression did as much
damage to notions of "eternal truths" as any industry accountant. By the
1930s, American commercial film was experiencing an artistic resurgence, with
numerous narrative innovations that frequently championed contemporary
wisdom and either ignored or satirized the past. DeMille's own *oeuvre* shifted
from critical cross-epoch comparisons of faith, gender, and consumerism to
predictable hagiographies of the country's western pioneers. Finally, the addition of synchronized sound had a pronounced and largely negative effect on
DeMille's art and preachment. While the director's melodious voice and precise diction made him the ideal radio spokesman for the industry—he served
from 1936 to 1944 as the national host of the Lux Radio Hour, where he
earned his title as "Mr. Hollywood"—as a director DeMille evidenced a tin
ear for dialog. Not only did this have the unfortunate habit of accentuating
his prescriptive and dated messages, but it also inserted a "voice of God" narration that effectively eliminated the need for historical testimony.

DeMille's story, his early use and then abandonment of time travel narration, and the rebirth of the genre in the latter half of the 20th century
underscore just how profoundly different the cultural production of the silent
era was from that which followed. DeMille's cinematic methods worked best
as chronological *modifiers* to his storytelling precisely because the commercial
opportunities were so varied and untested. As the industry matured and the
determining factors of profitable film-making became more obvious, men like
DeMille concluded that risky narrative experiments were simply too perilous.

A key part of this decision lies in the director's inability to fully imagine the ideological possibilities for the genre. While he never sought to establish time travel as a subject apart, the fact that a figure as experienced and headstrong as DeMille soundly rejected this opportunity speaks more to the studio's growing powers of cooptation than the mass audience's latent interest in the expressive genre to come.

A Spasso nella Commedia

Temporal Journeying Through the Transitional Landscape of Italian Film Comedy of the 1980s and 1990s

Giacomo Boitani

Time travel is a narrative motif that is, for obvious reasons, often connected with the science fiction genre. However, Italian national cinema represents an exception. Even in the 1960s and 1970s, when the Italian filmmaking industry experienced a period of great wealth and intense productivity, especially in relation to genre films, few science fiction films were produced in Italy. Brunetta writes that Italian film producers "abandoned science fiction films like relics after the public refused the first ones" (2004, 339).[1] Most of the few science fiction films produced in the 1960s, such as Ugo Gregoretti's *Omicron* (1963), Franco Castellano and Giuseppe Moccia's *I Marziani Hanno 12 Mani* (1964) and Tinto Brass' *Il Disco Volante* (1964), were primarily comedic films that relied on comedy stars. Indeed, the Italian genre in which time travel narratives have been utilized the most is comedy. This chapter discusses how adopting time travel narratives in comedies produced in Italy in the 1980s and 1990s changed the perception of their comedic practice. The modalities of time travel depicted will be analyzed in relation to the type of humor championed by three comedic phenomena from this period: the "nuovi comici," the Fantozzi franchise and the "cinepanettone." I argue that in each of these three comedic forms time travel is insightful in showing how the filmmakers involved dealt with the problematic legacy of "comedy Italian style."

Between 1958 and 1980 Italian film comedy experienced what is considered its golden age with the flourishing of the genre known as "comedy Italian style." "Comedy Italian style" coexisted with other Italian comedic genres, for instance, farce and "commedia sexi." Even though it was characterized by an emphasis on the contemporary social landscape of the Economic Miracle, a period of wealth experienced by the Italian economy between the mid–50s and early 60s, "comedy Italian style" did not shy away from representing Italy's past. The "national-popular" re-visitations of the past that "comedy Italian style" championed from *La Grande Guerra* (1959) onwards showed Italians their history "from below," with the average citizen at the center of their depiction. This was an attempt, inspired by the dissemination of the writings by Marxist philosopher Antonio Gramsci, to challenge the heroic rhetoric that had been promoted by the Fascist regime before World War II, which had resurfaced in the conservative political discourse of the liberated nation at different stages of its development from 1946 onwards. However, the realistic outlook of "comedy Italian style" determined that it never adopted the time travel narrative device and instead simply set films in the past. Time travel itself was left to a number of comedies that were produced when the "comedy Italian style" genre waned in the late 1970s. The landscape of Italian film comedy experienced an eclectic phase of transition that lasted from the early 1980s to the mid–1990s. During this period different comedic genres developed and reached popular appeal. This shift in the industry matched the country's own transitional phase from the Christian Democrat dominated First Republic (1948–1991) to the Berlusconi age (1994–present).

In this phase of transition a new generation of comedians, who also directed their own films and were described as "nuovi comici," emerged, including Carlo Verdone, Massimo Troisi, Roberto Benigni and Francesco Nuti. At the same time, a comedic franchise created by Paolo Villaggio, following the misfortunes of a vexed middle-class Italian bookkeeper, Ugo Fantozzi, developed into Italy's most successful comedic brand-name of the time. The first film in the franchise, Luciano Salce's *Fantozzi* (1975), was produced when "comedy Italian style" was still dominating the Italian comedic arena. During the 1980s, however, the Fantozzi franchise developed into something quite different from "comedy Italian style."

In the same transitional period, a series of Christmas comedies, eventually nicknamed by Italians "cinepanettone" films, started appearing in Italian movie-theatres after the success of Carlo Vanzina's 1983 comedy, *Vacanze di Natale*. Despite the fact that several of the "cinepanettone" filmmakers were biologically related to figures from the "comedy Italian style" generation, the Vanzina-directed Christmas comedy genre, which eventually became the dominant Italian comedic genre in the mid–1990s, is considered by Italian film criticism as a vulgar degradation of "comedy Italian style."

During the same era when these various changes were taking place, between 1980 and 1997, the time travel narrative was deployed most frequently in Italian cinema. This chapter analyzes three comedies that adopt this motif, namely the "nuovi comici" film by Roberto Benigni and Massimo Troisi, *Non Ci Resta Che Piangere* (1984), the fifth film in the Fantozzi franchise, *Super-fantozzi* (1986), and the 1996 "cinepanettone," *A Spasso nel Tempo*, in order to discuss how the use of time travel in each of these comedic genres reveals their relationship to the antecedent "comedy Italian style" genre. Absent in "comedy Italian style," the time travel narrative device, with its idiosyncratic elements of fantasy and multiple period settings, marks a shift in Italian film that demonstrates these new comedic practices in relation to the realist satirical genre that preceded them.

Nuovi Comici: Non Ci Resta Che Piangere *(1984)*

A few brief considerations on the wave of comedians labeled "nuovi comici" in the 1980s will now be made in order to contextualize the use and function of the time travel narrative in Benigni and Troisi's collaboration, *Non Ci Resta Che Piangere*. In contrast to the "comedy Italian style" generation, within which comedic stars were almost always deployed in socially engaged narratives criticizing consumerism, politics and later terrorism, the "nuovi comici" privileged more personal narratives. "Nuovi comici" films, however, were constantly compared to the socially circumstantiated "comedy Italian style" of the previous generation, partly because these "forefathers" were still making comedies. Also, "comedy Italian style," which had amassed a popular following in the 1960s and 1970s, was being reappraised by critics, especially in film journals such as *Positif*, precisely in those years in which the "nuovi comici" emerged. Time travel enabled two of the "nuovi comici," Roberto Benigni and Massimo Troisi, to distance themselves from these comparisons with their predecessors.

The premise of *Non Ci Resta Che Piangere* is that an elementary school teacher named Saverio and a janitor named Mario go on a road trip and halt in front of a railway intersection. A local employee of the national railway company explains to Saverio and Mario that a number of trains have to pass through and this means that there could be a very long wait. Mario decides to take a side street, hoping that it will lead them to a bridge over the railway. Instead, they are stranded in the middle of the countryside in a raging storm and take shelter under a tree. They see a light in the distance, which they investigate, and are eventually allowed inside a country house for the night. In the morning another guest opens one of the windows and starts relieving himself from the terrace. Mario and Saverio find it amusing, until the man is killed by a spear thrown by men on horses in the street below. They realize that they have somehow traveled back in time, the final proof being that the tree they used for shelter the night before is now a young plant.

The audience is offered no explanation as to why or how the time traveling has occurred. Also, for a long portion of the film we, like Mario and Saverio, are not fully aware of the time or the place to which they have traveled. As a result of the accents of the people in "Frittole," the imaginary small village in which they now reside, we know they are somewhere in Tuscany during the lifetime of Dominican preacher Girolamo Savonarola (1452–1498). Savonarola's followers are responsible for the murder of many members of the family of Vitellozzo, the owner of the country house in which the two protagonists stay. However, whenever Mario and Saverio ask any of the peasants of Frittole if they truly are in the 1400s, they are never given a precise date, but are simply answered, "Yes, almost 1500s"! Only in the last third of the film does Saverio find out that it is 1492, the year in which Christopher Columbus arrived on the American continent. Similarly, while most of the action in Benigni and Troisi's film takes place in the imaginary village of Frittole there is ambiguity about its geographical location. When the two ask "what city is close to here? If we leave Frittole, where do we get to?" they are always given the answer "Frittole." Even when Mario and Saverio eventually leave and travel towards Spain, we only see them in the middle of the countryside or in late-medieval traveling lodges, without knowing for certain where they are (with the exception of Palos in the last scene of the film). This sense of indeterminacy marks a stark contrast with the "comedy Italian style" films set in specific historical periods and in real parts of Italy. The elements of ambiguity in the historic and geographic setting of *Non Ci Resta Che Piangere* create a surreal atmosphere, particularly in comparison to the social commentary of the "comedy Italian style" historical films.

Another aspect that differentiates *Non Ci Resta Che Piangere* from previous comedies set in the past is the fact that it questions history as we know it. Mario and Saverio attempt to stop Columbus sailing to America because an American jilted Saverio's sister. Saviero plans to arrive before August 3, the day Columbus sailed. However, when they arrive in Palos they discover he left on July 12. The "national-popular" re-visitations of the past that "comedy Italian style" championed re-contextualized history by highlighting the role of the "common man" in significant junctures, but never question the occurrence of reported events. However, Benigni and Troisi distance themselves from "comedy Italian style" by avoiding the socially centered humor typical of the genre and, in some instances, "quoting" earlier comedy. For instance, in one scene where they write a letter to Savonarola, pleading with the monk to free Vitellozzo, they pay homage to a scene in Camillo Mastrocinque's *Totò,*

Peppino e la Malafemmina (1956), a purely escapist "farsa" from the 1950s. Whereas "comedy Italian style" films set in the past usually avoided parodying historical figures, a humorous practice typical of less realist comedic forms and often deployed in time travel narratives (as in the case of *Time Bandits* [1981], or *Bill & Ted's Excellent Adventure* [1989]), in Benigni and Troisi's comedy we are offered a humorous version of Leonardo da Vinci to whom Mario and Saverio try to sell ideas for present-day technology: the train, the thermometer, the card-game "scopa" and, most importantly, the water-tank/toilet plumbing apparatus, of course without knowing how any of those actually work. This scene also offers insight into how Benigni and Troisi avoid the class characterization typical of the "comedy Italian style" genre. Although Benigni (Tuscan) plays a teacher and Troisi (Neapolitan) a janitor from the underdeveloped South, when they walk by Leonardo's camp exchanging scientific information to capture the inventor's attention, Saverio is shown to be as simple-minded as Mario. Whereas regional background served an ongoing discourse about national identity in "comedy Italian style," here it is made to be socially irrelevant, thus confirming that the "nuovi comici" were interested in a less satirical type of humor.

In the last scene of the film the two protagonists hear a train's whistle blow in the distance and run down a hillside to see the heavy piece of machinery coming to a halt. Excited, they now believe that they have somehow returned to the present, only to be greeted by Leonardo, who reassures them that they are going to get their percentage for the invention. Mario and Saverio's time travel journey is never concluded with a return to the present and the audience's relationship with the characters is left open-ended. The open-ending, a realist narrative strategy that "comedy Italian style" often implemented in its satire of the present and avoided in its "national-popular" and somewhat heroic representations of the people's role in history, is repurposed here. It is deployed in a narrative that is indeed set in the past, but which features elements of fantasy and the surreal, rather than a socially circumstantiated narration about the struggles of Italian people through major historical junctures.

For Benigni and Troisi, time travel (and specifically the "unexplained" and "indeterminate" type of time travel they chose) offered an opportunity to challenge expectations associated with the "national-popular" representations of the past found in the "comedy Italian style" of their predecessors. They did not comment on the state of the country, nor offer a testament to Italian national identity like the historical comedies of the previous generation, but simply pursued their personal humor in an unorthodox historical setting.

The Fantozzi Franchise: Superfantozzi *(1986)*

In comparison to the personal humor of the "nuovi comici," the *Fantozzi* franchise (1975–1999) started out by offering a critique of consumerism and its empty promises. It did this by pursuing a cartoonish and carnivalesque humor that set it apart from the realism of "comedy Italian style." The franchise was inspired by the success of Paolo Villaggio's novels featuring the bookkeeper Ugo Fantozzi, an ever-vexed middle-class employee of a multinational based in Italy. The first two film adaptations of the character, *Fantozzi* and *Il Secondo Tragico Fantozzi* (1976), were directed by Luciano Salce, a director previously involved in the realist "comedy Italian style" genre. The two Salce-directed films featuring Fantozzi resembled the social commentary of many films of this earlier genre and were at times harsher in their critiques. If the characters of 1960s "comedy Italian style" films attempted to find shortcuts to becoming integrated into the Economic Miracle elite of those years, conversely Fantozzi is shown to have no chance of victory or escape from mediocrity. Fantozzi and his colleagues work in a massive grey building as instruments of a world of bureaucracy that they do not comprehend, but break their backs to appease. As Giacovelli noted "Fantozzi is not just ruled by his literal boss, the mythical and almost ethereal 'mega-galactic C.E.O.': he is 'owned' by consumerism, by the mass-subculture that promises happiness in the very same instant in which it makes it impossible to reach it" (1998, 159).

The way in which the Fantozzi character is constantly subjected to ever more extreme social circumstances than the average Italian of the "comedy Italian style" genre is by letting go of realism. Paolo Villaggio explains in an interview released during the making of the first film, which appeared in the daily newspaper *L'Unità*, "Fantozzi is going to be comparable to some of the animated characters from America rather than the characters of 'comedy Italian style': his naivety, the physical and spiritual immunity that derive from his ignorance, make him similar to [the *Looney Tunes* character] Sylvester the Cat" (Grieco 1974, 9). Fantozzi, as a fictional character, is immune to the laws of mortality: he can be punished by his employers and be put on the top of the company building to serve as a human lightning rod and survive this assignment. Nonetheless, in the first two films of the series Salce managed to balance this cartoonish aspect with a social critique of the Italy of the 1970s.

The franchise was taken over by director Neri Parenti with the third film, *Fantozzi Contro Tutti* (1980). In the review of this film in *L'Unità*, the reviewer notes "possibly the character created by Paolo Villaggio [...] is becoming like the types embodied by ['comedy Italian style' star] Alberto Sordi: if not a symbol of the habits of today's average Italian, at least a significant aspect of them" (L.P. 1980, 9). The comparison with Sordi and the use of the word "today's" give the impression of a strong relationship with contemporary Italian society. In this context—the reviewer laments—"the repetitions and the voice-over typical of the franchise slow down the action too much" (9). In this sense, these films repeated the tendency to reflect and comment on social reality that thrived in "comedy Italian style," but in doing so clashed with the cartoon-like humor previously established in the franchise.

Parenti's third directorial effort and the fifth film featuring Villaggio's character, *Superfantozzi*, deviates from this model by presenting a series of vignettes featuring Fantozzi in different epochs. The action opens in the Garden of Eden. God is unhappy with his first attempt to create a human being, which resulted in Fantozzi. He creates Adam, a handsome, strong and better-endowed specimen, to whom he gives a beautiful companion, Eve. Fantozzi receives an ugly wife. Eve seduces Fantozzi into picking the Forbidden Fruit from a tree and, as a result, Fantozzi and his family are condemned to an eternal existence as vexed subjects of the powerful. Thus, we find Fantozzi among the cavemen, doing his best to carve a wheel out of stone, unappreciated by society.

From there on the film moves through a series of historical epochs in which Fantozzi is always in the wrong place. In Jesus' times, for instance, he is Lazarus' nephew, entitled to a fortune that will finally turn things around for his family once his uncle passes. As soon as this happens, Jesus brings Lazarus back from the dead. In every historical vignette, the audience's expectations, bound to prior knowledge of the given epochs, are parodied in scenarios where expectedly/unexpectedly Fantozzi is ultimately the victim. In Medieval England, Robin Hood steals a bag of gold coins from an aristocrat and donates it to Fantozzi's family of underdogs. After two minutes are spent celebrating the fact that they are finally rich, Robin Hood returns and takes the bag of gold explaining that "I steal from the rich to give it to the poor." During the French Revolution, Adam is about to be guillotined and the underprivileged are finally about to be vindicated. However, the guillotine gets stuck and, when Fantozzi walks onto the scaffold to check the machine, he guillotines his own penis. And so on, until the final vignette, in which Fantozzi is in the future and has to give his automated shuttle-house to Adam, who needs to borrow it to seduce a woman while Fantozzi, floating in space, is hit by a meteorite.

Even though we are not presented with a time travel device, some aspects of time traveling and narrative continuity are parodied in the film. The stone-carved wheel built by caveman Fantozzi, for instance, can be found in other epochs, even in the future as a visual reference to the monolith in Stanley Kubrick's *2001: A Space Odyssey* (1968). At times, Fantozzi is shown ducking when the short-sighted Filini is about to do something potentially dangerous, almost as if he remembers getting hurt in similar scenarios from vignettes set in prior epochs. This would indicate that, rather than there being multiple Fantozzis, one for every generation of the human race, the man on screen is one person who exists in different eras.

Ultimately, the dimension that the use of time travel (in the sense that multiple timeframes are united in the one narrative journey) adds to the franchise is straight-forward: Fantozzi, a character who had cartoon-like aspects from the start, is removed from the context of the 1970s employee who is vexed by consumerist society and turned into "the vexed human being" *sui generis*. From a character—albeit a cartoonish one—who embodied the habits of the average Italian from a specific societal timeframe and who resembled Alberto Sordi's "comedy Italian style" types, he is transformed into *maschera*, an archetypal character in the tradition of *commedia dell'arte*, or an embodiment of one of humankind's universal attributes (in Fantozzi's case, vexation). Fantozzi's suffering is not the expression of a particular social malaise anymore, but rather a metaphor for the hardship of life itself.

After *Superfantozzi*, five more films were produced in the franchise over the next thirteen years and Villaggio's "maschera" was transposed unproblematically into the Italy of the 1990s. As with Benigni and Troisi's *Non Ci Resta Che Piangere*, time travel in the *Fantozzi* franchise is indicative of the problematic legacy of "comedy Italian style" realist humor and was used to steer the franchise in a different comedic direction. The heavy-handed social element of the third and fourth installments of the franchise was abandoned in favor of a universal scope in which the cartoonish gags typical of the franchise were more appropriate.

Cinepanettone: A Spasso nel Tempo *(1996)*

The third comedic wave that emerged within this transitional landscape, the "cinepanettone," emphasized regional background, an element it shares with "comedy Italian style." Christian De Sica is most often cast as a Roman on holiday, while Massimo Boldi is his Milanese counterpart. The "cinepanettone" protagonists are also, like the "comedy Italian style" average Italians, on-screen embodiments of societal customs, although their aim is not to find shortcuts to power, but most often to find shortcuts to "getting laid." The heavy reliance on female nudity in the "cinepanettone" films connects them to "commedia sexi," a farcical low-budget genre from the 1970s, rather than "comedy Italian style." Christian De Sica often attempted to create a connection with "comedy Italian style" in his "cinepanettone" appearances, having his characters mimic some of the Roman-accented antics typical of Alberto Sordi or Neapolitan-accented actions typical of his father, Vittorio De Sica. The Vanzina brothers, the most prominent writers and directors of "cinepanettone" comedies, also played with the notion of being the 1980s and 1990s heirs to "comedy Italian style," specifically in *Sapore di Mare* (1983), a comedy set in a seaside resort in the 1960s. With the use of nostalgic pop music and period accurate décor, the film appropriates the iconography of some of Dino Risi's "comedy Italian style" films shot in similar beach locations during the 1960s (such as *Il Sorpasso* [1962] and *L'Ombrellone* [1966]).

In most cases the Vanzina-directed "cinepanettone" films are considered by Italian film criticism to be a vulgar degradation of the "comedy Italian style" genre. The annual profits of these films are regarded as an indication of the cultural regression of the country and they have often been read as an expression of "berlusconismo," the superficial culture of mass consumption of media based on formulaic repetition rather than meaningful content. "Berlusconismo" is epitomized by the content offered on the television channels owned by the former Prime Minister, Silvio Berlusconi. Vanzina's early films focused on the teenage generation that was the by-product, culturally speaking, of Berlusconi's media empire and, as filmmakers, the Vanzina brothers often relied on female pin-ups and male entertainers who gained popularity on Berlusconi's networks. The sense of repetition and cultural regression associated with "berlusconismo" is evident in the Vanzina "cinepanettone" films since, as noted in an article published in *L'Unità*, they "revisit for the umpteenth time just the worst aspects of 'comedy Italian style'" (Vecchi 1996, 28).

A Spasso nel Tempo, the 1996 time travel "cinepanettone," offers insight into the genre's relationship with "comedy Italian style." The film opens, like many "cinepanettone" installments, with two Italian families on vacation, in this case in California. Ascanio is a Roman aristocrat who takes pride in his city's status as the capital of the country. Walter is the Milanese owner of a multiplex. We later learn that Walter votes for the Lega Nord, the Northern political party often allied to Berlusconi's Polo delle Libertà, which promotes a secessionist agenda and displays racist hostility towards illegal immigrants and Southern Italians. After some bickering, the two happen to sit side by side on an amusement park ride offering a "virtual reality" experience of different epochs. As they begin what is supposed to be a virtual journey, the ride malfunctions and, as Professor Mortimer, the American scientist responsible for the invention of the ride, explains, the two travel back in time.

The first thing to note is that, unlike *Superfantozzi*, this franchise—*A Spasso nel Tempo* and its 1997 sequel, *A Spasso nel Tempo 2: L'Avventura Continua*—features an actual time machine, as in *Back to the Future* (1985) and numerous other U.S. science fiction films. When the two protagonists are transported to a given age, the time machine automatically equips them with period appropriate clothes. Additionally, Ascanio still has his mobile phone, which at times works in different epochs and allows him to speak to his family and to Professor Mortimer in California in 1996. The comedic mechanism of the two films is quite simple: as Professor Mortimer attempts to bring them back to the present with the defective virtual time machine, Ascanio and Walter visit different eras, which become settings for toilet humor vignettes. A dinosaur wraps its extendable tongue around Walter's penis, while later Ascanio and Walter sexually attack a group of half-naked cavewomen, and so on. In the first film, the two visit Florence during the Renaissance, Venice in the 18th century, Italy during the Nazi occupation and the seaside town of Capri in the 1960s. Here a younger Ascanio is courting his wife-to-be (played by Manuela Arcuri, a pin-up who became popular for her appearances on Berlusconi's Italia Uno network) and the time-traveling Ascanio attempts to stop him so he will not end up being stuck to his "ball and chain" in the present. The scene in which the older Ascanio takes the place of his younger self, who is being distracted by Walter, gives the film's humor the vulgar, even morally questionable, dimension championed by the "cinepanettone" comedies. Seeing Arcuri's bare breasts, Ascanio decides to renounce his mission and copulate instead; when she hesitates, objecting that "she is a girl from an honest family," he thuggishly replies "you're from an honest family?!? Then I'll do you from behind"! and has his way with her. Thus the narrative potential of exploring a character by having him relive his own past is quickly put aside in order to privilege the commercial potential of a popular object (Arcuri's body, which is objectified by the character in the film as it had previously been objectified in print and on television).

The commercial mindset applied here foreshadows the film's approach to any product of popular culture. For example, while in Renaissance Florence Ascanio and Walter contribute to the invention of "calcio fiorentino," the progenitor of soccer, and meet Lorenzo the Magnificent, who they encourage to found Fiorentina F.C. (the modern soccer club that represents Florence in the Italian Serie A league), to sign Batistuta (the Argentinian star center-forward of Fiorentina at the time in which the film was shot) and to become a soccer mogul "like Cecchi Gori" (the owner of Fiorentina at the time and, incidentally, a rival of the film's producer, Aurelio De Laurentiis). Most of the antics of Boldi and De Sica follow this formula of decontextualized puns on popular culture referents from the present. When Walter hears someone saying "cavaliere," the Italian word for "knight," instead of looking out for an actual 15th century knight he immediately associates the word with the Italian honor of

"Cavaliere della Repubblica," which Berlusconi received, and frantically asks: "Cavaliere? Berlusconi is here? Did we end up in his villa in Arcore?" When Ascanio and Walter test Pico della Mirandola's scientific knowledge with a series of questions, De Sica and Boldi imitate the voices of Corrado Mantoni and Mike Bongiorno, two quiz-show hosts who worked for decades on Berlusconi's networks. In this context, when Ascanio, Walter and Lorenzo the Magnificent run through the streets of Florence, slapping the faces of horse cart passengers, they quote a famous scene set in Florence's train station in Mario Monicelli's classic "comedy Italian style" *Amici Miei* (1975). *Amici Miei*, which Walter tellingly identifies as "the box office hit of 1976," is not used as an example of the type of socially engaged filmmaking produced by the earlier generation that the "cinepanettone" has to live up to. It is simply addressed as something very popular (it made a lot of money), in the same way that Berlusconi is popular (he gets a lot of votes), Manuela Arcuri's breasts are popular (they sell a lot of magazines), and the film's international cultural referents, such as *Back to the Future* and Aqua's 1997 dance hit "Barbie Girl," which is played in the opening credits of the *A Spasso nel Tempo* sequel, are popular. Usually, all of these popular elements, which are indiscriminately mashed together, help the annual "cinepanettone" become popular and profitable itself.

Thus, the use of time travel in the *A Spasso nel Tempo* "cinepanettone" franchise is revelatory in identifying how, in this wave of comedies produced in the Berlusconi era, "comedy Italian style" and other traditions of Italian cinema are not regarded as "social" texts with their own meaning and impact, but simply as byproducts of consumerism. Gone is the discourse about national identity and gone is the socially engaged criticism of consumerism. From the "cinepanettone" point of view, "comedy Italian style" is nothing but a consumerist "object" that Italians buy into. The use of time travel in *A Spasso nel Tempo* is indicative of an Americanization of the "cinepanettone," despite its relationship to "comedy Italian style" and the frequent "nods" to some of this genre's texts. This impression is reinforced by the fact that the type of time travel mechanism chosen by the Vanzina brothers mimics the modalities of time travel in American films produced before *A Spasso nel Tempo*, which may have inspired it (the *Back to the Future* franchise and the *Bill and Ted* series), and after it (*Hot Tub Time Machine*, 2010).

Conclusion

As a result of the lack of a strong science fiction tradition in Italian cinema, time travel is a narrative trope that the Italian film industry has adopted most often in a comedic context and, specifically, in the transitional landscape of Italian comedy that the gradual disappearance of the "comedy Italian style" genre created in the 1980s and 1990s. "comedy Italian style" was a satirical means of representing social reality and it set a high bar for the comedic practices that followed it. Exploiting time travel narratives, the "nuovi comici" Benigni and Troisi distanced themselves from the precedent set by "comedy Italian style" in order to pursue their surreal humor. The Fantozzi franchise used time travel to transition from social commentary into a vehicle for a universal "*maschera*." The "cinepanettone" comedies embraced it to commodify "comedy Italian style" as a pop culture referent to be exploited commercially. If "comedy Italian style" satirized social reality, the use of time travel in Italian comedies of the 1980s and 1990s marked an attempt on the part of Italian filmmakers to clarify that their approach to reality was going to be different. Whereas "comedy Italian style" *engaged* with and *satirized* reality, the "nuovi comici" often *transcended* it, the Fantozzi franchise *mythologized* it, and the "cinepanettone" films *commodifed* it.

Note

1. This quote and all others from Italian sources have been translated into English by the author.

Remembering the Past for the Future

The Function of Museums in Science Fiction Time Travel Narratives

DOLLY JØRGENSEN

As the Doctor, a traveler in space and time, walks through the Delerium Archive, "the biggest museum ever," he comments on the exhibit labeling: "Wrong. Wrong. Bit right, mostly wrong. I love museums" (*Doctor Who*, "The Time of Angels," 2010). The Doctor finds several artifacts that he himself has had a hand in creating or saving in the past, exclaiming, "Ooo, one of mine. Also one of mine." A visit to a museum is a pleasant experience for the Doctor because there is a personal connection to the artifacts. However, the exhibit visit is more than pleasurable; it is also a way to obtain information from the past, for the museum is history's switchboard, relaying messages across time. The Doctor sees an object with a message to him in Old High Gallifreyan burned onto it, which was sent by his companion River Song. He jumps into the Tardis to go 12,000 years into the past to help his companion who guessed that one day the Doctor, a frequent visitor of museums, would visit the Delerium Archive. Unlike the standard visitor, the time traveler has the ability to go back into the past to the origin of an artifact and take action.

The Doctor's encounter with artifacts that both amuse and educate him is not unlike our modern encounters within the museum's walls. The role of a modern museum is significantly different from the cabinets of curiosities of the early modern age, which focused on the act of collection for knowledge-making and exhibition for status-gaining (Findlen 1994). In the 20th century, museums shifted from display for entertainment alone to incorporate education and interpretation. Specifically from the 1980s onward, museums moved from "static storehouses for artefacts into active learning environments for people" (Hooper-Greenhill 1994, 1). The new focus on museums as learning spaces fits the original meaning of the word museum in Greek: "the place of the muses." The muses were the personification of knowledge and arts and the nine daughters of the god Zeus and Mnemosyne, the personification of memory. The name for our institution, which serves as a repository of knowledge and art, is inextricably linked to memory, but the memory is not only for the past; it also leads to inspiration from the muses to create new knowledge and art.

There are five essential functions of modern museums: collection, conservation, exhibition, interpretation, and service (Alexander and Alexander 2008).[1] Although all of them exist in one form or another in all museums, they may vary in importance at different times and in different contexts. However, in all cases, museums collect and preserve items of the past in the present that in some way are deemed useful for the future. The visitor to the museum is a time traveler in a sense, experiencing objects and even replicated environments from the past. As Ludmilla Jordanova observed, "The most common kind of knowledge claimed to derive from museums is a sense of the past. ... It hinges upon our ability to use objects as means of entering into and living vicariously in a past time" (1989, 25).

At their core, museums are in the memory business. Jens Brockmeier has argued that remembering is "organizing and reorganizing the selected fragments of memory into meaningful schemata," which is precisely the work of a museum (2002, 22). Museums serve within the cultural geographies of remembering and forgetting as "temples of memory," becoming particularly common as modes of creating "lasting" memories in the face of rapidly changing modern societies. Museums cultivate collective memories, the "common experiential ground of coherence and belonging," by curating individual memories preserved as texts and artifacts into narratives (Brockmeier 2002, 18). Susan Crane summed up the relationship between museums and memory in this way:

> Being collected means being valued and remembered institutionally; being displayed means being incorporated into the extra-institutional memory of the museum visitors. ... What they then learn and perceive, and preserve as memory of that museal experience, becomes mobile and takes the museum beyond its own walls [2000, 2].

But as Björn Krondorfer (2008, 240–241) has cautioned, preservation and remembering are not the same thing; if too many things are collected, they may not be able to be integrated into a coherent historical narrative.

Paul Ricoeur (2004) reminds us that collected objects become the texts and artifacts that are remembered in the act of doing historical research and writing history, yet those things which are left out can create lacunas which inspire the writing of history. Museum collections are not objective about collecting the past or present. They are curated and interpreted; some things are collected and others are discarded; some things are remembered and others forgotten. According to Ricoeur, things forgotten and things destroyed erase the past because the past "is lost in forgetting; the destruction of archives, of museums, of cities—those witnesses of past history—is the equivalent of forgetting. There is forgetting wherever there had been a trace" (2004, 284). Ricoeur makes a distinction between memory, which for him is an event, and forgetting, which is the non-event or failure to make a memory, but more recent research has started exploring intentional forgetting as well (e.g., Golding and Macleod 1998). Forgetting can be a tool to overcome loss and embarrassment, or simply to make room for additional information. As this chapter will show, museums can function both as sites of remembering and as sites of forgetting.

Science fiction as a genre has often invoked museum settings as places of memories. Robert Crossley has argued that science fiction literature and museums have much in common:

> A museum operates as a place that is at once social, impersonal, and contemplative; it also, necessarily, constitutes an artificial world that disorients spectators in time and space. As a locale, therefore, the museum is ideally suited to science fiction, that form of fantastic literature most concerned with the speculative and the epistemological, most focused on humanity at large rather than the private self, and most at home on other worlds and in times to come [1991, 78].

In the science fiction discussed by Crossley, a visitor who lives in the future encounters a museum to uncover something about a past civilization, often resulting in an epiphany about social change. In his view, the museum represents the past and science fiction represents the future (Crossley 1991, 79).

How does that change when a science fiction time traveler encounters a museum? In this chapter, we will travel with three time travelers as they encounter a museum: the unnamed adventurer of H. G. Wells' novella *The Time Machine* (1895), the Man of Chris Marker's featurette *La Jetée* (1962), and the Doctor of the television series *Doctor Who* (1963–1989, 1996 and 2005–present). In these stories, the museums the travelers encounter have fallen into disuse and the collections are left up to interpretation, but the travelers still find value in their visits because they bring their own memories through the museum's doors. As a result, what will be remembered and what will be forgotten is at stake.

Time travel narratives fold together past, present, and future, so the time travelers' encounters with museums expose the entangled relationship between time, objects, and memory. For these museum visitors, there is a tension between remembering and forgetting, between conservation and decay. Time is central to the processes of memory. Brockmeier suggests that we "conceive of memory as a movement within a cultural discourse that continuously combines and fuses the now and then, the here and there" (2002, 21), but for the time traveler, the future also enters the memory narrative. The time traveler is a subversive visitor of the museum because he brings personal experience from the past or the future to interpret artifacts in ways that contemporary museum visitors cannot.

Museums then are both repositories of the past and creators of the future. Science fiction time travel can re-envision the museum as a house of memory *and* forgetfulness, which may help us to draw some conclusions about our own modern museum experience. Can we, like River Song, use museums as repositories of the past for the future?

Shiny Porcelain and Dusty Floors

In H.G. Wells' *Time Machine*, in the year 802701 the time traveler sees an enormous green building in the distance with a façade shining like porcelain. He is at first curious about this Palace of Green Porcelain, but visits it only when he eventually decides to seek refuge from the Morlocks, who prey on the Eloi and presumably would take him as well. From a distance the building's tall spires are shiny and impressive, but when the time traveler gets closer, he sees that it is deserted and decaying. Upon entering, he realizes at once that the building was a museum.

The collection at the Palace is extremely varied, as might be expected for a large and impressive museum. The time traveler visits the Galleries of Paleontology, Mineralogy, Natural History, Industry, Chemistry, and Ethnology, in addition to a library and armory. The Palace is clearly modeled on the Crystal Palace, erected to house the Great Exhibition of 1851, and its successor the South Kensington Museum (later renamed the Victoria & Albert). As the time traveler exclaims, "Clearly we stood among the ruins of some latter-day South Kensington!" (153). Patrick Parrinder has observed that the Palace of Green Porcelain is "precisely what a late Victorian visitor might have expected" with the museum having the same position and function as it had in the late 19th century (1995, 74). In spite of the claim that the museum is from the time traveler's personal future (sometime after 1895), the collection was constructed as a 19th century version of encyclopedic knowledge. This should remind us that science fiction is always written at a particular moment in time with a historical basis. Wells envisioned the museum of the future to contain the types of things that the most impressive museums of his day contained.

The impressive collection at the Palace was not, however, well preserved. A layer of dust blankets the tile floor and the objects are as decayed as the building's exterior. Time hangs heavy in the air—as remarked by the traveler, "the thick dust deadened our footsteps" (154). Time has taken its toll on the collection, although some artifacts appeared to have preserved, which the time traveler attributes to their cases being airtight. In the galleries, the time traveler notes that some specimens have been removed from their cases: the Eloi have used rare fossils as beads and the Morlocks have presumably taken away some cases altogether (154). The natural history collection is particularly hard hit, as the specimens have decayed beyond recognition: "A few shriveled and blackened vestiges of what had once been stuffed animals, desiccated mummies in jars that had once held spirit, a brown dust of departed plants: that was all!" (156). The books in the library have likewise disintegrated, leaving only warped boards and metal clasps behind. "Gallery after gallery, dusty, silent, often ruinous, the exhibits sometimes mere heaps of rust and lignite, sometimes fresher" (165)—the overwhelming feeling is of a place time forgot.

The exhibition space had at one time been lit by both natural and artificial lights. Cases lined the walls with small artifacts and large dinosaur skeletons loomed over visitors. The description of the exhibition infrastructure matches the cutting edge museum developments of the late 19th century, including new glass cases in the British Museum and lights in South Kensington (Crossley 1991, 86–87). Wells describes a gallery system with dedicated spaces for each scientific discipline, creating a focus on specific objects instead of holistic visions of nature and culture. There is no interpretation in the Palace museum of 802701—the time traveler sees no signs or boards, no labels on the exhibits. Everything he knows about the specimens on display comes from his own experience. It is he who knows that a skeleton on display is a brontosaurus (153) and that saltpeter was not in the mineral cases (155); he finds a box of matches in one of the airtight cases and knows how they can be used to make fire (161–62). The museum of the future holds the artifacts but no memories. As Krondorfer suggested, preservation does not equate to remembrance.

The time traveler is not interested in interpretative education (in fact, the museum offers none), but is instead interested in repurposing display objects for real world use. The public service of the museum of the future is as a warehouse of raw materials, which were originally displayed out of context and will now be taken by a time traveler out of the museum into a new context. In 1895, Wells portrayed the museum as a futile endeavor subject to "universal decay" (163), an "enormous waste of labor" (161). The forgetfulness of man seen in the forgotten museum weighs heavily on the traveler. In this dystopian vision, only objects that might be used for something practical matter in the future because all knowledge eventually turns to dust.

When *The Time Machine* was made into a full-length feature film in 1960, the museum was transformed into a library room and its function was twofold: to show that all written knowledge has passed away by 802701, and to reveal that the Morlocks and Eloi are divergent evolutionary human forms. Whereas the time traveler figured this out himself in the book, in the film he is given the information. This change partly reflects the move from text to film, but it also hints that by 1960, some people thought of libraries as more significant places of knowledge collection than museums. In the 2002 film version, the museum is replaced by the New York Public Library, which the time traveler visits in 2030 and again in 802701. Like the Palace of Green Porcelain, the library contains all knowledge, but this time literature, audio and video are accessed through an interactive hologram. The hologram is the internet embodied, containing all knowledge in the 21st century. Once again science fiction writers have created a "museum" based on their own experience of what constitutes a universal collection.

The 2002 film version does not read the destruction of the library with the same futility as Wells' original tale of the museum. Instead, at the end of the movie, the hologram is functional and retells the stories of civilizations long past to the Eloi. In this telling, the knowledge of the library is still useful in the distant future without modification, without being taken out of its museum context. This may reflect the growing emphasis on public service in the museum sector, in so far as museums are seen as having wide relevance for eliciting cultural and social change. Perhaps in the 21st century we are more confident that the knowledge contained within texts will not be forgotten.

Wells' *Time Machine* cautions that the museum is useful to a time traveler, but not for the purposes that a curator today might plan for. Interpretations of the exhibits and the knowledge that is supposed to be gained from visiting a museum are entirely missing from the Palace of Green Porcelain in 802701. A museum that was carefully curated to represent universal knowledge becomes a compendium of objects out of context and out of time. There is also a real risk that the museum space and the objects within it will not be conserved and thus will lose their original educational value. The museum itself becomes a site of forgetting, because only the time traveler can remember what the objects are and what they were for. While a museum may be shiny porcelain on the outside, inside the contents turn to dust with time.

Museum Memories

Chris Marker's short film *La Jetée* (1962) recounts the story of a man who travels into both the past and the future in order to save Earth's civilization and, like Wells' time traveler, is never named. After the Third World War, the Earth has become uninhabitable above ground. A group of men begin experimenting with time travel, using prisoners as their test subjects. They hope to send a man into the future to obtain food, supplies, and energy sources. However, in order to access the future, they first need a man who can become accustomed to time travel and the way to do that is to find a man who has a strong memory connecting him to the past. The man, the film's unnamed protagonist, is the perfect candidate because of a childhood memory of seeing a woman on the jetty at Orly airport in Paris from shortly before the war. This memory will allow him to travel into the past near the time of his memory, and will eventually make him strong enough to travel into the future to get help. In his travels to the past, he falls in love with the woman he had seen as a child at the jetty. Even after his task of contacting the future and acquiring help has been accomplished, he desires to return to the woman. With the help of the people in the future, he returns to the jetty and runs toward the woman. He catches a glimpse of one of the experimenters from his own time, who has come to shoot him. As he falls, he realizes that his vibrant childhood memory was witnessing his own death.

The story of the man is intricately tied to two museums. The first museum supplies the setting for the man's present day. When the survivors moved underground, they moved into the underground storehouses of the Palais de Chaillot, which served as the filming location (Harbord 2009, 105). Palais de Chaillot was built atop the Trocadéro, a hill in Paris, for the Exposition Internationale of 1937.[2] Like the Crystal Palace that inspired Wells, Chaillot was built to house exhibitions, in this case the Musée des Monuments Français (sculpture) and the Musée de l'Homme (ethnography). In making a former museum into one of humanity's final shelters, Marker shows the potential repurposing of the museum in the future. The museum is serving the future, but not in the ways a curator had intended. Just as the time traveler sought refuge in the Palace of Green Porcelain, survivors of the third World War also reuse the museum spaces at Chaillot as shelter.

The Musée des Monuments Français is particularly important to the film because the experimental chamber and the passageways to it were clearly shot in the underground storehouses for the museum. This particular museum specializes in casts of French sculptures from the medieval Romanesque and Gothic periods, particularly decorative sculptures from churches, although there are some earlier classical works from Greece and Rome. In the film, the corridors through which the prisoners walk are filled with these sculptures— in stacks, on wooden pallets, partially hidden under tarpaulins. One artifact is labeled "tête apôtre" (head of an apostle), while accession numbers, the numbers used by museums to index their holdings, are visible on some of the others. The statues all portray medieval saints and apostles, except the Boy Struggling with a Goose, which is a Roman copy of a Hellenistic original. The film's viewer is invited to see this collection of artifacts, which have survived the war only because they were in storage rather than on display above. The stone bodies had been carefully curated and conserved in the past, but that no longer matters because they will never be shown in their intended spaces. The sculptures are reminders—memories—of a time before the war, but at the same time, they and their histories have been forgotten. The statues are figures frozen in time, yet that time has been lost to the people after the war.

It is among these museum pieces that the time travel occurs. The man walks through an outdoor garden with statuary. These statues are not in a museum per se, but like the ones in the storeroom of the Palais de Chaillot, they are heavily damaged, with broken noses, missing faces, half an arm, or headless. They are tangled and maimed, even though these are museum pieces seen by the man in a time before the war. These statues converge on the man as his memory of one event in the past allows him to travel to and from the past more generally. The narrator's comment that "other images appear, merge, in that museum which is, perhaps, his memory" invites us to ponder whether memory is indeed a museum, or even more critically, whether a museum is memory.

The answer to these questions might be found in the most extended sequence in the film, an encounter in the Muséum national d'Histoire naturelle. The museum scene has previously been analyzed as a quintessential element in *La Jetée*'s innovative cinematographic style: a *photo-roman*, a series of still photos (although there is one short film sequence) which are nevertheless infused with motion through the use of cuts, fades and camera positioning to connect the images (Harbord 2009, 32). The film's construction is a mode of making time into instants instead of a continuous stream; the stasis inherent in the sequence of stills is in tension with life, which is always in motion. In this vein, the museum, with its taxidermied specimens and skeletons on display, has been understood as a way of juxtaposing stillness/death and motion/life (Kawin 1982; Harbord 2009). Life has been frozen in time.

The man and woman visit the zoology gallery of the Muséum national d'Histoire naturelle, which was opened in the form shown in the film in 1889. Ironically, it closed to the public only four years after the film was made and would remain closed until the new Grand Gallery of Evolution took its place in 1994 (Blandin 2001, 479). During the man and woman's visit it is clear that they are interested not only in each other, but also the exhibition objects. When the couple stand before the antelopes, the man points out a specimen high up on the display; when looking at the big cats, the woman gestures toward one. These gestures allow the audience to imagine the couple talking about the creatures, wondering about why they have big horns, long legs or striped coats. The woman puts her hand over her mouth in surprise; they laugh together as they look at the exhibit. When they view the wild horse they lean over to read its label through the glass. The gesturing even turns to physical contact when the woman touches the tapir's nose with her index finger. The museum encounter is thus about creating a relationship with the collection, experiencing the exhibit both emotionally and intellectually. The service aspect of modern museums has moved beyond education and become entangled with tourism and entertainment, such that the public should enjoy going to a museum (Stephen 2001). This is most certainly the case with this time traveler and his companion. The museum becomes a place to make memories both of the collection and of companions.

However, this visit to a natural history collection also asks the viewer to rethink who or what is on display in a museum. When the couple moves from where the animals are displayed in the open to see the ones behind glass, they peer into the case with the big cats. The camera angle is then changed so that the vantage point is from behind the cats in the case looking out on the couple. This is followed by a similar view in the avian exhibit, with the photo taken from inside the cabinet looking out at the man and woman. This encourages the audience to wonder who it is actually behind the glass: who is on display? This is even more acute in the final two images of the sequence: in the first, the woman points at a bird behind the glass; in the second, the camera zooms in on her finger to show a reflected finger reaching out from the other side of the case. Is she inside or outside? Crossley observed that science fiction encounters in museums often lead to the protagonist looking at himself in the reflection of a glass case, serving as a reminder "that in the showcases of science fiction's museums we are what is chiefly on display" (1991, 99).

La Jetée invites the viewer to think of a museum as memory and memory as a museum. The museum is a space that displays artifacts to visitors so that existing memories can be invoked and new memories made. According to Conway and Rubin, memories are stored in groupings that relate them to each other, including life periods ("when I lived in city X") and general events ("meeting friends at location Y") (1993, 109). New personal experiences become autobiographical memories through the thematic or temporal relatedness of the event to prior memories through these groups (Conway and Rubin 1993, 108). This means that people create new memories by first accessing old ones and then relating the new events to them. A museum displays old memories—things that have been collected in the past—in order to spur visitors to create new memories. In the reverse, when a person recalls a memory, it is like looking through a glass case at something collected in the past. The man has been able to perfect time travel because his memories of the past are like museums that can be visited to forge new memories in the present.

Memories in the mind are not that different from artifacts in the museum. The museum, whether mental or physical, is not a place of stasis, but one that uses the static lifelessness of old things to enable vibrant new life. In *La Jetée*, the museum is a site for making memories that harness the past to move society into the future.

Deliberate Forgetting

Early on in the long-running science fiction television program *Doctor Who*, the Doctor, a Time Lord from the planet Gallifrey who travels through time and space with various companions, visits a museum on a planet other than Earth. In this four-part serial, "The Space Museum" from 1965, the Doctor confronts the museum space as both a place of desired remembering and a place of deliberate forgetting.

The Doctor and his three companions, Ian, Barbara, and Vicki, materialize unexpectedly next to a large building filled with rocket ships. The Doctor remarks that the items come from different periods, which he interprets as evidence that they are seeing a collection rather than a working armory or space station. The museum, full of space rockets, mechanical equipment, and spacesuits to celebrate the military triumphs of the Morok Empire, is designed to fit contemporary expectations of a museum. As the Doctor's companion Ian notes, "We might almost be in a museum at home."[3] Cases and cabinets of artifacts line the walls and litter the walkways, going on "for miles," as Ian puts it. Like Wells' futuristic museum, which met Victorian expectations of such institutions, this museum is what a 1960s visitor would expect.

A museum on another planet is not altogether unexpected according to the Doctor: "After all, you have objects of historical interest on Earth, so why not a museum in space? I always thought I'd find one someday." Collecting and displaying the past is taken to be a reasonable part of civilization.

In spite of its similarities to Earth's museums, from the beginning the travelers feel that something is not right about the museum. The building has no prominent exits, unlike an "ordinary museum" according to Vicki, and no windows. When the group finally does get outside, they find that the planet "appears completely dead." There is dust everywhere in a thick layer and that an eerie silence hangs heavy in the air. Ian likens the planet and the museum to a "graveyard" several times. "The Space Museum" reflects the same kind of dystopian angst about museums that Wells showed through the Palace of Green Porcelain. Just as in Wells' description of the Palace, the dust and silence at the Space Museum indicate ruin. The museum on Xeros has fallen out of favor over time. As the planet's Governor comments, "People tire of their heritage. Three hundred mimmians ago, sightseers filled this planet, marveling at what they saw. Today, the occasional spaceship from Morok calls." The museum is in a state of decay—it is being forgotten.

After seeing the desolation of the planet, the time travelers are shocked to see themselves on display in an exhibit case. Unlike *La Jetée*, which asks the viewers to metaphorically consider museum-goers as museum objects, the Doctor nearly becomes an actual museum object himself. In a complex time travel narrative, the group has arrived in their own future in non-corporal form because they are out of sync with the time dimension. In this form they are able to see that they will become part of the exhibit. While peering through the glass, Barbara, one of the group, expresses disgust at seeing themselves fixed in eternity: "Well, it's horrible. Those faces, our faces, just staring." Not only will they become exhibits, but Ian fears that they will be forgotten: "Exhibits in a forgotten museum, eh? Is that how we are going to end up?"

Seeing oneself in the exhibit provokes disgust and fear because the exhibited object is lifeless. Artifacts in a case lose their context, history, and vitality. Before encountering themselves, the group had seen a Dalek, one the Doctor's archenemies, in a case. The item was labeled only "Dalek, Planet Skaro," so its significance had to be interpreted by the time travelers. Vicki notes that she had read about them in her history books because they had invaded Earth in her personal past, but that the Dalek in the case looks friendly, "not a bit the way I imagined it." Barbara and Ian, who had personally encountered Daleks during their time traveling, are quick to correct the girl about the Dalek's demeanor. Such an exchange between visitors could have happened someday in front of the exhibit of the Doctor and his companions. Who are these people and why are they here? Nobody would be able to answer. Thus, preservation of the artifacts would not result in them being remembered.

All is not lost, however. When time finally catches up to them (or backs up to them, if that is possible), they become corporal and the bodies in the case disappear. Their future is no longer manifest. Thus for the remainder of the serial the Doctor and his companions try to avoid becoming exhibited objects. The Doctor comes the closest to becoming a museum artifact when he is captured by the Governor and subjected to a deep-freezing process to preserve him as a specimen. Luckily his companions rescue him in time to reverse the procedure. After the rescue, when the Doctor could turn the tables on the Governor and make him into a museum object, he comments that his conscience will not let him do it. The act of collecting is rejected, seen as tyrannical.

The tyranny of the Governor and the Space Museum is finally toppled by the planet's conquered and oppressed native people, who are encouraged to lead a rebellion by Vicki. The first action the rebels take after driving the Moroks off Xeros is to dismantle the museum. The museum represents the Moroks, their wars, and the locals killed in the Morok conquest of Xeros. Nothing is spared. One of the rebels comments, "We only want on Xeros what belongs to Xeros." The museum objects are not repurposed in the future nor is the museum built on as a way of rewriting history; new history is only constructed by completely obliterating the museum. The decaying museum must be deliberately destroyed and its collection forgotten. The people of Xeros are expected to move forward from a blank slate.

Every item in the Space Museum collection is destroyed, except one machine component that is given to the Doctor as a souvenir. Since a souvenir is an object collected from a journey in order to remember it, the Doctor and his companions have been given permission to remember the Space Museum. However, that remembrance will be restricted to times and places far away from Xeros and its rebellion. In this ending, there is a tension between remembering and forgetting. The museum as site of remembrance is destroyed because it remembers the "wrong" things. An artifact is taken as a souvenir and trophy because it recalls the triumph of "right." The future lies beyond the museum.

"You've got a time machine. What do you need museums for?"

During the Doctor's romp through the Delerium Archive which opened this chapter, his companion Amy asks him a poignant question: "You've got a time machine. What do you need museums for?" This is the ultimate question for all three of these time travelers. It is the question behind this inquiry into the function of museums in time travel narratives, but it is also a question applicable to the modern museum experience.

Museums are a place to make memories of the display objects as well as our companions. Similarly, our memories are like museums that store up the things of life and display in our minds the experiences we have had so that they too can be revisited and repurposed over time. Visitors are the curators of those memories—some things will be chosen to remember and others will be forgotten. At the end of the episode "The Day of the Doctor" (2013), the Doctor sits alone staring at a landscape painting hanging in the National Gallery in London. He comments to himself, "I could be a curator. I'd be great at curating. I'd be the Great Curator. I could retire and do that." In many ways the Doctor has been a curator all along, selecting objects that should be taken out of collections (including himself and his companions) and reinterpreting the histories of others. Some things may be better left forgotten. Memory-making opportunities may be the most important service a museum can offer.

Museums are a place in which the visitor arrives with their own previous memories in order to make new ones. Objects will be reinterpreted based on the visitor's own knowledge and serve as springboards to action. The time travelers in these three stories interpret and reinterpret artifacts on display. While the museum holds objects that were collected and exhibited for particular reasons, the stories show us that, for all their good intentions, curators are often wrong about the meaning of objects in the future. Objects may be repurposed to serve a specific practical use, like a piece of machinery, which the time traveler breaks off a machine in the Palace of Green Porcelain to use as a mace. Museums may lose their cultural value, like the Musée des Monuments Français and the Space Museum, over time. We cannot assume that a museum collection can remain stagnant and still be valued. A top-down approach to knowledge production might not always be productive. This does not mean, however, that labels are unnecessary—we see that the man and woman in *La Jetée* read them—and museum studies show that real visitors do indeed read labels (McManus 1989). Giving information to the visitor about a museum object can be valuable.

At the same time, designers of museum exhibits need to leave room for the visitor's own experience and knowledge to play a part in their interpretation of the artifacts. Modern exhibits are often designed to affirm individual meaning making and personal interpretation (Hein 1999). This constructivist approach to exhibition, which developed along with postmodern thinking, allows more narratives and voices in the museum and sets it up as a communicative space (Hooper-Greenhill 2000). A museum is thus a space to engage the visitor to create new knowledge built upon his or her own experiences in the museum and outside of it.

All three of the time travelers in these science fiction stories go unnamed. They are simply the time traveler, the man, and the Doctor. Leaving them unnamed, the writers suggest that they could be anyone. They could be us. Thus, their experiences in the museums could be ours. Although we cannot physically travel in time, we can mentally travel in time. We can visit the past in a museum exhibit, but we can also envision the future through it because the memories made in a museum may be later recalled and put into action. The museum is our own personal time machine. Remembering the past becomes a way forward to the future.

Notes

1. The first edition of this book included research as a core function, but it was incorporated into some of the other functions in the updated edition.

2. The Palais de Chaillot replaced the older Palais du Trocadéro on the same spot. The older building was not entirely demolished, but rather extensively renovated and renamed. For a discussion of the palace's placement in the Exposition's landscape, see James D. Herbert, "The View of the Trocadéro: The Real Subject of the Exposition Internationale, Paris, 1937," *Assemblage* 26 (1995), 94–122.

3. Space museums were not typical in 1965. The U.S. National Air and Space Museum would only add "space" to its name in 1966 and was housed in a tin shed behind Smithsonian Castle until 1976, when its current location was opened on the Mall in Washington, D.C. The Royal Air Force Museum in London, which includes space exploration, was not opened until 1972, while the UK's National Space Centre in Leicester only opened in 2001.

*Narrative and
Media Forms*

"Harmonious Synchronicity" and *Eternal Darkness*

Temporal Displacement in Video Games

Paul Booth

In June 2002, a year after the debut of its GameCube console, Nintendo released its first (and only) "rated M for Mature" game. Although not as popular as its more family-friendly franchises like *Super Mario Brothers* (1985–present) or *The Legend of Zelda* (1986–present), Nintendo's *Eternal Darkness: Sanity's Requiem* (2002) became a cult favorite for the GameCube audience, winning "Outstanding Achievement in Character or Story Development" at the 6th Annual Interactive Achievement Awards and featuring in many critics' "best video game" lists.[1] A Lovecraftian-themed horror game, *Eternal Darkness* tells the temporally-linked stories of various members of the Roivas family, their ancestors and other figures from the past as they all fight with, or become enslaved to, an inter-dimensional being that exists outside time itself. Despite its complex narrative, detailed mise-en-scène and critical acclaim, *Eternal Darkness* is rarely analyzed in academia. Analyzes of the game have mentioned it within larger studies of the survival horror genre (Chien 2007/2008, 64), or have noted its interactive format (Garritano 2010, 111). In contrast, I propose to examine *Eternal Darkness* as a particularly ludic representation of video game time travel, which integrates player/character identities into an interactive environment.

By proposing this, I immediately throw into suspicion my analysis to anyone that's played the game, as technically no character actually travels in time in *Eternal Darkness*. To call it a "time travel game," then, requires a revision to popular conceptions of what "time travel" is or can be. Therefore, I want to make a correlated argument: our understanding of time travel has, since its inception, been discursively constructed by narrative and narratological principles, what I have previously called "temporal displacement" (2012). I use *Eternal Darkness* to represent a new mode of understanding time travel, which takes as its focus the interactive potentiality of time travel through (drawing the language from *Eternal Darkness* itself) "harmonious synchronicity," the drawing together of multiple timeframes within a coherent whole.

I first identify *Eternal Darkness* as an exemplar of an emphasis on temporal synchronicity within the time travel genre. Second, I examine traditional representations of time travel as narratively/spatially bound, and then offer a particular reading of time travel in video games that augments the time travel genre through ludism. Integrating "harmonious synchronicity" more fully into the time travel genre opens up new opportunities for the genre. Specifically, notions offered by traditional conceptions of time travel rest in a spatial metaphor of "travel"—a literal movement from place to place (or, rather, time to time), facilitated by a displacement in time frames. Conversely, an additional level of structure to consider within gameplay relies on a temporal metaphor of synchronicity—a subjective translation between time frames within a single identity as constitutive of time travel. Ultimately, by using *Eternal Darkness* as a case study, I illustrate that time travel in games may have less to do with displacing time than it does with augmenting the bond between character and player.

Eternal Darkness

There are twelve playable characters in *Eternal Darkness*. During the game, the narrative switches perspective through each of them, although the player always returns to the point of view of the game's protagonist, Alexandra Roivas (Alex). This character/perspective switching reveals a form of temporal displacement in the game, as players are literally displaced (and de-timed) from one temporal location to another. As the game progresses Alex discovers an ancient, fleshy book titled *The Tome of Eternal Darkness* in her family's centuries-old mansion that transports the player (and Alex) vicariously to different points in time and place. At each point the villain, Pious Augustus, a Roman centurion who has become inhabited by the essence of one of the "Ancient Ones" (interdimensional aliens who battle for control of the Earth), attempts to assemble relics, artifacts, and magick (the supernatural power of the Ancient Ones) that will mark his return to power. Augustus has survived for thousands of years and only Alex can defeat him by learning the ancient, magickal secrets of her family, using weapons from the past, and applying her experiential knowledge of the Ancient Ones. Throughout the game, the characters instruct the player how to use different weapons and how to practice various magickal spells, which she then embodies when later playing levels set in the contemporary era via Alex, who has also learned these same spells and weapons. These skills are also linked to the powers of the various Ancient Ones—magick (the power of the spirit), strength (the power of the body), and sanity (the power of the mind).

Through Alex's reading of the Tome, the twinned identities of Alex and the player "live" through the experiences of those in the book. This twinning occurs because Alex's consciousness transfers to the different characters, whom the game player then plays as avatars. A clear example of this dual embodiment takes place with the character of Anthony. Played relatively early in the game, Anthony is a messenger sent to deliver a message from Charlemagne to the leader of the Franks. The message, it turns out, is cursed by Augustus and corrupts Anthony's soul, turning him into a decaying zombie-like creature. At the end of his chapter, after successfully defeating the boss, Anthony dies, but not before learning one of the major magick spells Alex will need to defeat Pious Augustus. Anthony never reveals this magick to another and Alex never actually encounters Anthony, but his knowledge of the spell does transfer to her after the player completes his chapter. Furthermore, when playing as Augustus, the player first learns to wield the Roman gladius sword. Upon returning to Alex, the player finds that Alex too has learned how to use the weapon.

This affective interaction between player and character in *Eternal Darkness* illustrates what James Paul Gee (2007, 50) terms the "projective identity," a concept that stresses "the interface between—the interactions between—the real-world person and the virtual character." For Gee, the more a player embodies a character, the more developed the projective identity can become. That is, the "real-world" identity of the person playing the game develops by imbricating play into the persona of the player; the "virtual" identity of the character within the game progresses because the real-world identity of the player makes choices that affect the development of that character. Although Gee is mostly describing long-term characters in role-playing games, the similarities between his work and *Eternal Darkness* are striking. The player of *Eternal Darkness* must embody multiple characters, each one facilitating the amalgamation of character and play. Only by developing a theory of temporality that takes into account not only the character and the player, but also the interaction between them, can a fully-fledged understanding of video game textual temporality emerge.

The time travel in *Eternal Darkness* therefore relies not on the narrative progression of the story, but on the interactive potential between character, player, and projective identity, an interaction unique to games. This potential is enacted in multiple ways throughout the game. Most saliently, the first time through the game the player interacts with various characters throughout time, whose particular knowledge of magick, swordplay, gunplay, ancient runes and/or medicine help Alex, as previously discussed. Alex's virtual identity (tied to the player's via the projective identity) develops from this knowledge, as each of the other characters' traits (also tied to the players' via their particular projective identities) transfers across time. In *Time on TV* (2012, 30–31) I referred to this type of time travel as "memory temporality," as the audience's memory enacts a form of subjective time travel for the character: "the audience must piece together events from the future (that have not yet happened) with those from the present (as they are happening)." The player's mind must constantly be in two temporal locales at once, both remembering Alex reading in the "future" and playing the character in the "past." In effect, this dual embodiment distances the player from her own timeframe; her "present" is always deferred. There is a more complex type of "projective identity" created in *Eternal Darkness*—the player must simultaneously identify with more than one character, in more than one timeframe. This multiple identity connects player to characters across times, projecting more than just a singular sense of being within the game. As I described:

> The coherence of an audience to a temporally-displaced character functions because the character is not the only thing displaced in time: by following the character's adventure, the representation of the narrative in the show also jumps in time, and the audience likewise is forced to re-assemble the timeline in a non-linear manner [2012, 91].

In other words, this mental time travel, as the first type of time travel in *Eternal Darkness,* highlights the separate but connected temporal plots running through the game as embodied by the various characters. (In the next section, I'll problematize this notion of "plot" as a spatially-oriented understanding of narrative.)

The second type of time travel in *Eternal Darkness* is more subjective and more complex than the first. To fully complete the game—that is, to encounter the true "ending" of the story within the game—the player must play through the entire game three times. The larger backstory of the game involves not one interdimensional being, but rather four of them, each described as an Ancient One. Like a cosmic game of rock-paper-scissors, three of the Ancient Ones are in constant battle. Each of these three—Ulyaoth, Xel'lotath, and Chattur'gha—has a central power that it can wield. Ulyaoth's power is magick, and can damage a character's spirit; Xel'lotath's power is mental acuity and can force insanity; Chattur'gha's power is physical strength and can cause bodily damage. Ulyaoth is stronger than Chattur'gha yet weaker than Xel'lotath; Chattur'gha is stronger than Xel'lotath yet weaker than Ulyaoth; Xel'lotath is stronger than Ulyaoth yet weaker than Chattur'gha. All three are bound together by the fourth Ancient One, Mantorok—the "Keeper of the Ancients"—who maintains equilibrium among the other three Ancients Ones by ensuring that they are bound to fight against and destroy one another (see Figure 1). Mantorok lies dormant on Earth while the other three Ancients Ones appear in our dimension when summoned by evil-doers and villains like Augustus.

Early in *Eternal Darkness*, the player makes a decision as to which Ancient One will be the enemy throughout the game—Chattur'gha, Xel'lotath, or Ulyaoth. Whichever enemy she chooses, that Ancient One's particular power becomes dominant in the game. So, for example, if one were playing the game and chose Xel'lotath as the Ancient One to fight, most of the enemies in the game would be able to use powerful sanity-draining effects, making the player's characters' minds weak. At the same time, that Ancient One's particular weakness is a dominant weapon—so, in fighting enemies, brute strength tends to triumph more than using magick or sanity would.

Once the player has beaten the game for the first time, it appears to be over—whichever Ancient One the player was fighting has been destroyed (or, at least, sent back to the dimension from which it sprung). However, defeating

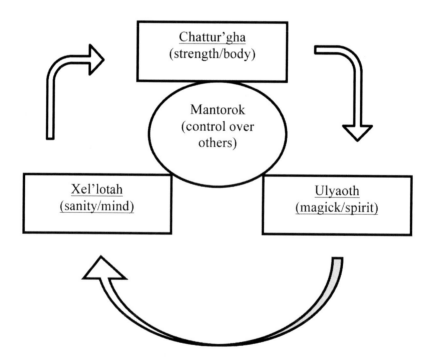

Figure 1. The Ancient Ones and Their Powers.

just one Ancient One still leaves two unaccounted for and the player can play through the entire game again, only this time with a different Ancient One as the main enemy. Once the player has beaten the game three times, a final cut scene of all the Ancient Ones being destroyed is revealed, and our heroine's grandfather, Edward Roivas, speaks to Alex from beyond the grave with the ominous words:

> The mighty Chattur'gha has obliterated the insanity of Xel'lotath. The madness of Xel'lotath has overcome the power of Ulyaoth. The boundless Ulyaoth has decimated the power of Chattur'gha. All at once, separate and simultaneous, for the Universe is made of many timestreams, many possibilities, all in harmonious synchronicity. Only Mantorok remains, slowly dying...

Thus, this meta-game time travel forms a type of symbolic synchronicity in and of the game itself. Only by triumphing over multiple iterations of the game can the player complete her task, of ridding the world of the influence of these interdimensional Ancient Ones. This is unlike time travel as it is traditionally deployed in the genre—although multiple trips through the same "time stream" are common (Shane Carruth's *Primer* [2004] provides an excellent example when Aaron and Abe see their past selves after time traveling to the future), these synchronous dimensional shifts are less frequent in narratives. That is, the third time through the game, the player does not meet herself playing, nor does she see Alex from previous iterations, nor are the characters and previously vanquished Ancient One "dead." Rather, these appear to be subjectively differ-ent but linked journeys through the same timescape. The narrative elements of time travel are here overshadowed by the ludic medium characteristics of har-monious synchronicity. However, this type of synchronicity across time frames requires an interpretation of the projective identity of the player-character interaction. Alex (as a virtual character) has not time traveled per se; nor has the player (excepting that the player has moved forward in time just as long as it has taken to play the game). Rather, the projective experience of the player's "real-world" identity as combined with the character's own virtual identity has shifted temporal plots at least three times. The time travel aspect of *Eternal Darkness* rests on this player/character interaction, realizing the projective iden-tity through time travel rather than in either the real-world identity of the player or the virtual identity of the character.

Harmonious Synchronicity in Video Games

The history of video game studies has been shaped by two particular schools of thought (Frasca 2003a): the ludologists and the narratologists of game theory (Aarseth 1997; Frasca 1999; Frasca 2003b; Jenkins 2004; Pearce 2004). Narratologists believe that games should be analyzed, at least partially, as types of stories. Ludologists see the study of game play as central to the study of games. The debate has lessened over time; there seems to be a general consensus today that narratology and ludology are not as polarized as once believed (Zimmerman 2004). As this discussion has shaped the development of game studies, however, it is a useful discourse through which we can start to look at the representation of time travel in *Eternal Darkness;* that is, as a particular narrative construct, time travel in video games already foregrounds a particular way of thinking about temporal displacement.

This temporality in *Eternal Darkness* reveals how time itself becomes a core mechanic of video games, and harnesses one of the key characteristics outlined by Salen and Zimmerman (2004, 152–155) as elemental to all games: that of complexity. In their terms, complexity describes a property of a system with multiple variables that have various outcomes dependent on those variables. Temporality is one type of complexity, as "looking at how the relationships in the system change from moment to moment can help determine whether the system is exhibiting complex behavior" (155). By examining the role that time plays in a specific game, a game system (a collection of simple games and puzzles that, when put together, forms a complete whole) can be analyzed for its inherent complex modality. Salen and Zimmerman also note that complex experiences of temporality can be more (or less) pleasurable for the game player, as "the participant's sense of time can stretch or shrink" in games, which "not only change[s] our perception of time but also offer[s] freedom from its tyranny" (338). That is, asserting control over time—through repeated gameplay, through saved games, through regulated failure like character deaths—actually produces the complex pleasures of meaningful participation in one's own temporal existence.

Although many video games have made use of temporal aspects in their gameplay, few actually use time travel as a narrative device (Zagal and Mateas 2010). An early exception is LucasArts' *Day of the Tentacle* (1993), in which the three main protagonists are separated by a time machine into three different time periods, again echoing in harmonious synchronicity. The game mechanics use time travel to facilitate puzzle solving; sometimes, certain inventory items can be "shared" across time. As game reviewer Mark Langshaw describes *Day of the Tentacle*:

> Changing the course of history was an essential component. For instance, one puzzle required Hoagie in the past to remove a tree as Laverne becomes entangled in its branches in the future. Another conundrum had the player ensuring that the original American flag design received a tentacle twist in the 1700s so Laverne could use it as a disguise in future [2010, para. 4].

The time travel mechanics in *Day of the Tentacle*, just as in *Eternal Darkness*, serve a particular ludic function—and as such, the three different time periods in the game create a similar type of harmonious synchronicity across the characters and player. The projective identity of the player/protagonist must negotiate between the time periods to produce the ludism of the game.

At the same time, a second type of time travel mechanic exists in *Day of the Tentacle*—a ludic self-referentiality, as Bernhard Rapp (2010, 260) notes. *Day of the Tentacle* is actually a sequel to LucasArt's *Maniac Mansion* (1987) and, as such, aspects of the original game manifest in the sequel. Further, Rapp (2010, 260) describes a scene in *Day of the Tentacle* that features a computer on which the player of *Day of the Tentacle* can actually play *Maniac Mansion*. The "retro" aesthetic of *Maniac Mansion* contrasts with the (at the time) more detailed graphics and gameplay of *Day of the Tentacle* (although of course both are heavily "retro" today), subjectively transporting the player to a different time period within the gameplay itself. The same "retro" aesthetic can be seen in Ubisoft's *Prince of Persia: The Sands of Time* (2003), in which players can unlock the original *Prince of Persia* (1989) game, as well as in Nintendo's *Animal Crossing* (2001), in which players can play original NES games. It's not just that the characters travel in time; it's that the subjective experience of the projective identity created by the amalgam of player and character experiences a harmonious temporal synchronicity.

Another game that makes use of harmonious synchronicity, quite literally in some levels, is the Jonathan Blow's adventure/puzzle game *Braid* (2008), which follows the adventures of Tim (note the etymological connection to "time") as he tries to save a princess from a monster. Unlike the traditional console games that *Braid* superficially emulates (like *Super Mario Bros.* [1985], which is even directly referenced in *Braid* when a dinosaur tells Tim that his "Princess is in another castle"), Tim does not progress linearly through the game, but rather has to manipulate time itself in order to advance. As Arnott (2012, 436) notes, these time-based manipulations become aspects of *"implicit puzzle making"* (emphasis in original). The player has to think through the entire level, using the time mechanics, to solve the puzzles. For example, Tim has the power of "time rewind," which means that at any time (including a character death) time can be rewound and everything in the level reverts to its original starting places (excepting some "exempt" items, which the player must make use of). Tim is a time manipulator quite literally, as his powers also include slowing time down, making time move forwards and backwards, depending on his movement, and even "doubling" himself and interacting with his other self, which Arnott (2012, 437) describes as "Tim and his shadow ... perform two actions at the same time some distance apart. The solution to the puzzle ... requires Tim to use his shadow to pass an otherwise inaccessible key back to Tim himself." Like the characters in *Day of the Tentacle*, Tim is also a traditional time traveler—that is, he physically traverses the boundaries of the linear experiences of time. More saliently, Tim's time travel only becomes relevant and emotionally satisfactory when viewed through the discursive lens of the projective identity. Tim may travel in time, but it is the player that makes sense of it, adding her own unique perspective onto the subjective synchronicity of the temporal dislocations.

With *Braid*, as with *Day of the Tentacle* and *Eternal Darkness*, time travel within the game is less focused on physically traveling from one time period to another (although that does occasionally happen) and more focused on the subjective experience of the projective identity of the player/character as she comes to terms with and solves puzzles that focus on different temporal existences. This differs significantly from previous narratological conceptions of time travel, which tend to highlight cause/effect relationships within adventure stories. As Paul Nahin (1993, 10) describes in his authoritative *Time Machines*, our most common assumptions of time travel involve using a machine to physically dislocate a character from a time stream. Although other types exist, our narratological assumptions hinge on this more specific definition. Nahin (1993, 7) quotes Franklin: "when one says time travel what one really means is an extraordinary dislocation of someone's consciousness in time," but he argues this is too broad to apply to traditional time travel. The reason for this traditional application may be because time travel has traditionally been heavily influenced by narrative development. In the next section, I will look at how the shape of narrative (via narratology) has influenced how we traditionally conceptualize time travel within spatial terminology and assert how video games offer a different conception of time travel as temporally-oriented.

Narrative Time Travel

The harmonious synchronicity of *Eternal Darkness* portends a shift in the way time travel can be interpreted within multiple genres and media. As a genre, time travel has always been associated with narratological developments and, as such, has been interpreted as a spatial phenomenon. For example, one of the first major time travel stories, H. G. Wells's *The Time Machine*, is significant not just for its exploration of time travel in literary form, but also for how Wells misinterprets the relationship between time and space. In the story, the titular machine moves in time but not in space; however, as Nahin (1993, 14) describes, "such a machine would ... run into itself"! That is, if

Wells's time machine stayed in the laboratory (as he described), then in traveling back in time it would literally occupy the same space as its past self—leading to, at the very least, nuclear annihilation. Space must be taken into account in discussions of temporality, at least for logical coherence.

Indeed, in narratological terms, time travel is always associated with a spatial understanding of narrative. For example, Nahin indicates basic rules about how time travel should work within traditional narratological instances:

> (1) if your story has a single time track or line, the events around a closed loop in time must be consistent; e.g., you cannot have a time traveler changing the past ... and (2) if your story does depend on changing the past, you must also introduce multiple time tracks as with a splitting universe [2011, 3–5].

Note his use of spatial language ("time track") in the description of how time travel functions. In fact, the English language makes it exceedingly difficult to describe time travel in anything other than spatial terminology—the idea of "movement" necessitates spatial understandings. Narratives are often seen as types of spaces. As narratologist Laure Ryan (2001, 73) has described, narrative can be interpreted as a "virtual reality," a "story"-space that contains all the elements of the narrative in an alternative experience. This spatial understanding of narrative echoes in the works of Herman with his concept of the storyworld. For Herman, the viewer's reconstruction of "the [story's] surrounding context or environment embedding existents, their attributes, and the actions and events in which they are more or less centrally involved" helps to build the storyworld as it encompasses both "the temporally [and] spatiotemporally structured" events encountered by the reader (2002, 14). As Jones has shown:

> the appeal of ... vast, transmedia fictions lies precisely in their invitations to immersion and interactivity; they are constructed, marketed, and used by fans not as "texts" to be "read" but as cosmologies to be entered, experienced and imaginatively interacted with [2002, 84].

My own (2012, 35) term "temporal displacement" uses the linguist base of "place" as a spatial phenomena, even as I qualified the term with a time-based adjective. Any similar linguistic attempt to describe travel time temporally becomes frustratingly difficult—it seems space and time are connected linguistically as well as physically (Nahin 1993, 89–97).

In his discussion of time travel literature, Wittenberg discusses the narratological impact of time travel as a genre. He describes time travel as a

> "narratological laboratory," in which many of the most basic theoretical questions about storytelling, and by extension, about the philosophy of temporality, history, and subjectivity, are represented in the form of literal devices and plot [2012, 2].

Indeed, his literary analysis underscores the larger point here, that all time travel literature (and, by extension, films and games) has developed a robust connection to narratological issues of cause and effect, spatial coordination, and the philosophy of storytelling. It may be that narrative as it is presented in linearly-based media (literature, film, television) will always retain elements of spatiality. By eliminating temporal "play" from the experience of the narrative, these linear media encourage viewers/readers to experience the text as it unfolds. Even if there are temporal ruptures in the telling of the tale (as in flashbacks, flashforwards, ellipses, and/or slow motion, e.g.), the viewer is encouraged to reconstruct that narrative in a linear fashion. Temporality exists to linearize traditional media. The contemporary media environment makes this point even more directly: the temporal messiness of social media problematizes this spatial metaphor and offers new invitations to explore the way time travel can be interpreted outside strict physical movement. For example, binge-watching DVDs of television programming changes the temporal situation of the show (Kompare 2006; Gillan 2010), while communication with and through a show's webpage, Twitter interactions, Wikipedia articles and Facebook profiles can change the relationship between viewers and the text (Booth 2010). At the same time, it can also make the temporal situation of the main text that much more difficult to pin down.

Anders argues that time travel works best in narratives when it is "messy." She contrasts the "neat" type of time travel storytelling, when "everything falls into place and you realize that the rubber duckie at the beginning of the story was actually put there by the guy at the end of the story" with the more realistic type, where

> adventures are messy and unpredictable. Therefore, the best time travel stories are untidy, rather than obsessed with providing the cheap "Aha! That's how it all fits together" moment. Life is a glorious, crazy mess in general—why should time machines make it any different? [2012, para. 26].

In a narratological sense, time travel can be messy because cause and effect can synchronize in multiple ways—an effect can be significantly different (or changed) than its requisite cause. However, with a video game, especially puzzle-based games like *Eternal Darkness*, the need to solve the puzzles in order to progress in the game forces coherence in time travel. Effects have to have particular causes. In order to progress, a player must complete the necessary steps, usually in the proper order. The necessity of narrative coherence means video game time travel must be "neat." Messy time travel does not work when it is about finding solutions to puzzles.

Any "messiness" within time travel in video games, therefore, has to come from the way audiences "play" with the subjective experience of time rather than the way time itself can be changed. When time travel based video games attempt to represent narratively-based (spatial) time travel, they are forced to remediate linear media. Take, for example, the classic arcade game *Teenage Mutant Ninja Turtles: Turtles in Time* (1991). Despite the fact the game is touted by Konami as a time travel game (villain Shredder sends our Testudine heroes into a time warp), in actual game play the fact that the Turtles are back in time makes little difference to the progression of the narrative: it is simply a plot device to put the Turtles into different locations. Rather than playing with time, the game treats time and space as synonymous. In effect, this type of (quite literal) temporal displacement remediates the way time travel works in linear media. For Bolter and Grusin (1999, 5), "remediation" describes the way any medium is constructed of previous media: e.g., cinema is remediated photography; television is remediated radio. Video games, in this deterministic sense, remediate filmic attributes and traditional board game attributes (Howells 2002, 110). In Bolter and Grusin's estimation, all "new" media remediate older media as an instructive genealogy of the history of media development. *TMNT: Turtles in Time* remediates the spatial time travel of the cinema. *Braid* remediates previous puzzle-based literary experiments, including Calvino's *Invisible Cities* (1972) and Lightman's *Einstein's Dreams* (1992) (Arnott 2012, 434).

For video games to develop their own type of time travel mechanics, we must interpret time travel within games differently than we have interpreted linear media's time travel. As McMahan (2003, 69) notes, most video game players become "so engaged with a game that [they reach] ... *deep play*," a state of being completely immersed in the game, a "measure of a player's level of involvement." To encourage players to reach deep play, games must be engaging to play but understandable to win—an outcome must be possible. Therefore, to make a coherent game, puzzles have to be solvable; to solve a puzzle in a game one must have been presented with the appropriate information earlier in the game. There must be consistency between cause and effect in order for the player to progress. However, the inherent interactive properties of the video game medium—that player actions can influence the development of the on-screen action (Aarseth 2004, 49; Wolf 2003, 49)—offer an alternate exploration of time travel in video games' "interactive narratives": the interaction between the player/character projective identity and the timeframes within the game generates a playful fluidity to the interpretation of the events on screen. What came before and what comes after the moment of play in the game can be influenced by the projective identity of the player/character and her knowledge of the other temporal moments in the game. This subjective temporality in *Eternal Darkness* offers a way of examining the synchronous movement of knowledge across time frames within a single space.

As time frames change, according to Zagal and Mateas (2010, 847), the "temporal frame" within video games provides a thorough grounding in the temporal play of the exploration of time in video games. For Zagal and Mateas, multiple timeframes in and around the playing of video games creates "multiple simultaneous perspectives, including the purely structural as well as cognitive and sociocultural aspects of time." The increase in this type of temporal understanding of video games arrives because of the particular techno-cultural moment of our society. We are in a time of "harmonious synchronicity." In a literal sense, our social media lives are synchronizing with our physical lives as we integrate the virtual more fully into our everyday existence (Thomas 2006, 388). Smart phones and wearable technology (like Google Glass and Apple Watch) make our digital worlds part of our physical ones through augmented reality (de Souza e Silva & Sutko 2011, 299). We live in multiple iterations at the same time, in a harmonious synchronicity with our own digital footprint. This "series of relationships, as a space, and as a metaphor for understanding how we as a species relate to knowledge and history becomes apparent in the way that our everyday media reflect network characteristics" (Booth 2012, 204). Yet, *Eternal Darkness* pre-dates much of what we now call social media, and its multiple temporalities foreshadow this shift in our understanding of multiplicity, becoming itself an instantiation of temporal synchronicity. Perhaps the fact that the time travel mechanic of "harmonious synchronicity" is apparent in video games that predate social media (going all the way back to the Nineties and *Day of the Tentacle*) reflects not just the unique medium characteristics of ludological narrative, but also how far back temporal displacement really goes. Our contemporary moment may not be as contemporary as we think.

Conclusion

The temporal complexity of *Eternal Darkness* highlights the affective influence of video games to develop players' larger interpretations of temporality in the world around them. In this way, the words of Edward Roivas, stated at the conclusion of the game, ring true not just for protagonist Alex, nor just for the player of the game, but for all contemporary opportunities for temporal connection: "All at once, separate and simultaneous, for the Universe is made of many timestreams, many possibilities, all in harmonious synchronicity." We are all always embedded within multiple possibilities, our own life narratives based on possible futures.

Eternal Darkness represents key changes in the way the time travel genre is represented in video games. Rather than seeing "space" and "time" as inseparable, concomitant elements of time travel, *Eternal Darkness* demonstrates that time travel is less about physical movement and more about mental acuity. One must necessarily pay attention to the key developments of plot, character and theme to understand the narrative of *Eternal Darkness*; and to realize the time travel elements requires a more robust understanding of the relationship between memory, history and identity. Although not a traditional view of traveling in time, this chapter's description of "harmonious synchronicity" presents subjectivity as the key component of mediated temporality. Although Alex is not a time traveler in the classic sense of the term (that is, physically she does not shift temporal situations), she is a mental time traveler.

For Zagal and Mataes (2010, 845), fluctuating temporality is a perspective within the game itself. Temporality is just one characteristic among many possible ones. However, their analysis looks at the game itself and elides the game player. Building on their perspective, my analysis of *Eternal Darkness* reveals that an additional level of temporal structure to consider within gameplay is that of the projective identity between character and player. Alexandra only travels in time with the participation of the game player, who must make the connections for her. Knowledge, magick and identities are shared across the multiple times within *Eternal Darkness*, forming a network of relationships that converge on the player. The multiple character identifications and temporal appearances make *Eternal Darkness* a precursor to what Papacharissi (2013) calls the "networked self," the multiple personae that exist online, but that together reveal a whole person. The contemporary self is always constructed from elements of multiple time frames; the interaction between "characters" from online personae open up to reveal entire selves.

The representation of subjective and mental time travel within the video game world demonstrates the impossibility of separating historical antecedents and contemporary realities. What *Eternal Darkness* represents is that such networking is not just a technological manifestation; it is not a product of social media. Far from just a game, *Eternal Darkness* reveals key truths about what it means to know the self. Video games themselves offer opportunities to explore the development of temporal fluctuations: playing levels over and over again, respawning once the character dies, going back to the beginning to pick up a missing element: these are key elements of temporality that play out in video games. *Eternal Darkness* goes one step farther, though, demonstrating not so much the way time travel can be played in a game, but rather how a game itself can become emblematic of the necessary mental play of identity, history, and memory.

Note

1. *Nintendo Power* ranked the game 101st out of all Nintendo games, the readers of *IGN* named it the 96th best video game of all time, and the *Official Nintendo Magazine* listed it as the 48th best Nintendo game. Additionally, it has consistently topped polls of the scariest video games of all time.

"I belong to the future"
Timeslip Drama as History Production in The Georgian House *and* A Traveler in Time

Victoria Byard

Timeslip narratives, stories in which children travel backwards or forwards in time by fantastic rather than scientific means, have been a part of British children's television drama since its earliest conception. One of the first drama serials for the newly instituted BBC Children's Programmes department was a 1951 adaptation of Kipling's *Puck of Pook's Hill*, in which Puck, "the oldest Old Thing in England," showed children Dan and Una events and individuals from the history of the British Isles. The form and genre rapidly became useful across British broadcasting, particularly in the 1970s, due to its ability to be mapped onto the developing and discursive model of children's television and the child audience. The values and concerns of the timeslip fantasy, its focalization through child protagonists and their subjectivities, use of time travel as a *bildungsroman*, and incorporation of history as part of a didactic model, corresponded with the ongoing development of British children's television as a child-centered discourse of citizenship, didacticism and subject-formation (Buckingham 1999, 34–35). This essay examines the potential reasons behind and implications of this generic upsurge through two children's timeslip dramas of the mid and late 1970s, *The Georgian House* (1976) and *A Traveler in Time* (1978).[1] I argue that both of these children's dramas use the timeslip form to explore contemporary social and political anxieties with particular reference to the shifting priorities and forms of history and education within Britain.

The Development of a Genre

Children's timeslip fantasies first developed in literature. Linda Hall (1998, 2003) locates their origins with Kipling and E.H. Nesbit, but they were

149

swiftly taken up by children's television. From the late 1960s, the provision of children's programming by the BBC and ITV had become increasingly valued as a benchmark of public service broadcasting. When broadcasting hours were increased from 1972, the development and expansion of children's television as a schedule and a discourse in both the BBC and ITV accelerated. However, underpinning and affecting the increased production of children's television drama was the *zeitgeist* of the 1970s, including social, political and economic changes which affected contemporary concepts of childhood, history and British identity. McArthur suggests that these cultural changes may have impacted upon television drama, stating "it seems reasonable to suppose that a society going through a period of historical transition and finding it immensely painful and disorienting will therefore tend to recreate, in some at least of its art, images of more (apparently) settled times, especially times in which the self-image of society as a whole was buoyant and optimistic" (1980, 40). McArthur attributes the popularity of the historical drama on television in the 1970s, such as *Upstairs, Downstairs* (1971–75), *Poldark* (1975–77) and *Edward the Seventh* (1975) among others, to this discursive shift within British society, although as Cooke (2003) suggests part of the appeal for "TV companies in producing multi-episode historical drama series [resided] more in their potential for maximizing and retaining audiences" (113).

Economically and culturally, timeslip dramas, as a generic hybrid of historical and contemporary drama, were a useful form in 1970s children's television. Their historical, and often literary, associations could satisfy the "quality" and didactic criteria for which children's television was scrutinized while using contemporary backgrounds and characters as framing devices. This allowed the child viewer more equable access to the narrative, the past, and its difference from their own lived experience. At the same time, the timeslip narrative as a nexus of popular memory, identity and genre could respond to the demands of televisual popularity and social anxieties specific to the production period. In this respect, timeslip drama, regardless of "what period history-writing or historical drama is ostensibly dealing with, in reality [...] is providing for the ideological needs of the present" (McArthur 1980, 40–41). Central to the ideological needs of the 1970s was a need to work through the idea of childhood, education and citizenship in a changing Britain; children's television drama was an ideal form for British broadcasters to interrogate such tensions.

The two programs under discussion provide a useful comparative basis, falling neatly into the two cycles which Wheatley (2005a) identifies in British children's television: "a cycle of original serial drama produced for ITV in the 1970s, much of which was created by a core creative team at HTV," and "a cycle of Gothic costume dramas for children produced by the BBC in the late 1970s and the 1980s" (386). While Wheatley rightly sees these as Gothic dramas, my concern is rather to explore the use of the timeslip within *The Georgian House* and *A Traveler in Time* as a way of investigating contemporary intersections of education and childhood with ideas of history, identity and citizenship. Both serials reflect social, political and pedagogical changes in post-war society by questioning, if not critiquing, the dominant practices of historiography in education and the heritage industry. Production spaces, form and aesthetic do not only re-produce history but reflect changes in the pedagogy of history since the early 1960s and into the 1970s. These educational shifts were largely formulated and disseminated through several dedicated "Schools Council" projects [which] questioned the assumptions about pedagogy and teaching which underpinned the "great tradition'" in history education (Husbands, Kitson & Pendry 2003, 10). These shifts ran parallel to the theorization of postmodernism throughout the 1970s, corresponding to what Lyotard described as the defining feature of postmodernism, an "incredulity towards metanarratives" (1984, xxiv).

The timeslip fantasy drama was particularly suited to investigating historical paradigm shifts and the breakdown of metanarratives, such as imperialism, national identity and the concept of a "great tradition." According to Cosslett (2002), the timeslip fantasy in children's literature opens up space for "history from below." She states:

> [T]his genre provides ways out of some of the dilemmas and negative features of "heritage" as a concept and a practice. In many of its variants, the time-slip narrative offers an openness to "other" histories, rather than the potentially nationalistic search for roots; it problematizes the simple access to the past promised by the heritage site; it critiques empty reconstructions of the past; and because of the way it constructs childhood, it evades the dangers of nostalgia [244].

The capacity of the literary timeslip to unsettle comfortable orthodoxies of time, history and childhood is also present in the television dramas under analysis. Both serials use time travel to articulate continuities and change within education, society, and the concept of the past in the 1970s, and to interrogate the place of the child in society and in history.

"Look to Your Future": The Georgian House *(1976)*

The Georgian House was produced for the ITV children's schedules by HTV West and transmitted in the after-school schedule in January and February 1976.[2] Children's television schedules were traditionally carved up between the "big five" ITV majors who had a stranglehold on the national network; for a regional company to even produce children's television was an economic gamble. HTV West, half of franchise holder HTV which broadcast to Wales and the West of England from 1968 onwards, took a calculated risk in trying to get onto the national network with children's drama. However, HTV West's venture paid off and by the late 1970s the company had built up a popular and critically acclaimed canon of children's drama, much of it fantastic and not a little terrifying.

In *The Georgian House*, a museum in 20th-century Bristol becomes the backdrop for a timeslip drama in which two modern teenagers are transported back to 1772. Middle-class Dan and working-class Abbie are thrown back two hundred years to the newly-built Georgian house in which the Leadbetters, a merchant family involved in the Bristolian slave-trade, reside attended by their own slave, Ngo. The doubled space of the Georgian House as heritage site and home was modeled around the Bristol heritage site The Georgian House Museum, previously the residence of a merchant, John Pinney, and his family. While later lauded as one of the founding fathers of Bristol trade and society, Pinney built much of his fortune through the use and trade of slaves for his sugar plantations on the island of Nevis. *The Georgian House* drew on Pinney's business, family, and the "other," lost history of their slave, Pero Jones, for its narrative. It functions as an adaptation, re-producing regional history to unsettle Bristol's identity, heritage and history and recover "history from below" for black Britons, the working class and others excluded from the dominant discourse. In so doing, it also establishes another history that counters the popular historical dramas in which those dominant discourses were presented as unproblematic or reconcilable.

Both contemporary and historical time periods in *The Georgian House* were constructed in the naturalist mode; the timeslip itself was the sole nexus of the fantastic, constructed visually through electronic effects and narratively through Ngo's conviction in the ability of his cultural beliefs and artifacts to intercede in his fate. Shot entirely on videotape and in color, it was a studio-bound production, confined to the elaborate domestic and heritage spaces of the house itself, creating a sense of claustrophobia. While the use of videotape enabled Chromakey (color separation overlay) and other electronic effects to be used in representing the fantastic appearances and disappearances of Abbie and Dan, it also created a textural stability between the textual past and present. Consequently, the anxiety of *The Georgian House* was not displaced onto the unknown inherent in the fantastic, but was instead located in the ideological difference between 1970s Britain and the Georgian era and the subsequent threat to all three adolescent protagonists. In this respect, it uncovers several "other" histories and conflicting ideological models, as per Cosslett's analysis, creating a more politicized representation of pedagogy, capitalism and regional history than might otherwise be expected in a children's drama.

The first of these conflicts is in Abbie and Dan's understanding of the Georgian era. Both are students of history who have been accepted to take part in an historical interpretation project within the Georgian House Museum. Dan's enthusiasm for the Age of Elegance, which "is rather [his] thing," is based upon bourgeois society and its relationships, while Abbie's passion is for the relationship between labor and material culture, offering a potential working-class "history from below." She proposes using a flat-iron in a demonstration of Georgian household skills, much to resident custodian Ellis' disbelief, and waxes rhapsodic about the architecture and decor in the recreated drawing room: "Incredible craftsmanship," she says of a carriage clock. "Imagine anyone taking such care today!" "Or commissioning it," Dan says. "You'd have to be a Paul Getty," "Or a Tory Town Council," says Abbie slyly, and Dan responds, "Or a trades union." *The Georgian House* thus sets up its contemporary narrative within a discourse of labor, class and economy, a discourse complicated further by the timeslip to the Georgian era. The focus and accuracy of Abbie and Dan's historical knowledge, as well as their identity, is challenged when, post-timeslip, their social roles have been reversed: Abbie, originally from a council estate, becomes Miss Abigail Ventnor, the Leadbetters' cousin, and Dan, the public schoolboy, becomes her servant. Unaccustomed to the roles they must now play or the social and labor structures they may access, both must "let go of mistaken stories or theories about the past," as "the simple access to the past promised by the heritage site is problematized" (Cosslett 2002, 244). Their understanding of the historical period through empiricism and the heritage space is challenged when they are made subject to and complicit in social, political and racial discourses antithetical to their 20th-century beliefs. Foremost among these is the right of the Leadbetters to own and dispose of Ngo as a possession. The slave trade then flourishing in Bristol is naturalized within *The Georgian House* as part of Bristol's civic identity and British nationality. Thomas Leadbetter, the patriarch of the house, declares that his involvement in the slave trade contributes to the prosperity not just of his house but of the nation as a whole: "[W]hy, the whole balance of our land would collapse were it not for men such as I." His rhetoric establishes the slave trade as part of British and Bristolian history, but goes further in presenting it as part of a systemic ideology of national and imperial power. Even socially progressive elements of Georgian society, such as the Leadbetters' guests Hezekiah Allsop and Madame Lavarre, are revealed to be invested in the status quo, returning Ngo to Leadbetter after he tries to escape with them.

The Georgian ideology is therefore not presented as glossy and unproblematic, as per many costume dramas, although its nostalgic connotations are reinforced as part of the 20th-century heritage experience: Ellis tells Abbie, "You just tell them that the Leadbetters were rich, and that the rich do not have any problems." Nor is the narrative of slavery in Britain shown through an isolated and dramatic incident, but as part of an axiomatic discourse. Racial, gender and class inequalities within historical British society are inherent at every level, and represented and reinforced through the domestic spaces of the Georgian House. Ngo and Dan are relegated to the kitchen, sleeping under the table and regularly threatened with violence. Abbie, as a relation of the Leadbetters, has her own bedroom, but as a young woman her movement and agency are constrained to the upper floors.

While Abbie is threatened with a return to Cornwall when she resists Georgian ideology, Ngo faces more immediate and physical threats. Leadbetter intends to send him to Jamaica as a field slave, underlining Ngo's textual and historical status as a "commodity form." Once again, Abbie and Dan's knowledge and enthusiasm for the Georgian period is undermined: Abbie is made aware of the troubling history behind the "beautiful things" she admired and the tyrannies of capitalism, and Dan is awakened to the oppression and marginalization inherent in "elegant" society. Ngo, the most oppressed character, is even marginalized within the *mise-en-scène*, framed within sets and narrative in the same way as furniture: in several scenes, the white characters are foregrounded as they engage in dialogue whereas Ngo is visible but mute, static and out of focus in the rear of the shot. As part of this framework of race and objectification, Ngo is also used as a fetishized commodity. Not only do the Leadbetters outfit him in exoticized livery, reinforcing his status as part of the household furnishings, but in contemplating the loss of Ngo from the Leadbetter household to the dangerous labor of the plantation, their friend Lady Cecilia muses, "[T]hink what delicious fun you'll have looking for a new one." While Abbie protests that Ngo is a human being, the ideology of the period including a naturalized view of race-based slavery is presented through trade, patriotism, family life, gender roles and domestic spaces as "the 'social cement,' in Gramsci's terms, whereby the power of dominant groups is maintained without regular and widespread recourse to physical coercion" (McArthur 1980, 1).

Race and its treatment within British society is the key paradigm shift for *The Georgian House*; correspondingly, Ngo is more than a cipher or a victim. The production makes him the locus for values of individualism, multiculturalism and national identity, but it avoids the trap of making the white characters his saviors. The timeslip that transports Abbie and Dan to the past is generated by a carving belonging to Ngo, which, although later appropriated by Leadbetter, reflects the power and resistance of a subaltern subject through culture, history and voice. He emancipates himself through his own agency and intelligence, and his collaboration with Abbie and Dan. In a decade when Race Relations Acts were breaking down color bars in labor and society, this seems a valuable reflection of changing attitudes to race, class and British identity, despite the ongoing popularity of more problematic programs such as *Love Thy Neighbour* (ITV, 1972–76), *The Black and White Minstrel Show* (BBC, 1958–78) and *It Ain't Half Hot, Mum* (BBC, 1974–81). However, *The Georgian House* does not merely reflect contemporary changes in British society, but attempts to recover a black experience of the slave trade, an "other" history obscured until recently in cities like Bristol and Liverpool. The Mansfield Judgment acts as the narrative and temporal pivot of *The Georgian House*: its enactment on 22nd June 1772 guaranteed the freedom of slaves in Britain and therefore effectively ended the slave trade as a profitable enterprise. It also made those disenfranchised slaves British citizens, but, as Ngo comments, the freed slaves "are desperate, so they betray each other. [...] They have no money, no work, no hope. I do not know why they decided to free us without making any provisions for our wellbeing."

Ngo is as much a part of this discourse of British identity, integration and citizenship as Abbie and Dan. The final episode uses historical documents to resolve Ngo's fate. A regional newspaper reveals that, in 1816, "Mr. Ngo Aboyah, the wealthy timber merchant of Sierra Leone and co-founder of the new city of Freetown, was welcomed by the Bristol Society of Merchant Venturers following his arrival in our city." It adds that Ngo intended to "endow a fine charitable institution for the housing and education of former slaves and their descendants," affecting civic history, spaces and identity and indicating the contribution of black Britons to contemporary and historical Britain. This ending suggests that British national identity and citizenship is constituted through contemporaneous British values of multiculturalism, civic engagement and personal identification and contribution to the nation-state, but it also introduces new methodologies of historical interpretation. *The Georgian House* exposes tensions within historiography by contrasting easy concepts of nostalgia and aestheticism with the hierarchized oppression through race, class and gender which produced the material culture and national identity, an approach which also reflected contemporaneous shifts in the teaching of history within national education.

The British Schools' Council was influential in the debate about the purpose of British education in the 1970s, and in the subsequent implementation of changes in curriculum: in 1976, it published *A New Look at History*, a project originating in the concerns of "teachers of history [...] obliged by the current waves of curriculum reform to question the purpose and method of history in the classroom" (1976, 2). First initiated in 1972, it sought to justify the place of history within the educational curriculum, how adolescents between 13 and 16 could most productively approach and synthesize history, and which teaching modes would best facilitate this. It proposed new approaches to teaching history, such as Marxist history, the use of historical documents and the invocation of lived experience to encourage a more holistic approach to historical study. *The Georgian House* reflects these concerns and approaches in its construction of education and history by incorporating quotidian historical events and documents such as *Felix Farley's Bristol Journal*, a historical regional newspaper, to reveal not only narrative but the mechanics and glossing of ideology which worked to brutalize and repress its characters. Likewise, the production's representation of "lived experience" and its spatial and social restrictions, inequalities and naturalization throws into relief the complex interaction of heritage, nostalgia and social responsibility. The "dominant ideology," as described by McArthur, which "refines itself out of existence, the *dominant practices* in social institutions and groups becoming naturalized," was unearthed and questioned by *The Georgian House*, not just for the Georgian period but for the 1970s as well (1980, 7).

When Ngo manages to timeslip to the future, he rejects the 1970s' ideology and spaces as Abbie and Dan rejected those of the Georgian era, describing contemporary Bristol as "a hell" with its noise, pollution and "madness." Ngo's discontent with the present, and an ending in which Dan and Abbie are dismissed from the Museum by Ellis for their attempts to change the past, suggests that while racial, gender and class politics had improved in two centuries, they remained far from utopian. *The Georgian House*'s refusal to valorize either past, present or future, along with its representation of "other" histories, may be attributed to changing conceptions of race, history and education in the 1970s. Similarly, its articulation of race and nationality was located through the changing conceptions of Britain in the wake of the 1948 arrival of MV Empire Windrush which carried the first large-scale immigration from Jamaica; a Britain in which multiculturalism was not a set of values quickly or easily arrived at, but an uneasy and ongoing negotiation, organized through politics and media as much as through social relationships. Bristol was not immune from these tensions: an influential boycott of Bristol buses in 1963 was organized to protest the bus companies' employment color bar, and the Bristol riots of 1980 were linked to increasing racial tensions within the city throughout the 1970s. Kowaleski-Wallace suggests that such "political tensions between the city's black and white populations ought to be traced to a missing history of slavery" (2006, 26).

Twenty years before the formation of the Bristol Slave Trade Action Group and subsequent acknowledgements of Bristol's role in the Atlantic slave trade, then, *The Georgian House* attempted to recover, at least in part, this missing history and "other" histories from below, incorporating and transmitting new pedagogies and new British values and identities.

"Time everlasting": A Traveler in Time *(BBC, 1978)*

The BBC's adaptation of Alison Uttley's *A Traveler in Time* was broadcast two years later in January 1978, and was directed and produced by Dorothea Brooking, known for her sensitive, polished children's dramas for the BBC. The original text, first published in 1939 and reflective of Uttley's nostalgic memories of her own Derbyshire childhood, told the story of Penelope Taberner, one of three children who go to stay with their aunt and uncle at Thackers, an Elizabethan farmhouse. In the historic house, Penelope is able to step back through time to the 16th century when then-owners of Thackers, the aristocratic Babington family, were involved in a plot to free Mary Queen of Scots, held at nearby Wingfield Manor at the order of her cousin, Elizabeth I. This escape plot was based on the popular legend that while Mary was imprisoned there she was visited by fellow Roman Catholic and admirer Anthony Babington disguised as a gypsy. He would subsequently conspire with English and Spanish Catholics to assassinate Elizabeth and put Mary on the throne in the ill-fated Babington Plot. While the events of the novel are fictionalized, therefore, the places, characters and political background are real.

Like *The Georgian House, A Traveler in Time* is located around a fictionalized representation of quotidian historical events, and this tension between history and drama is located around the material and mediated re-production of historical space. Where the HTV production recreated the Georgian House in painstaking and expensive detail in the studio, down to "door handles and lock escutcheons" (Network DVD notes), the BBC adaptation complicates levels of reality and fiction by filming within the quotidian historical spaces on location. Thackers was recreated at Dethick Manor Farm, previously Dethick Manor and Uttley's original inspiration for the novel. The farmhouse was the locus for the historical narrative and was also central to the escape plot in which the Babingtons and their retainers attempted to tunnel from Thackers to Wingfield Manor to free the Queen of Scots. However, not only was the Babingtons' ancestral home used as a location, but the Queen's captivity was filmed in the ruins of Wingfield Manor itself. The location of the drama in and around quotidian historical locations is reminiscent of McArthur's critique of the narrator within factual historical programs:

> This locating of the narrator in the actual substance of his narration offers a quasi-talismanic guarantee of truth: the place actually exists, therefore what is said must be true [1980, 29].

A Traveler in Time's location of characters in the actual substance of the drama creates a space through which contemporary ideas of history, heritage and education could be invoked and problematized. The timeslip becomes a nexus of not only historical periods but a way of troubling the binaries of knowing and learning, reality and fiction, belonging and exclusion, and childhood and adulthood.

In her analysis of children's timeslip literature, Cosslett suggests that Penelope is one of those "[c]hild protagonists who rediscover a sense of territorial belonging, by simply returning to ancestral homes and connecting to their 'real roots'" (246). Penelope is however not a Babington, although her 20th-century education allows her to move among them. Penelope's "real roots" are with Dame Cicely Taberner, the Babingtons' cook, suggesting a "history from below." Affiliation with Thackers in the past, as in the present, is not associated necessarily with ownership but with community, responsibility and continuity. The feudal ideology of the narrative is consequently glossed over in favor of a dialectic of past and present values. Penelope can, like Abbie and Dan, move between the physical and ideological spaces of the past, and suggest "a new version of the national past," located "in the practices of oral, local and family history, and [...] particularly evident in the way that history is taught in the schools, and in the institution of 'heritage' sites and activities" (Cosslett 2002, 244–245). However, the disjuncture between the two historical ideologies is subsumed in the continuity of Thackers itself.

While Thackers is shown as an historic house, it is also a contemporary domestic space, making it a site of lived and "living history." Elizabethan objects are used by the Taberners as everyday items in the 1970s, as are old traditions, such as herbalism, thereby constructing the rural as the site of historicity and continuity. Penelope rejects the London of her family and home, stating that their modern kitchen "is not warm and comfortable" like Thackers', adding later that "I wish I lived here. I'd stay here forever." Penelope's visits to Thackers in the novel take place over several years, accompanied by her family from London, but in the adaptation her visit is made in isolation and only lasts several weeks as she recovers from pneumonia. The adaptation therefore further compresses and dislocates time, making Thackers a place where staying forever might be possible. Penelope's ability to see the Babingtons "quite alive, like you and me!," a hereditary trait of the Taberners, makes her "always-already" part of a family and community identity, organized around the house and to a lesser extent the landscape. Perry Nodelman points out that Thackers is both the narrative and ideological locus of the production: "the heart of the novel's meaning," indicating that "[t]he passage of time means that everything must change, so that everything must die; but the continuance of the house and of old ways for doing things within it means that time's passage does not matter, for despite it, things do continue in the same way" (1985, 8). The use of the quotidian locations reinforced these values of authenticity and continuity within the serial, but necessarily had implications for its aesthetics.

In contrast with *The Georgian House*'s studio-bound production on videotape, *A Traveler in Time* was shot largely on location in Derbyshire on film and around the actual physical sites associated with the historical events and characters.[3] The BBC serial, like the HTV production, questioned the concept of history, childhood and learning in the 1970s, but its exploration of the historical ideology had a different focus. Where *The Georgian House* located history and pedagogy within a museum and used timeslips to expose the characters to lived history, *A Traveler in Time* used a farmhouse that had been in the family for centuries and the persistent traditions, timeframes and language of the locality to make contiguous the lived histories and heritage separated by four centuries. History in *A Traveler in Time* is always-already there, not just as part of the heritage discourse but as part of everyday, domestic life. The house, traditions and artifacts are shown being used in both time periods, establishing a continuity of regional and family history: modern-day Aunt Tissie "still stick[s] to the old-fashioned herbs" to keep moths from the linens, a practice also shown in the historical narrative, and later declares that "This old pan's been at Thackers as long as I can remember, and before that. It's almost as old as the house." "Perhaps," suggests Penelope, "it was used by the Babingtons"! Thackers' domestic spaces and practices are history, a "rootedness" arguably lost in the 1970s. The production's expansive, even cinematic, aesthetic created by the primarily filmed production of *A Traveler in Time* on location in the houses, landscape and culture of Derbyshire contributes to this construction of place and mood, reflecting Peter Hunt's statement that within English fantasy, "places *mean*" (1987, 11).

Penelope therefore enters another time, but due to the construction of the past as accessible and ideologically contiguous through place and family, she does not reject the "social cement" of the historical period as Abbie and Dan do. Just as the places, spaces, and objects exist in both eras, so too do the values of loyalty to the land, the local community, and the continuation of

Thackers. Despite the nationwide, historical shifts in religion and state, the serial suggests that these can be reconciled if core local values are maintained; it is implied that Anthony Babington's plot fails because he in turn fails to uphold the sanctity of Thackers and his responsibilities to the land and his estate. He places the national above the regional: Francis says to Penelope, "I'm afraid Anthony will be ruined, whether he saves the Queen or not. The money is running away like the River Darrant." Penelope might turn away from the dominant national ideology and history located around the Virgin Queen, but she does so in order to protect Thackers. Paradoxically, she attempts to change history in order to preserve history. The ideological conflict is therefore displaced from the difference between past and present to other historical tensions: regional and national histories, Catholic and Protestant, received history and lived history. Consequently, *A Traveler in Time* is less radical in its recovery of history than *The Georgian House*, while still incorporating the resistant formal strategies that Cosslett identifies in timeslip fantasies: "other" histories and other epistemologies.

These other histories may be meta-textual as much as diegetic: MacKinnon posits that Uttley's original text "voiced counter-narratives that demonstrated personal (predominantly but not exclusively female), collective and national threads in the historical narrative, such as gender roles, fighting for religious and political tolerance and women's rights" (2011, 813). "Furthermore," MacKinnon points out, "Uttley was contributing to a long matriarchal tradition of historical fiction about Mary, Queen of Scots, that questioned the standard masculinist British History narratives" (811). These counter-narratives suggest some of the previously marginalized discourses that the new pedagogical emphases of history in the 1970s, "[i]nnovative methodologies, an interest in the experiences of the dispossessed and oppressed and a new openness to influences from sociology and anthropology" (Husbands, Kitson and Pendry 2003, 10) could recover both in education and, I argue, children's television drama.

These alternative historical perspectives, the revelation of previously hidden information, and new understandings of time, reality and learning are also suggested in the aesthetic of *A Traveler in Time*. The slipperiness of narrative time and subjectivity is reinforced by the use of unusual perspective shots. The serial opens with an establishing shot of the Derbyshire landscape from *within* the train Penelope is traveling on, rather than as a wide, exterior shot. Upon her arrival at Thackers, the house is viewed first from inside the moving Land Rover before it cuts to an exterior, static shot. Later in the serial, an Anglican mass opens with a shot from the empty pulpit before moving through the church itself, suggesting alternate subjectivities, temporal shifts and relationships with spaces. This is reinforced most strongly in the final episode when Penelope visits Wingfield Manor. As her uncle's Land Rover pulls up to the ruined castle, it is seen from one of the empty windows, high above, suggesting that it is being watched by some unknown viewer. Subsequently, a similar window is seen in the Queen of Scots' room. These alternate subjective shots work as part of an aesthetic of mutable space and time, suggesting different perspectives on the *mise-en-scène*; a hidden history to be revealed depending on where the camera moves. This is reinforced by Brooking's use of cross-cutting or reverse shots from alternate perspectives, reframing angles of vision that reveal additional information within the scene. One of these occurs within the sequence with Queen Mary when, prior to the timeslip, Penelope is shown sitting on the same ruined stone window frame. This shot then mixes into one of the Queen sewing and the following scenes focus upon her exchange with her lady in waiting, Seton. Subsequently, a reverse shot of a wider view of the set reveals Penelope still sitting on the same windowsill as a contemporary, but secret, audience to this historical event. This perspectivist approach to editing, alongside the alternation between subjective and objective shots, works to create an unstable relationship of time and reality.

The grammar of television, therefore, creates time travel within *A Traveler in Time*, complicating the difference between past and present. There is no fantastic touchstone for the timeslip, such as the African carving in *The Georgian House*; there are however several artifacts that appear in both time periods and *indicate* rather than effect the timeslip. Chief among these is the locket containing a portrait of Mary, Queen of Scots, which Anthony Babington loses in the 16th century and Penelope finds in the twentieth. Another is the ribbon that Francis purchases for Penelope at a fair, which she loses when she timeslips back to the future. Its appearance and disappearance from scene to scene indicates the time periods through which Penelope is moving, and its restoration by her aunt who has found it in an old chest marks her departure from Thackers in the serial's finale. Thackers is haunted not just by the Babingtons but by the physical objects they made, used and loved, creating a contiguous heritage and suggesting phenomenological approaches to history that may again correspond with suggested changes to teaching history. "For example," states the Schools Council's *A New Look at History*,

> many history teachers have noted that adolescent pupils, given the opportunity, can respond to the past in a positive way; they can get excited when they touch some object which has survived from the past, or when they see Elizabeth I's signature, whether actually or in facsimile [1967, 7].

These phenomenological encounters reflect the strongly subjective and sensuous reactions Penelope has to the world in and around Thackers in the original text, but also reflect an increasing drive in pedagogy to move outside the merely empirical into the affective. These objects, whether in terms of everyday use or the haptic encounter within pedagogy, collapse time and encourage historical learning about objects' production and use. This occurs diegetically when Penelope is given the bobbin boy, a carving made by Jude the kitchen boy, which she admires in the 1970s before encountering its maker in the 16th century. The bobbin boy also condenses space, allowing a trapped Penelope to communicate psychically with the mute Jude, a lovely sequence that cuts between Penelope and Jude spatially located to the left and right of the screen, as if in dialogue. The Schools Council publication continues:

> [M]any adolescents have an ability to imagine the past, to recreate its actions and its thoughts in drama or role-play, to sympathize with people from the past in discussion or dialogue and even to hero-worship and identify themselves with some of the people of the past. Finally, [...] most pupils are capable of the more passive ability of receiving the past and of escaping from the present into it, whether through a story told by a teacher, or through film, or through a book (either of history or historical fiction) [7].

A Traveler in Time is therefore arguably as historically valuable as *The Georgian House* or even pedagogical methods in writing, re-writing and perhaps more importantly creating a sympathetic interest in history for child and adolescent viewers, a view endorsed by the Schools Council and its pedagogical initiatives of the 1970s.

Conclusion

Following this analysis, it can be seen that both serials open up spaces to question contemporary ideas of history and historiography. The use of the timeslip in both dramas not only creates a dramatic narrative of fantasy and estrangement, but also articulates "other" histories and other historiographical approaches. Their unsettling of orthodoxies of history in teaching, television drama and the national past reflects changing priorities in the construction of British citizenship, constitution and childhood. However, each serial also uses the timeslip to suggest divergent possibilities for the present and the future through different inflections upon the value of difference, continuity and change within British society, culture and education.

Rather than making these other histories the site of rupture and radicalism as *The Georgian House* does, *A Traveler in Time* makes them a locus for loss, reconciliation and romance. Penelope attempts to change history to ensure that the values and community of Thackers and the Babington family, and her romance with Francis, will survive, and her ultimate effect upon history is left ambiguous. The events of the Babington Plot and its tragic consequences, the execution of Anthony Babington, his co-conspirators and the Queen of Scots, are not altered by her allegiance to the Babingtons; the serial acts as a prologue to the doom of the family and the Queen of Scots, a fate which the adaptation truncates. The ultimate tragedy in the serial is the loss of childhood and therefore access to the past, as embodied in the ill-starred romance between Penelope and Francis Babington. Its incorporation of working class and feminist histories as well as its emphasis upon the continuities of family and regional identity "offers an openness to 'other' histories" (Cosslett 2002, 244) and to other historical approaches, decentering previous historical and national metanarratives. Ultimately the serial reaffirms the transhistoricity of *local* values made material and contiguous in Thackers and in kinship.

In contrast, Abbie and Dan's actions in *The Georgian House* result in changes to both the past and present, but upset the certainty of valorized national and local identities and the dominant ideology of the 1970s. *The Georgian House* ends with the dismissal of Abbie and Dan from the museum. Ellis, the ex-military custodian, rejects their changes to history and the positive implications for British citizenship, democracy and multiculturalism. "I do not want to know," he declares upon seeing the timeslip return them to the present, "I do not want anything to do with it. If you'd put some time in some of the places I'd served, you'd know there are some things you do not meddle with. You leave them alone and they leave you alone. You'll learn, I hope." Abbie and Dan do learn but, unlike Ellis, they learn through the new affective, multicultural pedagogies of the 1970s, enabling them to recover other histories and thereby formulate new models of British and Bristolian identity and citizenship.

Both serials' protagonists ultimately are forced to leave the site of their historical experience, perhaps suggesting the need to apply these newly developed identities and ideologies within the wider world and signifying a move from poïesis to praxis. Despite the differences between the aesthetics, production spaces and ideologies in these children's television dramas, the timeslip narrative allows them to examine the potentially dangerous difference between past and present, the recovery of lost or marginalized histories, and the role of the child as a British citizen. Both *The Georgian House* and *A Traveler in Time* re-produce and interrogate the changes to education and historiography during this period, as well as construing the child audience as an active and potentially radical force within British society and national identity. They thereby locate British children's television in the vanguard of the nation's socio-cultural shifts in the late 20th century.

Notes

1. My thanks to MACE and the BFI through whose offices I was able to view *A Traveler in Time*.

2. *The Georgian House* does not survive as a complete audio-visual text. Three episodes are available but the other four only exist as shooting scripts, which are made available as PDFs on the Network DVD. Any analysis of *The Georgian House* is therefore necessarily an archaeological, and occasionally a speculative, enterprise as there is no guarantee that the drama as seen in the scripts would have remained the same throughout the contingencies of filming.

3. While there seems to be a common belief that the production was wholly filmed on location, the visual aesthetics and the credits make it clear that videotape footage shot in studios was used to suture several interior scenes together.

"Who knows about the future? Perhaps only the dead"

Configuring the Transtemporal Timespan of Planet of the Apes as a Transmedia Saga

MATTHEW FREEMAN

Everything seems different ... Time bends, space is boundless (Col. George Taylor in *Planet of the Apes*).

In *Escape from the Planet of the Apes* (1971), three speaking simians—each dressed like human astronauts, fully equipped with space station technology—mysteriously crash land in America in the 1970s. At a Presidential Commission called to unravel the means by which so-called intelligent apes could have fallen from the stars, one of the apes explains to the bemused council that they have traveled back in time 2,000 years "from your future." In a later scene, Dr. Otto Hasslein, interviewed on *Eyewitness News,* attempts to describe the nature of time travel by using the example of a freeway with multiple lanes:

> Time is like a freeway with an infinite number of lanes, all leading from the past into the future. However, not into the same future. A driver in lane "A" may crash, while a driver in lane "B" survives. It follows that a driver, by changing lanes, can change the future. In the dark and turbulent corridors of outer space, the impact of some distant planetary, even galactic, disaster jumped the apes from their present into ours.

This analogy of conceptualizing time travel as multiple lanes on a freeway, each streaming in the same direction, carrying a multitude of events, seems to share some central characteristics with what Henry Jenkins has called transmedia storytelling. This chapter examines the extent to which the time-bending narration employed in and across the *Planet of the Apes* saga can be seen as a means of articulating socio-political messages—the choices we make now will determine the world we create for our children, for instance. Moreover, this transtemporality can also be conceptualized in terms of transmediality, with each of the lanes on this proverbial freeway occupying different lanes of media, each carrying the larger transmedia story from one point to another. It is this unique relationship between the telling of a story that crosses and jumps over its timeline through its production in and across multiple media and the nature of a story that is itself *about* time travel that will sit at the heart of this chapter. In what ways and for what purposes does time travel make a narratological puzzle out of the spatiotemporal reality of a story—and how might this story be constructed across media?

According to Jenkins, transmedia storytelling can be defined as "stories that unfold across multiple media platforms, with each medium making distinctive contributions to the storyworld—a more integrated approach to franchise development than models based on urtexts [a model of adaptation wherein an original version of a text is replicated] and ancillary products" (2006, 334). In Jenkins' model of transmedia storytelling, media platforms take on a specific meaning relating to the creation of a wider, coherent, fictional storyworld that is delivered to the audience in multiple forms and platforms. Transmedia storytelling can be understood as an industrial strategy whereby multiple media texts converge in order to build a storyworld and to narrate the adventures of that storyworld in a way that better serves the story itself. This then fleshes out and fills in the gaps from one medium with the stories from another. For Jenkins (2006, 21), "[t]o fully experience any fictional world, consumers must assume the role of hunters and gatherers, chasing down bits of the story across media channels [in order to] come away with a richer entertainment experience." To demonstrate this Jenkins uses the example of *The Matrix* franchise, which consists of three films, a collection of animated shorts called *The Animatrix* (2003), a series of comics, and a video game titled *Enter the Matrix* (2003), all of which contain storyline elements necessary to an understanding of the whole. The animated short "Final Flight of the Osiris," for example, features a protagonist called Jue, who sacrifices herself to send a message to the crew of the Nebuchadnezzar, an event referred to in second film in the franchise, *The Matrix Reloaded* (2003), when the characters discuss the last transmissions of the Osiris (Jenkins 2006, 104). In that same film, Morpheus and Trinity are rescued by Niobe, who seems to appear as if from nowhere—but players of the video game encounter a mission designed to get Niobe to precisely that rendezvous point (Jenkins 2006, 105). Essentially, transmedia storytelling, configured within an increasingly converged culture of media production, hereby encourages its media-hopping audiences to consume and comprehend what becomes a geographically vast storyworld as a transtemporal tapestry.

The type of integrated transmedia Jenkins explores in this example of *The Matrix* saga places emphasis on narrative events, where the plot is distributed across media in ways that create, to borrow Jason Mittell's terminology, canonic integration, with interwoven story events that must be consumed across multiple films and indeed multiple media for full comprehension (Mittell 2011). This canonic integration elevates textual stories to the level of narratological puzzle pieces—each dispersed segment of a story representing one piece belonging to a much larger jigsaw that the audience must piece together text by text. Transmedia storytelling, the art of world-building, thereby permits the expansion of narrative breadth—a single storyworld may exist over centuries, with any number of accumulative plotlines and character backstories accruing within what Mittell calls its "temporal vastness" (Mittell 2011). With these transmedia texts taking place in-between the story gaps of the others, each unfolding, potentially over many years of story-time, the role of the audience is thus akin to that of the time traveler itself: in consuming this multitude of story content, the audience jumps back and forth in time, as it were, from one point in the timeline to another, perceiving the storyworld non-linearly from different temporal perspectives, one piece at a time. Transmedia storytelling may have been branded exclusively as a contemporary phenomenon— understood most pointedly as a practice emerging in recent years out of the advent of media conglomeration and the rise of digital media technologies that allows content to flow across the borders of media platforms more easily—yet work is now beginning to be done that seeks to trace the history of such transmediality (Scolari, Bertetti and Freeman 2014).

Rather than using the original *Planet of the Apes* franchise (1968–1977) to historicize transmedia storytelling, however, this chapter will examine this particular saga from a conceptual perspective, exploring time travel as a narratological strategy while questioning what it might mean to understand time travel *as* transmedia storytelling—or, indeed, transmedia storytelling *as* time travel. What function does time travel have in articulating the philosophical and socio-political messages of this saga as a whole—and in what ways does transmedia storytelling reinforce such messages in this particular case? I will argue that in exploiting time travel as a narratological strategy, the *Planet of the Apes* saga—spanning five films, two television series, a comic book series, and a range of tie-in promotional materials, all produced between 1968 and 1977—contributed to the popularization of narratological attributes of world-building and transmedia storytelling that have since become dominant features of contemporary franchise production. Even without the benefit of common production personnel working across these various texts, time travel—as a thematic and narratological structuring device—will thus be positioned and understood as the feature that enabled the development of the *Planet of the Apes* saga as a transfictional and indeed transmedial enterprise. Time travel, in this sense, construed here as a facilitator of transmedia storytelling, would serve to articulate the saga's themes as narrative pieces of a puzzle plot across media.

On Screen

Few film series produced during the 1960s and 1970s attempted to create transfictional and transmedia extensions that offered the degree of canonic integration between multiple texts as defined more recently by Jenkins and Mittell. Film sequels, while certainly not uncommon, were still mostly maligned by audiences in the late–1960s. As Dale Winogura wrote in a *Planet of the Apes* edition of *Cinefantastique* magazine in 1972, "[e]very film series of a fantasy nature up until the series of *Planet of the Apes* films has existed on a simple repetitive plane, continually reusing the framework of the original film" (1972, 3). *Planet of the Apes* was unique, then, in its narratological approach to continuing the series beyond the first film: "The sequels to *Planet of the Apes*," Winogura continued, "have extended and further explored the concepts of the original film, rather than merely repeating its formula, and therefore do not deserve their a priori dismissal as being purely commercial ventures with nothing to offer" (1972, 3). In its review of *Escape from the Planet of the Apes*, the third film, *Variety* called the series as a whole "not just three separate films, but one great work that has the promise of being the first epic of filmed science fiction" (1970, 33).

This sense of epic stemmed from its narratological structure, with the *Planet of the Apes* films structured as a time loop. The first film's narrative events exist both as the effect and as the cause of its later sequels, taking place both before and after those sequels. In terms of temporality, the saga spans over 2,000 years, "beginning" in 1972 and "ending" in 3978. Many of cinema's most iconic time travel films, such as *The Terminator* (1984), *Back to the Future* (1985), and *The Time Machine* (1960), reflect this particular characteristic: such films travel mostly in time, rarely in distance. In the case of *Planet of the Apes*, its principle utilization of time travel invokes philosophical concepts such as the predestination paradox, a narratological device functioning to create paradoxes arising from time travel. Predestination paradoxes occur when a time traveler is caught in a loop of events that both precede and succeed the time traveler traveling back in time. This predestination paradox occurs because if Colonel George Taylor had never traveled forward in time in *Planet of the Apes* (1968), the apes of this future Earth would not have found his space craft in *Beneath the Planet of the Apes* (1970), an event that enabled three apes to travel back in time in *Escape from the Planet of the Apes* (1971) and become integrated into society. Over time, this latter event triggers a revolution among the now enslaved apes in *Conquest of the Planet of the Apes* (1972). This gives rise to a nuclear war prior to the events of *Battle for the Planet of the Apes* (1973), wherein an attempt to form a co-existence between man and ape ultimately fails and leads to the apes becoming the dominant species on Earth, as lived first-hand by George Taylor in *Planet of the Apes.* Paul Dehn, screenwriter of each of the four *Planet of the Apes* film sequels, once emphasized this notion of circularity explicitly in interview, commenting to *Cinefantastique*:

> The whole thing has become a very logical development in the form of a circle. I have a complete chronology of the time circle mapped out, and when I start a new script, I check every supposition I make against the chart to see if it is correct to use it.... While I was out there [in California, producer] Arthur Jacobs said he thought [*Conquest of the Planet of the Apes*] would be the last so I fitted it together so that it fitted in with the beginning of Apes One, so that the wheel had come full circle and one could stop there quite happily, I think [Winogura 1972, 28].

Despite such time-bending circularity, the only films in the series to actually feature time travel are the first and third—and it is only in the final frame of the former that time travel between alternate points in Earth's history is revealed to have occurred. On first viewing, *Planet of the Apes* (1968) leaves audiences shocked. Its twist ending, wherein an alien planet ruled by a species of intelligent simians is finally revealed to be Earth thousands of years into the future, reveals the secrets of the story. The image of the Statute of Liberty, half-buried into a cliff-face, symbolizes the eventual fall of humankind, forecasting such downfall as a consequence of its self-destructivity. And, yet, the jarring juxtaposition of this final scene's imagery provides a mechanism of temporality confusion that both radically alters the story being told and creates a puzzle out of its climactic twist. The film's narrative strategy is characterized by its tendency to hide more than it shows, with an emphasis on concealment and discovery. Unlike many of cinema's most iconic time travel films, including the aforementioned *The Terminator*, *Back to the Future*, and *The Time Machine*, which each establish their time travel premises early on with scenes of background exposition detailing the creation, function and narrative context of time travel as that which propels the story, *Planet of the Apes* unfolds its narrative in a way that actively conceals or camouflages the presence of time travel. That the *Icarus*, Taylor's space craft, has traveled not in distance to an alien planet light-years from our own, but rather in time to Earth's distant future, is withheld until the end, while Dr. Zaius' knowledge that apes had once inherited the planet from man—a clue to this revelation—is similarly masked throughout. In one sense, the film's status as time travel cinema thus belongs to its most significant narratological ellipsis, since the image of the Statue of Liberty is synonymous with the time-traveling of the story. In another sense, this utilization of a time-bending space craft and its infinite, inconsistent narratological possibilities paved the way for an entire mythology, one that spans 2,000 years of time, and which could only be unraveled piece by piece through a multitude of sequels and additional media texts. Writer Paul Dehn implied as such: "The plot of Apes 2 was suggested by the memorable last shot of Apes 1: the half-buried Statue of Liberty. This implied that New York itself lay buried beneath what the apes called 'The Forbidden Zone'" (Winogura 1972, 26). Dehn here acknowledges the role of what Jenkins has termed world-building in his approach to continuing *Planet of the Apes* as a series. Jenkins (2006, 335) defines world-building as "the process of designing a fictional universe that will sustain franchise development, one that is significantly detailed to enable many different stories to emerge but coherent enough so that each story feels like it fits with the others." This process of world-building, as Jenkins (2003, 20) also argues, implies that transmedia stories utilize unexplored dimensions of the storyworld, such as characters and locations. This might well leave narrative gaps that other texts can bridge. Similarly, in visiting the desolate city beneath The Forbidden Zone—a location from the first film's storyworld mentioned only by name—Dehn's first sequel, *Beneath the Planet of the Apes* (1970), can be seen to have utilized such a strategy, expanding the storyworld by escalating and quite literally deepening the saga's world-building and mythos-making across the construction of an additional text.

This process of world-building, itself sprung from the film's adoption of time travel as a narratological strategy, was only the beginning. This world-building would soon expand the mythology of *Planet of the Apes* much further in ways that would provide fragments of a temporal puzzle plot that only altogether—each textual piece scattered across multiple texts over multiple media—answered one particular question: How did apes come to dominate the future of Earth? Audiences may have discovered that Earth will one day fall during the denouement of the first film, but they did not yet fully understand how, why, or when. Moreover, the science fictional trappings of time travel here served to establish the basis of an additional mystery, one which would springboard across further sequels and which concerned a more philosophical question: *will* the Earth one day fall? Is the end of the world in 3978, as witnessed in the first film, necessarily inevitable, since it has already happened, as it were, or perhaps avoidable, since the circularity of the ensuing saga means that its history is simultaneously its future, a future that is both ingrained in its past and unfolding in its present? Dr. Otto Hasslein had mentioned the theoretical possibility of altering history in his aforementioned freeway analogy in *Escape from the Planet of the Apes.* Hasslein's notion of multiple lanes of time is echoed by Virgil in *Battle for the Planet of the Apes* (1973), and seized upon by Cornelius and Zira's son Caesar, who seeks to avoid the Earth's apocalyptic future 2000 years later having gained foreknowledge of this eventual destruction. "I went looking for the past," Caesar declares at one point, "but I found our future." Whereas the first two films in the saga placed viewers in the middle of a story, in a skewered timeline that left more questions looming than answered, the final three films formed something of an origins trilogy that showcased more precisely how, why and when Earth came to be as it is depicted in *Planet of the Apes* and *Beneath the Planet of the Apes.* In essence, the series indeed replicated the act of time traveling—first taking its audience to a strange new world thousands of years into the future, only later to explain the origins of the characters, stories, and settings of this world by taking the audience back in time, jumping them across a vast, complex timeline.

On Paper

Such complex storytelling and world-building strategies indeed transcended the medium of cinema and extended across to a range of other media including television, comic books, and, most interestingly, promotional tie-in materials. It was the role of this "spin-off media," as it was more commonly branded at the time, to more thoroughly flesh out and fill in the gaps of the *Planet of the Apes* timeline, feeding into the film series while providing audiences with the narrative content not disclosed in the films. Distributed to the audiences attending *Planet of the Apes* cinema screenings in 1968, for instance, was *The Ape News*, a mock promotional newspaper sent allegedly from the fictional world of the film. The faux newspaper would produce "in-universe" articles that added new narrative information about the characters and events from the film itself, contributing to the mythology of the storyworld even before its development into a series. The debut edition of *The Ape News*, published Friday, March 1, 3978, featured information about the Simian Museum that Taylor runs through during his escape attempt in the film, as well as revealing smaller details such as the age of Nova, one of the film's characters. *The Ape News* was re-issued for each subsequent sequel, on each occasion featuring new narrative content to accompany the films. These faux newspapers would thereby continue the mythos-making process of the saga, revealing snippets of world-building that altogether unfolded *Planet of the Apes* as a transmedia narrative. The second edition, for example, released as a giveaway item to cinema-going audiences in 1970, revealed that the leader of the mutant resistance to the ape invasion—a mutant race seen during the events of *Beneath the Planet of the Apes*—was named Ygli VII, whose responsibility was to train the population in the use of mental deterrents against the apes. *The Ape News* had served simultaneously as a narrative bridge between the films and as an advertisement for them—mixing content and promotion to produce components of a larger, circular tapestry of transmedia storytelling.

Such circularity, as discussed via the film series, served to articulate complex and ambiguous philosophical meanings—most notably, that our future may be lost through the barbarities of our past, and that, in turn, our future may no longer exist at all. These themes would also be examined further in the pages of *Planet of the Apes Magazine*, a series of comic books published under license by Marvel Comics between August 1974 and February 1977. With *Battle for the Planet of the Apes*, the final film, released in 1973, it was the role of the comic book to effectively continue the saga, providing audiences with new information relating to the puzzle of how, why, when, or indeed if, the apes come to dominate the Earth. The comic book's writers Gerry Conway and Doug Moench set out this responsibility in their editorial, mapping out the saga's circular, time-travel-formed timeline, writing in issue #1:

> The first two Apes films featured characters traveling into the future, but it wasn't until the third film that the series ventured into real paradox territory. Having the characters travel into the past and participate in events which lead to their future creates a closed loop (or perhaps strange loop would be a better term). How could Zira and Cornelius, in their past, set into motion the events which lead to their future? This leads us to a problem of reverse causality—the future causing changes in the past... Is there an answer to the questions of time travel? [1974, 2].

This transtemporality indeed came hand in hand with transmediality—the comic introducing previously unknown facets of the *Planet of the Apes* mythos with a variety of new stories taking place across different regions and eras of the storyworld in order to provide the answers to these questions of time travel. Original stories published in the comic book included "Kingdom on an Island of the Apes" and "Future History Chronicles"—both of which aligned with the continuity of the film series, rooting different adventures in different points of the timeline set in-between the events of different films.

In "Kingdom on an Island of the Apes," for example, published inside issue #9 in June 1975, readers followed the exploits of a scientist named Derek Zane, who, in 1973, believed that the ship carrying Taylor had been propelled into the future and constructed his own time machine with the intention of rescuing the astronaut. The subsequent story follows Zane as he time travels to the year 3975, landing in The Forbidden Zone. From here Zane begins a journey to find Taylor, only to be attacked and later trapped forever in the future as one of the primitive humans encountered by Taylor in the original film. *Planet of the Apes* was thus developing as a transmedia saga founded, most prominently, upon science fictional conceptions of time travel. While transmedia storytelling has since become commonly understood as a means of accelerating strategies of world-building—expanding the geographical parameters of the storyworld while exploring those broadened spatial parameters in and across different media—in the *Planet of the Apes* saga it had operated also as a means of bridging the vast temporal parameters of a story told circularly and in tangents across multiple millennia of fictional time.

In *Planet of the Apes Magazine* #11, published in August 1975, a supplementary feature titled "Outlines of Tomorrow" provided readers with a detailed timeline that would reconcile all five films with the upcoming television series and indeed the spin-off comic book adventures into one coherent timeline, adding facts omitted from other media so as to create a comprehensive picture of the future. One such fact included the revelation that the virus that killed all cats and dogs on the planet, an event mentioned by Cornelius in *Escape from the Planet of the Apes* that led to apes being trained as slaves in *Conquest of the Planet of the Apes*, also caused the accelerated evolution of apes as well as the gradual de-evolution of humans, thus explaining to audience why all remaining humans are dumb and mute in *Planet of the Apes*. This sense of canonic integration between the time-traveling transmedial texts of the saga was evidently formed as part of its franchise construction, in turn elevating each of its textual stories to the level of narratological puzzle pieces. Each segment of the story, dispersed over multiple media covering a vast temporal timespan, represented one piece of a much larger jigsaw that the audience, operating like hunters and gatherers, to paraphrase Henry Jenkins and his description of contemporary transmedia-minded audiences, must piece together.

At Home

Thus far this chapter has attempted to explore the ways in which the circular, paradox-inducing application of time travel storytelling in the *Planet of the Apes* saga—itself serving to obliterate linear understandings of past and future—operated across both multiple films and across multiple media in order to construct its themes. In expanding the narrative events of the storyworld across multiple film sequels, promotional tie-ins, and comic books—each text feeding into the circular story arc—this utilization of transmedia storytelling functioned as an effective narratological strategy for communicating philosophical concepts about time travel as well as political themes about the potential destruction of humankind. This complex structural design of the storyworld would soon expand into a further medium—television.

In much the same way as minor or supporting characters from the storyworld of *The Matrix* films became promoted to central protagonists in subsequent transmedia texts in Jenkins' more contemporary example, Dr. Galen, a character mentioned by name in the first *Apes* film—here branded "a corrupt surgeon" by Dr. Zaius during the trial of Taylor—becomes the central ape protagonist in the first television series, where he is played by Roddy McDowall. *Planet of the Apes*, the television series, aired on CBS on Friday nights, premiering on September 13, 1974, and ending on December 20, 1974. Running concurrently with the monthly publication of the comic books, the narrative events of this first *Planet of the Apes* television series take place in the year 3085, thus "time-traveling" its audience back in time a little under 900 years from the events of the first film, yet forward a little over 400 years from the events of the fifth and final film. The television series is set in a post-apocalyptic California after its destruction by the nuclear war that took place between the fourth and fifth films. A number of episodes revealed glimpses of the devastated city ruins of San Francisco, mirroring the half-buried shot of New York's Statue of Liberty and its remains beneath The Forbidden Zone in the earlier films, thus providing audiences with a broader geographical comprehension of what its American storyworld looked like after the aftermath of the off-screen nuclear war. In one episode, characters also discovered a photograph of a futuristic New York from the year 2503, effectively revealing the height of the city's technological prowess prior to its ruination around 2670, the year in which the story is picked up in *Battle for the Planet of the Apes*.

Despite being produced under a more scattered industrial model than today's conglomerate-formed transmedia entertainments—with all subsequent *Planet of the Apes* texts licensed by film studio 20th Century–Fox to a host of unaffiliated third-party corporations—each franchise text was indeed closely interwoven with the story, storyworld, and mythology of *Planet of the Apes*. Constructing each consecutive piece of spin-off media as transmedial extensions that, to recite the earlier praise written by *Cinefantastique* magazine in

1972, "further explored the concepts of the original film rather than merely repeating its formula" (Winogura, 3) had established each of these spin-off incarnations as artistically valuable and commercially coveted components of *Planet of the Apes* via their ability to contribute new explanations to the ever-perplexing time travel mysteries established in the original film.

These time travel mysteries thus encouraged further innovative concepts of transmedia storytelling in the *Planet of the Apes* franchise. In addition to the comic book and television series fleshing out and filling in the story gaps of the saga's circular timeline, other franchise spin-offs exploited strategies of parallel transmedia storytelling—narrating adventures in one medium that take place alongside the adventures already witnessed in another medium in order to reveal previously unknown narrative content. The first employment of this strategy seems to have been a series of audio adventures—or "Little LPs"—released through Power Records that expanded the stories and characters of the *Planet of the Apes* television series. Parallel expansions of the storyworld continued much more emphatically, however, with a second television series—this time an animated series called *Return to the Planet of the Apes*. Premiering on September 6, 1975, and broadcast until September 4, 1976, *Return to the Planet of the Apes* was set in 3978, the same year as the events of the first two films, with its narrative running in parallel to those earlier films and even featuring a number of characters from both *Planet of the Apes* and *Beneath the Planet of the Apes*. Cornelius and Zira, for example, parents to Caesar, leader of the ape uprising in later/earlier centuries, discover further details in this television series regarding how their simian society was established long after human society had deteriorated—a discovery mentioned only briefly in the original film. Believing that humans should at last be offered equal rights to those of apes, and while digging for further ancient evidence that the apes plan to present as part of their proposition to the Senate, Cornelius and Zira discover the discarded spacecraft of Taylor, which, as narrated in *Escape from the Planet of the Apes*, enabled the ape couple to travel back in time to 1973 moments prior to the destruction of the Earth, bringing with them the seeds for the eventual uprising of the apes. The future in which mankind will come to its downfall and the ascendancy of the apes beginnings is instigated by this specific discovery, thus knotting itself together with the arrival of Taylor in the original film in a way that influences—not to mention profoundly complicates—a cause and effect narrative logic across multiple media. Is it right, as the apes discuss in the *Return to the Planet of the Apes* television series, to use Taylor's space craft to escape to the planet's past—especially as audiences would certainly have known by this point that this very act of responding to time travel with further time travel effectively distorts the figure of Taylor into the cause of the apes' uprising? Time travel essentially transforms the hero into the villain.

Conclusion

This chapter has highlighted how, if audiences had wished to experience the storyworld of *Planet of the Apes* fully during the late–1960s and early 1970s, they were in fact required to act like hunters, as Henry Jenkins puts it, gathering story information from different media sources. The complete circularity of the *Planet of the Apes* timeline was not available in any single medium—even cinema, which jumped as many as 2,000 years between its sequels. Rather, audiences were required to consume each and every media component, including the products of cinema, comic books, television, and promotional tie-in materials, if they wished to experience the story, storyworld and mythology of *Planet of the Apes* in full. Different media contributed different stories, taking their audiences backwards and forwards in time, bridging the mysteries of one medium with the adventures of another. It was the narratological concept of time travel, moreover, that served as both the source and means of such transmedial world-building. The time-bending, climatic twist of the first film paved a circular timeline that unfolded across media, each medium providing audiences with new entry points, which in turn accentuated the saga's underlying themes.

In his review of the film for *Newsday* magazine, Joseph Gemlis called *Planet of the Apes* "a first-rate science-fiction adventure with serious moral, theological, and social implications" (1968, 21). "The world seems ready to destroy itself and *Beneath the Planet of the Apes* asks you not to contribute to that destruction," once asserted that film's director, Ted Post (Winogura 1972, 22), continuing:

> Our days on this planet at this moment are numbered and the reason for our finite, unrosy future is that we are corrupting ourselves out of existence—with our double standards, hypocrisy, injustice, anarchy, shortsightedness, very shallow forms of self-delusion, profound national disarray, sickness, a cold war that does not end, a hot war that does not end, a draft that does not end, and a poisonous race conflict that does not end [*ibid.*].

Post's emphasis on destructive actions without end was precisely what was emphasized via a circular narratology, which ultimately denied the prospect of a future and a past in favor of an endless loop of violence. More than a time loop, the metaphor of the Möbius strip perhaps more accurately represents the structure of the *Planet of the Apes* saga—the destruction of the entire world during the denouement of *Beneath the Planet of the Apes* representing the twist in the Möbius strip, the moment where the topside is transferred to the underside as the apes of the future travel back in time to the Earth of the past, and the cycle of events unfolds again. Moreover, this aforementioned film's final scene represents the moment where the two edges of the Möbius strip are connected together, which in collapsing causal binaries—in this case, beginning/ending or past/future—reasserts the saga's philosophies by suggesting mankind's entrapment within an endless cycle of violence. This structural design also echoes the words of philosopher Jean Baudrillard and his suggestion that science fiction, the generic housing of *Planet of the Apes*, "will never again be a mirror held toward the future, but a desperate rehallucination of the past" (1994, 125). The circular narratology of the *Planet of the Apes* saga's transtemporal transmediality ultimately quite similarly serves to deny its representation of humankind both a future and a past—its existence is "from the start … without origin, immanent, without a past, without a future" (Baudrillard 1994, 125). Transmedia storytelling thus becomes a uniquely interesting way of exploring the time loop. The telling of a story that crosses its own timeline—taking its audience non-linearly from one point in the story to another—is mirrored and indeed accelerated by the transmedia format, which, in unfolding one expansive narrative across media, itself serves to take its audience from one corner of the storyworld to another, from one point in the timeline to another. The audiences of transmedia stories are nothing if not time travelers across the borders of media.

Tropes, Narratives and
Generic Cycles

Time Travel and the "Afterlife" of the Western

PETE FALCONER

Time travel movies often employ tropes from various genres in their portrayal of the past and future. Particular genres frequently come to be associated with particular periods, either because of their characteristic settings (the historical epic, science fiction) or because of their popularity or prominence at a specific time (horror movies and the 1970s, teen movies and the 1980s). The conventions of a genre, then, can also be used to evoke an era with which it is associated. As Lucy Fife Donaldson points out, each of the main periods visited by Marty McFly in the *Back to the Future* trilogy is connected to a particular genre: "the teen movie of 1955," "the science fiction of 2015" and "the western of 1885" (2010, 74). Donaldson goes on to argue that this use of multiple genres across the *Back to the Future* films, situated in "a wider context of science fiction and comedy," helps to draw attention to some of the connections and affinities between the different genres involved (74).

Framing individual genres within a time travel narrative can also reveal much about how these genres are perceived and represented at a particular time. To treat a genre as a time travel destination is to contrast it implicitly with the present, however that is defined. This contrast will often reflect some of the ways in which the genre and its history are understood at the time of production. In this essay, I will examine the representation of the Western genre in two time travel movies, *Back to the Future Part III* (1990) and *Bill & Ted's Excellent Adventure* (1989), and the particular connections this suggests between time travel and the recent history of the Western.

By the 1980s, the Western had ceased to be a consistent part of mainstream Hollywood production. The genre had not disappeared entirely, but Westerns were no longer released in the same quantity, or with the same regularity, as they had been in previous decades. This shift has had a significant impact on the ways in which the Western genre has been treated and understood in the past thirty years. New Westerns have come to be regarded not as continuations of what Kitses described as an "American *tradition*" (1969, 8), but as revivals of a once-popular genre that is understood to have come to an end. The forms in which the Western continues to exist can be perceived as a kind of "afterlife," in which the residual traces of the genre's mainstream status endure in transformed contexts. These are the specific conditions within which the use of the Western in *Back to the Future Part III* and *Bill & Ted's Excellent Adventure* seems to operate.

Time travel is an apt trope for engaging with the "afterlife" of the Western; a major characteristic of the genre's latter-day identity is a sense of inherent retrospection. The Western is understood as belonging to the past, not just in its portrayal of a period in American history, but also as a popular form strongly associated with previous eras of filmmaking. To use or to evoke the Western in its "afterlife" is, in a sense, a form of time travel—to return to the genre is to return to the past.

The two films I will be discussing make this connection explicit. Both show their main characters traveling back in time to the Old West. In *Back to the Future Part III* (hereafter *Future III*), most of the action takes place in a Western setting, in and around Hill Valley, California in 1885. In *Bill & Ted's Excellent Adventure* (hereafter *Bill & Ted*) there is only a short episode in the Old West revolving around Billy the Kid, who subsequently joins the characters in their travels. However, both movies treat the Western genre in the same retrospective fashion. The West is visited by time traveling characters whose contemporary sensibilities clearly distinguish them as outsiders. The sense of distance from the genre that this creates reflects a number of wider tendencies in the "afterlife" of the Western.

"A voyage into the Old Western"

Although both films present their characters' destination as the historical West, the primary point of reference in each case is Western movies. As Collins observes in relation to *Future III*, "When the characters travel back in time to the Old West, their trip is actually a voyage into the Old Western" (1993, 248). This is also reflected in my argument, in which I will be discussing the films primarily in relation to the Western genre, rather than in relation to the historical past. The emphasis on the movie West is especially emphatic in *Future III*. Marty McFly travels from 1955 to 1885 via a kitsch Western-themed drive-in movie theatre against the backdrop of Monument Valley, and adopts the alias "Clint Eastwood" while in the Old West. As noted below, *Future III* also contains a number of allusions to specific Westerns, particularly those of

John Ford and Sergio Leone. The intertextual elements in *Bill & Ted* are less pronounced, but the film's West is also an amalgam of movie tropes. This is apparent in two musical motifs that occur when Bill and Ted arrive in 1879. A grizzled Westerner can be heard humming "Oh! Susanna" while settling down in an outhouse. Stephen Foster's song has been used extensively in Westerns; as Peter Stanfield notes, the song "rings out time and again " in the movies that made up the mainstream revival of the higher-budget Western in 1939 (1996, 33), including *Jesse James* (1939) and *Dodge City* (1939). After Bill and Ted's time-traveling phone booth lands next to the outhouse and scares the Westerner away, we also briefly hear a fast, descending string figure on the non-diegetic soundtrack. In its pitch, rhythm and orchestration, the figure evokes the syncopated strings that open Jerome Moross' famous theme from *The Big Country* (1958).

Since both *Future III* and *Bill & Ted* clearly define their Wests in relation to Western movies, their portrayal of the West can be seen to reflect the contemporary status of the Western genre when they were made. I want to argue that although the two movies, especially *Future III*, seek to evoke aspects of the Western, the popular profile of the genre in its "afterlife " means that they are only able to do so within quite narrow and restricted parameters, and in ways that emphasize its distance from the films' construction of the present.

Containing and Condensing the Western

One aspect of the "afterlife " of the Western that is evident in both movies is the perception of the genre as a finite, finished body of work. Both films present or allude to specific, self-contained locations that seem to summarize the genre. The Pohatchee Drive-In Theatre in *Future III* is the most obvious of these locations. Its décor revolves primarily around stereotypes relating to Indians in Westerns, including a tepee, a men's bathroom labeled "Braves" and a mural of warriors on horseback under the cinema screen itself. Other generic elements are also incorporated into the scene: in preparation to travel to the Old West, Marty changes into garish pseudo–Western clothes, described by Exshaw as "the sort of embarrassing B-movie Western costume worn by series " "fantasy cowboys " like Tom Mix and Roy Rogers " (2010, 98). The Hawaiian-style shirt worn by Doc Brown also features cacti, rodeo riders and lassos. The overall effect is of the intense concentration of Western tropes into a single location.

It is also significant that this location should be very clearly bounded. A fence encircles the drive-in, connecting to the Indian mural under the screen.

The distinctive rock formations of Monument Valley, familiar from the Westerns of John Ford, can be seen beyond the fence. The red sandstone buttes form an outer layer to the boundary, further accentuating the self-contained quality of the location. This persists when Marty arrives back in 1885. Throughout the scene in which Marty faces first Indians and then the U.S. Cavalry charging towards him, the buttes continue to form strong horizontal lines across the background of many shots, creating the impression that the open desert is somehow fenced-in.

The Western is also connected to a single, self-contained location in *Bill & Ted*. When Bill and Ted arrive in the West, Ted remarks that it is "just like Frontierland," the Western-themed section of Disneyland. The West in *Bill & Ted* does, in some respects, resemble a theme park. The action seems to be perfectly poised and choreographed, as if performed for outside visitors. When Ted makes his "Frontierland" remark, a blacksmith steps into the center of the frame and cools a horseshoe in water, before returning to the darkness of his shop. The blacksmith's actions resemble those of a theme park automaton, emerging to perform a pre-programmed gesture for the passing crowds. This seems to support Ted's comparison to Frontierland and suggests that we are seeing another condensed and localized version of the West.

Although the West in *Bill & Ted* is reminiscent of a theme park, it differs from the actual theme park in *Westworld* (1973). The robotic Western resort in *Westworld* caters to a clientele familiar with the Western genre. The film is set in an unidentified future, but one clearly extrapolated from the early 1970s, when Hollywood Westerns were still made and released relatively frequently. The theme park's visitors (and, implicitly, the film's contemporary audience) grew up with the Western. Bill and Ted, by contrast, come from an era in which the Western was less prominent. Frontierland is presented as one of their primary frames of reference for understanding the West. This can undoubtedly be viewed in terms of postmodernism—Ted's remark that New Mexico in the 1870s is "just like" its Disneyland imitation seems like an exemplary instance of the postmodern simulacra described by Baudrillard, who remarked that "Disneyland is a perfect model of all the entangled orders of simulation" (1981, 174). However, the kind of cultural and historical situation outlined by Baudrillard would seem to apply equally to all genres (indeed, to all forms of meaning). I am concerned here with identifying some of the ways in which the two films reflect the specific historical conditions of the Western genre in its "afterlife."

It is perhaps necessary for the narratives of *Future III* and *Bill & Ted* to represent the Western genre as if it were a single visitable location, which can function as a clear destination for time travelers. However, this representation also implies a wider perspective on the genre as something that can be condensed and summarized into a single representative form. This in turn can only be possible if the Western is understood to be finite and complete, and thus able to accommodate a retrospective overview. There is little sense in either film that the genre might continue to proliferate and produce new narratives. The stories of the Old West have already happened—they can be interacted with and even revised, but only by rearranging elements that are already in place. Bill, Ted and Marty's adventures cannot generate new Westerns; the characters can simply participate in Western narratives that already exist.

Harwood-Smith and Ludlow note that the narrative of *Bill & Ted* is predicated on a fixed timeline, in which Rufus must travel back in time to help Bill and Ted preserve a future that already exists: "The future society of *Bill & Ted* know they must insert someone into the past to bring about their present, but there is no indication they believe this involves changing history" (2010, 237). Harwood-Smith and Ludlow contrast this to the "changeable timeline" (236) of the *Back to the Future* trilogy, in which radically different futures can be produced by actions in the past. The West in *Future III*, however, remains a fixed and stable entity. Erisman compares the moment where Doc Brown and Clara Clayton dance at the Hill Valley town festival to the famous and celebrated dance in *My Darling Clementine* (1946), to which the scene clearly alludes. Erisman observes that

> Ford's dance takes place in the full light of day, bathing landscape and society with an illuminating clarity that promises communal growth and endless progress. Zemeckis' takes place at night, the surrounding darkness shutting out the land and thereby focusing attention upon the integrated, self-sufficient community, complete within itself and concerned with problems within rather than progress without [1992, 30].

Again, we see the West presented as discrete and self-contained, without the promises of renewal and boundless possibility frequently associated with its wide-open spaces in earlier incarnations of the Western genre. In addition to this sense of spatial containment, there is also a temporal dimension. The future of the Western town in *Future III* is assured—it is an older version of Hill Valley, the town that the previous films in the trilogy have already shown us in 1955, 1985 and 2015. As Erisman suggests, the West of *Future III* leads inevitably to a familiar future, from the perspective of which it is viewed:

> in contrast to Ford's affirmative picture of the progress of conventional American culture within a surrounding and hostile wilderness, Zemeckis offers a meditation upon a century and more of community, technology, and the evolving West [30].

Hill Valley in 1885 is not a precarious frontier community that could potentially succeed or fail. The Western genre is simply a phase through which

Hill Valley passes on its way towards becoming something else. Again, the logic of the movie is based on the presumption that the Western has come to an end, that its possibilities have already been explored and defined.

This view of the Western is also manifest in the nature and range of the intertextual allusions in these films. The implicit definition of the Western that is offered, particularly in *Future III*, consists less of a wider set of generic conventions than a number of more specific motifs from a few canonical directors, primarily John Ford and Sergio Leone. I have already mentioned the use of Monument Valley and the allusion to the dance in *My Darling Clementine* in *Future III*. Collins notes that "one of the most famous shots" in *Stagecoach* (1939) is replicated "almost exactly" (1993, 242), and Exshaw (2010, 99) points to the similarity between Buford "Mad Dog" Tannen and Liberty Valance in *The Man Who Shot Liberty Valance* (1962). Marty McFly survives his face-off with Tannen by using a trick from *A Fistful of Dollars* (1964) and the film features a version of the famous crane shot rising over the town in *Once Upon a Time in the West* (1968). Leone is also the clearest specific point of reference in *Bill & Ted*, with another version of the same crane shot and Billy the Kid's long "duster" jacket (also worn by Doc Brown in *Future III*) similarly evoking *Once Upon a Time*.

This relatively narrow pool of allusions defines the Western in relation to a small, settled canon of works. Again, this is a retrospective view, in which particular aspects of the past have already been picked out for preservation. This identification of the genre with a small number of "classic" movies is a recurring characteristic of the "afterlife" of the Western, but it also reflects tendencies that extend beyond this context. *Bill & Ted* presents a similar approach to history in general. Bill and Ted travel through time, picking up historical figures to help them with their high school history report. As well as Billy the Kid, other figures include Socrates, Joan of Arc and Abraham Lincoln. Each is treated as being able to represent all that is worth remembering about their historical period. Another connection can be made here to postmodernism, to Jameson's observation of the various ways that the representation of the past is mediated in postmodern works, including through "stylistic connotation" in the "nostalgia film" (1991, 19) and through representative historical figures in E.L Doctorow's novel *Ragtime* (23–24). In *Bill & Ted*, the Old West is one of a number of historical periods that are evoked in this way. The allusions to a narrow range of Western directors in *Future III* and *Bill & Ted* suggest that the Western as a genre is itself considered to belong sufficiently to the past to be accommodated within this wider approach to history.

The Uncertain Status of the Western

Retrospective appreciation of "classic" movies and directors is also a much safer position to take on a genre that is no longer considered either reliably profitable or easily understood by contemporary audiences. This continues to be a prevailing attitude towards the Western, despite occasional revivals. *Future III* and *Bill & Ted* were released before one such revival, led by two prestigious and acclaimed early 1990s Westerns: *Dances with Wolves* (1990) and *Unforgiven* (1992). While these films did bring popular attention back to the genre, they did not ultimately result in a return to the regular production of Hollywood Westerns, which continued to be considered to be too far outside the mainstream. Shortly before the release of *Unforgiven*, Thompson remarked that "while [Clint] Eastwood, [Walter] Hill, and [John] Milius know how to make Westerns, many other top directors are afraid to hurt their commercial viability by revealing that they do not" (1992, 53).

Many of the ways in which the Western has been treated across its "afterlife" seem to reflect a sense of uncertainty about the levels of popular familiarity and appeal that the genre has been able to retain. This can be seen in a number of moments in *Future III* that seem to offer some of the conventional pleasures of the Western but also frame these pleasures in ways that set them apart from the genre. For example, Marty and Doc have to steal a train in order to push their DeLorean time machine fast enough to send them back to the future. The action involved in the early stages of this would not feel out of place in a more conventional Western. Marty and Doc gallop after the train on horseback, leap onto the back of it, make their way along the top of its still-moving carriages, mask themselves with bandanas and hold the driver at gunpoint. However, when the driver asks, "Is this a hold-up?" Doc replies, "It's a science experiment." This acts as a comical reminder of the non–Western contexts that frame the scene's Western action. It also points towards the more technologically-focused action that follows, featuring multi-colored smoke from Doc's customized fuel logs, frequent cutaways to gauges and digital displays, and the decisive intervention of the futuristic "hoverboard" first seen in *Back to the Future Part II* (1989). The train hijack sequence quickly shifts from action reminiscent of a Western to something closer to science fiction, a more familiar and commercially successful genre in recent decades. The uncertain status of the Western in its popular "afterlife" means that the genre can only bear a limited and contained significance in the film's climactic moments.

The Present vs. the Old West

The containment of the genre in this example is part of a wider aesthetic in both *Future III* and *Bill & Ted* that insists on the separateness of the Western from contemporary styles and perspectives. Both films emphasize, for comic effect, the incongruity of 1980s teenagers in a Western setting. Sometimes, this is simply the basis for amusing juxtapositions, like Bill's laughable and short-lived attempt to maintain a poker face in a card game, or the reaction of Buford Tannen's henchmen to Marty's straight teeth and white Nike sneakers. At other points, however, the sense of separation is more pronounced. When Marty first arrives in the Old West, the charging Indians into whose path he drives appear to be charging anyway, and do not seem to especially alter their course to pursue him. The cavalry who are chasing the Indians do not seem to register Marty's presence either, even before he returns to his hiding place in a cave. The only indication that any of the charging riders notice him at all is a retrospective one: the Indian arrow that Marty pulls out of the side of the DeLorean. During the charges themselves, there is little to suggest that Marty is anything more than incidentally involved in someone else's chase.

Similarly, the brawl that erupts in the Western saloon in *Bill & Ted* appears, in its early stages at least, not to touch the two characters at all. Bill and Ted remain in their seats, still holding their cards from the poker game, as the fight takes place around them. They are positioned as if they were an audience, sitting back and enjoying the spectacle, exclaiming "Excellent!" as a woman swings on a rope and crashes through a window with a man. The two young men are eventually dragged into the fight, but continue to play a relatively passive role. They are both thrown along the bar and end up, to their delight, with their heads through the wall of the saloon girls' dressing room. For most of the fight, Bill and Ted are framed as spectators, rather than participants, just as Marty has been described as "little more than an onlooker" (Exshaw 2010, 109n) in much of *Future III*. In both films, the contemporary characters seem oddly inert in the midst of iconic Western action. It is as if they are unable to fully participate in the genre, their status as 1980s youths rendering them incompatible with it.

The young protagonists in each film may not always appear to be fully present in the West, but this does not mean that they are safe from danger. Bill qualifies Ted's "Frontierland" comparison by saying, "Yeah, but you can get shot here, Ted." Some distinction is suggested between the theme park version of the West and the authentically dangerous Western milieu visited by the characters. This distinction, however, serves to further emphasize the sense of separateness associated with the Western genre. The tone of benign comic fantasy in *Bill & Ted* means that the dangers of the West aren't developed much beyond Bill's remark and the barroom brawl, but *Future III* takes this dimension somewhat further. Marty travels back to 1885 to prevent Doc Brown from being shot in the back by Buford Tannen. Donaldson points to the distinct sense of danger associated with the Western in *Future III*, as exemplified through Tannen. Comparing Marty's encounter with Tannen in the saloon to his confrontations with Tannen's descendants Biff in *Back to the Future* (1985) and Griff in *Back to the Future Part II*, Donaldson observes that the construction of the sequence seems to "insist on Buford's dangerousness" (2010, 86) to a greater extent than the scenes in the previous films do with later Tannens. Furthermore, Donaldson argues that Tannen's dangerousness is articulated in relation to the Western genre, connecting his "specifically masculine and threatening physicality" to "the kind of masculinity more commonly encountered in the Western" (2010, 85). Buford Tannen's Westernness represents a new type of danger that Marty has not faced before, and their first encounter ends with Marty being roped, dragged behind Tannen's horse, and nearly hung, "a modulation that indicates just how dangerous Buford, and by implication the world of 1885, is in contrast to Biff of 1955 and Griff of 2015" (Donaldson 2010, 87).

The particular level of danger associated with the Old West in *Future III* emphasizes its sense of separateness by distinguishing it from the other periods that Marty visits in the *Back to the Future* trilogy. This forms part of a wider insistence on the difference of the West in physical terms. Part of this is technological—we are repeatedly reminded of the advantages that are unavailable to Marty and Doc in the 19th century. Marty erroneously assumes that he will be able to obtain gasoline for the DeLorean in 1885 Hill Valley, and Doc constructs elaborate machines for preparing breakfast and making a single ice cube. A larger part of the physical difference of the West, however, is suggested by portraying aspects of it as grotesque. Buford Tannen's grubby, hirsute Western masculinity is exaggerated to the point of monstrosity. When Marty's Irish immigrant ancestors, Seamus and Maggie McFly, take him in, his discomfort at the dinner table is played on for comic effect as he is served brown water and rabbit meat with shot in it. Marty also jumps back into a pile of horse manure to avoid a stagecoach after he first arrives in town. This emphasis on the dirty and the scatological in the West can also be seen in *Bill & Ted*. As I have already mentioned, Bill and Ted's phone booth time machine lands between two outhouses, one of which is occupied. As the two friends walk into town, Bill warns Ted to "watch out for the horse crap," and we see Ted steer himself around another pile of manure. It is a curiously specific parallel that both films should connect their main characters' arrival in a Western town with the dangers of stepping in equine excrement. Among other things, this motif functions as an explicit demonstration that the characters have arrived in a world that is different to their own. In contrast to the implied norm of the clean, Californian present, the Western genre is associated with the dirt and inconvenience of the past.

The roughness of the West is the basis for another point of contrast with the present. Part of the danger associated with the Western in the two movies comes from its presentation as a site of frequent and ready violence. This can be seen, for example, in the suddenness with which the brawl erupts and takes over the saloon in *Bill & Ted*. In both films, the violence of the Western is associated with the past through contrasts to more peaceful modes of contemporary behavior. As they are dragged into the brawl, Bill protests that he and Ted are unaccustomed to violence: "Look—we're totally weak. We can't possibly fight you." In *Future III*, Marty's encounter with violence in the Old West forms part of the process through which he learns to be less short-tempered and susceptible to taunting. As Harwood-Smith and Ludlow point out, "Time travel helps rid Marty of ... hotheadedness" (2010, 249). In *Back to the Future Part II*, Marty is shown to be sensitive to accusations of cowardice, and particularly the label "chicken," which repeatedly causes him to act rashly. This quality persists in *Future III*—Marty agrees to a gunfight with Buford Tannen after Tannen calls him "yellow." However, on the morning of the scheduled face-off, Marty finally learns to ignore such goading. In the Palace Saloon, with Tannen yelling insults outside, an old-timer warns Marty that, if he does not fight, "everybody everywhere will say Clint Eastwood is the biggest yellow-belly in the West." The comical reference to Marty's choice of pseudonym, the invocation of the codes of public honor associated with the Western hero and the echo of the phrase "fastest gun in the West" clearly frame the showdown in relation to the conventions of the Western. Marty rejects this conception of heroism, dismissing Tannen as "an asshole" and aiming to escape to the future with Doc. He is eventually forced into facing Tannen anyway, but prevails through a combination of cunning (the trick taken from *A Fistful of Dollars*, where he uses a stove door as concealed armor) and less lethal violence (knocking Tannen out with a punch). In this way, Marty can be shown to have acquired a calmer and more mature attitude to violence, but can still triumph. The violence associated with the Western, which threatens to be fatal to either Doc or Marty himself, functions as a negative example from which Marty can learn. The exaggerated, aggressive masculinity that Marty encounters in 1885 presents him with the dangerous excesses in his own temperament in a form sufficiently removed from himself for him to reject.

The type of masculinity that *Future III* associates with the Western is not treated as idealized or heroic. Rather, it is presented as dirty, dangerous and in need of improvement. In order to be a better young man from the 1980s, Marty must learn to behave less like a character from a Western. Again, the implication seems to be that contemporary youth is incompatible with the Western genre. If the present in *Future III* and *Bill & Ted* is associated with youth, the Western is associated with age. One example of this is the trio of old men repeatedly seen in the Palace Saloon in *Future III*, played by Pat Buttram, Dub Taylor and Harry Carey, Jr., veteran character actors with a history of Western roles. The three men are only ever seen sitting around the same table in the saloon—another example of the tendency to localize and condense the Western genre. Clint Eastwood, the model of the Western hero with which Marty seems to be relatively familiar, was 55 in 1985, the year the film offers to us as the present. At this point in the trilogy, Eastwood is already associated with the older generation—in *Back to the Future Part II* we see Biff Tannen, who is the same age as Marty's parents, watching *A Fistful of Dollars*.

A particularly striking aspect of the association between age and the Western in *Future III* is that the white-haired Doc Brown seems to make a more suitable Western hero than the boyish Marty. Doc rescues Marty with his sharp shooting and grim resolve when Tannen tries to hang him, plays the Wyatt Earp role in the homage to *My Darling Clementine* and seems more physically at ease than Marty does in the Western milieu. He also forms the film's central romantic couple with the newly-arrived schoolteacher Clara Clayton. Marty's relative passivity and inertia within what the film suggests is an older man's genre makes room for Doc to step into a more heroic role.

Bill & Ted's representative Western figure is the youthful Billy the Kid, but he seems strikingly atypical in the film's Western milieu. All the other men that Bill and Ted encounter in the Old West are considerably more grizzled—grey hair, beards and moustaches seem to be the norm. The fair-haired, clean-shaven Billy seems to have more in common with Bill and Ted themselves than he does with his contemporaries in 1870s New Mexico. The film develops this apparent kinship, and comes to present Billy the Kid as almost a prototypical 1980s Californian. By the time that Bill and Ted take their group of historical personages to a shopping mall in the present, Billy has started to pick up aspects of their distinctive "Valleyspeak" idiom. When Sigmund Freud embarrasses Billy and Socrates in front of two young women, Billy exasperatedly remarks, "Way to go, egghead." Later, when security guards tackle him and Genghis Khan, he exclaims, "Bogus!"

Of all the historical figures that Bill and Ted pick up, they trust Billy with the most responsibility—he is left to guard the phone booth and look after Socrates in medieval England, he lassos Freud when they capture him from his own time and he acts as the master of ceremonies for Bill and Ted's spectacular school history report. When they arrive in the medieval period, Bill congratulates Billy for "dealing with the oddity of time travel with the greatest of ease." Billy's ability to do this seems to be connected to the implication that he does not quite belong in his own time—he is set apart from the film's version of the West, and seems more easily detachable from it. Indeed, the "greatness" of *Bill & Ted's* various historical figures appears to be partly defined by their capacity to adapt to contemporary tastes and values. Joan of Arc takes up aerobics, Beethoven embraces rock music and Abraham Lincoln proudly declaims Bill and Ted's motto, "Be excellent to each other, and party on, dudes!"

The association of the Western with age and the past, then, needs to be seen in conjunction with the implied superiority of the present. This perspective can certainly be identified in *Future III*. Exshaw remarks that the entire *Back to the Future* trilogy presents "the Eighties All-American high-school kid" as the "high pinnacle of human evolution and adornment of Western civilization" (2010, 105). Elizabeth McCarthy characterizes Marty as an implicitly superior figure who "fixes the future by fixing the past" (2010, 148). Whenever Marty travels to the past, knowledge from his own time is shown to give him a decisive advantage. In the Old West, he recognizes a Frisbee brand pie tin as something that can be thrown, demonstrates shooting skills learned from the video arcade game *Wild Gunman* and defeats Tannen using a trick borrowed from *A Fistful of Dollars*. In this last example, Marty does not so much take on the mantle of Western hero as exploit the fact that, as we are repeatedly reminded, no one in 1885 knows who Clint Eastwood is. Marty's relation to the Western is one of retrospective dominance—his limited but effective knowledge of movies is offered to us as just one aspect of his more generally superior perspective.

The superiority of the present is treated with more irony in *Bill & Ted*. From the beginning of the film, the premise that a utopian future society could be structured around the values and musical aspirations of two cheerfully vacuous 1980s teenagers is presented comically. This is apparent in Rufus' introductory description of the world of 2688, in which its advancements are measured by the standards of 1980s suburban Californian leisure culture: "Bowling averages are way up; mini golf scores are way down. And we have more excellent waterslides than any other planet we communicate with." This description of utopia is explicitly framed as comedy by its delivery as a monologue, directly to camera, by a character played by George Carlin, more famous as a stand-up comedian than as an actor. In its extrapolation of a utopian future from two teenage boys' dreams of forming a rock band, the film subjects the values of contemporary youth to a certain amount of affectionate mockery. As a consequence, *Bill & Ted* takes a less overtly superior attitude to the Western than *Future III*, but its focus on the contemporary still means that the genre is viewed from a predominantly outside perspective.

The Far Country

The perspective of the outsider on the Western that characterizes the two films reflects the wider context of the genre's "afterlife." By the time of *Future III* and *Bill & Ted*'s release, the Western genre had come to be regarded as at best peripheral to contemporary popular culture. The prevalence of the outside perspective at this time can be seen in two further examples: *Dances with Wolves* (which I have already mentioned) and *City Slickers* (1991). Neither film opens in a Western setting. Instead, the West is a place to which the characters have to travel. In *Dances with Wolves*, Lieutenant John Dunbar requests to be posted to the frontier, ostensibly to see it "before it's gone" but also to seek freedom and solitude away from the ongoing American Civil War, in which he has fought. In *City Slickers*, Mitch Robbins and his friends pay to take part in a cattle drive in New Mexico as a temporary escape from modern urban life. Both of these scenarios draw on long-standing conventions of the Western genre, in which the West is a portrayed as a site of liberating male adventure away from the pressures and restrictions of civilization. Alongside this, however, the West is also presented as a more remote space, explicitly away from the worlds that the characters come from. Unlike the majority of previous Westerns, the characters do not inhabit the West from the outset. The Western genre, which both *Dances with Wolves* and *City Slickers* seek in different ways to evoke, is treated as a location to be visited, like Frontierland or the Pohatchee Drive-In Theatre. The standard contemporary perspective, the norm that each movie establishes, is assumed to come from outside the world of the genre. Its perceived distance from contemporary culture (which is treated as a source of exotic appeal in both movies) is expressed in geographical terms, as the remoteness and separateness of the West.

In *Future III* and *Bill & Ted*, the trope of time travel enables the films to acknowledge the historical basis of this sense of distance. Time travel narratives allow different periods to be treated as separate and distinct temporal entities, to be accessed as if they were geographical destinations. This acquires a particular resonance with the Old West as represented through the Western genre, because the genre itself has come to be regarded as a popular form of the past. The two films demonstrate the extent to which time travel in films involves not only returning to previous eras, but also to previous tropes, conventions and modes of representation. Beyond that, the movies show some of the effects that changes in the contexts and attitudes surrounding popular forms can have on the forms themselves. Looking at the Western genre in relation to the films' construction of the past can also help us identify characteristics of their particular representation of the present, and which aspects of the Western might be accommodated within this. In the context of a time travel narrative, the sense of the past associated with the Western can be confronted, and ways of understanding and relating to the genre in its "afterlife" can be proposed. Some of these ways are better able to recognize the complexity and value of the genre than others, and it is certainly possible to detect an element of condescension in some of the ways in which it is framed in relation to the present. However, for the Western to continue to exist in any meaningful form, the historical shifts in its place within popular culture must be recognized. The trope of time travel provides one way of making this recognition explicit.

Temporal Prosthetics and Beautiful Pain

Loss, Memory and Nostalgia in Somewhere in Time, The Butterfly Effect *and* Safety Not Guaranteed

TRAVIS L. MARTIN *and*
OWEN R. HORTON

In the *Mad Men* episode "The Wheel" (2007), Don Draper pitches a marketing strategy for Kodak's new slide projector. While the Kodak executives want to emphasize the novelty of the product's technology by calling it "The Wheel," Draper believes its power is more elemental and rooted in a personal appeal to nostalgia. He cites an old copywriting mentor's definition of nostalgia as "the pain from an old wound," in this case a loss of the ability to return to the physical site of memory: the past. If nostalgia is a romanticized version of the past, Draper posits that it is more pain than pleasure. Still, he argues, we cling to the transportive power of memories: "This device is not a space ship, it's a time machine. It goes backwards and forwards. It takes us to a place where we ache to go again." Although the slide projector does not have the ability to alleviate the pain of loss, it does have the ability to psychically transport the viewer to a time and place of his or her choosing.

Draper's pitch presents time travel not as a scientific or metaphysical act of fiction, but as an everyday function of memory compelled by the "ache" of nostalgia. This chapter argues that the characters in *Somewhere in Time* (1980), *The Butterfly Effect* (2004), and *Safety Not Guaranteed* (2012), like Don Draper, experience this compulsion following a traumatic loss. Specifically, we argue that what is lost becomes a psychic wound for the subject, creating a separation between memory and identity. The moment of trauma is a line of demarcation in which the subject can look back and see a stable, linear past as well as a whole identity. Simultaneously, memory paints the moment of trauma as a nostalgic locus, the

194

point in which that identity was irrevocably changed. It is in understanding the nature of trauma—how it functions within the creation of self and memory—that we begin to understand the nostalgic compulsion of time travelers.

This chapter explores the role of time travel in memory and identity formation, including an analysis of the device or ability itself as shown in three films. In *Somewhere in Time*, the time traveler is summoned to the past by a woman he is destined to fall in love with. In *The Butterfly Effect*, the ability to travel in time is inherited through paternal lines, enabling the protagonist to move throughout different—often traumatic—points in his life by reading about them in childhood journals. *Safety Not Guaranteed* most closely depicts Don Draper's ache. In that film, the heroine is caught between a time traveler and a third character's nostalgia. The choice to travel in time is tantamount to faith. In each of these films we found temporal prosthetics fueled by nostalgia, functioning as ghost limbs, producing pains and longings in the time traveler that result in a compulsion to invent a device capable of transporting the time traveler to a physical site in the past.

We use the term *temporal prosthetics* as both a reference to the tool granting time travelers their abilities and as a nod to Alison Landsberg's (1995) essay on "prosthetic memory." The tool emerges from a nostalgic compulsion to return to the historical site of trauma. The separation between the subject and his or her past at that site exists as it might to an amputee, a specific moment of pain resulting in feelings of loss and lack in the present. What goes missing after trauma, for time travelers and amputees alike, once contributed to an aesthetic sense of wholeness. In the films we examine, time travel is possible due to a *beautiful pain*, a source of potential derived from the unique properties of traumatic experience enabling time travelers to overcome the loss causing Don Draper's "ache." These films each illustrate how the lines between that which *was* experienced in the physical world of the past and that which *is* experienced in the psychic world of the present as nostalgia are blurred. Through both failure and success, the protagonists come to understand that trauma and loss are not located in the past. Rather, temporal prosthetics, created as a result of nostalgic compulsion, reveal pain and loss as constituent parts of the time traveler's identity in the present. When realized, a reinterpreted past creates a new identity, allowing the time traveler to progress forward into the future.

Temporal Prosthetics and Unclaimed Experience

It will help us in our later analysis to set forth the terms by which we frame the compulsion to travel in time. We've already said that a temporal prosthetic—a time machine or the ability to return to the past—is often the product of a compulsion. Even in those films where the ability to travel in time is discovered accidentally, temporal prosthetics enable the traveler to revisit or work through past events that were foundational in the construction of that character's psyche as it exists in the present. In the films we analyze, this compulsion derives from a trauma or loss in the past and manifests as nostalgia in the present. Nostalgia, as Pat Gill argues, is "a response to the historical combination of an uncertainty about the continued usefulness of historical and traditional forms and formulae, the nature of unpredictably changing political situations, and the score of indeterminate technological innovations" (1997, 164). Certainly, cultural nostalgia is the result of a desire to return to simpler times. Although Gill is hesitant to agree with Frederic Jameson's implication that nostalgia is postmodern (163), he concurs that rapid technological progress is at the root of a modern nostalgia for simpler times. Reminders of these times, no longer limited to literature and music, trigger nostalgia through a variety of media and confuse the mind's understanding of linear time. The wholeness of post-trauma identity is perpetually threatened by the possibility of a simpler, pre-trauma space in the past. The very existence of this possibility—as well as the popularity of the time travel genre—is made possible through the alienating speed of technological progress.

The proliferation of means through which we can put the past within our grasps (such as photographs, television, and media on the internet) intensifies our awareness of the void it creates in our present. Gill's later assertion that "[t]he recent past, one that seems much simpler and slow and still (almost) graspable, becomes a reassuring construct that allows for a stabilizing self-definition in the present" (164) is important. Temporal prosthetics remove the parenthetical *almost* from Gill's statement, transforming a past understood *symbolically* as a lack into one interpreted *literally* as a physical place to which we can return. For Don Draper, time travel is less about physical location and more about emotional and psychic existence. This presentation of time travel anticipates (or rather, reflects) Landsberg's concept of "prosthetic memory." Prosthetic memories are "memories which do not come from a person's lived experience" (1995, 175). Landsberg uses the films *Total Recall* (1990) and *Blade Runner* (1982) as examples, arguing that prosthetic memories occur in reality when implanted by mass media. Interestingly, she takes issue with films that distinguish between "real" and "prosthetic" memories and present prosthetic memories as dangerous and false. For Landsberg, the importance of prosthetic memories, or any memories, is not in whether or not they come from actual lived experience, but in the ways in which they contribute to the formation of identity and self. She argues that memory and identity are intertwined—that our desire to distinguish between "real" and "prosthetic" memories is pointless. Memory, she argues, does not function in the past, but in the present: "memories are less about validating or authenticating the past than they are about organizing the present.... Memory ... is not a means for closure ... but on the contrary, memory emerges as a generative force, a force which propels us not backward but forwards" (176). The authenticity of a memory does not matter in this sense. What matters is the way in which memory—existing psychically in the past—impacts an individual's identity in the present. Landsberg helps us understand the connection between nostalgia and time travel as a compulsion rooted in memory.

Still, there exists a disconnect between the nostalgia of the present and the pain of the past that temporal prosthetics promise to repair. Nostalgia serves as a symbol of past pain in the present, but also as an unconscious drive to return to the site of traumatic loss. The temporal prosthetic, then, makes conscious that unconscious drive. Freud (2006) calls into question the prevalence of "forgetting," arguing that patients tend to "shut out" rather than forget trauma entirely. What Freud's patients shut out is precisely the ability to differentiate between past and present. In distinguishing between those who remember and those who do not, Freud explains that patients can recall "screen memories" through hypnosis, containing all "essential elements of the patient's childhood" (393). In subjects haunted by their pasts, progress in treatment depends on the analyst's ability to "identify the resistances ... and mak[e] the patient conscious of them" (391–92). By isolating and defining the nature of the patient's resistance, the analyst can help him or her conceive of ways to overcome repressed trauma.

Temporal prosthetics function psychically in a way similar to the analyst in Freud's account. The time travelers of *Safety Not Guaranteed*, Kenneth and Darius, hope to return to the past and undo the deaths of loved ones. They have direct knowledge of the traumatic event and the temporal prosthetic's function is straightforward. The film complicates this process in the case of its third main character, Jeff, a man who is not a time traveler, but whose nostalgic compulsion returns him to his hometown only to learn that some things are better remembered than re-experienced. In the case of Darius and Kenneth, a time machine removes the resistances preventing them from returning to the death of their loved ones. In Jeff, due to a lack of awareness about his compulsion to reclaim the past, what was lost remains unspoken and the wounds of loss prove more difficult to mend.

Likewise, Freud found that some patients cannot remember—that they require an additional step in treatment that makes traumatic memories accessible. These individuals, like Jeff, "act out" repressed memories through a "repetition compulsion," which "takes the place of the impulse to remember" (395). We see an unconscious compulsion to return to the past in both *The Butterfly Effect* and *Somewhere in Time*. In the former, Evan Treborn acts out the scene in which his father attempts to kill him as a young boy in the new realities that emerge when he attempts to fix the past. In the same way, *Somewhere in Time* presents a time traveler, Richard Collier, who is summoned to the past by a lover, Elise McKenna, years before he would ever know about their relationship. At the center of both *The Butterfly Effect* and *Somewhere in Time* we see a paradox: the requirement of action in the present *before* that which requires it in the past is realized.

An understanding of traumatic memory helps us to unravel this paradox. It is not dissimilar to the one described by Caruth: "Traumatic experience, beyond the psychological dimension of suffering it involves, suggests a certain paradox: that the most direct seeing of a violent event may occur as an absolute inability to know it; that immediacy, paradoxically, may take the form of belatedness" (1996, 91). If traumatic experience is not "fully assimilated as it occurs" (5), emerging instead in the survivor's unconscious attempts to "master what was never fully grasped in the first place" (62), it stands to reason that trauma is a prerequisite to time travel. Caruth argues that "[r]epetition ... is a history that is experienced as the endless attempt to assume one's survival as one's own" (64). In *The Butterfly Effect,* Evan realizes, in his numerous attempts to undo the series of traumas resulting from his father's attempt on his life, that *he* has a life to sacrifice for his friends. In *Somewhere in Time*, Richard lays claim to a love he never knew he had. In *Safety Not Guaranteed*, Darius and Kenneth embrace life in their journey to undo death. In each case, a trauma from the past causes pain in the present. This pain compels the time traveler to return to a repressed, forgotten, or not-yet-experienced physical space, a space in which the time traveler lays claim to his or her status as savior, lover, or survivor in the present.

Loss: Somewhere in Time

Time travel promises mastery, an ability to repair traumatic events by revisiting them and negating loss. The time traveler is in control and *chooses* when and where to visit. This control is not always apparent. In *Somewhere in Time* the protagonist, Richard, falls in love with the portrait of a woman at a hotel and, with some coaching, learns a process through which he can time travel using a form of self-hypnosis. He discovers he can travel back to a moment of his choosing if he induces a sleep-like state and removes all reminders of the present from his room. He succeeds and travels from 1980 to 1912 to meet Elise McKenna, the woman whose portrait ensnares him in the hotel lobby. His trauma—the loss of a love object—is not revealed until the end of the film. As Richard and Elise celebrate their love and its defiance of temporal barriers, attention turns to the time-appropriate suit Richard procured for his journey. He goes through its pockets and pulls out a penny minted in 1979, a violation of the means through which his presence in the past remains possible, resulting in physical pain and an immediate, traumatic return to the present. The events unfold in a way similar to the recovery of repressed memories: the space separating Richard and Elise, sixty-seven years, is meaningless. This lost love is as vivid to Richard in 1980 as it would be to a traumatized subject who uncovered a repressed trauma following any period of latency. Richard, as the survivor of loss, experiences physical and mental anguish following the recognition of this traumatic loss.

We do not want to suggest that *all* time travel narratives are the unconscious fantasies of traumatized subjects. Rather, when it comes to time travel and trauma, the real and the symbolic are reversible. But mastery almost always functions in a way that informs present identity. Ragland argues that "what appears in narrative accounts of trauma are the pathetic, suffering, passionate, and affective dimensions that literary language and genres have always sought to embody and recount" (2002, 75). The plot-structures in metaphysical time travel narratives correlate with the real in the shared processes of repetition and return. Ragland suggests that "art cannot be seen as separate from life, or as separable from a certain normal affectivity which is the very domain of literary language" (76). So, if we treat time travel narratives as real representations of trauma, we learn about the symbolic implications of time travel, and vice versa.

In *Somewhere in Time*, the only hint that Richard has of his impending trauma is a visit from a woman eight years prior to his traveling back in time. The woman, an older Elise he has yet to meet in his own narrative, hands him a watch and says, simply, "Come back to me." The event has already happened in 1912, but Richard, who will not travel back to meet Elise for another eight years, has *not yet experienced* it. The time travel narrative lends credence to the act of repression by physically—rather than emotionally and intellectually—postponing the experience of trauma. Repression, Ragland claims, "is not the repression of some base symbol, nor of a secondary reflective meaning. It is the repression of an actual event, doubled in an imaginary story, fleeting image, or vague affect. In other words, the symbol is realistic" (84). The *not-yet-experienced* loss for Richard is tantamount to the *not-yet-experienced* loss for the survivor of trauma. What's more, both parties find in themselves a compulsion to repatriate Caruth's "unclaimed experience," or the process of returning to the site of trauma and experiencing what was never experienced in the first place.

Memory: The Butterfly Effect

In *The Butterfly Effect* Evan uncovers repressed memories that include being filmed in a child pornographic film, watching helplessly as his friend Tommy murders his dog, Crocket, and witnessing another friend, Lenny, detonate a stick of dynamite in a mailbox, killing a young mother and her newborn child. However, it is the repression of meeting his father at an insane asylum, his father's subsequent attempt to kill him while yelling "you cannot play God," and witnessing him being bludgeoned to death by a guard, that transforms trauma into a compulsion to repeat for Evan. His childhood-self experiences blackouts that correspond with each of these events, symptoms that result in the prescription of journaling through his adolescent years. As an adult, reading this journal enables the protagonist to travel back to the moments in which the entries were written. While there, he inhabits his childhood body but can change the past. However, these changes have unintended consequences: Evan suffers from brain hemorrhaging as he assimilates decades of new timelines into his brain; things often change for the worse; and, in those timelines where mastery succeeds and things improve, Evan recreates the violence of his father's death and his own near-death in the lives of his loved ones.

Evan disrupts each new reality created through his ability to travel in time by unconsciously recreating the scene with his father at the asylum. Resolution of the subsequent traumas ceases to matter. In the "Director's Cut" Evan concludes that his only option is to return to the womb and end his life before it can begin. This decision appears to be informed by the "death drive," postulated by Freud as a "primal" effort to restore the subject to "an earlier state" (2011, 76). Freud proposes that repetition compulsion is closely tied to the death drive to explain how it bypasses the pleasure principle to work through trauma. Just as Freud finds in the word "uncanny" a dual meaning, containing at once "two sets of ideas, which are not mutually contradictory" (2003, 131)—"that species of the frightening that goes back to what was once well known and had long been familiar" (124)—repetition takes the subject back to repressed trauma to learn that, a traumatic loss or experience threatened the ego. More importantly, the ego survived the experience and can master it.

However, Evan sets his sights on the wrong traumatic experience in each visit to the past. Mastery cannot take place before the unknown goals of the death drive and repetition compulsion are made clear to the patient. In *The Butterfly Effect*, Evan fails to realize that his compulsion results from those formative experiences with his father. This early trauma leaves behind what Linda Belau calls the "internal determinant," allowing for trauma to occur in the psyche (2002, 168). She continues, "The compulsion to repeat, which drives the subject, is a compulsion to repeat a prior impossibility, an earlier state of things. This is the compulsion the subject suffers as the logic of its own impossible genesis, and it is where the misery comes from" (168). Evan is not *compelled* to repeat sexual abuse, the murder of his dog, or the accident that kills the young mother. He attempts to *master* them. The "impossibility" that ruins each timeline is not in the trauma he shares with his friends, but the trauma he shares with his father.

As Evan reads through his journal and uncovers a series of repressed traumas he never considers returning to the events that led to his father's death. Caruth claims that "the most direct seeing of a violent event may occur as an absolute inability to know it" (91) and, if this is the case, Evan fails "to know" that he survived his father's attempt to kill him. Instead, he acts out the repression in alternate timelines. In one sequence, Evan and Kayleigh's college romance is marred by her brother, Tommy. In rescuing Kayleigh from her pedophile father in one trip to the past, Evan tells the man, "Let's just say you're being closely watched, George.... You screw this up again, I'll flat-out castrate you. What you need to do is discipline your son Tommy, because the kid is one sadistic fuck." Evan levels judgment on Tommy in this instance, unaware that the previous timelines in which Tommy assumed the role of villain were tainted by *his own* trauma with his father. As a result, Tommy grows up the victim of abuse and resents Evan's romance with his sister. As adults, the two men find themselves face-to-face: "You ruined Lenny's life. You killed Crocket. You killed that woman and her baby. Now you're trying to kill me." Tommy assumes the role of Evan's father in the scene; Evan blames him for all of those things that began at the asylum. In his compulsion to repeat, the hero assumes the role of the guards, bludgeoning Tommy to death just as they did his father.

The role reversals in *Butterfly Effect* represent the aim of repetition compulsion. Ragland argues that this aim is "to reconstitute oneself as a being of consistency, recognizability, and unity; to reconstitute oneself as having a position or place within the symbolic and imaginary order of things and people" (2002, 100). Certainly, a number of traumas intersect in *The Butterfly Effect* and each character brings his or her need to work through childhood events to the film. However, Evan alone possesses the ability to travel in time.

Unfortunately, the initial trauma with his father does not figure into his attempts at mastery. As a result, escaping one trauma results in another visiting his friends. Such is the case with Lenny. When handed a metal shard to protect Crocket, he uses it to kill Tommy. Evan returns to the present and finds Lenny in an asylum and Kayleigh working as a drug-addicted prostitute. This scenario plays itself out again and again. Each time, Evan returns to the wrong site of trauma—the pedophile's basement, the junkyard where his dog is murdered, the mailbox containing a stick of dynamite—and fails to realize the elements of the original trauma playing themselves out in his actions and the lives of his friends.

All of Evan's actions are informed by a *compulsion to repeat* his father's death and his own survival in the timelines he creates. The traumatic event is unassimilable; it cannot take place within the traumatized subject's conception of reality. It is only in the beginning of the film, when repression maintains a fictionalized, but stable reality, that Evan is not controlled by this compulsion. Following the return to the asylum, and in the throes of repetition compulsion, the only outcome Evan can conceive of involves his own death. As Evan strangles himself on his mother's umbilical cord in the "Director's Cut," the viewer may be left wanting an alternative. These are provided in the two "Theatrical Endings" where Evan sabotages his first encounter with Kayleigh. In each ending, Evan lays claim to the life that the death drive asserts *should have* ended in the asylum, using it to save his friends at his own expense. Symbolically, by negating their death and suffering, Evan's compulsion to repeat concludes when he is unable save his friends in place of his father.

Nostalgia: Safety Not Guaranteed

Svetlana Boym writes that "[t]he nostalgic feels stifled within the conventional confines of time and space" (2001, xiv). Temporal prosthetics offer escape from these confines. They need not be time machines, but could also come in the form of a Kodak slide projector (*Mad Men*), hypnosis (*Somewhere in Time*), forgotten journals (*The Butterfly Effect*), or anything that can trace nostalgia back to its roots in the past. Boym describes the plight of the nostalgic as "the irreversibility of time that plagues the human condition," mirroring the compulsion of the time travelers we have examined "to revisit time like space, refusing to surrender" (xv). Nostalgia, which we have likened to the ache of an amputee's ghost limb, contains within in it the compulsion to create temporal prosthetics that reunite the time traveler with that which was lost at the historical site of trauma. Temporal prosthetics, like the artificial limb of the amputee, promise to make their creators whole.

According to David Mitchell and Sharon Snyder "[n]early every culture views disability as a problem in need of a solution" (222). The desire to "solve" disability rests in the belief that disability is an aberration of the natural condition: ability, or the *whole* body. Similarly, nostalgia posits that there was a time when everything was better and that a temporal prosthetic can take you there. These are both tempting myths. Temporal prosthetics, like physical prosthetics, represent a mastery over disability. The mind desires order and rationality, despite those being antithetical to actual lived experience. Just as the writers of *Mad Men* imitate societal nostalgia through the prostheses of their characters, who in turn propose a temporal prosthetic of their own in the Kodak slide projector, the time traveler in *Safety Not Guaranteed* is one who employs prosthetics in a myriad of ways to make himself whole.

The film begins not with the physical time traveler, Kenneth, but with apathetic protagonist Darius and her question: "How far back to you want me to go?" From there, she embarks on a nostalgic return through her college and high school years to the last time she was happy: childhood, before her mother died. Later, Darius acknowledges this pre-trauma past as her nostalgic locus, or the site of the void that compels her to return to the past. Darius' nostalgia is not one of space; she is physically at home. It is one of circumstance, of time. Such circumstance is the catalyst through which the director, Colin Trevorrow, endears her to the audience. Her disaffected nostalgia is universal; her affliction is the audience's affliction. In fact, the early portions of the film are structured around the development of Jeff, Darius' womanizing journalist boss. Like Darius, Jeff experiences the pull of nostalgia; unlike Darius, the object of his obsession is still alive and in the place he left her.

In many ways, Jeff's nostalgia is the most common. While Darius desires to return to a time before her mother died, Jeff simply wants to return to his hometown and into the arms of his childhood sweetheart, Liz. Jeff not only normalizes nostalgia, he also pathologizes it. When offered the opportunity to cover the story of Kenneth, a purported time traveler understood more as a joke or a meme by his magazine, Jeff is incredulous: "Who would not want to go back [in time]?" he asks his editor. This question sets the rest of the film in motion. The question behind *Safety Not Guaranteed* is this: How can anyone resist the lure of nostalgia-made-real?

Unfortunately, Jeff's return home is predictably depressing. Liz has aged, but Jeff, like the audience, finds himself caught in the fantasy that the past is graspable—that maybe, somehow, she exists in the present as he remembers her, that all of our pasts are still there, somewhere, as we remember them. Liz is an idea and, though Jeff is initially disappointed, he convinces himself to give his old flame a chance. Naturally, his courtship only leads to heartbreak.

Jeff's proposition to her that they should rekindle their relationship reveals a regression of the character: optimism and naiveté rule his choices. The fact that he is not viable in the present in this regressed state, however, forces him to recover from his compulsion to reclaim the past. He realizes there is no "home" waiting for him in Ocean View; that version of his hometown exists only in his mind.

Kenneth's need for a partner is what brings the reporters to Ocean City. He does not believe he can time travel (again) without another person's help. Both Darius and Kenneth choose to go back to the locus of their nostalgic compulsions. While Darius wants to save her mother, Kenneth wants to prevent the death of his girlfriend, Belinda. Unlike Jeff, Kenneth's temporal prosthetic makes his return "home" possible. The prosthetic becomes challenged, however, when Darius' investigation leads her to an alive-and-well Belinda. When she confronts Kenneth with Belinda's story, he reasons that his previous mission was successful: he saved Belinda's life by sacrificing the relationship. The temporal prosthetic in this view is functional, yet useless. It does not so much negate loss as it does disguise and relocate it. When Kenneth discovers that saving Belinda will force him to give her up, he realizes the danger of nostalgia. There is no "home" to which he can return. There was never a home to begin with. Like the fantasy of the whole, healthy and functional body, the past is a myth.

At one point, Darius discovers that Kenneth has a prosthetic ear. Kenneth panics and tries to cancel the time-traveling mission. When asked why he reacted so strongly, he simply tells her: "It's fake. My flippin' ear is fake." While this does not specifically answer Darius' question, it does point toward the connection Kenneth makes between his malfunctioning prosthetic and his ability to travel in time. For Kenneth, a perfectly functioning body is analogous to ability. When the truth of the prosthetic's past is exposed, it compromises its user in the present by revealing Kenneth's compulsion. What he learns, especially after acknowledging that Belinda is still alive, is that the past as he remembers it is not a place to which he can return. Kenneth's nostalgic pain is the impetus for his journey through time—the space in which the temporal prosthetic emerges—as well as a foundational part of his identity. This pain, if it is harnessed in a way that does not erase the past and, instead, appropriates it to chart a new future, allows the time traveler to move forward. When Kenneth tells Darius that his mission is "not just about a girl, it's about a time and a place" he rewrites the moment of trauma, creating a narrative in which Darius fills the void created in Belinda's absence, reconstituting a fragmented identity.

Conclusion: Generating Memories

At the conclusion of her essay on prosthetic memory, Landsberg suggests that *Blade Runner* and *Total Recall* show how "we should never forget" and "we should never stop generating memory" (1995, 187). In *Safety Not Guaranteed*, Darius *rewrites* rather than *repeats* her loss. The difference is that the former generates a new interpretation of that loss, defines it, and uses it to heal a damaged identity in the present. To replace or blot out the past by way of time travel would be to further disrupt that which is foundational to a whole self. This type of disruption haunts Evan's attempts to replace the past in *The Butterfly Effect*. In each attempt to replace memories in his notebook with new ones, relationships fundamental to his understanding of himself are perverted or destroyed. The delicate line that time travelers walk between past and present serves as a metaphor for the *connection* Landsberg sees between memory and identity. Her call to "never stop generating memory" asks us to understand identity as iterative, reflexive and fluid. Memory, then, is always capable of reinterpretation.

That compulsion that produces temporal prosthetics at first seems to reject notions of growth or progress. After all, to relive trauma is to experience pain. In *Somewhere in Time*, Richard, like Evan, fails to understand the true meaning of his loss. As he languishes over lost love, he recognizes the pain but is unable to see the potential also contained in those memories. That potential, which Caruth describes as an inherent aspect of any traumatic experience, is in the copious amounts of emotional detail traumatic memories carry into the present. Nostalgia, as Don Draper suggests, "aches" because of the intensity of those emotions. Traumatic memory is always present, and it is capable of being channeled by something as innocuous Evan's notebooks, Richard's painting from a hotel lobby, or Kenneth's prosthetic ear. These items, as real symbols of temporal prosthesis in each time traveler, represent the power of nostalgia. Our protagonists fail because they do not see how memory exists simultaneously in the present and the past. It could be that we need them to fail. Rather than the brand of redefinition found in *Safety Not Guaranteed*, we need characters like Evan and Richard to remind us of our own beautiful pain. Once reminded, we find ourselves capable of either traveling to the past (where we experience the doomed project of repeating loss), or to the future by reinterpreting it.

Try Again

The Time Loop as a
Problem-Solving Process in
Save the Date *and* Source Code

VICTOR NAVARRO-REMESAL *and*
SHAILA GARCÍA-CATALÁN[1]

The hero of the story has been there many times before and knows exactly what is going to happen. He has seen the girl die repeatedly and has failed to prevent each of these deaths. "There" is not a real place but a virtual reality that can be repeated and manipulated, a time loop that he needs to explore in order to obtain some vital information. Only with this will he be able to save the girl and achieve a happy ending.

This description fits both the film *Source Code* (2011) and the video game *Save the Date* (2013), two narratives that feature a closed, repeatable and editable period of time. There are many variations of the time loop, but these two works illustrate the basic principles of the trope.

Source Code is a mainstream Hollywood movie that can be framed in the trend of "mind-game" films (Elsaesser 2009), complex narratives that aim to challenge the viewer with the construction of their narratives. *Save the Date* belongs to the visual novel genre, whose games are composed mainly of static screens and text descriptions, in which the player is frequently presented with several options to choose from. Both works are clearly inspired by *Groundhog Day* (1993), a movie in which the main character relives the same day multiple times, and both add layers of complexity typically associated with their genres, trends and media to the time loop trope.

While *Groundhog Day* keeps the causes of the time loop deliberately vague, these two stories make its mechanisms and logic explicit. The virtual space of the time loop becomes a playground where the hero can use specific tools and techniques to solve a mystery. Diegetically, the time loop becomes a problem-solving process; extradiegetically, it reveals the inner workings of the media formats and genres of these stories in a metadiscursive manner. Through our analysis in this chapter, both of these aspects offer useful insight into the nature of both media—films and video games.

The time loop is similar to, yet different from, circular time travel stories, where the traveler's actions in the past are the causes of the travel itself in the future, as in *The Terminator* (1984) or *Timecrimes* (2007). These loops are unchanging and self-originating, whereas the time loop is constantly rewritten, as in Richard A. Lupoff's short story "12:01 PM" (1973) or *Groundhog Day*. Every time a certain condition is met—the clock reaches a particular time, someone dies—time bounces back to where the loop began, but someone retains memories of the previous repetitions and can alter the chain of events. As there are no real consequences to their actions, this traveler can learn about the repeated events using trial and error, but their achievements within the loop are lost when it resets. The traveler usually has only one way out: to acquire knowledge. Memory is the sole means of progression.

Both the loop traveler and the audience witness the chain of events many times, memorizing and learning from them. Both need to focus on the differences caused by the protagonist's actions as well as the constants, obsessively running through the same scene again and again to unravel its mysteries. This way of presenting the narrative as a puzzle is typical of mind-game films and can be linked to Ryan's observations about the aesthetics of interactivity (2004, 34). For her, while the aesthetics of immersion present the text as a world, interactivity configures the text as a game, language as something to be played with and the reader or audience member as a player. Time loops allow the media producer to build complex narratives that can be seen both as worlds and games. The narrative use of the time loop therefore combines time travel tropes with the very ways in which texts are consumed and contemporary trends in narrative. It establishes a strict internal logic and a self-referential deconstruction of the nature of narration.

The Narratives of Source Code *and* Save the Date

For our analysis, we first need to delineate the nature of the time loops depicted in our two case study texts. *Source Code* follows Colter Stevens, an amnesiac soldier caged in some kind of pod or machine that connects his mind to the Source Code, an abstract technology that can recreate portions of the past and project someone's consciousness into them. The researchers in charge of the machine use it to recreate the bombing of a train and order Stevens to take on the role of Sean Fentress, a passenger on that train, to find the person responsible. The recording of the past lasts for eight minutes and can be repeated as many times as he wishes, but there is a clear deadline: the terrorist will act again in a matter of hours. Fentress' time is frozen and malleable; Stevens' is dominated by a sense of urgency.

Unknown to Stevens, the pod is, in fact, another virtual space. He is actually connected to a life support machine and his mind is alternating between two fake realities. While in the Source Code, he begins to fall in love with Christina Warren, Fentress' traveling partner. Love, as in other postmodern fictions, such as *Lost* (2004–2010), acts as the constant in an inconstant time. Although the creators of the Source Code refer to it as a simulation and not actual time travel, Stevens sets out to change the past, stop the bomber and save the girl. In a final repetition of the loop, he manages to do so, creating an alternative timeline and a happy ending for the narrative in which he is alive and well, Christina is saved and they start a new life together.

Save the Date is a much smaller work. It is a short piece written and designed by one author, Chris Cornell, and distributed freely online, so it can be seen as part of the current trend of independent and experimental games created outside the dominant production houses of the media industry. In this game, the player starts in her or his bedroom picking up the phone. A conversation with a girl called Felicia ensues: the player's avatar has previously arranged a date with her and they discuss the details. They can go to several restaurants and, in each one of them, some hazard will appear out of nowhere, killing the girl in progressively more complicated ways.

The game needs to be played more than once for the complete text to be revealed. It makes use of a technique called persistent data: the system registers the player's choices and opens up new choices deriving from them. If the girl dies because she is allergic to peanuts, the player can warn her against eating them next time. In order to advance to its final stages, more than one playthrough is required. That is, the girl needs to die several times. There is initially no narrative path that leads to the girl surviving the events at the different restaurants, but the player can question her to open up new options and convince her that they are inside a video game. A metanarrative conversation starts; the girl asks about the game's look and design and questions the player's motivations for playing, as well as the designer's for creating such a story.

At the end of that dialogue, the girl talks about the nature of stories and narrative and encourages the player to quit the game and make up her or his own happy ending. If the game is not turned off, she dies again. The only way to end the game with her surviving is to cancel the date at the very beginning or to use a cheat that opens up a parody of happy endings, including unicorns and crystal castles. The player can play as many times as she or he wants with no limit, but the text is not infinite. When every option has been activated, the only choices left are to relive the date and kill the girl again, cheat or reject the story by quitting the game.

Time Loop Machines

Most stories about time travel involve some means for such travel, whether these are magical, scientific, or metaphysical, and a logic system, however vague, behind those means. Stevens talks to the scientists behind the Source Code and discusses the technology with them. They reluctantly give him more information, to the point where he knows about the two virtual spaces: the train and his pod. As we already mentioned, this complicated set of realities links *Source Code* with the wave of "thrillers of the mind" that question our notions of reality and our perception of it, such as *Memento* (2000), *Open Your Eyes* (1997) and *Shutter Island* (2010). These films present a deceptive and complicated narrative in which the author uses the film as a "scene of the game" (Sorolla and García-Catalán 2013, 113) and acts as a schemer who develops his trick, as in the case of *Source Code*, around a detailed set of rules. Even the twist at the end, that the Source Code is a parallel universe where events can be changed, is built around the specifics of the imagined technology. Stevens is just a pawn; he has no control over the machine and needs to negotiate with its operators to be sent back one more time once his main mission is completed to try to save the girl.

Save the Date does not feature a time machine at all. Instead, the existence of the previous repetitions of the date is acknowledged by simply stating that it is a game. The player can explain that he knows what is to come because "I reloaded from a saved game." In the final moments of the game, this idea is reprised and expanded as the characters try to find a way to "beat the game." The game itself is the time machine; its menus and mechanics allow the traveler to go back to the time loop. The "Start Game" and "Load Game" options on the main title screen are the time machine's buttons. Since these are common elements in many video games, this implies that they are all, in fact, time loops. To understand these "time loop machines," we have to explore the nature and limits of represented time in film and video games.

The repetition of events is a mandatory part of how many video games are played, not least since characters die and sections must be tried again. Designers are bound by it but, at the same time, can explore this dynamic and its limits to create meaning. The power of the designers lies in the rules they build and the freedom of the players in exploring the limits set by them. In this way, video games are discourses of "directed freedom" (Navarro 2013, 33). They are cyber-texts, systems capable of generating multiple discourses depending on the player's actions. There is a constant dialogue between designers and players.

If the designer is akin to a demiurge acting in the shadows, *Save the Date* makes him visible by pointing at him and questioning his motives. It is not, however, the first game to allow some kind of manipulation of time. *Braid* (2008) is famous for its various mechanics concerning time, especially the ability to rewind freely. In *Prince of Persia: The Sands of Time* (2003) the rewind mechanic depends on a finite resource, the titular sands, and the player needs to collect more sand to be able to escape death. *Catherine* (2011) grants the player the ability to undo his last move. *The Legend of Zelda: Majora's Mask* (2000) features probably the most famous time loop in video games: the world will end in three days and, when this happens, the player can go back to the first day to attempt to avert the disaster again. They can also slow time down or speed it up. In *Superhot* (2013), a first-person shooter, time only advances when the player moves, turning its shootouts into intricate puzzles.

Time transforms the relationship between the player and the video game, between the consumer and the consumed. The idea of time was vital in the constitution of photography and cinema as media and visual arts, and video games have given it their own twist. All art forms based on time have to manage the duality of the viewer's time and represented time, or the time of their fictional worlds. Juul (2004, 131) talks about play time, "the time used by the player to play the game," and event time, "the time of the events in the game." Video games have turned event time into something to experiment with, as explorable as space. Time, then, loses familiarity and becomes sinister, in a Freudian sense, as Sherlock (2012, 84) states. It was something that we used to perceive as familiar, but not anymore. Time, explains Sherlock, depends on "its own representation in the game" (80) and can become "a controllable good" (77). There is a distancing and an estrangement between natural time and the gaming idea of time. Every video game is a series of events that the player can repeat, explore and experiment with to some extent, but only some of them turn this manipulation of time into what Sherlock refers to as "a narrativized fact" (77). Only some games acknowledge this manipulation of time and integrate it in their narrative. The repetition of events in *Save the Date* is acknowledged and consequently, "narrativized."

While films are not traditionally designed to be interactive, time is no less important in them. Film time is not constricted by natural time and film-makers can speed it up, slow it down, invert it, repeat it, break its linearity and so forth. The deconstruction and estrangement of time, both as a narrative and a formal element, seems to be a main trait of "mind-game films," as can be seen in *Memento* or *Inception* (2010). The first movie builds its plot by inverting the natural order of events, while the second one uses multiple realities or "dreams within dreams" where time passes at different speeds. The interpretation of the time of the story and the plot in these films is not interactive, but it demands an effort from the viewer and poses a challenge. The viewer is never completely passive. The text, as Ryan (2004, 34) affirms, can be seen as a puzzle, a riddle or a game, and that is clear in "mind-game films."

Source Code is quite straightforward in its formal use of time and states its diegetic rules clearly, but its main concept forces a rupture of natural time. The movie makes use of editing to show each repetition of the train incident. There are seven recurrences of the simulation and none is as long as the full eight minutes that we are told the events in the film take. The longest one is seven minutes and thirty seconds. Certain small events are shown several times to reinforce the notion of a repeated loop, but most of them are ignored in the later journeys, following a standard sense of rhythm and narrative economy in mainstream Hollywood films. It can be argued that the filmmakers are exploring time, skipping the previously seen parts of the loop and focusing on the changes, just as *Save the Date* allows the player to skip messages that have already been seen and highlights unseen parts. In both cases, story events are filtered and re-arranged to create an interesting plot.

Source Code shows several limits to its time: firstly, the duration of the simulation; secondly, the next terrorist attack, which serves to provide a countdown and a deadline; and thirdly, from a formal point of view, the film's running time. It has a clear sense of linearity as a narrative as it moves towards the next bomb attack. As a formal discourse, it is also linear: a film is an object with a more or less foreseeable length and an end in sight. *Save the Date*, on the other hand, allows the player to go back to the date as many times as he wants. Each play session usually lasts for approximately five minutes and all the branches can be seen in less than two hours, but there is no diegetic time limit to add urgency since the player can explore the narrative at his own pace. There is no climax, closing credits or other marks that indicate that the narrative is over, so the linearity of this game is much weaker than in a film. The time loop in *Save the Date*, just like its plot, never actually ends.

The Time Loop as a Thematic Element

Thus far we have studied how time and the time loop work in *Source Code* and *Save the Date*, but what do they use these devices for? What thematic elements are associated with the time loop in these texts?

Narrative traditionally depends on conflict. The idea of a hero overcoming obstacles, fixing problems and solving mysteries lies at the heart of many tales. Where there is a story, the audience expects there also to be a problem and a reward for overcoming it. When a viewer or player is presented with a time loop, she can assume that there is something wrong in that chain of events that can be corrected and that there is a reason why it needs to be repeated. There cannot be a tomorrow, or even a today, until the past is fixed. Phil, the main character in *Groundhog Day*, escapes the time loop by helping everyone and maturing. In *Source Code*, in addition to stopping the bombing, Stevens takes on a self-imposed mission, to save Christina, find a way to live his life with her and prove that time can be changed. The hero, then, does not have a single mission, he has three: to save the world, the girl and himself. In *Save the Date*, there is nothing forcing the player to experience the loop again and again. The "game over" screen reads: "The End. Your date has ended in disaster." Not "Try again" or even "You failed." However, everything seems to point to a personal mission that can be completed with a positive result. The title itself can be seen as an imperative. Video games show virtual conflicts and have end states or, at least, desired states that have a positive or negative value. In *Save the Date*, however, there is no traditional happy ending. Felicia keeps dying to provide the player with a conflict. The only ways to save her are either to stop playing or to walk away from the date. She points to the existence of a designer who takes advantage of the audience's interpretation of a time loop as the repetition of a terrible event that needs to be prevented.

This presumption turns these stories into cycles of death that have to be stopped. Time, as Derrida argues, cannot be separated from metaphysics (in Sherlock 2012, 71). Time is what our existences are made of and death is the end of time. This is "one of the major phenomena of repetition, one of the essential norms of the cyclical construction of being and societies" (Balló and Pérez 2005, 147). The time loop creates a rhetoric of repetition based on the notion of limits and their constant negotiation. Time and death are immovable, but the idea of a time loop dismantles and diminishes them. If time is not definitive, we can fantasize about changing it and its limit, death. If the girl dies within the time loop, we can take on the mission to save her and take her out of the loop alive. Each death of the girl is a failure and also a reminder of this mission. In the seventh and final repetition of the loop, Stevens proves that the past can indeed be changed: all the knowledge gained from his previous trips through the time loop can be applied to avert the tragedy. The painful events that happened are now the painful events that would have happened. Tragedy serves as a reminder of the importance of the hero's presence.

Almost every journey through time in *Source Code* and *Save the Date* ends with one or more deaths, but this is just a motivation to try again and make things right the next time. Death is only real if the present is the only time we can live in. As García-Catalán explains, "Present time is the time of responsibility: only in it can we decide and accept our actions" (2012, 331). In video games, the importance of player actions makes the present more evident and undeniable. Video games are the domain of the present and films, even if they are perceived as present time, seem to point to an unchangeable and recorded past. In video games, the tragedy is happening before the player's eyes; the passive spectator has to become the active savior.

Juul (2013, 115) writes about the paradox of failure in video games. Players accept failure or "unpleasant experiences (for ourselves or for fictional characters)" because they compare their short-term frustration with the pleasures of the long-term success that comes with mastering skills (2013, 116). The player is made responsible for the fate of the world and its inhabitants since "failure connects us personally to the events in the game; it proves that we matter, that the world does not simply continue regardless of our actions" (2004, 122). This responsibility is stronger in video games than in other narrative forms because "regular non-interactive stories shield us from responsibility in a way that games do not" (2004, 117). However, if the past can be corrected so easily, players can feel responsible only for the final end state of the game, not the minute-to-minute events. Failure within a closed system of rules implies that this system can be understood and its mechanics mastered. It implies the promise of a happy ending. Near the end of *Save the Date*, Felicia tells the player, "You seem convinced that it's even possible to 'win' this game," and one of the available answers is "There is kind of an implicit contract, when someone gives you a puzzle, that it has a solution." Freed from the uniqueness of the events and with multiple chances to find this solution, the loop traveler can become trapped by his own obsession and the impulse to give it another try after each defeat. If the events can be rearranged, the loop traveler can—or so it seems—produce the best of all possible worlds.

Since death in these stories can be theoretically averted, we can separate it in two categories: temporary death, the kind the hero faces during his many trials and errors, and final death, the one that closes a story. The player in *Save the Date* has to see Felicia killed many times to learn how to save her. There is a sense of instrumentality to the interactions with the girl. The player tests the causes and consequences of the loop using trial and error, while Felicia's death loses importance because it is seen as temporary, a learning process leading towards the positive end state, where final death will be averted. This can be connected with the game designer Daniel Cook's (2007) idea that games are played in skill atoms, "self-contained atomic feedback loops" that teach a new skill and are connected in "skill chains." Video games do not progress in a linear fashion but through repetition and the accumulation of knowledge. The time loop seems to favor this same logic. Stevens never accepts death as final and keeps trying to save Christina. In virtual spaces, death becomes, as Klastrup (2007) states, "a non-event, as natural almost as breathing" and the same could be applied to time loops. The hero keeps indirectly killing the girl on each journey and she keeps being reborn.

Saving the girl at first seems to undo all her previous deaths, but both the game and the film avoid this assumption. *Save the Date* keeps score of all the times and the ways Felicia has died and the ending of *Source Code* seems to imply that each journey to the simulation creates a new timeline, one that does not cease to be once Stevens leaves it. Even though the protagonist and the viewer want to believe that the "happy ending" is the only real ending, both works seem to consider each loop as a valid telling of their stories. They do not replace one other but coexist in displaced time. The loop journeys can be considered as an eternal limbo of multiple, equally valid realities inhabited by the ghosts both the player and Stevens left behind when they returned to the time of the living.

Another thematic element of great importance in both narratives is memory and, to be exact, its persistence. When time is periodically rebooted in time loop stories such as *Groundhog Day, Source Code* and *Save the Date*, the only changes that can be preserved are memories. All the protagonist's actions will be undone; only the knowledge he has gained will remain. Memory, then, is the only key to solving the problems of the time loop. In *Source Code*, Stephen's memories are routinely erased. Stevens is an amnesiac hero, a trope widely used in postmodern fiction such as *Eternal Sunshine of the Spotless Mind* (2004). Amnesiac heroes are often the result of experiments with the brain, mental illnesses, virtual realities or altered states of the mind. This can be seen as a product of the neuroscientific thinking of our age and the rise of digital environments. We question reality because we can alter it. If our memories, as empirical evidence, are our personal compasses in this new worldview, losing them or finding out that they are fake, as in *Blade Runner* (1982) or *Dark City* (1998), makes us doubt our own identity.

Amnesia in *Source Code* works as a starting point, a thematic substrate and a plot device that articulates the narrative as a quest towards the discovery of oneself. It changes completely the way Stevens navigates the time loop and even the way he understands himself. This opens up a new opportunity. As Balló and Pérez claim, "The protagonist's amnesia gives us the chance to imagine, for a while, one of the hidden possibilities of every fiction: the adventure of constructing an alternative personality" (2005, 111). Only when Stevens starts remembering pieces of his previous travels to the loop, does he have the opportunity to understand the loop, anticipate its events and, more importantly, work towards his personal freedom. The exploration of the time loop, and the escape from it, allows Stevens to rebuild himself, not as the soldier he was but as another person, Sean Fentress, with a new life. The time loop becomes, as in *Groundhog Day*, a space where the protagonist can explore himself and build a better self. Stevens conquers the time loop, his memory and his self.

In *Save the Date*, the protagonist is very vaguely characterized. He does not have a name or even a gender. The "avatarness" in this game, or the way the player is functionally and fictionally embodied within the game (Navarro 2013, 36), aims to put no distance between the player and the role she takes when playing. The main character's memory, just like the character itself, is irrelevant to the loop. What is important is what the player remembers and especially the fact that Felicia does not. There is no need for an amnesiac character since the player is the one acting within the time loop. The conflict and its solution depend on Felicia's memory. The use of persistent data allows the player to use the information obtained in previous plays to convince her that they are inside a time loop. The file where the game and its persistent data are saved is, as Sherlock (2013, 79) states, "a personal history of the player that is rewritten as the game is played," an extradiegetic element, a piece of the digital stage machinery that exists behind the fiction, which the designer uses to direct the plot and structure of the game. However, since the game uses time as a "narrativized fact," it becomes a part of the plot too and helps the player prove there have been previous plays. Felicia never remembers these previous plays and, at the end of the game, after every frustrated attempt to change her fate, she encourages the player to end his pursuit and make up his own ending for their story. In this regard, she is asking the player to conquer his memory more than Stevens ever does, by creating his own fake memories.

Thematically, both works reflect on the nature of drama and narrative conflict, the importance of death and the relationship between memory and identity.

The Time Loop as a Meta-Discursive Element

We have analyzed the mechanisms of the time loop as a narrative and structural device and its thematic integration in *Source Code* and *Save the Date*. In this section, we take a closer look at the way these aspects collide to reveal the nature of the media and genre of these two works.

Source Code uses the time loop as the center of a recognizable thriller structure. It is, at heart, a detective story. Such stories always demand a constant return to a major event that needs to be clarified: the time loop makes this return literal. Stevens travels to the crime itself and inspects it from within, not unlike the way Deckard inspects photographs in *Blade Runner*, Edward Lyle looks at surveillance footage in *Enemy of the State* (1998) or Alan Hakman reviews recordings of an entire life in *The Final Cut* (2004). The analysis of the crime from within articulates the management of knowledge. In *Source Code*, the clues are not objects or recollections by witnesses, but the actual memories of the victims: the time loop acts as the main tool for the investigation.

This conjunction of traditional detective stories and postmodern tropes is one of the defining elements of the mind-game films. In them, the formal aspects of the narrative, and not the case, are the main mystery, and they are planted with clues and red herrings that the viewer has to find in a kind of game with the narrator, "a silent enunciation that plots against the spectator" (García-Catalán and Sorolla 2013). The narrative traits of the thriller are, somehow, "narrativized": the Source Code simulation is a text that Stevens reads and analyzes in search of meaning, as the viewer analyzes postmodern films. When trying to figure out where he is, he even comments on the plausibility of the scene, telling Christina that she is the pretty girl and that "there is always one." Talking to himself, he states that "they" would not put his target in front of him, referring to some unknown demiurges behind everything, as if he were wondering about his story's author. He seems to be questioning reality as a constructed, archetypal fiction. If the virtual realities are considered different diegeses, some lines can be considered as metalepses, ruptures of the fourth wall, as when Stevens hits a passenger and affirms "It's OK, he's no more real than you are." He even has some spectators within the film—his supervisors are watching him—with whom he debates the events and authenticity of each layer of reality. This film is not only a genre piece, but also a deconstruction of the genre tropes.

However, all these nuances do not change the thriller as a genre, nor do they negate the spectator's willing suspension of disbelief and acceptance of fiction. On the contrary, even the simulated worlds end up being real, and the possible worlds of the narrative prevail. The nature of fiction and reality is questioned but remains unchanged. In this way, *Source Code* updates the thriller by taking it into the realm of the "thriller of the mind" and reaffirms its validity by proving that it can accommodate postmodern ideas and anxieties.

Save the Date uses the traditional structure of a visual novel, with the addition of persistent data, to present a reflection on narrative in games, happy endings and player motivations. The player can try to save Felicia as many times as he wants, effectively becoming trapped in the loop not by an automatic reboot or the pressure of external agents, but by his own obsession. As Felicia says, "You've already been mangling the story by reloading, restarting, and undoing your choices after you see where they lead." She tries to understand the idea behind the game by reflecting about "how stories work": in her opinion, a story "lives in the brain of whoever's listening to it." Narrative is a collaborative effort between a narrator and a listener who pretends to believe the story and its world. Narrative in video games, Felicia affirms, is even more collaborative, and she encourages the player to quit the game and imagine his own ending. If he does so, his role in the game is expanded and the demiurge disappears, giving the floor to the player. The directed freedom of video games becomes complete freedom and the player's responsibility is not in his actions any more, but in his imagination, in his mind, in the memories of Felicia's fate that he decides to create. *Save the Date*, then, is a deconstruction of the dynamics of video games and visual novels and it encourages the player to position himself within the process of the creation of the narrative.

Conclusions

Source Code and *Save the Date* both are built around a time loop, the death of a girl, the quest to avoid it and memory as the only way to accomplish this. Their loops are not automatic but rather depend on a mission, on a sense of responsibility and the promise of a positive outcome. These texts adapt these ideas to the particular features of their media and contexts. *Source Code* is a mainstream film with postmodern traits, but it still follows well-established narrative patterns and tropes, tying everything in its plot together by the end. It may test the validity of the possible worlds and accepted realities of fiction, but in the end the test is passed. There is a logic to the loop and an "official" escape. *Save the Date*, on the other hand, is built around the notion of a problem that is unsolvable no matter how many times we try to fix it. Even more than in *Source Code*, the loop is a space of ghosts and obsessions. If the player refuses the date after having seen the invading aliens—the last major threat that can kill Felicia—the final messages affirm that this is, perhaps, the best option, and a closing title appears: "The (or at least an) End." This is the only solace the player can take, the only "official" closure that he can achieve, and it seems deliberately unsatisfactory. The time loop and its resolution in *Source Code* renew the way stories are consumed, but *Save the Date*'s loop invites us to embrace stories by accepting that they are not real. We have described how the time loop works in both cases as a narrative device and as a catalyst of contemporary thematic elements. The exploration of time, narrative events and space within these time loops allows the audience to reflect on the way stories are told and the importance of their role as consumers. If the storyteller is the true architect of the loop, the viewer or player is its active explorer.

Note

1. This study has been carried out with the help of the Universitat Jaume I-Bancaja Research Project entitled "Anhis a del videojuego" code 111301.01 / 1, during the period 2012–14 under the direction of Dr. Javier Marzal Felici. The authors would like to thank Ana Burguera and Simon Berrill for their revisions and corrections.

A Stitch in Time

Film Costume as a Narrative Tool Beyond Time Linearity

ELENA TRENCHEVA *and*
SOFIA PANTOUVAKI

Time travel is about transporting bodies through time: bodies that are naked or en-cultured through costume to construct identities. Joanne Entwistle (2000, 326) writes that "conventions of dress transform flesh into something recognizable and meaningful to a culture and are also the means by which bodies are made 'decent,' appropriate and acceptable within specific contexts." The appropriate dress en-cultures the body, putting it into boundaries of behavioral manners, restrictions and freedoms created by a specific society. A culturally determined garment imposes on the body active signifiers to delineate an identity, because "costume assimilates bodily signifiers into character, but body as a whole engulfs the dress" (Gaines 1990, 193). The interplay between the presence or absence of costume and the way it connects to the body to express identity in time travel film is the focus of this chapter.

According to Geoff King, "time travel broadens the visual scope of science fiction because it allows its stars to be shown in various costume styles and interacting with important historical events. This tends to reduce history to simply a difference in visual style that is often figured in terms of film genre conventions" (2000, 26–27). Body representation and costume play an essential role in time travel narratives, a role which has not yet been addressed in depth. Britton (1999) addresses the authorship of the costume designer in the TV series *Doctor Who* (1963–1989, 1996 and 2005–present) in his article "Dress and the Fabric of the Television Series." In "Fashioning Masculinity and Desire," Gilligan (2010) focuses on the central role costume plays in relation to representations of masculinity, gendered identity and sexuality in *Torchwood* (2006–2011). Sobchack (1999), Jenssen (1987) and Trencheva (2009) critically address costume in science fiction from different perspectives, but none of them traces its functions in time travel film. Separate time travel films are critically analyzed in themed volumes and specialized articles, but costume stays marginal to these accounts. Among these, the collective volume of critical essays on *Back to the Future*, *The Worlds of Back to the Future: Critical Essays on the Films* (Ní Fhlainn 2010) also omits discussion of costume.

In this essay, we aim to explore costume in time travel films as a narrative tool beyond time linearity. We argue that the meaning and importance of costume in time travel films exceed the portrayal of a character on screen or the creation of stylistic dissimilarity in the style of attire worn by the character in different periods. Costume—or its absence in some cases—plays a crucial part in time travel narratives by pointing to the passing of and through time. Exploring the functions of costume as a character delineator and a tool for supporting narrative progress, we utilize concepts of time travel and identity developed by David Lewis to frame our discussion. We employ Lewis' concept about "discrepancy between time and time" (1976; 145)—the two types of time referring to the duration of the travel and the distance traveled in time—to describe how persistency and change in costume underline time travel by creating visual discrepancies.

In addition, we expand on the notion of *continuity* (Lewis 1983) to argue that in order to pictorialize a journey through time, the time traveler's costume usually violates the practice of continuity through which the different psychophysical states of a person are causally connected. This chapter is about how bodies traveling through time interact with costume in versatile ways to embody specific meanings. Our aim is to point out different costume design practices that support the time travel process as depicted within the story, and to analyze the different functions costume acquires in relation to the narrative. The costume-body interaction incorporates signifiers associated with the time's politics, ideologies, economies and social life, reinforcing the critique embodied by the narrative towards reality. We trace this signifying function in three emblematic films. To set the basic function of costume in relation to the traveling body we analyze *The Time Machine* (1960) as a seminal film. We employ the binary opposition of change and persistency to highlight how costume signifies the act of time travel, how it enhances the "discrepancy between time and time" (Lewis 1976, 145), and how it connects to the traveler's body to underline certain character traits according to the narrative. Other films we examine reflect the political climate of the time in which they were created: the *Back to the Future* trilogy (1985, 1989, 1990) and *The Terminator* (1984). In these films costume is a visual representation of two types of masculinity strongly associated with the ideology of the Reagan Era, which according to Jeffords (2010, 156), "depended on the successful reproduction of certain images and definitions of masculinity." Therefore, our study introduces three concepts of the body and costume in time travel films: (i) costume as an agent of persistency/continuity, which is crucial in understanding the move forwards or backwards in time, examined through *The Time Machine*; (ii) the naked body as "nude costume" revealing connotations beyond sexual desire and indicating the hyper-muscular male, an embodiment of force freed from clothing-related representation, analyzed through *The Terminator*; and (iii) costume as time homogenizer and time spatializer, examined through the teenage protagonist of the *Back to the Future* trilogy.

Identifying Costume and Time Travel

Depending on the type of time travel and the means of accomplishing it, we can identify different kinds of time and travel relationships in narratives: inactive, recurring, and active time travel. In inactive time travel the main character is hypnotized, falls asleep, recalls the past or experiences flashbacks, as in *Somewhere in Time* (1980), or *Peggy Sue Got Married* (1986). The protagonist dresses consciously (*Somewhere in Time*) or unconsciously (*Peggy Sue Got Married*) to find themselves in a certain past period. Self-hypnosis as a travel method, incorporated in *Somewhere in Time*, requires high concentration and a sharp focus on the point in the past the traveler wants to reach. It requires appropriate clothing to dissociate the traveler's body entirely from the present and to foster impulses and associations, helping the mind to travel back in time. In *Peggy Sue Got Married*, if Peggy was not dressed for a retro party, she would barely fit so well in the 1960s.

In recurring time travel the characters are transferred through time recurrently until they find a solution to a problem, as in *The Butterfly Effect* (2004) and *Midnight in Paris* (2011). Their travel is not shown or explained. Costume helps the audience to identify a certain time in the past of the protagonist to which he/she is transferred. Waking every morning in the same hotel bed, wearing the same pajamas, or the same costume during the day, indicates the repetitive events in *Groundhog Day* (1993). In *12:01* (1993) the whole world loops and experiences the same day recurrently except the protagonist, who gets an electricity shock which pushes him out of the loop. The different costume he wears on each different morning underlines that he is the only one who knows what is happening.

Active time travel films portray characters who literally travel through time. These narratives are usually situated in the domain of science fiction. A main characteristic of the genre is that it often builds its stories by extrapolating and exaggerating contemporary mass fears, trends and problems and finds an illusory solution to them. Thus, active time travel stories try to foster understanding of contemporary problems by depicting the past or future through a journey in time in which a hero experiences, explores and finds a solution to a range of issues. In films of this kind, costume and body actively signify time travel in different ways. Some bodies travel naked, leaving behind uninhabited clothes (*The Time Traveler's Wife*, 2009) or en-culturing the character through acquired clothes (*The Terminator*); others use special costumes that support the travel (*Looper*, 2012) or fit in with the visited time (*The Time Tunnel*, 1966–1967). Regardless of the different design practices, the process of time traveling is underlined by persistency in the traveler's appearance.

Costume Change and Continuity as Time Travel Indicators: The Time Machine

In the original novella *The Time Machine* (1895), H. G. Wells presented his vision of the future of mankind as a satirical commentary on British society: the protagonist builds a time machine and, driven by curiosity, travels to the distant future to find a socially degraded world. In *The Time Machine*, producer-director George Pal adheres to the time in which the book was written by embodying the aesthetics of Victorian England in the film's interiors, exteriors, and costumes to underline the temporal distances and the passage of time. The Victorian aesthetic in costume serves the narrative on several levels: it defines the period in which the film's action initially takes place by relying on culturally determined codes and underlines that the traveler is out of his time by embodying particular mores and imposing certain actions and constraints on his body. To make the unbelievable story about time travel believable, its visual elements have to have some connection with the prior knowledge of the audience, with some stereotypical notions they already have about Victorian society. Thus the costume following the aesthetics of Victorian fashion prepares the audience for a fictional story and, at the same time, gives the film the needed verisimilitude—the conventional historical costume is used to create a notion of credibility.

In general, costume design practice conforms to the notion of *continuity* as a device for supporting the progress of narrative time and temporal time in a credible way through a gradual change in a character's appearance. Continuity supports the flow of a story in showing, for example, the aging of a character, the passing of time, and the development in the story from point A to point B. In these cases, costume is characterized by continuity even if it actually changes; it is not the specific visual form but the concept behind the costume that transfers ideas about who a person is.

Costume also reflects changes in the psychophysical condition of a character. If a character experiences a new situation, this is often shown in the change of costume. The change in time is inevitable due to the world we live in. In the same way, if something that leads to a change in the state of identity happens in a story, it is often visually reflected through a change in costume.

As a tool for recognizing this shift, costume functions as a "bond of similarity" and a "bond of lawful causal dependence" (Lewis 1983, 55–56). These concepts are developed by Lewis in arguing that the successive mental states of a person have *connectedness*, as "direct relations of similarity and causal dependence between my present mental state and each of its successors," and *continuity*, as "the existence of step-by-step paths from here to there, with extremely strong local connectedness from each step to the next" (1983, 56). These notions ensure a connection and gradual change in the appearance of the different psychophysical states of an individual. Analyzing costume in film, Gaines (1990, 196) points out that "narrative realism dictates that costume be curtailed by conventional dress codes; continuity requires that it be monitored for the telltale continuity error; economy requires that it reinforces causality." All these requirements are violated in the costume of the time traveler.

The time traveler's costume disconnects from its causal dependence, since the cause and effect processes that impose changes on the psychophysical appearance of the character do not affect him/her. His/her costume stays the same throughout the travel process, securing the traveler's body from the inevitable changes caused by the passing of time (e.g., aging). The visual identity of the time traveler's body disrupts the sense of causality associated with gradual changes occurring over time and is instead characterized by persistence. This costume-created persistence of identity forms a "gap" of stillness, a safe, unchangeable mode of transition between the starting point in time and the time in which the traveler arrives. It also proves in the eyes of the audience that the traveler stays the same and has the same personal identity.

In active time travel films, costume is the perfect vehicle for displaying the journey of the traveler through time: when everything around them changes, he/she is costumed persistently. The persistency in costume acts as a device pointing out that the wearer is in a "safe mode" of transition through time. As the time machine creates a sort of isolated space, untouched and immune to the passing of time, shielding its contents from acquiring any visible change, so the costume functions as a shell around the traveling body, signifying its inviolability. This is visualized literally by the 2002 film version of *The Time Machine*. The protagonist forces the villain out of the "safe traveling mode" of his machine. Outside the machine, the villain's skin and bones are dissolved by the fast pace of time, while his hands, which remain inside the machine, are unaffected.

One more concept should be introduced here: the interplay of continuity and persistency in costume reinforces the temporal discrepancy inherent in time travel by creating visual discrepancies. The discrepancy in costume points to different time periods the traveler visits by utilizing culturally determined, conventional notions of historicity (if going back in time) or futuricity (if traveling to the future). In *The Time Machine* (1960), the appearance and dress of the time traveler, George, differentiates him from the inhabitants of the age he visits by visually underlining the anachronism through the stylistic dissimilarities between his costume and the inhabitants' costumes. Arriving in the Lost Eden wearing his Victorian apparel, George appears out of time. The persistency of his appearance connects him with the time he comes from. In *The Time Machine* (2002), when George stops in 2030, a woman dressed in a futuristic biking suit comments on his costume ("Nice suit! Very retro!"), underlining his out-of-time appearance. This differentiates the past and/or the future from the starting point in time—the present.

The persistency/change opposition underlining the fast pace of time in *The Time Machine* (1960) is lyrically visualized in a sequence which shows a clothing shop window equipped with two models dressed in the fashionable attire of Victorian England. In front of the spectators' eyes, the fashions in the window display change rapidly, indicating the passing of time. The audience witnesses the characteristic Victorian style changing into the fashionable attire of the 1910s, the 1920s and so forth up to 1966, when the machine stops. The change of popular fashion highlights the passing of time and is visually and stylistically opposed to the protagonist's unchanging attire. In that sense, the costume of the traveler is not subject to change due to the elapsed time. It is defined by persistency and transgresses the principle of fashion change and underlines the journey through time. This sequence also reveals costume to be a time and place indicator. It constructs notions of different times through creating stylistic dissimilarity and oppositions in the style of clothing worn by the time traveler and the inhabitants of the times he visits. Costume defines the different periods the main character passes through while seated comfortably in the armchair of his time machine by utilizing popular sartorial signifiers associated with various periods.

The journey of Pal's protagonist to the distant 8000th century reveals a world reminiscent of the Lost Eden, filled with light, beautiful flowers and carefree people—the Eloi. The costumes play an important role in creating the image of this utopian heaven. Pal and the film's designers created costumes conforming to Flügel's idea of the "utopian dress." In *The Psychology of Clothes* (1930) Flügel describes a collective utopia, where the production of clothing is regulated by the government, which creates egalitarian, functional and elegant apparel, demonstrating the political and social equality of the wearers. This resonates with Thomas More, in whose *Utopia* (1516) all people wear identical uncolored clothes, which have the same shape and fitting. More's Utopians "have no tailors or dressmakers, since everyone on the island wears the same sort of clothes ... and the fashion never changes. These clothes are quite pleasant to look at, they allow free movement of the limbs, they are equally suitable for hot and cold weather—and the great thing is, they're home-made" (More 1516/2003; 55). Following More's idea, in *The Time Machine* (1960) the clothes of the Eloi are also identical. The garment is the same for men and women and differs only in color: a short tunic, whose hemline reaches the knee, with a robe belt. Therefore, the costume is a tool that places everyone in the same category, erasing individuality. The Eloi are kept in an "artificial" paradise supplied with plenty of food and leisure time. Their costume gives a hint that it is mass-produced, in keeping with the fake rural environment, suggesting that this lost Eden is an image of a degraded world.

Pale skin monsters called Morlocks live beneath the Earth's crust. They provide daily food and clothing for the Eloi with a single purpose: to fatten them up as a food source. The Morlocks' human features have degenerated due to centuries spent underneath the ground and they have acquired a thick colorless fur. The Eloi have degraded mentally—they are deprived of the ability to reason. This is Wells' critique of the class system in Victorian England, in which the upper classes (the Eloi) survive through the hard labor of the working classes (the Morlocks). In his Victorian costume, George, the protagonist, is an outsider who initiates a revolution that seeks to regain the Eloi's freedom. He is a portrayal of outmoded and long-forgotten human qualities, an embodiment of the upheaval evident at the end of the 19th century in the field of science through the explorations and inventions that abounded. He is costumed in Victorian attire, which suggests the morals and behavior of that time. He is the "old-fashioned hero," a stereotype associated with the time in which the novel was written. The zeitgeist, with its inventive spirit and new scientific ideas, is embodied visually in his appearance, conforming to Parrinder's suggestion that Wells "writes a visionary satire on the utopian idea which reintroduces the romantic hero as explorer and prophet of a menacing future" (1976, 15).

In that distant time the main character undergoes a transition from an awkward intellectual to an action hero. The transition is externalized by a slight change in costume: the jacket is gone, as the awkwardness is. The jacket, as part of a formal suit, restricts the body's movement, thus limiting the potential for the individual to take bold action. The suit changes one's posture by imposing a more formal behavior pattern. The body becomes more disciplined and stands straight. Hollander (1994, 55) writes that "the modern suit ... has gradually provided the standard costume for civil leadership for the whole world." Dressed in a suit, George is "predestined" to become the leader in a degraded world; clothed in power he will lead the mindless Eloi to regain their freedom. Hollander continues: "The masculine suit now suggests probity and restraint, prudence and detachment; but under these enlightened virtues also seethe its hunting, laboring, and revolutionary origins" (55). Once the jacket is gone, the hero's body is freed from its restraints; part of his hidden, wild nature is externalized in the more casual look and he is able to be the revolutionary leader. Once the body is freed, George is able to undertake a serious action to rescue his friends: he whips and wrestles with the Morlocks. If he had not removed the jacket, he would not have been able to act in that way.

The concept of the persistent appearance deployed by *The Time Machine* (1960) is used not only in the remakes from 1978 and 2002, but also in almost every active time travel film. In some films the travelers change their outfits to fit into a new period. For example, in an episode of *The Time Tunnel* entitled "Rendezvous with Yesterday" (1966), one of the characters from 1968 dresses in early 20th century costume to infiltrate the Titanic in 1912. The costume secures for the character an appearance that will fit the time. This can also be seen elsewhere, as in *The Blue Yonder* (1985), where a boy from 1985 re-clothes after his arrival in 1927 to elude confrontations that would risk the success of the trip. Of course, there are exceptions. Sometimes the traveling body departs in one costume and arrives in another. In *Quantum Leap* (1989–1993), Dr. Beckett is regularly transported into someone else's body in different time periods. The different clothes witness the change of the body (and the date) because Beckett is played by the same actor in each episode.

In this section we have analyzed persistency in the time traveler's appearance as a basic function of the relationship between costume and body in *The Time Machine*. The traveler's persistent appearance, violating the practice of continuity, creates stylistic discrepancies in costume to reinforce the idea of time travel in a visual way and to signify the traveler's unchanging state.

"Nude" Costume as an Open Frame for Identification: The Terminator

The story of *The Terminator* begins in 2029, when an artificial intelligence network has taken over and plans to eliminate a handful of human survivors who have discovered how to overcome the machines. The machines send a cyborg, or Terminator, back in time to kill the mother of the future leader of the resistance, Sarah Connor. The rebels send a man, Kyle Reese, after the Terminator to rescue Sarah. Both Kyle and the Terminator are sent to the past naked through a special Temporal Transfer Field (TTF).

The film introduced a new type of time travel to cinema, utilizing an idea presented for the first time by Anthony Boucher, a science fiction writer, who "has, in fact, made an interesting observation that 'the nude' may actually be the most reasonable way for a time traveler to make his appearance." As we are told in "Barrier" (Boucher), nakedness is the one costume common to all ages, and we are asked, "Which would astonish you more, a naked man, or an Elizabethan courtier in full apparel?" (Nahin 1999, 40). As presented in *The Terminator*, the TTF works only on living tissue, "because nothing dead will go through" the field. Pavis argues that "as far as nudity is concerned, it does not constitute the degree zero of costuming; instead, this would be a costume that represents a degree zero through its familiarity and appropriateness to our values. Nudity can embrace a wide range of functions: erotic, aesthetic, "disturbing strangeness," and so on (Pavis 2003, 175). Stripped from any signifying references usually transmitted by costume, nudity opens a space for reading the "emptied" body in the context of the surrounding environment and in the contexts of the film and reality.

Susan Jeffords analyzes the film through the context of Reagan Era America. In *Hard Bodies* she argues that the Hollywood films of the 1980s epitomized a new type of masculinity—the hard body—which represented all the qualities admired by Reagan politics, such as "strength, labor, determination, loyalty, and courage" (1994, 24–25). These aggressive, determined and heroic hard bodies reflected different aspects of the nation's desire to restore the economic, military and spiritual strength of America. Placing the film in that context she states that "*Terminator* ... works to put to rest fears about the logical extensions of a hard-body mythology—that that body would become so hardened as to forget that it was human, or 'natural,' at all" (105). In the film the hyper-muscular hard body "stood for the aggressive militaristic and business strategies of the Reagan period" (Cornea 2007, 121), underlining the president's pro-technology militarism directed against the Soviet Union.

As Jeffords notes, in the Hollywood films of the 1980s the male body "became increasingly a vehicle of display—of musculature," in which "the outer parameters of the male body were to be the focus of audience attention, desire, and politics" (1993, 245). The disturbing strangeness of the naked, hyper-muscular Arnold Schwarzenegger, who plays the Terminator, redirects the audience into reading the body. It is a "characterization coded by the

Schwarzenegger body itself" (Mizejewski 1999, 155) and by the political climate of the Reagan Era. In this way, the body reveals connotations that go beyond sexual desire—a notion that is underlined by the director's desire to create "an indestructible machine ... coming phoenix-like out of fire" (Chute 1985, 57). The cyborg has a militaristic, violent, aggressive, hard body, which stands in for the militaristic and business strategies of the Reagan period. As Cornea argues, "the enormously threatening and coldly mechanical figure of the Terminator can be read as a critique of a then dominant, but warlike and dehumanized, masculinity" (2007, 122).

Inside the synthetic living tissue, the Terminator is represented as an inhuman killing machine that does not feel pain, as visually connoted by the sequence in which he opens up his arm to adjust the technology inside. Its body is an incarnation of the violence planned not only against the future leader of the resistance, but also against the whole of humanity. His extreme power is signified by his excess muscularity and "when his weapons empty or are discarded, the Terminator becomes simply an embodiment of implacable force, the imperative of programed desire, the image of technological power itself" (Telotte 1995, 172). As the film's director, James Cameron, puts it, "[the public] sees [Schwarzenegger] from the beginning as this implacable, sexless, emotionless machine—in the form of a man, which is scary, because he's a perfect male figure" (Chute 1985, 58). Without costume the naked body is "all surface, exposed, a visible function, there is little point to considering motivations or to holding some special knowledge ... scant space is left for human identity" (Telotte 1995, 177). On the other hand, the naked cyborg body, deprived of identity as it is mass-produced, has the possibility to acquire "appropriate" clothing and to adopt signifiers that do not belong to and are not associated with the body. In a process of disguising itself, the Terminator obtains a leather jacket and biker accessories. The dressing-up adorns the naked, menacing body in an even greater viciousness not only through the act of forcibly taking the clothes, but also through the culturally determined signifiers associated with the type of clothing acquired. It relates him to earlier transgressive models of masculinity pictured in biker movies like *Easy Rider* (1969) or *Hells Angels* (1969). It reinforces the meaning of the hypermuscularity, stripped naked and desexualized, as violent and aligns it with the anarchic ideology as a subcultural movement driven by a desire for breaking the social order.

To summarize, *The Terminator* utilizes the naked, time traveling body as a new type of costume-body interaction to construct the traveler's identity not only by embodying the ideology of the time, but also by reinforcing it through the adoption of a subcultural trend's aesthetic.

Dress to Fit the Time: Back to the Future *and Costume as Time-Homogenizer and Time-Spatializer*

The *Back to the Future* films portray the adventures of Marty McFly, a young teenager who travels to 1955, 2015 and 1885 to alter the past in his struggle to create a perfect family and to ensure the existence of the present. Some scholars see the trilogy as an embodiment of Reagan's ideologies of domesticity and family (Jeffords 1994, Ní Fhlainn 2010). Jeffords argues that the films "figured anxieties between the past and the present explicitly as a father and son relationship" (67), interweaving "the strategies of Reagan America—to rewrite the recent past" (70) and to ensure a better present. It is a story of personal growth, reflecting the shift in masculinity toward the end of the Reagan Era. To accomplish this personal journey, "heroes must return to the time before things went wrong—the 1950s ... and reinvent the characters who would shape the future" (Jeffords 1994, 70) or learn by their own mistakes and grow up. This growth is incorporated in the way the costume connects with the body to construct a shift in Marty's identity from his early uncertainty to a mature, sensitive and decisive masculinity through a constant interplay of persistency and change. As this section of the chapter notes, in the first film in the trilogy this is achieved in relation to the film's use of the idea of time-homogenization, or the merging of signs of different time periods into one, reducing the distance between the past and present to "a spatial 'nowhere' in time" (Sobchack 1999, 274) and "collapsing the inter-generational gaps" (Ní Fhlainn 2010, 4) between fathers and sons. It is also achieved through *Back to the Future*'s utilization of the concept of time-spatialization, or "the use of spatial modes for time conception and measurements" (Gross 1981, 59). If spatialization signifies the overall sense of social space, typical of a time, place and culture, we can extend it to time-spatialization to indicate that culturally articulated signs of spaces, places and cultures can construct notions of a specific historical times.

Time-spatialization in *Back to the Future* operates to fabricate a desired past "that has no connection with 1955 as a 'real' historical past" (Sobchack 1999, 274), but which is presented as unproblematic and is dressed in nostalgia, reconstructed as "a dreamscape desired to be returned to, rather than learned from, in the cultural climate of the 1980s" (Ní Fhlainn 2010, 20). As such, Sobchack observes that "*Back to the Future* is a generic symptom of our collapsed sense of time and history" (1999, 274). It presents an idealized version of the 1950s, nostalgically constructed "as more benign than the liberal or decadent 1980s, in which the local picture house has become a porn cinema" (King 2000, 26). The past conforms to the conventional image of a bygone time and is glossy, polished and presented as pure nostalgia. Jameson has argued that "the nostalgia film was never a matter of some old-fashioned 'representation' of historical content, but instead approached the 'past' through stylistic connotation, conveying 'pastness' by the glossy qualities of the image, and '1930s-ness' or '1950s-ness' by the attributes of fashion" (Jameson 2001, 19). The film's costumes certainly touch on the fashionable New Look silhouette, using a few markers to suggest the 1950s, such as the slim waist of the "hourglass" feminine shape or the hairdo worn by Marty's mother, Lorraine. They suggest historicity by employing highly conventional and culturally determined visual codes, which conjure up the era through associations with images from popular culture. As Ní Fhlainn points, "We subscribe to a visual authenticity of an era via its visual artifacts—the cars, dress, logos, and colloquialisms of the period—which distinctly capture the period from cultural memory onscreen" (2010, 12). Through its nostalgic presentation of period fashion, *Back to the Future* encompasses pastness created through pastiche.

However, in *Back to the Future* these codes do not always connect neatly to the correct era. In 1955, Marty's father has the same haircut and clothing style as the audience has seen him with him thirty years later. Biff, a local bully, and his gang have the same shirts with rolled-up sleeves that Marty wears in the 1980s, which puts their appearance "out of time" and connects them to the film's present. The spatialization of time is evident only in the fact that the young hero changes outfits to fit the periods he visits, but even when reclothing himself, Marty's appearance is strongly connected to the present. His white sneakers, blue jeans and a plain t-shirt—a typical fashion of the 1980s teenager—act as time-homogenizers, merging the past, present and future through the persistency surrounding his traveling body, and thus erasing any associations with the era in which he will arrive. The audience is never sure if Marty has returned to the right time or where exactly he is going due to his persistent look. The constant merging of historical and cinematic references adds to the homogenization on several levels: the facetious adoption of costumes associated with images from popular culture diminishes the temporal distance and creates a comic effect; the past and the future are presented as extensions of the present by incorporating the visual dimensions of the costume from the present. The fashion of 2015 is a *bricolage* extracted from the present with the colorful spandex of 1980s disco culture surrounding the well-shaped sporting bodies. In the third film, he has brand new boots to suit 1885, but they do not fit and his sneakers are symbolically grounded in the 1980s. In 1955, when advised to "get yourself some '50s clothes," the only thing Marty adds to his appearance is a leather biker jacket, associated more with the image of James Dean as a 1950s rebel or with Marlon Brando in *The*

Wild One (1953) than with the dominant moral values of the decade. Marty rebels against his present in his desire to rebuild his future.

His altered appearance imposes on Marty a specific set of behaviors associated with the visited era. It allows Marty to shift to the appropriate *habitus* (Bourdieu 1977): the lifestyle, values, dispositions and expectations of a particular social group. The historical time and the geographic place are connoted by the costume. For example, in the third film in the series, he visits the "Wild West"—not the historical West, but the one known from the Western film genre. In his new pink shirt, he is a parodic embodiment of the iconic image of Clint Eastwood's protagonist in *Bronco Billy* (1980), and of the culturally accepted stereotype of the cowboy hero, who is supposed to fight against the villains. It seems unlikely that he will be able to perform the actions expected of him in this fancy pink shirt, not only due to Marty's own remark that "Clint Eastwood never wore anything like this," but also because of the witty observation made by Doc, the scientist who facilitates his journey through time: "You have to do something about those clothes. If you walk around town dressed like that, you might even get shot!" This ends up in Marty visually quoting another iconic costume—the poncho, hat and boots that Eastwood wore in *A Fistful of Dollars* (1964) and in *The Good, The Bad And The Ugly* (1966).

This journey, from the teenager willing to alter his family in *Future I*, to Marty's indecisive behavior in *Future II*, to his maturation in *Future III*, is underlined by constant refashioning and the adoption of iconic imagery. The spatialization of time through costume is not reached by a true historical representation, but through cultural references that usually create a comic effect. The direct reference to Eastwood's iconic image is not just a tool for creating parody. It points to a shift in the representation of masculinity towards the end of the Reagan era and embodies the idea that if anything must be done, it should be done by decisive individual acts. The *Back to the Future* trilogy extends the opposition of change/persistency to concepts of time-spatialization and time-homogenization to reflect the shift in the traveler's identity by employing signifiers known from popular culture. It also reflects the political climate of the 1980s by nostalgically constructing an idealized version of the past.

Conclusion

In this essay we have analyzed three cases in which costume and body interrelate in different ways to indicate time travel. Through *The Time Machine*

(1960) we have explored the dichotomy of persistency/continuity in costume. With *The Terminator* we have introduced the concept of the naked time traveling body as a "nude costume," able to reveal ideologically inscribed meanings in relation to the contemporary political and cultural climate. In *Back to the Future* and its sequels we have examined costume as a time-homogenizer and time-spatializer, which constructs an idealized and desired past, mirrors the maturation of the protagonist, and consequently reflects the shift in masculinity associated with the end of the Reagan Era.

Costumes and bodies construct identities, delineating various character traits and reflecting shifts in characters' psychophysical conditions. Costume in time travel films is an artistic device that contributes to the narrative beyond merely suggesting specific historical periods. It distinguishes the past, present and future by creating visual dissimilarities, but it simultaneously connects them by maintaining a visual persistency in the traveling body's appearance. The costume and body interaction varies from film to film and plays an active part in reinforcing the film's specific meaning and critique of reality. The study of costume in time travel films can be developed to examine more than just its basic functions in relation to character and narrative. Costume creates its own discourse for the traveling body, revealing its changing psychophysical dimensions and situating the body in the film by visualizing it as a social construct.

Case Studies

"Downwards is the only way forwards"

"Dream Space," Parallel Time and Selfhood in Inception

CHARLES BURNETTS

The worst thing you can do according to Dom Cobb, as an "architect" of virtual worlds in *Inception* (2011), is create places drawn from one's own memory. He issues this warning to his new tutee Ariadne as they explore the streets and bridges of Paris as part of a shared collective "dream space," something that we learn is made possible by a new technology known as the PASIV device. He tells her this because she has been handed over the reigns as a "dreamer," a role that permits her to create and modify the virtual world within which they interact, which she reasonably enough decides to populate with her own memories of places she has walked by in the real Paris. However, recreating places from memory risks no longer being able to distinguish between "what is real and what is dream." This is a fate that Cobb himself has experienced first-hand and which persists as an "idea" that continuously undermines his own sense of reality. Such a condition is analogous to those moments in certain time travel films when a character meets his own relatives, or perhaps even him or herself as a younger or older person, and experiences what might still best be understood in terms of the Freudian uncanny and its "involuntary return to the same situation" (Freud 2003, 144). In fact, when Cobb issues his warning to Ariadne in this scene, it is because the Paris bridge they pass by has triggered Cobb's own memory of a happy day once spent there with his now deceased wife. In this doubling of worlds, where the traveler or dreamer is subjected to an unreal experience of the familiar, time seems to have folded in on itself, threatening to undermine the perceiver's sense of reality.

Such parallels and analogies with the time travel genre abound in *Inception* owing to its foregrounding of temporality, duration, memory and ageing. However, *Inception* is not strictly a time travel film. With an emphasis on virtual worlds that are mapped in parallel by the PASIV device, time is less linear or sequential than in the typical time travel film. The topos of travel moreover becomes the mind rather than any externally rendered set of locations/periods, and as such points to a rather different kind of time traveler, one for whom the contemporary world more or less collapses into that of the self and his or her own memories/cognitions. The discussion below seeks initially to identify points of comparison and departure between *Inception* and more traditional time travel films in order to establish its common concerns and anxieties with what remains a key genre of science fiction cinema. The essay then frames the film's treatment of time alongside newer tendencies in contemporary American cinema, drawing in particular on concepts such as the "mind-game film" (Elsaesser 2009, 13) and the "post-cinematic" (Shaviro 2010, 16), theories that both attempt to map out the intersections between contemporary cinema, subjectivity and newer media forms like DVDs, music videos, video games, cyberspace and social media. The discussion turns finally to how the film quite overtly negotiates video game aesthetics and the ambiguous tension it invokes between narrative and video game, one that is indexed furthermore to debates between literary theory and games scholarship, or ludology. Examining *Inception* alongside such traditions and theories allows us, I suggest, to understand *Inception* in terms of a broadened sense of time travel and narrative, while signaling new issues relating to the virtuality of new media technologies and the challenges of global capital and labor.

Time/Travel

The first thing to establish when approaching *Inception* is that it is not a time travel film in accordance with our usual understanding of the genre and its standard conventions. If a key ingredient of time travel involves the premise that character(s) are able to either go backwards or forwards in an externally rendered universe of different temporal periods, usually through the technological means of a time-machine, the same is not strictly true for Nolan's film. Taking place in the dream-space of characters, time is not so much traversed as compressed and virtualized by the PASIV technology used by Cobb and his associates to manipulate the mind of Robert Fischer. Fischer is the heir to the corporate entity Fischer-Morrow and Cobb and his associates aim to induce Fischer to break-up the conglomerate using a technology that allows them to psychologically tap into his dreams. We are told that time elongates in the dream compared to real time "up top." Giving themselves eleven hours on board a flight from Sydney to Los Angeles to get the job done allows Cobb and his aides to operate for much longer within the virtual world of the collective dream-space. Moreover, since their mission involves the creation of multiple dream layers, dreams within dreams, where each further layer expands time exponentially in relation to the previous layer, the time perceived by characters while "under" is elongated significantly. However, Cobb recruits his associates without giving them crucial information about dying while "under" on this particular mission. While they would ordinarily merely wake up in the event of their virtual death, or from any kind of physical jolt or "kick" to their dreaming body, they find out here that death on this mission results in a potentially interminable "limbo" state of heavily sedated non-consciousness. Thus they must follow Cobb into further dream layers in order to carry out the mission as planned, their motivation provided (in a similar way to the time travel genre) by the need to survive the perilous conditions of the parallel world itself. As Cobb puts it, "downwards is the only way forwards."

Notwithstanding the film's foregrounding of virtualized or parallel times rather than time travel, the film's structure thus emulates the usual co-ordinates of the time travel film in narratological terms, where narration usually differentiates visually between the time *from* which characters travel and the time *to* which they travel. Although the more sophisticated of these films might begin in the time traveled *to*, it is rare that audiences of the genre will be wholly denied a vision of the future or past worlds from which they emerge. Key to the time travel genre is thus the differentiation of time-worlds along the axis of a usually linear story, punctuated by the actual moments of time traversal between time-worlds. This is usually effectuated narratologically by the cut, which has of course become the cinema's conventional grammar for temporal elision and spatial differentiation. Although *Inception* is not about time travel in conventional terms, we might say that it shares its grammar in its rendering of a variety of distinct temporalities/locations traversed by characters while under the influence of the PASIV device. Using terms deployed by David Bordwell and the Russian formalists, the "fabula" or story of *Inception* differs significantly from time travel films, but its plot or "syuzhet" is in fact quite similar, in as much as the film is about characters that cross temporal and spatial divides in order to intervene in a predetermined turn of events (Bordwell 1985, 48–62).

Nevertheless, if we subject our understanding of the time travel genre to a more detailed scrutiny, we find that certain logical criteria for establishing time travel are too narrow to include the kinds of temporal distortions seen in *Inception*. William J. Devlin, for instance, drawing on a key definition of time travel laid down by philosopher David Lewis, argues that

> someone travels through time if and only if the difference between the traveler's departure and the arrival times in the surrounding world does not equal the duration of the traveler's journey [2008, 106].

Going by this logic, films like *Back to the Future* (1985) or *The Terminator* (1984) adhere clearly to time travel schemata owing to the essential instantaneity with which time travelers reach the past or the future. If the journey takes no time at all, then the only way to account for the arrival of Marty McFly in 1955 and Arnold Schwarzenegger's assassin cyborg in 1984 is that they traveled *through* time. When we turn to *Inception* by comparison, we may at first feel quite uncertain as to whether time travel has occurred owing to the film's play with temporal distortion rather than time travel as such. If dream spaces mediated by the PASIV device are constructed from the residues of different people's subliminal pasts, the film seems to offer a less concrete sense of where anyone is in temporal or historical terms, making any determination difficult as to the length of journey undertaken and thus whether time travel occurs between distinct periods.

Applying these criteria to the engagement of characters with the PASIV device in *Inception*, we thus find that the criteria of differential arrival and departure times apply in particularly subjectivized ways. We learn for instance that Cobb and his wife Mal have lived out their lives to old age in a collectively dreamed world of their own making, only to be returned to their younger corporeal selves when they finally disconnect from the device. They become "old souls" in young bodies, with each character experiencing a passing of time that is shown to be discrepant to the real time of non-connected reality. Saito, the shady corporate mogul who bankrolls the inception mission and insists on joining Cobb and his associates when they "go under" to manipulate Fischer, also has a similarly long-term experience. Although we first see him in the film as an old man, it is eventually revealed that this version of him exists only within the dream-space, while his real, much younger, self is still connected to the PASIV device on the eleven hour flight to Los Angeles. Saito experiences his own aging process in a subjectively real way, only to have Cobb finally find him and bring him back to consciousness. His experience, alongside Cobb's and Mal's, signals a definite differential between journey time and historical time, while falling short of constituting time travel in conventional terms. In as much as Saito endures his time in as real a way as possible (when in fact he is in "limbo"), his return to real consciousness when he finally disconnects from the PASIV device signals a radical, and rather traumatic, subjective experience of distorted time, or a long-term hallucination.

"Mind-Game"

The film therefore foregrounds a sense of time that is not only subjective and personally endured, but also relative; an unfixed and unstable experience of duration that cannot be fully objectified and measured. The dream-spaces of *Inception* share a different *ontology* to those of the time travel genre while articulating its concerns with change, continuity, escape and return. By ontology, we would be referring to the way reality is accounted for both by the film and its spectator, particularly with regards to the important distinction between character perception and externally rendered events and locations. For instance, the images of family that haunt Cobb (his dead wife and abandoned children) as embodied manifestations of his memory problematize the ontological basis of what he deems real "up top." Dream-spaces are moreover designed by "architects" and populated by the conscious demands and subconscious cognitions of dreamers. Such environments conflate artifice with memory in a way that contrasts with the fully externalized but self-contained pasts or futures of the time travel genre. As we see when Ariadne manipulates the entire geography of Paris by turning buildings on their head, the dream-space also obeys a different set of geometrical and temporal laws to that of cinematic realism, adhering to the demands of its architect while simultaneously allowing for the free movement of actors within the worlds themselves. While the places visited by the time traveler share a similar basis in a fundamentally linear reality and allow him to maintain a sense of self in relation to altered time, *Inception's* distortions of time undermine distinctions between past and present, real and virtual. As one of the men in Mombasa who supervises a group of dreamers who spend more (actual) time within dream-space than "on top" says to Cobb, the "dream has become their reality. Who are you to say otherwise?"

The film poses a problem then to the feasibility of a rational ordering or policing of subjective experience. No one can legislate on another person's reality, for reality is presented here as a set of subjective impressions and memories rather than fixed events and temporalities. Such emphasis on parallel or forked narratives and relative possibilities in recent cinema has occupied a wide range of theorists, where a "puzzle" aesthetics has proven a particularly fertile line of insight. Thomas Elsaesser writes, for instance, of the "mind-game film" as a key "tendency" in contemporary American cinema (2009, 13). Sharing aspects of the European "art-film" tradition and the "New Hollywood" film, the "mind-game film" recasts the traditionally Romantic trope of alienation through the mold of a blockbuster aesthetic. Sporting big-budget special effects and a high-concept premise, such films are looser in terms of narrative and character stability and more ambiguous in their rendering of clearly externalized worlds. By contrast, the defining diegesis of the mind-game film is the mind and the trope of the genre *par excellence* is that of the protagonist (usually male) who cannot be sure that he is experiencing either dream or reality, and who lacks vital information with regards to the constitution and origins of his own identity. From Quaid (Arnold Schwarzenegger) in *Total Recall* (1989), who realizes that he is the deposed leader of a democratic rebellion on Mars, to the more romance-driven *Eternal Sunshine of the Spotless Mind* (2004), unreliable memories and the problems of recovering a sense of self are key to such films. The self is foregrounded as a puzzle of contradictory memories, meanings and traces, reflected by the interweaving plot strands and parallelisms of a complex narrative. Elsaesser also notes of the mind-game film that what counts more than a linear story and astonishing effects is the creation of a virtual world where a new set of physical laws apply, and where the focus lies in the imparting of new "rules." Thus

> mind-game films, we could say, break one set of rules (realism, transparency, linearity) in order to make room for a new set, and their formal features—whether we examine them from a narratological angle, from an ontological, epistemological, psychopathological, or pedagogical perspective (for all of which they provide credible "entry-points")—represent a compromise formation, which is itself flexible, adaptable, differential, and versatile: not unlike its ideal (implied) spectators [38].

Elsaesser's point here then is to emphasize the ways that versatility and differentiality take over as a key logic in such films, a destabilization of Hollywood narrative and grammar that expresses a variety of shifts in contemporary culture and subjectivity. Hollywood's traditional externalization of narrative, or its "transparency" (38), is undermined here by doubt and the ongoing possibilities of trickery or psychosis on the part of the narrator(s). Truth becomes a game or puzzle that depends as much on being familiar with the new rules of engagement as with more traditional cultural values or virtues, such as a character's courage, morality or self-conviction.

It is also worth noting that the spectator of the "mind-game" film factors in the above as a significant subject of enquiry, the "ideal" instance of whom will reflect the indeterminacies and versatility of such films themselves. Films like *Inception* thus imply a changed form of spectatorship that speaks to an unprecedented level of adaptability, flexibility and uncertainty as conditions of engagement, mindful as Elsaesser is here of the various technologies utilized by the film. In this, he invokes a line of enquiry that touches on the anti-humanist philosophy of critical theorists such as Michael Hardt and Antonio Negri (2000, 289) and Steven Shaviro (2010, 3–4). These theorists account in particular for how a condition often analogous to the "posthuman" (Shaviro, 33; Hayles 1999, 3–26) is arrived at in an age of unprecedentedly flexible flows of capital and labor in a globalized culture, where traditional, localized loci of power (governments, military forces, national institutions) give way to the more obscure, virtualized regimes of networked finance, con-

glomerates and "big data." We see this thematized, for instance, in the slippery
networks of power and influence represented in *Inception*, where questions of
who is working for whom are unclear and provisional. Mission briefs are issued
on a need to know basis, where each agent in the chain of command (including
the seemingly powerful Saito) is subordinated to a larger framework of impersonal information and privatized knowledge. Those who survive in such circumstances are flexible enough to adapt to permeable boundaries and a set of
rules that must be in perpetual flux. Moreover, identifying with such characters
is fraught with the risks of our own restricted knowledge about them as spectators, relationships that are characterized by doubt and our own provisional
assessments of truth at any particular point in the film.

We can even go so far as to consider *Inception* as an example of what
Shaviro has termed "post-cinema" in relation to a range of contemporary
media texts that rework, enhance or intensify cinema's negotiation of other
media. A form of "post-cinematic affect" applies for Shaviro to works as
differentiated as feature-films and music videos, distinguished for him by their
foregrounding of a formal "flexibility" and "modulation" (2010, 13) of the
human form and the cinematic image. He relates these ideas in turn to
Deleuze's theory of subjectivity in a "control society." Thus he argues that

> in the control society, or in the post–Fordist information economy, forms can be
> changed at will to meet the needs of the immediate situation. The only fixed require-
> ment is precisely to maintain an underlying flexibility: an ability to take on any shape
> as needed, a capacity to adapt quickly and smoothly to the demands of any form, or
> any procedure, whatsoever [14].

The virtue of post-cinematic videos and films in such respects is that they
reflect, or better, enact a pervasive state of "modulation" (156) in a global,
neoliberal society, dramatizing its costs and sacrifices while highlighting the
"schematic and implosive" character of its underlying logic (13). Compared
to the more visually escapist, or purely aestheticized, visuality of mainstream
cinema, "post-cinematic affect" is more about capturing the reality of our
"real subsumption" (53) by global media and a capitalist "networked society"
(183) and looking for alternative forms of being.

These aspects of "subsumption" seem important to *Inception* in its foregrounding of Cobb's agency, as well as subordination, in relation to corporate
espionage and the knowledge economy. Information and data are the most
valued commodities across all the domains surveyed by the film, a situation
that has a deep influence on Cobb's affective orientation towards his wife and
children as both a workaholic, globe-trotting agent of corporate capital and
a fugitive from U.S. justice (as he's deemed to have murdered Mal). Immersed
in a "mind-game," Cobb's remove from reality seems the logical result of his

own occupation, where ideas and desires can be extracted and inserted at the behest of the market, leading him to become uncertain of his own reality. Consider such a situation alongside Shaviro's description of the commodification of virtual events, a situation wherein "corporations value nothing more than innovation," and thus "increasingly commodify and market pure virtualities, in the form of events, experiences, moods, memories, hopes, and desires" (45). In such a landscape of virtual commerce and the commodification of subjective experience, we might say that Cobb and his cohorts both profit and pay a price for their labor and its spatial/temporal/moral flexibility, attaining the power to access and manipulate the consciousness of others while subjecting their own minds and bodies to the indeterminacies of the global marketplace and its unquenchable desire for information and innovation.

Notwithstanding *Inception*'s foregrounding of virtuality and globalized labor, it is necessary to be cautious about aligning *Inception* too closely to Shaviro's concept. His examples of "post-cinema" tend to be differentiated from blockbuster films like *Inception* in their avoidance of "high" production values and big budgets. Significantly, while *Inception* poses a puzzle and invites a rational reconstruction of its tangled events, "post-cinema" tends rather towards an excessive polysemy as well as an overall mood of restlessness, hyperactive nihilism and smart humor. In other words, while *Inception*, as others have noted, seems to want to be an "art-film,"[1] "post-cinema" is rather more concerned with cinema's invocations of popular culture, like music videos, comics, video games and trashy B-movies. Being mindful of such differences, the film's concern with issues of subjectivity, virtuality and dislocation nevertheless raises interesting questions in relation to post-cinema, as do many "mind-game" films. Foregrounding the sub-genre's concern with unreliable narration and puzzles, *Inception* looks to new technology with a sense of nervous trepidation as a sophisticated 21st-century blockbuster film, particularly with regards to how new media can be harnessed, represented or negotiated. It is also deeply invested in issues of globalization and the demands made of capital on an increasingly mobile, transnational labor force. The costs of such demands are foregrounded here as those endured by a fragile human body and psyche that plays games with his social or familial self, where only the most flexible (and emotionally disconnected) can succeed.

Gaming the Self

Indeed, if *Inception* is still quite classical in its linear "heist" structure and sometimes feels a little too self-important in its self-conscious nods to deep philosophy (for instance Mal's contemplation of a Francis Bacon "grotesque" in Saito's compound), it is highly invested in issues of selfhood in a world of new technologies and new media. As a particularly literalized "mind-game," *Inception* invokes gaming technology in particular as a key analogy, in its foregrounding of level-design, strategy and task repetition. Conceived of as gamers, the conspirators in *Inception* are hooked into technologies of multiplayer simulation and virtual environment, their bodies rendered inert while under the influence of powerful sedatives designed to keep them asleep. The PASIV technology thus emulates the conventions of interactive gaming, where player attention is fully submerged in virtual space (such as one's own computer screen, mobile device, etc.). The physical integrity of the time travel hero as he crosses different time dimensions is split here between body and mind, where the latter is freed from its usual physical and ontological constraints and permitted to exercise the full extent of imagination and memory. As with gaming too, what becomes of most importance in *Inception* is timing, familiarity with levels and mental versatility as much as the more traditional skills of strength and physical dexterity. Although the characters in *Inception* still require these latter attributes, they in many ways become subordinated to the mental, strategic and, above all, dispassionate mode of affect.

These skills, the preserve of the computer whizz rather than the athlete, are perhaps epitomized in Cobb's right-hand man, Arthur. As an expert in strategy and the precise organization of missions, Arthur represents the technological labor of information-technology and other knowledge industries, where painstaking attention to detail and a sober, unrattled confidence is held at a premium. Yet unlike intellectuals of earlier time travel films, such as Doc Brown in *Back to the Future*, such a character is no longer permitted to merely orchestrate the action from behind the scenes, because his gaming skills are too valuable. Arthur is integral to the mission's execution and indeed it is he who must improvise the "kick" necessary for all of the dreamers to successfully emerge out of the dream-space at the film's climax. He does this while engaging in hand-to-hand combat with various henchmen in a zero-gravity environment, recalling the "wire-work" of films like *The Matrix* (1999) and its hero Neo, arguably the paradigm of geek-hero characters in recent cinema.

Inception thus in many ways "remediates" (Bolter and Grusin 2000, 46) a video game, foregrounding a spatialized logic as opposed to the more temporal variations of the traditional time travel film. While time travel films usually set the story-world as a constant against which time is a variable, *Inception* is like a video game in its rendering of heterogeneous levels within which the mission takes place. Such spaces do not exist independently of the dream's participants, but are rather designed by specifically appointed "architects," who set the terms or rules for what can occur on each level while leaving the details to the participants themselves. Determining what will occur relates to both traditional models of story and narrative but also to less predictable, participant-oriented factors that usually fall within the province of "gameplay."

There are, as such, contending ways to describe the situations represented in *Inception*, depending on whether one chooses a game or a story as its key referent. Video games have become a major object of interest to media studies in the last twenty years, and debates continue with regards to the utility of narrative as a governing rubric around which to comprehend their structures. Game theorists, also known as "ludologists," often argue from a position that seeks to align games with a new paradigm, positioning them as a unique departure from older, narrative-based media like cinema or the novel. Approaches from literary studies often take an opposing position, drawing comparisons rather than distinctions between games and older media, particularly with regard to the way games tell stories.[2] However, a cursory analysis of films like *Inception* and various video games reveals a far more nuanced situation with regards to claiming either narrative or ludology as a governing aesthetic. Consider for instance the following from Henry Jenkins on the importance of space or "spatiality" in games as a compromise-term between ludology and narrative:

> The discussion assumes that narratives must be self-contained rather than understanding games as serving some specific functions within a new transmedia storytelling environment. Rethinking each of these issues might lead us to a new understanding of the relationship between games and stories. Specifically, I want to introduce an important third term into this discussion—spatiality—and argue for an understanding of game designers less as storytellers and more as narrative architects [2004, 121].

The notion of a "narrative architect" seems tantalizingly comparable to the "architects" of *Inception*, figures that seem equally immersed in considerations of gameplay, space and narrative. The above alerts us moreover to more flexible approaches to authorship, by conceiving of games in terms of what Jenkins later refers to as "spaces ripe with narrative possibility" (119), or "authoring environment[s]" (128). This "middle-ground position" (119) between ludology and narrative becomes applicable too for Jenkins to certain kinds of film, those that belong in particular to genres characterized by "world-making and spatial storytelling" (122). Some films are thus less open to narratological analysis than others, particularly those that foreground "spatiality" in favor of more traditional character construction and linear narrative, such as in the fantasy or science fiction genres.

Such theory has key applicability to *Inception*, notwithstanding the film's adherence to storytelling and exposition of character psychology. The film is, of course, a feature film produced in Hollywood, one that clearly adheres to narrative conventions in a way that many games cannot. However, the film also foregrounds issues associated with game-design, particularly in terms of the creation of authoring environments. The figure of the "architect" is key here, as epitomized by Cobb or Ariadne, characters that are immersed in considerations of "gameplay" as much as story. They seek to guarantee an advantage to the conspirators in the important business of information "extraction" or "inception" in the film. They thus use space strategically to manipulate Fischer, ensuring that he is policed by a pre-conceived story caste by their manipulation of its spatial and temporal coordinates. The luxury hotel bar where Cobb meets Fischer, for instance, is designed on the basis of Cobb's plan to win Fischer's confidence in an unthreatening public space, so he can successfully manipulate him later.

Facilitated by the parallelism and virtuality of game "worlds" over the concrete historicity of real places, *Inception* therefore partially upholds the "ludology" perspective, allowing space and "world" to govern narrative while characterization is suspended. Consider for instance the job designated to each character in the film—Ariadne as "architect," Eames as "forger," Arthur as "point man" and Saito as "financier"—foregrounding a sense of depersonalized function over story and character depth. In all instances, game, strategy and function trump considerations of character and backstory, allowing the film's open-ended plotting and sophisticated visual spectacle to dominate. Time and identity are *informational* rather than physical in the world of shared dreaming, with the effect that Cobb and his associates are cynical calculators of risk and probability compared to the more "embodied" heroes of *The Terminator* (1984) or *Superman* (1978). While the latter films are structured around the binary of good versus evil, the moral universe of *Inception* does not allow for such easy clarification with respect to its characters.

At the same time, the validity of a literary approach is hardly exhausted for this Hollywood film, as borne out, for instance, by consideration of both Fischer and Cobb's subplots. Fischer's experience is a linear, traditionally Oedipal narrative of conflict with his father, followed by a staged acceptance by him and the eventual assuming of the father's position. He is subjected to an engineered melodrama with its compulsory abandonments, recognitions of virtue and cathartic deathbed reconciliations. Cobb must by contrast play the role of the haunted widower in a Gothic romance, complete with a mad wife who (literally) hides in the basement of his imagination, while he and Ariadne (who serves here as a kind of "Rebecca" figure who threatens to both uncover and usurp Mal) shuttle between realities in his mental elevator. Although Cobb's story involves a more complex, modernist game of interwoven events and possibilities, there can be little doubt as to its correlation with certain literary, narrativistic models.

Considering the film alongside both ludology and literary paradigms seems thus the best means of clarifying some of its indeterminacies, particularly those surrounding issues of flexibility and selfhood. With a complex narrative structure, *Inception* emphasizes the ways that contemporary cinema remains in perpetual negotiation with non-cinematic media technologies. No longer able to court its public solely in cinematic terms, it also embodies the multi-platform conditions around which it will be consumed in order to be both profitable and engaging, whether in terms of a video game or as a DVD product that can be watched over and over again to discover new clues and secrets. By being as "flexible" and "versatile" as its projected users, the film allows for as many "entry-points" (Elsaesser 2009, 38) as possible, but by so doing, also disengages itself from the usual criteria of realism and transparency that cinema has relied upon on in its classical phase. Fitted to co-optability as game, DVD product and website content, *Inception* enacts the very mise-en-abymes depicted in the Paris dream sequence discussed above, where time is conceived as a confluence of parallel dimensions, or better, interfaces, as opposed to synchronous, causally-related events.

While time travel in film is often structured around the cinematic presumption of linear time and a related set of causal relations, *Inception* tries to incorporate the new formal logics and ontologies of digitization. More open-ended and hermeneutically flexible than its classical antecedents, the film in many ways celebrates this changed media landscape, virtualizing the time travel genre in order to prepare the spectator for more interactive forms of narrative media. As a blockbuster movie, the film retains the production values and stylistic polish of an expensively made Hollywood film, yet at its core is a problem relating to the indeterminacies faced by media users in the 21st century. Such problems affect character psychology and morality as a function of the more diverse and multiple entry-points through which he or she can be understood, allowing for a Cobb that is a devoted father, negligent/insecure husband, Bond-style secret agent and bloodless international mercenary. These identities are too numerous to be credible along the trajectory of a character's development in classical, linear time, and are thus rather better understood in terms of performance and game. Time essentially folds into itself and can no longer be conceived of in terms of an ongoing procession of unfolding events, a condition that requires the subject to more or less gamble with the certainties once ensured by time travel, and derive faith from whatever provisional reality he or she currently inhabits in his or her present. The instabilities and limitations of such a condition very much echo our own as fellow consumers and producers within the "networked" society, where leisure and work become confusingly intertwined in their subordination to digital temporalities. It is thus as if Nolan's film challenges its audience to realize the stakes of these new terms of engagement and accept its avoidance of narrative closure as a paradigm of contemporary choice and performance.

Notes

1. See for instance Steven Benedict's video-essay on the film, at http://www.steven benedict.ie/2013/02/analysis-of-inception/.
2. An excellent summary of debates is provided by Jenkins in Wardrip-Fruin & Harrigan, 118–130.

"A world without history"
Fate, Fantasy and Temporal Fractures in The X-Files

ELEANOR DOBSON *and*
ROSALIND FURSLAND

From its unassuming beginnings in a remote film studio in Vancouver, few would have predicted the success of *The X-Files* (1993–2002) as a cult science fiction series. It is a testament to the series' creator Chris Carter that his oddball show about aliens, monsters and the supernatural was to become not only a hit with audiences, but was also assimilated into the televisual canon of the 1990s. The disparate, and in many cases esoteric, sources that constitute an *X-Files* episode distance it from the conventional; as Douglas Kellner observes, *The X-Files* incorporates a hybrid of stimuli, drawing upon "classic figures of the occult, present-day horrors, and political conspiracies as material" (1999, 161). *The X-Files* also came to defy viewer expectations by rebelling against its own strictures, as well as the science fiction genre more broadly. Considering the profusion of narratives involving or alluding to unusual temporal phenomena across contemporary science fiction television, their relative invisibility across a series as celebrated as *The X-Files* might seem peculiar. Indeed, other cult television programs in this era with a parascientific or supernatural flavor, such as *Star Trek* spin-offs *Deep Space Nine* (1993–1999) and *Voyager* (1995–2001), *Stargate SG-1* (1997–2007) and *Charmed* (1998–2006) to name a few, feature story-lines where time functions abnormally with far greater regularity. In *Star Trek*, especially, attempts are made to control and suppress temporal anomalies within rigid scientific and moral frameworks that neutralize their threat. Of the two hundred and two episodes of *The X-Files*, just three explore temporal anomalies at their heart, and there is no defined set of regulations to police the boundaries between normality and abnormality. The attitude towards such devices is cautious at best; each of the three episodes addresses temporal anomalies in a distinct fashion that avoids creating a comprehensive philosophy to which the series adheres.

247

This chapter interrogates *The X-Files'* tentative approach towards time travel and related phenomena, focusing on the episodes "Synchrony" (1997), "Triangle" (1998) and "Monday" (1999). "Synchrony," the only installment to tackle time travel in its traditional sense, depicts the scientific realization of movement through time via the development of chemical agents that allow the human body to survive the journey into the past. The episode revolves around MIT researcher Jason Nichols as he works on developing a rapid freezing agent. It becomes apparent that a mysterious elderly man, who forewarns— yet cannot prevent—the accidental passing of another researcher, is Nichols' older self, who has used the freezing agent to travel back in time with the intention of destroying his, and his colleagues' work. "Triangle," meanwhile, deals with the concept of "time warps," suggesting that traversing the Bermuda Triangle offers a method of jumping between times. As Agent Fox Mulder attempts to reach a ship that has materialized on the border of the Bermuda Triangle, he supposedly journeys back in time to 1939, encountering doubles of colleagues and acquaintances from the contemporary world. The discovery of Mulder's unconscious body, however, and his subsequent conversations with his partner Dana Scully, indicate that Mulder's voyage was psychological rather than paranormal. Lastly, "Monday" centers on a time loop that repeats until the "correct" outcome is reached. Initially, the only individual aware of the loop is a woman named Pam, who experiences the same day repeated with minor variations. The day always culminates with the bombing of a bank by her boyfriend, Bernard. Eventually, Mulder is able to break the pattern through a sense of *déjà vu*, remembering that Bernard has a bomb. Pam sacrifices herself to save Mulder when Bernard tries to shoot him, the bomb is not detonated, and the loop comes to an end.

These episodes, categorized as standalone "monster of the week" storylines are perhaps not as detached and unconnected as one might assume. The broader extraterrestrial storyline of *The X-Files* often includes lost time as evidence of alien encounters. Inexplicable temporal anomalies thus come to signify brushes with the threatening unknown in the series, and the appearance of "Synchrony" after a two-part episode dealing with lost time as a result of the presence of extraterrestrials, the aptly named "Tempus Fugit" (1997) and "Max" (1997), may not be coincidence. Multi-faceted and complex, these various versions of temporal phenomena, as encountered by FBI agents Mulder and Scully, are manifested as greater threats in the way that they cannot be combined into a single coherent theory. Considered together, these episodes vary wildly in their representation of unusual temporal phenomena, ranging from realism to subconscious delusion and presenting conflicting notions of destiny and autonomy. Specifically, then, this essay analyzes how *The X-Files* introduces the notoriously complex idea of time travel into a context habitually defined by its devotion to realism, discusses notions of fate and free will, and ultimately comes to conclusions concerning the self-contradictory and paradoxical depiction of temporal anomalies across the series. Drawing upon time travel narratives across fiction, television and film, it demonstrates *The X-Files'* devotion to intertextuality, which creates a hybrid vision of unusual temporal phenomena, a subject that has hitherto escaped scholarly attention. Through analysis of its nuances and nods to earlier time travel narratives in their varied guises, *The X-Files* illuminates this theme within a complex and polyphonic web of allusion, itself revealing much about how time travel is confronted across media and genre: in multifaceted, contradictory and self-referential ways.

Realism and the Fantastic

The avoidance of a coherent picture of temporal phenomena in *The X-Files* is characterized by its suspension between notions of realism and the fantastic. Overall, the series emphasizes realism, with its trademark typewriter-style indications of exact locations and times in the manner of a documentary. The viewer is, thus, usually placed in a position of objectivity. Time travel is, nevertheless, a remarkably fantastic concept, resulting in its more frequent adoption by the contemporary television shows cited earlier, which do not assert that they exist within our *real* universe to anywhere near the same degree as *The X-Files*, but instead offer up fantastic *versions* or *reimaginings* of it. Conversely, the premise of *The X-Files* is that it could feasibly present "the truth," and as such relies upon—in most episodes, at least—realistic elements. However, the degree to which realism is upheld varies between the three episodes in question, perhaps partly as a result of the different writers and directors behind each of these installments, revealing the contradictory nature ascribed to temporal anomalies not just throughout this episode but across *The X-Files*.

"Synchrony" conforms the most to *The X-Files'* own brand of realism. Its time traveler actively defies the defined parameters that traditionally inform its practice in works of a more fantastical nature. As Susan Schneider puts it, in such formats, as "even the slightest change in the past can alter the future in momentous ways, travelers are instructed to use extreme diligence to leave the environment undisturbed" (2009, 12). Schneider goes on to recollect David Lewis' wry question as to whether, in the case of a timeline alteration, there is "a time policeman who races after her machine to stop her from altering the past in certain ways " (2009, 12), alluding to the time policing in narratives such as *Timecop* (1994), and more famously, the Temporal Prime Directive device used in *Star Trek*, a basic Starfleet principal employed as a means of policing the timeline and ensuring its coherency. Starfleet officers are strictly instructed to abide by the Temporal Prime Directive in order to refrain from interfering with the course of history or from time-traveling members of the fleet informing others about the course of the future. Despite Captain Janeway's characteristically scandalous breaches of the Prime Directive in *Star Trek: Voyager*, including conversing with and accepting guidance from her future self and negotiating a timeline swap to shave sixteen years from Voyager's journey, this trope proved an effective way for the writers to address notions of time travel in a moralistic sense. Janeway's seeming disregard for the Temporal Prime Directive, however, largely undermines the concept as a way of framing and explaining the rules of time travel in the entire *Star Trek* franchise. As she stated of the Directive in "Endgame" (2001), "it's less of a headache if you just ignore it." The Temporal Prime Directive is even seen to be policed by characters that evoke Mulder and Scully in the *Deep Space Nine* episode "Trials and Tribble-ations" (1996). In a tongue-in-cheek nod to *The X-Files*, Temporal Investigation agents Dulmur and Lucsly (their names almost perfect anagrams of Mulder and Scully) quiz Captain Sisko on his recent voyage into the past, claiming to be searching for "just the truth." While the obvious allusion to Mulder and Scully evokes the regimented protocols expected from an organization such as the FBI, in reality *The X-Files* only directly interacts with time travel in "Synchrony," in which there is a noticeable lack of guidelines within which the procedure is practiced. It is thus a portrayal of troublesome science in keeping with *The X-Files'* devotion to realism, in contrast to contemporary series with a more fantastic emphasis. Key to an understanding of *The X-Files* is its mistrustful skepticism and moral obscurity where other shows provide reassuring ethical frameworks and pre-existing guidelines.

The realistic depiction of time travel in "Synchrony" is further accentuated through its connections to genuine scientific theories, defying conventions of how journeys through time are commonly achieved in the context of science fiction television and its extended literary history. Contrary to the traditional notion of a time machine popularized by H. G. Wells' Victorian prototype, time travel in "Synchrony" is achieved through an unexplained process involving tachyons—common to contemporary science fiction dealing with time travel—and, more notably, a chemical catalyst that can reduce body temperature to absolute zero. The scientific theory behind "Synchrony" is revealing of the disparate sources drawn upon by the writers. Allusions are made to the work and philosophies of real scientists, including Albert Einstein and Stephen Hawking, while contentious scientific concepts that are referred to include the cryopreservation of human tissue and the aforementioned tachyons—hypothetical faster-than-light particles. Mulder refers to Scully's undergraduate thesis entitled "Einstein's Twin Paradox: A New Interpretation," quoting passages from it which seem to support his proposition that the discovery of time travel is unavoidable. Her thesis, contrary to the level-headed skepticism for which Scully is famous, notes that "although common sense may rule out the possibility of time travel, the laws of quantum physics certainly do not." Mulder, drawing on Einstein via Scully, also remarks on the work of Hawking, noting his suggestion that time travel might occur through wormholes, adding a sense of contemporaneity to the episode through references to current scientific thinking. Originally, the teleplay included a wheelchair-bound scientist inspired by Hawking, although this character was removed before shooting began (Meisler 1998, 207). Had this overt reference been included, the image projected would have been unmistakable to viewers, and the episode's entanglement with contemporary science made explicit. While Hawking has since altered his position on time travel, asserting that if time travel were possible time travelers would have made themselves known to us, he was more willing to entertain the notion at the time "Synchrony" was produced. The presence of his double in *The X-Files'* universe, then, would have signposted time travel's supposed practical feasibility within both its and our own worlds.

Gordon and Greenwalt were, for the writing of this episode, also reportedly inspired by physicist J. Robert Oppenheimer's comments to Harry S Truman on the 1945 nuclear bombings of Japan (Meisler 1998, 207). Oppenheimer, known as the "father of the atomic bomb" for his work on the Manhattan Project, which operated between 1942 and 1946 and developed the first nuclear weapons, became a strong adversary of the uncontrolled dissemination of nuclear technology. Appalled by his own creation, upon the atomic bomb's first detonation he quoted the ancient Hindu scripture, the Bhagavad Gita, saying that "now I am become Death, the destroyer of worlds" (Hijiya 2000, 123). Oppenheimer's dismay at the destruction in Japan, for which he felt responsible, is certainly akin to the themes addressed in "Synchrony." A scientist whose research ultimately caused destruction, Oppenheimer finds his contemporary counterpart in the character of Nichols, whose work emulates the atomic bomb in its potential for global devastation, on a cultural if not physical level.

Yet there are certainly also literary allusions and parallels present, fantastical elements working in tandem with notions of scientific realism. The image of frozen bodies evokes a visual pun of "freezing time," while the idea of the application of cryogenics to awaken the subject at a later date has literary precursors stretching back to Louis Henri Boussenard's *Dix mille ans dans un bloc de glace / 10,000 Years in a Block of Ice* (1889). Time travel brought about by chemical means has a rich literary history, with models as notable as Thomas De Quincey's *Confessions of an English Opium-Eater* (1821) (Nahin 2003, 7). Subverting audience preconceptions of commonly used methods of time travel in science fiction by evoking these less traditional devices, "Synchrony" instead creates a hybrid iconography from a diverse array of sources, blending the modern and the ancient, and attempting to marry the real with the fantastic.

Other characteristic elements of the series identified by critics include its "self-conscious intertextuality, unstable epistemology, mixture of genres, and periodic forays into self-parody" (Booker 2002, 125). Certainly, "Synchrony" is intertextual and presents a volatile and variable scientific discourse inspired by these numerous sources. Other episodes concerning temporal anomalies ("Monday" and "Triangle") frustrate generic boundaries and venture into the territory of pastiche. Considered independently and in conjunction with one another, these installments conform to an idea of unconventionality, "consistently undermining audience expectations and finding new ways to make the familiar strange" (Hersey 1998, 109). Directly contradicting the thematics of time travel depicted in "Synchrony," the other episodes that broach the issue demonstrate completely opposing interpretations on temporal theory. Furthermore, this lack of cogency on the complex theories of temporal phenomena in *The X-Files* perhaps arises from discrepancies in the disparate sources of inspiration for time travel narratives. The complexity of dealing with this theme in television, evident in the number of inconsistencies and errors that pepper these narratives more broadly, might offer some explanation as to why later episodes dealing with temporal abnormalities avoid the traditional and problematic time travel concept.

"Triangle" interacts with temporal phenomena theories associated with the Bermuda Triangle. As Jan Johnson-Smith notes, *The X-Files* "draws upon urban legends, the gothic, alien abduction and anything else vaguely unsettling to our impressionable minds" (2005, 35). The Bermuda Triangle, an area with a mysterious and deadly reputation, is one of the most notorious locations inspiring theories involving UFOs, government conspiracies and various physical anomalies and, as a result, lends itself well to the series through these associations. In this episode, Mulder goes to investigate the disappearance of a luxury ship, although on arrival he finds he has been transported back to 1939 at the outbreak of the Second World War. Mulder's discovery that the characters he encounters in 1939 are doppelgängers of his contemporary acquaintances immediately highlights the fantastical nature of this supposed voyage into the past, and is just one of the ways in which the episode acknowledges *The Wizard of Oz* (1939), which was released in the year to which Mulder— or at least, Mulder's subconscious—has journeyed. Like Dorothy, who awakens after her adventure in Oz, which is implied to be the result of a dream, Mulder regains consciousness in a hospital bed. The episode's events are suggested to be the result of a head injury sustained at sea rather than the "time warp" he suspects. This offers a convenient explanation for any historical inaccuracies in "Triangle" including musical items on the accompanying soundtrack produced post–1939; any mistakes are thus Mulder's, not the writers'. Hallucinations of time travel caused by "a knock on the head" hark back to Mark Twain's *A Connecticut Yankee in King Arthur's Court* (1889) (Nahin 2003, 9), with later notable instances in American comedy films including *DuBarry was a Lady* (1943) and *Peggy Sue Got Married* (1986). Other sources that made a more definite contribution to the episode's intertextuality include the music video for Semisonic's "Closing Time" (1998), with its distinctive use of split-screen, and Alfred Hitchcock's thriller *Rope* (1948), which inspired the episode's "wide-screen letterbox format" and "long continuous takes" (Booker 2002, 121). As a result, "Triangle" amalgamates diverse sources, creating a highly visually stylized version of time travel that emphasizes the comical and the whimsical, producing a narrative of subconscious introspective fantasy in direct contrast to "Synchrony."

Comedy and quirkiness also manifest themselves in "Monday," the final episode of *The X-Files* to use a temporal anomaly as its central plot device. Unlike "Triangle," the events are depicted as real, if presented in a self-consciously stylized manner. "Monday," therefore, attempts to find a middle-ground between fantasy and realism, diverging from the bleak tone of "Synchrony." Originally entitled "Mobius" after the one-sided surface which forms a twisted ring, "Monday" shares striking similarities in plot to *Groundhog Day* (1993). Both see the same day repeated until what is supposedly the "correct" outcome takes place, bringing an end to the time loop, a plot with successors including *Source Code* (2011). Writers Vince Gilligan and John Shiban claimed that *Groundhog Day* was in fact not the inspiration for this episode, instead citing "Shadow Play" (1961), an installment of *The Twilight Zone* (1959– 1964) as a key influence (Meisler 2000, 194). "Shadow Play" concerns a man who dreams that he is sentenced to death and executed every night, the looped event occurring during sleep. Significantly, and unlike "Shadow Play," the events of "Monday" are real rather than fantasy, and commence with waking, rather than sleep. The similarities to *Groundhog Day*, including the premise of a single, repeated day beginning at awakening, are many. As in this precedent, different versions of the same point in time are presented from varied camera angles in an effort by director Kim Manners to keep the scenes visually interesting, and dialogue is changed slightly with each version of the same event. A series of shots of a newspaper thrown down outside Mulder's apartment door in quick succession alert the viewer to a number of versions of the day that they do not get to see, symbolically condensed into these short fragments, also redolent of editing techniques used in *Groundhog Day*. Similarly, the day after the time loop is broken is also heralded by the arrival of the newspaper, creating a playful moment when the viewer is unaware of whether or not the next day has successfully begun. These comic devices draw attention to elements of pastiche in the episode that mimic the more fantastic mechanisms of "Triangle," yet ultimately "Monday" is meant to depict events as they happened (albeit, in some cases, condensed into comical fragments). The time loop—like the time warp in "Triangle"—is a hypothetical scientific concept that has established itself within the popular consciousness. Thus, the fusion of disparate concepts from a variety of earlier sources in each of these episodes dealing with unusual temporal phenomena exposes a desire to concurrently engage with time travel's complex mythological (fantastical) and scientific (real) theoretical history. Its fractured genealogical patchwork offers no concrete answers and confuses the authentic and the illusory experience.

Fate and Free Will

While the light-hearted "Triangle" avoids tackling subjects of fate and free will, these themes are central to the narratives of "Synchrony" and "Monday." Furthermore, in both, notions of fate specifically address the deaths of major characters. "Synchrony" explores predestination through the trials of Nichols, who sets to work attempting to alter the timeline of cryogenic research, which has resulted in the possibility of time travel. Unable to prevent the death of a scientist who might bring an end to the project's funding, the time traveler resorts to murdering the scientists (including his younger self) whose work made time travel possible. He injects his victims with a catalyst that brings their body temperature towards absolute zero, the same catalyst with which he needs to inject himself to negate the heating effects of time travel, which would otherwise cause him to spontaneously combust. He reveals that his grisly task is undertaken with the intention of averting a futuristic dystopia, itself the result of the practicality of time travel, attempting to save the world from a tragic and unspeakable end.

Contradictions in the timeline and the altering of the course of fate thus characterize the themes of "Synchrony." The episode, which, according to

Dean Kowalski, "raises a variety of philosophical issues: freedom, fate, and foreknowledge and questions in epistemology generally," presents juxtaposing answers to theoretical questions posed about the inevitability of one's fate and associated notions of predetermination (2007, 260). In the beginning it is implied that the course of fate cannot be altered, as Nichols tries to warn his former colleague that he will be killed by a bus at precisely 11:46 p.m. a prophecy which is seemingly irreversible. However, later in the episode, when it becomes clear that the elderly Nichols is the future self of one of the researchers with the intention of using time travel to sabotage his own research, the ultimate conclusion seems to be paradoxical. While Nichols is successful in deleting his files and injecting his colleagues with a not-yet-invented cryogenic enabler, it seems that even if the path of fate changes, time travel technology and the future dystopia remain inevitable. Nichols argues with his younger self after having imparted his ominous foretelling. Nevertheless, in prophetic disbelief, young Nichols provokes his older self, who forcefully embraces him then bursts into flames, incinerating them both. This is not enough, however, as Scully, ever doubtful of Mulder's fanciful beliefs, unknowingly interferes in Nichols' plan by reviving Lisa Ianelli, one of his former colleagues, from Nichols' cryogenically induced slumber. The final scene portrays Ianelli as she returns to her research and attempts to recreate the futuristic chemical compound introduced by Nichols from the future, much as the prosthetic arm recovered from a Terminator from the future allows more advanced technology to be reverse engineered in *Terminator 2: Judgment Day* (1991). The lasting image of Ianelli at her computer, staring at the chemical that will determine the world's fate, mocks the reassuring presence of Scully at the end of a number of episodes, typing up a report that subdues the threat of the individual case by containing it within textual form. Without this pacifying narrativization, there is little sense of closure: society's fate hangs in the balance.

This timeline of events in "Synchrony" implies that, while the course of proceedings is alterable, the ultimate conclusion may be predestined. Conversely, it is unclear as to whether it was Scully's involvement that foiled Nichols' plan, or whether it was her predestined fate to intervene, particularly significant in the light of her Catholicism. It may be that the outcomes would remain fixed, although the order or details of events changed as a result of a degree of individual autonomy. Moreover, it can be argued that Nichols' attempt to interfere with fate actually perpetuated and propelled humanity's damnation as a result of his conceded short-cut to the discovery of his chemical compound and hence a fast-track to dystopia. Gordon and Greenwalt thus interact with several existing theorems on the possibility of time travel, and moralistic and religious ideals concerning the inevitability of fate, ultimately culminating in an unresolved conclusion characteristic of *The X-Files*. Unfortunately, without a *Star Trek*-esque directive model, which acts to police any interference in the timeline or discrepancies in the course of fate, the time travel depicted in *The X-Files* catalyzes many further questions and is not entirely convincing. Moreover, the ambiguity with which the series deals with the course of fate becomes problematic when viewed alongside notions of temporal paradox, including the grandfather paradox. The theory of temporal paradox is strongly akin to the dilemma posed in "Synchrony." This is the concept that a time traveler may go to the past and alter factors that ultimately impede the possibility of the development of time travel in the future. However, having prevented this possibility by creating obstructions to time travel, these obstacles (themselves the product of *successful* time travel) would cease to exist, again resulting in its possibility. This perhaps explains the irrevocability of the fate of time travel and the unavoidable dystopia depicted in *The X-Files*.

Similarly, the grandfather paradox, first suggested by René Barjavel in *Le Voyageur Imprudent* (1943), may have been an equally effective means for Nichols to have prevented his invention, simultaneously erasing him from history. This theory poses the idea that a time traveler could kill his own grandfather before the birth of his parent, thus resulting in him never being born. However, the pivotal flaw in his plan arises because if he is not born, he is unable to travel back in time to kill his own grandfather and therefore he cannot destroy the hereditary chain, as was his original purpose. Indeed, Scully even refers to the grandfather paradox explicitly when she, disbelieving the theory of time travel that Mulder has proposed, teases "and if your sister is your aunt and your mother marries your uncle, you'd be your own grandpa." Here Scully reveals a cultural awareness of these paradoxes as popularized in fiction, such as Robert A. Heinlein's "–All You Zombies–" (1959), indicating that the characters themselves are all too aware of the events' inherent intertextuality.

The dystopian vision that foretells the impending future presented by "Synchrony" mirrors that of Wells' influential novella *The Time Machine* (1895). An unnamed time traveler, returning from his foray into the earth's distant future, reveals the bleak fate of the human race, which will divide—or rather degenerate—into two distinct species. The concept of dystopia relates to *The X-Files'* wider vision of government conspiracy and extraterrestrial invasion, and critics including Michael Valdez Moses have noted echoes of Aldous Huxley's *Brave New World* (1932) and George Orwell's *Nineteen Eighty-Four* (1949) in the sense of unease that pervades the series, embodied in its mantras "trust no one" and "the truth is out there" (2008, 219). While Moses claims that *The X-Files* is not as pessimistic as these earlier literary sources, "Synchrony" offers a version of the future that is, in Nichols' words, "a world without history, without hope." The image of "a world without history" is suggestive of the ruined museum that Wells' time traveler discovers in *The Time Machine*. In "Triangle" and "Monday," unusual temporal phenomena become tools of resolution, maintaining a sense of universal balance. The resulting harmonious conclusions stand in direct contrast to the dystopian future alluded to in "Synchrony," which generates an aura of disillusionment surrounding the moral ambiguity of murdering a few in order to avoid a terrible fate for humanity. Indeed, moral ambiguity characterizes *The X-Files*; as Beth Braun observes, it presents "a vision to morality that resists easy categorization" (2000, 94). Her acknowledgement that "characters may be heroic on one level, but presented as ambiguous and dangerous on another" corresponds to Nichols' predicament in "Synchrony" (94). Murdering his former friends and colleagues, he is certainly the antagonist of the episode, and yet his motives are revealed to be darkly honorable.

Fate and ideas of self-sacrifice also feature in "Monday," as the bank robbery and explosion that form the time loop change slightly with each repetition, but eventually conclude with the same result. In the end, Mulder increasingly experiences *déjà vu* until, in one version of the day, he remembers the bomb before it is revealed. Pam, who on the final occasion enters the bank, is killed protecting Mulder, and her death ends the loop. Consequently "Monday," like "Synchrony," sees a character trying to use their experience of a temporal anomaly in order to forestall the deaths of others that they have already seen occur. These individuals are warned in advance and yet the fatal outcome—in most cases—cannot be avoided. "Monday," however, is much more explicitly concerned with fate than "Synchrony." Mulder flippantly speculates that the *déjà vu* he experiences is the result of living the same moment again in order to "right some wrong or change fate," oblivious to the ironic accuracy of his statement. This view is later confirmed by Pam who tells Mulder that "things didn't end the way there were supposed to" and the day will keep repeating "until we get it right." While the different versions of the day suggest a degree of free will, the loop does continue towards a final, supposedly fated point.

Ultimately, it is Pam's death that is the predestined outcome, not Mulder and Scully's, who die in the explosion in every loop but the last. Matthew Van-Winkle offers an insightful analysis of "Monday" alongside the episode "Tithonus" (1999), which aired just a few weeks in advance of "Synchrony." He notes that "Pam has outlasted the destined moment of her death" like Alfred Fellig, the central character in "Tithonus," who circumvents his own demise and, remarkably, sees those whose death is imminent rendered in grayscale (2007, 305). Comparing "Tithonus" to an earlier episode, "Clyde

Bruckman's Final Repose" (1995), VanWinkle notes a striking continuation between notions of fate in these installments. In "Clyde Bruckman's Final Repose," the eponymous Bruckman, who can envisage the ways in which people will die, reveals to Scully that she will not. This cryptic comment, the subject of much speculation among fan communities, appears to be addressed in "Tithonus," where Scully, who has begun to appear in grayscale from Fellig's perspective, is seemingly mortally wounded (VanWinkle 2007, 305). After Fellig instructs her to avoid death's gaze, he meets the eye of death himself, effectively taking her place and apparently fulfilling Bruckman's prediction by transferring his immortality to her. While Scully's appearance in grayscale indicates the beginning of the end, it also intimates that this was the moment at which she was fated to die. Her fate is, however, avoidable, admittedly through the intervention of an individual with remarkable supernatural abilities. Yet the absence of a time loop in this case is suggestive. Considered alongside Bruckman's foreseeing of Scully's eternal life, we might read her fate to be this state of deathlessness all along, her near-death experiences part of some greater universal plan. This offers one explanation as to why Pam is trapped in a time loop until she dies, whereas Scully is not.

Temporal Fractures

Time travel as depicted in *The X-Files* provides an informed but fractured representation of the theoretical frameworks of temporal anomalies, as scientific hypotheses and fantastical speculations within the science-fiction genre itself. The episodes "Synchrony," "Monday" and "Triangle" do, however, encompass a broad spectrum of moral and logistical issues concerned with conventions of time travel, ranging from injury-induced time loops to temporal displacement. As a result of *The X-Files'* fleeting and inconsistent dalliance with notions of time travel, the contradictions and confusions evident within these episodes mirror both the incongruities of time travel theories themselves and the paradoxical and inconsistent nature of time travel across science fiction as a whole. Suspended between conceptions of realism and fantasy, and circumventing a definitive picture of fate, on a personal and global level, *The X-Files* thus presents a portrait of temporal anomalies that addresses notions of paradox, uncertainty and the fragmentary. Abstaining from definitively answering its most compelling questions, *The X-Files* resorts to the philosophy of its enduring refrain: the truth is, and will remain, at least for the time being, out there.

The Therapeutic Value
of Fantasy Revealed Through
the Colors of *Pleasantville*

ELISSA NELSON

Pleasantville (1998) occupies an unusual space as a time travel narrative because the past represented is one mediated through an imaginary television sitcom. Operating through the lens of fantasy, the narrative takes two teenagers from the 1990s back in time and into their television set to the world of the series *Pleasantville*, the television show within the film. David and his twin sister Jennifer go from a broken home to what appears to be an idyllic 1950s suburbia. However, even though the past is a fictionalized version of the real, it still represents a rendering of the 1950s that is linked to reality by association with actual events and similar sitcoms produced during the period. As a result, by setting events in the fictionalized past, the film differs from traditional time travel narratives that go to "real" pasts or futures. In *Pleasantville*, the primary reason for time travel has less to do with learning about or altering a timeline of events and more to do with changing the inner lives of its main protagonists. Instead of setting color and black and white, past and present, fantasy and reality in direct opposition, the film blurs these boundaries in order to highlight how mediated versions of the past decontextualize and personalize our understanding of history while at the same time facilitating character growth and development. As a fantasy film, *Pleasantville* shows how time travel can be used to achieve self-actualization.

In his discussion of time travel, Gordon (2004, 116) explains how time travelers in Hollywood films like *Back to the Future* (1985) and *Peggy Sue Got Married* (1986) go to the past in order to change the present and the future. Even in time travel films such as *Twelve Monkeys* (1995) and *The Terminator* series (1984, 1991, 2003, and 2009), films that depict characters who must go back in time to ensure a pre-destined future transpires in an ill-fated time loop, every action taken has an effect on the present-day world. One of the note-

259

worthy differences with *Pleasantville*, however, is that instead of using time travel to fix something in the past or the future with large-scale causal repercussions ensuing, the consequences of the heroes' actions focus on how they can better accept the unchanged present. While character development is important for all archetypical heroes' journeys, the time travelers' ability to effect only limited change in their real world sets *Pleasantville* apart. *Pleasantville* illustrates how traveling to a different time or place functions within the fantasy genre; the journey focuses more on characters' internal development rather than external change. Similarly to the way travel between different fantasy worlds functions in *The Wizard of Oz* (1939) or *Where the Wild Things Are* (2009), personal growth and acceptance become the apotheosis of the narrative because, while a version of the fantasy world might be susceptible to change, the real world the characters inhabit remains the same, with only the protagonists' perspectives on it changing.

In order to understand why the sitcom *Pleasantville* cannot change and to conceptualize where the fantasy world of the film exists, it is particularly helpful to look at Jackson's notion of paraxis: "This paraxial area could be taken to represent the spectral region of the fantastic, whose imaginary world is neither entirely 'real' (object), nor entirely 'unreal' (image), but is located somewhere indeterminately between the two" (1981, 19). The town of Pleasantville to which the teens travel (the fantasy world) is located between the image (the sitcom) and the lens through which it is seen—in this case the television, which itself is a reflection, albeit a distorted one, of reality.

Beyond fantasy, though, the film also works as a time travel narrative, with the concept of the paraxial positioning of the fantasy world (one with a relationship to reality) helping to explain this classification. As Jackson states, "the fantastic plays upon difficulties of interpreting events/things as objects or as images, thus disorientating the reader's categorization of the 'real'" (20). She relates this in-between space to Tzvetan Todorov's categorization of fantasy, which exists in between the "marvelous" and the "uncanny," or as a state where the viewer is uncertain whether to interpret events as either supernatural or scientific. This notion of uncertainty between the real and the imaginary is helpful in understanding how *Pleasantville* can be read as time travel. Both David and the audience can confuse the mediated, television version of the past with the actual real past of the U.S. in the 1950s. Audiences may logically know that TV shows are not actually real, but there is still an assumption that they are based on reality, that they are related to the cultural context in which they are produced or set. Even cartoon family sitcoms that are obviously cued as "not real," such as *The Flintstones* (1960–1966) and *The Simpsons* (1989–present), are still based on realistic human and familial relationships. Additionally, even if the sitcom *Pleasantville* is manifestly marked as a fictional television show, it clearly harkens back to programs that did exist, like *Father Knows Best* (1954–1960) and *Leave It to Beaver* (1957–1963). While these are fictional depictions of the ideal American family of the 1950s, they also offer representations of aspirational interpersonal relationships grounded in the realm of the real. By introducing the fantasy world in the film *Pleasantville* through the lens of the sitcom *Pleasantville*, the television show is marked as a cultural product of the society that produced it. It occupies a space (in the "real" world of the film) that is mass mediated and therefore, by its very nature as a television show standing in for similar programs that were produced in the 1950s, it has an indexical relationship to reality. This notion of the show functioning within the movie as a mediated version of the 1950s that holds up a (distorted) mirror to the real 1950s leads to an interpretation of the film as a time travel narrative because of the resultant conflation between the real past and the mediated past that David and Jennifer visit.

In addition to understanding how the film works as fantasy time travel, it is also important to stress how the therapeutic value of the film works in tandem with its fantasy genre categorization. Fantasy and therapy are actually closely related through the similar "need to construct narratives to explain the utterly inexplicable: what drives us, what terrifies us and why, and what our greatest desires might be" (Armitt 2005, 3). Armitt refers to authors who address two related views of what can be called a use-value for engaging in fantasy, both related to the potential educative and healing power of the fantasy world. Bettelheim (1991) discusses the way children repeatedly return to fairy tales as a form of therapy and explains that the interactions children have with fantasy texts are a "means of teaching children how to negotiate the world" (Armitt 2005, 201). Botting (1999) mixes post–Lacanian psychoanalysis and postmodernism when he states that in fantasy "the object of anxiety and desire appears the same" (Botting 1999, 3). In effect, fantasy offers a utopian ideal, but it is one that is not actually sustainable; it is aspirational and, because the ideal can never be achieved, it leads to dissatisfaction with reality and a desire for escape. In *Pleasantville*, after David has been in the television world for a while, submersion in the ideal makes him realize that the fantasy is not actually a utopia. Importantly, with the lessons he has learned from his therapeutic fantasy time travel adventure, he accepts that he is better off in the real world.

In the same way as a course of psychotherapy, *Pleasantville* ultimately reveals that we only have power over our own actions. While those individual actions may lead to seismic transformations, such as when David and Jennifer revolutionize the town of Pleasantville, the purpose of the time travel narrative in *Pleasantville* is not to radically alter the external world or to make material adjustments to reality. Rather, its primary purpose is to change the outlook and shift the perspectives of the time travelers in the present. In this fantasy film, time travel becomes history lesson, tolerance message, and therapy session, all elements that are predominantly geared towards personal development.

Pleasantville *as Constructed History*

Upon first examination, the history recreated in *Pleasantville* depicts a progress narrative replete with liberal ideologies about the nature of change—the film shows positive attitudes associated with individual freedom, civil liberties, and tolerance of difference. However, these messages and the overall historical trajectory of the narrative are essentially constructed to ascribe significance more to the development of the protagonists than to any historical actuality. When David and Jennifer go to Pleasantville, instead of fitting in and quietly embodying their respective roles as Bud and Mary Sue in the sitcom family, they bring with them modern-day sentiments about sex, knowledge, courage, and freedom. The twins begin to effect change in the town steeped in authoritarianism and traditional family values, and as the people in the fantasy world adopt or accept these new ways, they cease to be black and white and instead change to color. Through analogy, for example by the use of signs in storefront windows that say "no coloreds" to exclude people who changed, the history of the Civil Rights Movement from the 1950s is depicted. The tolerant members of the community battle the intolerant and messages of change, progress, and acceptance are proffered and idealized. However, it's important to note that there are no actual people of color to be found in *Pleasantville* and, for all the discourse about civil rights and acceptance, it is still a middle-class, white, heterosexual, male character who has the agency to instigate the changes that take place, albeit with help from his white, middle-class, heterosexual sister. As Spigel (2001, 396) suggests, "the white boy somehow emerges as the central hero in a story of women's liberation—rescuing his mom, sister, and girlfriend from the sexual repression and 'occupation housewife' role of the 1950s past." It is as though the privileged visitors from another time and place bestow knowledge upon the naïve natives. The situation is further complicated by the fact that *all* the people of Pleasantville change to color by the end of the film; in effect, they are all made the same again and their newfound tolerance ceases to be tested, thus limiting the film's interest in the history of liberalism and civil rights during the 1950s.

Further historical tensions are evident in the narrative constructed in

Pleasantville; the film chooses select topics to include by analogy, thereby limiting its progressive, linear logic. Although the sitcom is set in the 1950s, the events of the film seem more akin to counterculture movements of both the '50s *and* the '60s. The film depicts the advent of rock 'n' roll and the fight against literary censorship from the 1950s, and also the Civil Rights Movement which continued well into the 1960s, and the Women's Liberation Movement which gained more strength in the latter decade. Even more conspicuous absences in the reconstruction of this era are evident with the lack of mention of the Cold War, the Korean and Vietnam Wars, or fears of the atomic bomb. These lapses could perhaps be explained through the internal narrative logic of the film where the town is depicted as part of, yet isolated from, the rest of the nation. Even though there are shots of American flags throughout, before David and Jennifer's arrival, Pleasantville was completely closed-off; the beginning and end of Main Street looped back on each other, and the concept of a world "outside" Pleasantville did not exist. However, the film does still work under the rubric of time travel and, as such, the importance of the Cold War to the 1950s and the way it permeated so many aspects of government, entertainment, and everyday life cannot be overlooked. Granted, the film is a fantasy and not a historical document, and even if the film were trying to present itself as a historical text, "there are always more facts in the record than the historian can possibly include in his narrative [...] so the historian must 'interpret' his data by excluding certain facts from his account as irrelevant to his narrative purpose" (White 1990, 51). However, these elisions and omissions suggest that the aspects of the era the film chooses to depict and conceal reveal something greater about its narrative purpose.

A reason, then, that movements from the 1960s are addressed and that the geopolitical climate of 1950s America are not chronicled is the relative importance of these issues to David and Jennifer in the present. As Rosenstone (1995) argues when discussing the way historical narratives are brought to the screen, we create histories in terms of our underlying values and construct historical narratives as an attempt to make sense of the past. History on screen will never be complete and will tend to compress the past into a linear story (20, 22). Regardless of whether a text refers to actual historical occurrences or ones that are made up, the events are often constructed to satisfy the needs of the narrative and focus only those elements that are important to our values and understanding of the present. The Cold War thus becomes less of a concern in *Pleasantville*, even though it left an indelible mark on the world and its aftermath is still being felt, because it is not significant to the immediate anxieties of the film's protagonists, two teenagers from the 1990s. For David and Jennifer, the past that they travel to "is thus presented

as having been lived for the benefit of the viewer [or, in this case, the two sib-
lings], who can learn its lessons and apply them to contemporary life" (Marcus
1997, 362). The historical world that the film constructs is therefore extremely
restricted in scope since it exists only to facilitate the storylines through which
the heroes achieve self-actualization.

Pleasantville *as Postmodern History*

Though failing to include certain historical and cultural movements
denies their impact and legacy, the film's engagement with history attains complexity through other means. One example can be found in the way in which
the film purposefully leaves narrative threads unresolved, indicating a rejection
of grand, totalizing narratives and an acceptance of multiple perspectives.
This lack of closure indicates *Pleasantville* as a postmodern text. As Hutcheon
(2002, 67) argues, whether in fiction or historical writing, a postmodern text
"exploits and yet simultaneously calls into question notions of closure, total-
ization, and universality that are part of those challenged grand narratives."
Closure is suspect in postmodernism because of "both its arbitrariness and its
foreclosing interpretative power" (66). Indeed, the lack of a completely closed-
off view of history, where all questions are given neat answers, is one of the
more interesting aspects of the narrative structure of *Pleasantville*. The film
opens with teachers giving lectures about the poor state of the economy, disease and famine, issues to which the narrative never returns. Betty, the twins'
mother in the sitcom, embraces the sexual revolution and women's liberation,
but George, her husband, is slower to welcome the changes. Without really
giving George much of a chance, Betty finds a companion in the artist/soda
shop owner, Bill. The film ends with Betty sitting on a bench with her
estranged husband. Betty asks George what he thinks will happen. The camera
pans from a close-up of her face to his. George responds that he does not
know. The camera returns to Betty who responds with the same line. After a
pause, the camera pans over to the left again, but this time Bill has replaced
George on the bench. Bill states that he does not know what will happen in
the future either. A love triangle is thus established, but never resolved. At the
end of the film the future is still uncertain.

The scene is preceded by one where David is talking to his "real life"
mother after he has returned from *Pleasantville*. She is crying because she is
upset with how her life has turned out. In response, David describes to her the
lessons he has learned—that there is no one right way that life is supposed
to be and that there can be joy in an uncertain future. While this suggests a

positive outlook on the nature of change, that people can deal with whatever comes their way by being true to themselves and by accepting others, it is easy to lose the irony of the situation. David, the son of divorced parents who overhears his mother arguing with his father about how she cannot watch the kids over the weekend because she wants to go away with her new boyfriend, has, via fantasy, helped to create a world in which the "traditional" family has broken down. Eschewing a totalizing historical perspective, the value of such social change is left open to interpretation.

In addition to the lack of narrative closure and the multiple loose ends (such as Jennifer staying on in Pleasantville without a remote control to get her back to the present), *Pleasantville* also works in the postmodern vein of nostalgia. Jameson (2001, 563) describes the incompatibility of postmodern nostalgia with "genuine historicity." As noted, the film does take liberties with historical representation, which could easily fall in line with Jameson's seemingly more negative view of nostalgia texts and the way they reduce "history to historicity, to a stereotyped and clichéd set of images that pander to nostalgia rather than genuine historical understanding" (Kellner 2013). This issue of nostalgia in *Pleasantville* is essential to understanding how the text operates. David has seen every episode of the sitcom *Pleasantville* and can answer even the most obscure trivia questions about it. He does not have many friends in high school, he cannot summon the courage to talk to a pretty girl, and his sister thinks he's "lame." When David hears his mother arguing on the phone with his father he turns away in order to watch the happy family on the television set. He uses the show as an escape and when he enters the sitcom world he strives (in the beginning) to preserve order and to stop his sister from changing anything. To David, Pleasantville is an idealized world (regardless of whether or not it is presented with historical accuracy) where mothers cook breakfast, fathers come home when they are supposed to, and everybody says "hello" to one another when they pass on the street.

The changes that are brought to Pleasantville after David and Jennifer's arrival are initially a product of Jennifer's less traditional views about sex, and later result from chance and accident. When David arrives late to his job, something that would never happen to his television counterpart, he suggests something seemingly quite simple to Bill: if David is not there, Bill can accommodate this by changing around the order in which he performs the tasks necessary to open the soda shop. However, this leads to Bill seeing the whole world differently because he no longer has to fit into a rigid set of rules and expectations. It is only when David begins to see that this powerful obligation to conform has led to individual freedoms being trampled upon that he recognizes that maybe life in *Pleasantville* is not idyllic. His nostalgia and longing for the past set the tone for most of the film, but his appreciation of progress and tolerance for new ideas eventually take over the narrative. Whether those ideas originated in the culture of the 1950s or if they came from his own teen years in the 1990s, which were of course already influenced by the previous decades, does not seem to matter to him.

It seems, then, that *Pleasantville* is both a nostalgic text and a narrative about progress, a contradiction that Spigel has written about in broader terms. In *Welcome to the Dreamhouse* (2001), she uses a case study of students who had decided to write their term papers about the changing role of women on television. Often her students would decide that women had come a long way from the sitcom mothers of the 1950s because today they had more choices. Although this general consensus was framed by the logic of a progress narrative, there were some students who felt nostalgic for decades past, not because women did not have as many options, but because they were not faced with as many difficult choices about careers and motherhood. "However, even when students romantically remembered the past as a better place, they typically mixed this nostalgia with a firm belief in future progress. [...] Nostalgia in this regard is not the opposite of progress, but rather its handmaiden. Like the idea of progress, nostalgia works to simplify history into a timeline of events that leads somewhere better" (372). Ultimately, "television recontextualizes the past in terms of contemporary uses and perspectives," as when David watches reruns of *Pleasantville* on a cable channel, and "engages in a kind of historical consciousness that remembers the past in order to believe in the progress of the present" (362).

While David's initial nostalgic longing leads him to wish to inhabit the world of Pleasantville, it is not clear whether he wants to inhabit a sitcom from the 1950s or the 1950s themselves. It is not even obvious whether he makes this distinction. This conflation of real and imagined pasts mimics Edgerton's (2001, 1) observation that television has "transformed the way tens of millions of viewers think about historical figures and events" through both its "nonfictional *and* fictional portrayals" (emphasis added). As such, perhaps it does not matter whether David thought the televisual 1950s was the actual 1950s or not. What is important is that he wanted to be elsewhere, somewhere stable and idyllic, and that it was of little consequence whether this "elsewhere" was the real past, the televised version of it, or the version that David wanted to believe was true.

Pleasantville draws together a sense of both nostalgia and progress in order to rework history from the perspective of a 1990s teenager. Both Edgerton and Spigel emphasize that television (and, it should be added, films and popular culture) is often a source of historical knowledge, and the way it affects our understanding of history cannot be discounted. These mediated memories of the past can valorize history and criticize present conditions, or they can be used as a way to judge the past by how far we have come. As Pennebaker and Banasik (1997, 3) argue, "The ways people talk and think about recent and distant events is determined by current needs and desires. [...] Just as the key to the future is the past, the key to the past is the present." *Pleasantville* demonstrates how fantasy time travel films embody this approach to history. The past, which in Pleasantville is rendered free of "real life" consequences because of the protagonists' inability to change events in their "real" world, is a space constructed to revolve around the characters' needs to better accept the present.

Pleasantville *as Television Viewing*

Although what David and Jennifer go back to is not the actual 1950s but rather an imagined sitcom version of it, it appears that it is nonetheless easy for characters and audiences to conflate the reality and the fiction. While noting that television shows do not present reality, some critics at the time of the film's release argued that *Pleasantville* (the film) is inaccurate in its depiction of the actual 1950s. In his review of the film, Byrne (1998, 45) claims that "This movie repeats the tired metaphor that the '50s represent everything that is narrow-minded, repressive, racist, sexist, intolerant, insular, conformist and even fascist." He suggests that

> [this] was a generation that laid down its lives and treasures to end the horrors of fascism, and which still faced real threats to freedom posed by Communist states. The idea, floated four decades later, that this generation never was challenged, that it was scared to learn new things, is the product of either dumbfounding intellectual dishonesty or ignorance... In the movie, it took time travelers from the '90s to bring about the sort of changes that, in reality, were set in motion by the '50s themselves [*ibid.*].

Byrne is not alone in conflating the film's sitcom with a representation of reality. Wattenberg (1998) is astute in observing that the filmmakers were not only providing an allegory "about the lapse from innocence or the dangers of totalitarianism," but were also trying to assert a "more immediate political warning against those 1990s social conservatives who would turn the clock back to a postwar American Golden Age that never was" (38). In his argument, however, there seems to be a slippage between the real and the televisual: "There is no room in *Pleasantville* for [...] any ambivalence about the 1950s. The elders who rule static Pleasantville fear change above all. Does the generation that weathered the Depression, waged World War II, and watched the Iron Curtain fall across the heart of Europe really need another lecture on adapting to the new from a privileged segment of a generation whose idea of change was co-ed dorms, pass-fail grades, and junior years abroad?" (*ibid.*). It is not enough to say that these writers are mistaking a mediated fiction for reality. Rather, in their criticism, they seem to be addressing the ways people learn about history through television and media. The slippage, then, does not occur at the level of being unable to discern the difference between the fictional and the real. Instead it harkens back to Barthes' (1997, 37) point that "the literal image is *denoted* and the symbolic image *connoted*." What is problematic, therefore, is not the television sitcom world that David and Jennifer enter, but the historical world that it symbolizes and the relationship between the two.

Just as *Pleasantville* refers both to the real and the televisual 1950s, to the film and the sitcom, the town of Pleasantville itself is also split into two. There is the fantasy Pleasantville, which comes to embrace the moral lessons it learns from the time travelers, and the sitcom *Pleasantville*, which remains the same. When David returns home, he stands in front of the television set, remote control in hand, as the announcer says that the *Pleasantville* marathon that David had originally sat down to watch will be continuing. The image of the show on the screen is in black and white. Of course, *Pleasantville* the television show cannot actually change since it is embedded in the "real" world of the film, rendering it impervious to the siblings' fantastic visit. The only changes that are effected, therefore, are to David and Jennifer's characters. Traveling back in time and to the television show taught them the overt moral lessons presented in the film, but it also provided them with lessons on how to live their lives. David realized that his problems are not going to be solved by immersing himself in a make-believe television world and Jennifer learned, rather reductively, there is more to life than boys and being popular. People achieved "color" in Pleasantville by gaining what they lacked, by becoming more complete as characters who embrace a wider spectrum of human emotions and experiences. For many, Betty included, this meant learning about sex; for George, it was about accepting and expressing his emotions; for Bill it was art; for Jennifer, books; for David it was about developing the courage to stand up for and defend what he believes in. However, David and Jennifer are the only characters who "really exist"; when David gets his fill, when he has compensated for his lack, he returns home with his lessons safely engrained in his new outlook on life and etched into his toolkit for living. Jennifer, though, who has not yet had her fill or learned all her lessons, decides to stay on in Pleasantville, presumably to return home at a later time when she is mature and ready.

Learning about history through television, therefore, is not the main goal of the time travel, although some insights are gained about the past. Instead of learning facts, David and Jennifer learn life lessons. The history they are immersed in does not redress the ills of the present by revisiting the past. When David returns home, he comes back to a mother who is still divorced, to a country whose economic outlook is bleak, and to a world plagued by famine and disease. That present and that potential future have not changed because of David's trip to *Pleasantville*, nor does it seem like David has any intention of leading a social revolution that might address those problems. At the end of the narrative David has a better grasp on life and has learned how to face his personal problems. While this keeps the film in line with standard narrative construction and character development, it nonetheless tends to place any historical teachings, even if they are revealed by analogy, in the background. The personal may have become the political, advancing civil liberties during the 1950s and '60s, but in this version of history, the political exists to advance the personal. Ultimately, David's trip to Pleasantville is not about history, but is rather about learning a new approach to living life.

Conclusions

When interviewed about the film, writer/director Gary Ross pointed out that the sitcoms he watched during childhood did not mimic his life as the son of an out-of-work writer. He longed for stability and was envious of the lives of television characters (Stein 1998, E1). This response is in line with a reading of *Pleasantville* as a fantasy time travel narrative steeped in televisual nostalgia and the logic of a progress narrative. It is perhaps the unrealistic families that are presented on screen that pose a greater source of anxiety when viewers make comparisons to their own lives than if they did not have this supposed ideal as a standard in the first place.

One reason that viewers watch films and television shows is escapism, which allows people to avoid their everyday lives (a reason also commonly given for engaging in fantasy narratives). Additionally, the regularity that television offers is a source of stability for viewers and certain shows help with problem solving (Livingstone 1998, 56–57). Interestingly, these reasons reflect David's needs, both when he is an avid fan of *Pleasantville* and when he realizes that he no longer has to watch it so devotedly. At first, he tunes in regularly and watches the show in order to avoid his problems at home and at school. When he becomes a part of *Pleasantville* and then returns to the present after he has learned his lessons, he has the ability to face life's obstacles. His fantasy time travel experience in *Pleasantville* has served his personal needs and facilitated his growth as a person. David has in essence discovered how to live his life more fully through his immersion in a fantasy world.

Not only does the therapeutic nature of television viewing, of being able to work through one's own problems as a result of engaging with various programs, contribute to identity formation, but as White (1992, 178) points out, it can have a larger impact as well. It would be difficult to completely separate the narrative and social setting in which these discourses unfold from their therapeutic effects. "The therapeutic discourse projects stories as case histories, including the possibility of carrying both personal and social implications. The elaboration of narrative in terms of confession and therapy thus enables the production of a sense of context and history" (178). Accordingly, David is able to go to *Pleasantville* to learn about himself, but he can also then contextualize this knowledge in terms of a historical discourse. Watching and being immersed in television, therefore, teaches history *and* self-knowledge; the lesson about history and the lesson about the self go hand in hand. Just as the seemingly incompatible nostalgic aspects of the text satisfy the dictates of the progress narrative and the historical elements focus on the current needs of the historian, the text itself satisfies its quest for illustrating the drive for self-discovery and for providing a greater moral lesson.

Ultimately, the fantasy of being transported to another time and place that this film offers is more than just an analogy about tolerance and the need for change and individual freedom. Although *Pleasantville* may present itself as mere fiction, its historical implications are significant because of the ways in which its symbolic presentation of the 1950s is constructed through a 1990s mentality. Facilitated by the use of fantasy time travel, the film shows how history is written and rewritten and how self-knowledge is gained. *Pleasantville* does not just provide a moral; it speaks to the nature and use values of studying history, engaging with the media, and immersing in fantasy.

Woody Allen's (Post)Modern Nostalgia Games

The Critical Rhetoric of Cinema as Time Machine

Dario Llinares

I would like to go back in time, but just for lunch (Woody Allen)

Nowhere are cinema's properties as an allegorical time machine more overtly effected than in the films of Woody Allen. The director's extensive *oeuvre* demonstrates the use of formal cinematic techniques in order to traverse, fracture and rearrange temporal linearity. All filmmakers necessarily deploy strategies that reconfigure the relationship between real-time and film-time. However, Allen's films reflect a self-consciously experimental play with sequential logic through which the grounding of subjectivity in historical context is satirically questioned.

Comedic romanticization, which is often the fundamental viewing pleasure in Allen's films, is in many ways built on his sophisticated manipulation of time and space. The interrelationship between past, present and future underpins the structure and theme of seminal films like *Annie Hall* (1977) and *The Purple Rose of Cairo* (1985). *Annie Hall* deploys flashbacks which place the main characters, Alvy and Annie, in scenes of their past lives, thus framing a discussion of how these experiences define their present relationship. *Purple Rose* fantastically transports black and white matinee idol Tom Baxter from the silver screen into the color "reality" of adoring audience member Cecilia. In rejecting a "realist" logic of time and space, Allen ironically interrogates the contradictions and discrepancies of subjective memory, suggesting that in film, as in life, the past is a construction of unreliable fragments. But further than that such orchestrations of visual language exemplify Constance Penley's assertion that "cinema itself has the properties of a time machine" (1986, 70).

Woody Allen's use of cinema to represent past eras can obviously be aligned within the postmodern theoretical paradigm that highlights, and often maligns, a contemporary infatuation with nostalgia. The work of Fredric Jameson is central in conceptualizing the late 20th century zeitgeist, in which cultural production is replete with the "random cannibalization" of past forms, "the imitation of dead styles, speech through all the masks and voices stored up in the imaginary museum of a now global culture" (1991, 18). For Jameson the postmodern experience reflects a quixotic obsession with all things retro. The "nostalgia film" is defined as an indicative form that seeks to authenticate a past yet simultaneously iterates an empty signifying practice of "past-ness" through aesthetic mimesis of style, texture, mood and theme (Jameson 1998). Allen's use of time travel, through an internal narrative or via processes of formal experimentation (or both), deploys the intertextual referencing that Jameson decries, yet is imbued with what Linda Hutcheon describes as a double-coded politics that "both legitimizes and subverts that which it parodies" (1989, 97).

Through close analysis of *Sleeper* (1973) and *Midnight in Paris* (2011) this chapter reads Allen as occupying a liminal space, in cinematic terms, in which the unashamed visual pleasures of nostalgia are asserted, yet deliberately undercut through a dismantling of the structuring mechanisms that work to seduce the viewer into an idealized view of the past. In *Sleeper* the mild-mannered yet anxious Miles Monroe, played by Allen, awakes in 2173 to discover he was involuntarily frozen in cryostasis after a routine operation in 1973. This set-up provides the framework for a clash of generic and stylistic form and content, incongruously fusing the physical comedy of silent slapstick with the futurist aesthetic of 1970s science fiction. Consequently, the broad comedy emerges through visual *bricolage*, yet the text is riven with parodic flourishes, which call attention to the contradictions of historical epistemology and, in turn, its grounding of subjectivity.

In *Midnight in Paris* dissatisfied Hollywood screenwriter Gil Pender is mystically transported back to the era of his nostalgic ideal: Paris of the 1920s. The character serves as a surrogate for the viewer to engage in a sumptuous fantasy of flâneuring through the Jazz era parties of literary greats such as F. Scott Fitzgerald and Ernest Hemingway. The film paradoxically revels in its romanticized historical simulation, whist also confronting the audience with an inherent existential dissatisfaction borne out of nostalgic longing.

In order to frame this essay I begin by interrogating Jameson's invocation of "past-ness," specifically his critique of nostalgia as a bankrupt, commodified system of cultural production that precipitates a collapse between subjective present and idealized past. Using Linda Hutcheon's contestations of this postmodern reductivism, I read Allen's use of nostalgia, parody and irony as a critical strategy. The director's time travel cinema is a rhetorical device that allows the representation of the past as ideal to be constantly undercut through the foregrounding mechanisms of visual construction. *Sleeper* and *Midnight in Paris* are explored through their satirical unpacking of historicity as ideological, which confronts the contradictions of subjectivity between the modern and the postmodern.

Postmodernism, History and the Nostalgic Imaginary

The commodification of nostalgia is often viewed through a postmodern theoretical lens as having a rupturing effect on the metanarrative of history. In *Postmodernism, or, The Cultural Logic of Late Capitalism*, Jameson's opening assertion defines the postmodern as "an attempt to think of the present historically in an age that has forgotten how to think historically in the first place" (1991, ix). This reflection on contemporary experience can be read through myriad forms of constructed "past-ness": the endless recycling of material fashions under the banner of "retro." Examples might include the rebooting of kitsch 1970s TV shows into outlandish cinematic spectacles; theme park simulations offering an immersive yet somehow unreal journey through time and space; and buildings of the future made to look like relics of the past. Such forms are indicative of a late 20th century culture that has been defined through its obsession with nostalgia (Davis 1979; Tannock 1995; Grainge 2000).

Jameson's writing is profoundly critical of the implications of an era in which the fetishization of nostalgic artifacts, processes and representations has engendered a crisis of subjectivity. Such a malaise is rooted in a paradox:

> Everything in our culture suggests that we have not ... ceased to be preoccupied by history; indeed, at the very moment in which we complain, as here, of the eclipse of historicity we also universally diagnose contemporary culture as irredeemably historicist in the bad sense of an omnipresent and indiscriminate appetite for dead styles and fashions; indeed, for all the styles and fashions of a dead past [1991, 286].

The interrelationship of form and content, what Jameson calls "historicity," has traditionally configured a fundamental affinity between time, experience and culture. In other words, historical periods are given their veracity not merely in informational terms but through a connection with literary, artistic and even documentational styles.

In Jameson's estimation the simulated experiences of "past-ness" effect a decoupling of the specific cultural forms from their grounding in the very historical period they represent. This causes a fundamental disassociation with the present, a "process of reification whereby we draw back from our immersion in the here and now" (1991, 284). For Tim Shary the ubiquitous materialisation of "past-ness," or history consumed through symbolic language, "erases our concepts of past and future" (1998, 77).

Time travel is a narrative and thematic device that can interrogate these ideological and existential effects of nostalgic construction. Through the complex dynamics of temporal play the viewer can arguably be placed at a subjective distance from which the mechanics of "past-ness" are revealed and, in turn, a self-referential, knowing spectatorship is implied. This instills a critical potential for the nostalgic image. The fantastical nature of time travel is a constant reminder of the unreality of "past-ness." Allen's films are apposite in amalgamating the narratively diegetic and formally experimental in exploring the complexity of cinematic time travel and its relationship to history. Beginning with *Sleeper* I analyze how temporal play facilities the use of parody to interrogate the interrelationship between history and subjectivity.

Sleeper *as Parody of the Historical Self*

Of Allen's early films, *Sleeper* most overtly amalgamates the diegetic and formal in directly exploring the theme of time travel. Aesthetically the film parodies the sparse, minimalist futurescapes and technological quirkiness of science fiction classics, such as *2001: A Space Odyssey* (1968) and *THX 1138* (1971) and riffs upon dystopian themes such as paranoia, state control and the fear of technology. However, the aesthetic and thematic context of science fiction sits alongside references to the silent film slapstick of Chaplin, Keaton and Lloyd. The juxtaposition of these incongruous genres (science fiction and slapstick) underpins the humor but also, ironically, unravels the interconnection between specific artistic forms and their historical contexts.

The evocation of slapstick occurs on various levels. It is primarily rooted in Allen's absurdist physical performance, which is embellished by extravagant camerawork and underscored by jaunty ragtime jazz. The scene of Miles' initial revival relies on Allen's exaggerated facial expressions and physical clowning to reflect the disorientation caused by a 200-year cryogenic freeze. The ridiculousness of his enactments is augmented by the earnestness of the scientists as they work to bring Miles around in an intentionally lo-fi laboratory. The arrival of fascistic state security agents, whose authoritarian officiousness plays against Miles' erratic lunacy, again characterizes an incongruity of styles that ferments the joke. This initial sequence is essentially a blueprint for the film's method of contrasting absurdist slapstick gesture and form within the milieu and thematic content of '70s science fiction.

Further sequences follow a similar pattern. Doctor Melick tells Miles that he has been woken up in the future. Filmed in long-shot with no dialogue or diegetic sound, ragtime piano accompanies the histrionic gestures of Miles, pushing the Doctor away, hyperbolically miming laughter and waving his hands incredulously until he theatrically faints from shock. Later Miles pretends to be a servile robot—a prerequisite domestic necessity in *Sleeper's* imagined future—in order to evade government agents. With his face painted white, a metallic helmet and fake microphone wedged in his mouth—but still wearing the signature Woody Allen glasses—he becomes an embodied juxtaposition of science fiction and slapstick.

The antithetical generic fusion at play here decouples cinematic form from historical context in overt ways so as to be read in a knowing manner. Slapstick of the '20s silent era grafted onto a '70s science fiction aesthetic is obviously intended to be funny, yet there is an implicit complexity in the fracturing of film-time and real-time. Miles awakens in an imagined future, the year 2173, but it is the future as imagined in the '70s. The '70s that is Miles' origin in the film is also the present-day '70s of the film's production, and the assumed present-day of its initial audience (not to mention the further temporal complexity that results from the film being viewed in 2014). Furthermore, the textuality that is riven with stylistic affectations of '20s slapstick dislocates generic language from its historical fabric. The time travel device therefore disrupts the temporal continuum within the internal logic of the film, but there is also a complex knock-on effect in that the audience is dislocated from being able to historically position the representational aesthetics with any certainty.

It is clear that much of Allen's humor, in this film and many others, relies on the recreation and referencing of earlier cinematic forms. However, instead of a superficial postmodern mimicry—a pastiche or what Vera Dika (2003) describes as a "returned" image which lacks the aura imbued by an original context—the crosscutting of style is reliant on a "knowing" viewer: a viewer who is versed enough in the framework of film history to read when a work is being ironically mimicked. Without knowledge of the references, the interplay of forms would lack the points of contradiction that create humor.

Although cultural forms that borrow and imitate with the intention of deconstructive mocking have a history that spans back to ancient Greek literature, notions of parody, pastiche, intertextuality and bricolage are all asserted as intrinsic to postmodernism. Jameson is pessimistic about such inces-

sant cultural borrowing, decrying the lack of political intent and ahistoricism
that is indicative of pastiche:

> Pastiche is, like parody, the imitation of a peculiar or unique, idiosyncratic style, the
> wearing of a linguistic mask, speech in a dead language. But it is a neutral practice
> of such mimicry, without any of parody's ulterior motives, amputated of the satiric
> impulse, devoid of laughter [Jameson 1991, 17].

The endless avenues for imitation provided by postmodern culture lead
to artistic conservatism and derivative consumerism, which is exemplified by
the "nostalgia film." For Jameson the significatory veneer of the nostalgia film,
imbued with the illusory mechanism designed to seduce, amounts to "the cannibalization of all the styles of the past, the play of random stylistic allusion"
(18). The lack of artistic or historical origin is therefore indicative of the dead
language of pastiche.

However, Linda Hutcheon suggests that postmodernism is fundamentally parodic in a way that retains critical, political edge:

> Postmodern parody does not disregard the context of the past representations it
> cites, but uses irony to acknowledge the fact that we are inevitably separated from
> that past today—by time and by the subsequent history of those representations....
> Not only is there no resolution (false or otherwise) of contradictory postmodern
> forms in postmodern parody, but there is a foregrounding of those very contradic-
> tions [Hutcheon 1989, 90].

Hutcheon suggests cinema's use of parody "simultaneously destabilizes
and inscribes the dominant ideology" in a double play of meaning. In other
words there is an obvious calling of attention to, or interpellation of, the ways
in which the spectator is ideologically positioned by a representation in parody
while *reasserting the validity of the representative mechanics being parodied.*
The approach to understanding ideology and its formation of coherent subjectivity is perhaps a central difference between modernist and postmodernist
critical strategies. Modernism searches for "wholeness" of experience and selfhood amid a fragmenting culture, a search that is arguably the central aim of
Freudian psychoanalysis (through which, of course, Allen's film are often read),
Marxist theory and structuralist literary criticism. Postmodernism challenges
the very possibility of defining a continuous, unified, autonomous self.

Sleeper's parodic intent is indicative here of forms that produce historical
periodization only to simultaneously send-up the process of that very formation in a "metacinematic play." As I have discussed, the time travel narrative
enables parodic intertextual referencing of disparate cinematic conventions,
which points to how the textuality of cinema is bound to its conceptualization
of history. A further satirization of what might be termed "the historical
method" occurs in the scene where Miles is asked to help identify and explain

a series of famous people from the 20th century. Looking at a series of photographs, his descriptions obviously have comedic intent: Joseph Stalin ("Bad Moustache and Bad Habits"), Bella Lugosi ("Mayor of New York City"), Charles de Gaulle ("Talented French Chef"), F. Scott Fitzgerald ("Popular with college graduates and nymphomaniacs"), Billy Graham ("knew God personally"), Norman Mailer ("donated his ego to the Harvard medical school"). Underlying the jokes is an allusion to the fallibility of historical interpretation that society relies upon to provide knowledge of the past.

Since modernist epistemology is so ingrained, contestations of "official history" are often met with skepticism if not overt ridicule. Such a reaction from an audience is what Allen is counting on to engender the laughs. However, Allen's use of the time travel device also makes subtle political assertions directly related to '70s culture. At one point Miles is shown a film of Richard Nixon:

> DR TYRON: Some of us have a theory that he might once have been a president of the United States, but that he did something horrendous so that all records, everything was wiped out about him. There is nothing in history books, there are no pictures on stamps or money.
> MILES: Yes, he actually was President of the United States. But whenever he left the White House, the Secret Service used to count the silverware.

Sleeper, having been released in 1973, came towards the end of Nixon's time in office, although he had not yet resigned in the wake of the Watergate scandal. However, the implication here as to the political mood of paranoia and distrust of government at the time is clear and informs the narrative further as Miles goes on the run from the totalitarian state. The time traveler himself therefore becomes the benchmark of epistemological validity regarding the past, the comedic irony of which is again reliant on a knowing viewer.

The use of irony as a strategy woven through parodic form demonstrates how the link between history and politics is ideological and has a contingent relationship to the subject. Allen's cinema utilizes nostalgia, but rather than being a superficial construction of past-ness, the temporal play operates in a nexus between the modern and the postmodern, particularly with regards to how subjectivity is positioned through historical epistemology. On the one hand Miles represents the coherent protagonist of cinema who has been ripped out of his historical anchoring point. His search is for a valid subject position when all the signifiers of society, culture and history have changed. He could be read as a modernist figure whose wholeness requires the forging of a new self-hood based on integration with, and acceptance of, his new historical place in the future.

However, on the other hand time travel has revealed to Miles how his sense of self is based merely on culturally specific perceptions of time and place. The very structures that define history are exposed in *Sleeper* through satirical questioning of the subject's relationship to the past, present and future. The audience is implicated in this dislocation through the narrative, but also on a deeper level through the mechanics of cinematic play. For Hutcheon, Allen's films are postmodern because they effect an "insider-outsider doubled position." She states: "Through parody it [Allen's work] uses and abuses dominant conventions in order to emphasis the process of subject formation and the temptations of easy accommodation to the power of interpellation" (1989, 105). Allen thus exposes the very nature of cinema as a medium that simultaneously reinforces and undermines the link between history and the subject.

Temporal Flâneuring in Midnight in Paris

Time travel, both narrative and symbolic, which reiterates a nostalgic obsession with the past while exposing the contradictions of that obsession, is explored directly in *Midnight in Paris*. This film echoes many of Woody Allen's previous productions in its aesthetic construction of the past, which revels in the pleasures of nostalgia. Here, however, he uses the device of time travel to interrogate the contradictions of nostalgia in cinema and as a societal condition. The central conceit of having his protagonist mysteriously transported back in time to experience Paris of the 1920s, the period and place he romantically idealizes, allows the character (and the viewer) to directly confront his existential anxieties of nostalgic longing. Allen eschews a "realist" internal logic that might explain the time travel, while also foregoing experimental time distortion techniques, in favor of straightforward editing and a fantastical narrative set-up. *Midnight in Paris* has commonalities with *Somewhere in Time* (1980), *Peggy Sue Got Married* (1986) and *The Time Traveler's Wife* (2009) in that physical time travel facilitates a character's self-reflexive, psychological journey, which is bound up with an impossible romantic entanglement.

Gil Pender is a Hollywood screenwriter vacationing in Paris with his fiancé, Inez, and her parents. Though successful, he is dissatisfied with what he considers to be the superficiality of writing screenplays and has pretentions towards the "higher" form of literature. Taking inspiration from his surroundings, he enjoys wandering through the Parisian streets and imagining being one of the famous American expat literati who are part of the city's mythical past. Gil's daydreaming clashes with Inez and her materialistic parents, for whom Paris represents a consumerist paradise offering retro-culture artifacts to be imported back to the United States.

Gil's nostalgia is brought into sharp focus through a chance meeting with Inez's former professor, Paul, a smug intellectual with an infuriatingly conceited high-brow knowledge of art and culture. Paul, accompanied by his wife Carol, immediately pinpoints Gil's penchant for nostalgia as symptomatic of existential dissatisfaction as they discuss the lead character in his unfinished novel:

> INEZ: He works in a nostalgia shop.
>
> CAROL: What's a nostalgia shop?
>
> PAUL: One of those stores where they sell Shirley Temple dolls and old radios. I never know who buys that stuff, who'd want it?
>
> INEZ: Well, people who live in the past. People who think their lives would be happier if they lived in an earlier time.
>
> PAUL: Ahh ... and just which era would you have preferred to live in Miniver Cheevey?
>
> INEZ: Paris in the twenties ... in the rain.
>
> GIL: It would not have been bad.
>
> INEZ: When the rain wasn't acid rain.
>
> PAUL: Oh, I see, and no global warming, no TV and suicide bombings, and nuclear weapons, drug cartels.
>
> CAROL: The usual menu of clichéd horror stories.
>
> PAUL: Well, you know nostalgia is denial ... denial of the painful present.
>
> INEZ: Oh well, Gil is a complete romantic, he would be more than happy living in a complete state of perpetual denial.
>
> PAUL: And the name for this fallacy is called "golden age thinking."
>
> INEZ: Ah ... touché.
>
> PAUL: The erroneous notion that a different time period is better than the one one's living in. It's a flaw in the romantic imagination of those people who find it difficult to cope with the present.

Tellingly, Gil stays quiet during this conversation as Paul, Inez and Carol's sarcastic reactions reflect what they see as a rather infantile longing indicative of denial. This is perhaps epitomized by Paul's condescending reference to *Miniver Cheever* (1910), a poem by Edwin Arlington Robinson, which tells of a hopeless romantic whose pining for a romanticized past symbolizes a loathing for himself in the present. This scene could be read as Allen self-reflexively aiming an ironic barb at nostalgia culture (towards which, of course, many of his films could be seen to contribute). This scene also sets up a central dilemma: do we always idealize a past we cannot reach out of dissatisfaction with the present? At this point of course the question is rhetorical. However, the proceeding time travel narrative confronts Gil with the issue directly.

Having endured another evening with Paul, Carol and Inez, Gil makes his excuses and strolls once more into the Parisian night. When he stops on a street corner for a moment a nearby clock chimes out the twelve strikes of midnight. An old Peugeot Type 176 draws up slowly. The door opens and he is beckoned to enter by a group of revelers all wearing '20s garb. He is taken to a party populated by sophisticates also decked out as though at a retro-themed fancy dress party. As he wanders around the room he notices an uncanny Cole Porter "lookalike" playing the famous standard *Let's Fall in Love* on the piano. He then strikes up a conversation with a couple that intro-duce themselves as Zelda and F. Scott Fitzgerald. Gil understandably thinks that this is some kind of prank, but they are completely serious in their "per-formance" of these "characters." Gil accompanies Zelda and Scott to another bar where he is introduced to Ernest Hemingway.

This sequence does not really explain the mechanics of time travel (which are much clearer in *Sleeper*). Instead, like Gil, the viewer is asked to accept his arrival in the '20s as a device in service of the thematic conceit, allowing an overtly nostalgic character to interact with his artistic idols and ontologically experience the historical period. The viewer is encouraged to reject any initial skepticism or enquiry about how this could be possible, as Gil is seduced wholeheartedly into the experience of the past. How time travel "works" in terms of the internal logic of the film is never addressed. Allen rejects any overt use of special effects, instead simply using straight cuts between scenes to demarcate Gil's journeys through time. When Gil first gets in the car it is still in modern-day Paris, yet when he is taken to meet Hemingway, Paris itself has changed. After the meeting with Hemingway the film cuts to the front of his hotel, back in the modern day, giving no clue as to how Gil returns from the past. The effect here is to maintain an uncertainty as to whether the entire temporal excursion could simply be all a figment of Gil's imagination, and arguably to amplify the mystique of Paris itself.

Allen's films such as *Play It Again, Sam* (1972), *Stardust Memories* (1980), *Zelig* (1983) and *Shadows and Fog* (1991) have directly engaged with visual form, demonstrating the potential for cinema to be used as an allegorical time machine. Indeed, the structural relationships between film-time and real-time are numerous within film theory and philosophy (Metz 1974; Coates 1987; Deleuze 1989; Rodowick 2003). Cinema and time, as conceptual paradigms that sit within the struggle of a modern/postmodern dynamic, are theoretically brought together in Anne Friedberg's *Window Shopping* (1990). She outlines a genealogy of visual experiences that inform cinema spectatorship and sug-gests that time travel is implicit within the formal mechanics of film. Film is therefore the medium that symbolises the temporal mobility of modern life and which destabilizes the past, present and future.

However, instead of relying on cinematic mechanics to assert a "logic"

of time travel, *Midnight in Paris* uses location as a space of mythical reminiscence to produce and satirize the nostalgic idealization of the past. Gil's penchant for strolling around the streets of the city seems as though it is a
deliberate reference to the figure of the *flâneur*, which featured in the 19th
century poetry of Charles Baudelaire. It was Walter Benjamin, however, who
enshrined the *flâneur* as an icon of modernist culture through various writings,
most notably his immense and unfinished history of urban experience in mid–
19th century Paris: *The Arcades Project*. The *flâneur* was a central motif in
this new modern space, a figure who "strolls through the urban crowd as prosthetic vehicle of a new vision" (Jennings 2006, 9). Friedberg adapts the concept of the *flâneur* to conceptualize the transition from modern to postmodern
subjective experiences brought about by 20th-century technological and cultural change. She cites the cinematic and televisual apparatus as productive of
a mobile, virtual gaze that "travels in an imaginary flânerie through an imaginary elsewhere and an imaginary elsewhen" (1993, 2).

I argue that, through the time travel device, Gil is given the opportunity
to *flâneur* through Paris in the modernist sense, with us as spectators following
in his postmodernist wake. For both protagonist and spectator the journey
through time and space initially meets all expectations, suggesting that the
past, as created in nostalgic fantasy, is actually how it was. Hemingway plays
to the stereotype of the hard-drinking, brawling adventurer, speaking in the
sparse, yet potently direct, prose of his novels. Pablo Picasso, Henri Matessie
and T.S. Eliot are all encountered and live up to characterizations obviously
shaped by historical knowledge gained in Gil's present day. In a moment of
meta-surrealism (if there is such a thing), Gil discusses the problems of having
two women in different eras with Man Ray, Luis Buñuel and Salvador Dali.

Hutcheon's notion of a double play is once again apposite here. On the
one hand, Allen is reinforcing the historical significance of the art and culture
of this specific period, underlining the modernist mythology or artistic value
associated with these figures and their works. On the other, the time travel
device always asserts a distance, or reification, to use Jameson's term. Gil experiences Paris as a cultural theme park mirroring Inez and her family's consumerist shallowness in the contemporary setting. All the artists and writers
depicted are parodies, displaying stereotypical and symbolic behaviors that
feed a nostalgic desire, but pushed to the limit of comedic absurdity (particularly Hemingway and Dali). Confirmation of the historical narratives of
these great characters thus satisfies Gil's romantic imagination, but paradoxically infuses them with a cartoonish unreality.

It is not only the specific representations of Gil's artistic idols that are
interrogated, but also the sensibility of the tortured writer who is misunder-

stood in his own time. Gil refuses to let the insufferable Paul read his novel in the present, but he is introduced by Hemingway to Gertrude Stein, whose critique of his book is another moment of pointed irony:

> Now, about your book. It's very unusual indeed. In a way it's almost like science fiction. We all fear death and question our place in the universe. The artist's job is not to succumb to despair, but to find an antidote to the emptiness of existence. You have a clear and lively voice; do not be such a defeatist.

Stein's description of Gil's novel about nostalgia as being like science fiction is a wonderfully precise iteration of history as reification. The past can only ever be accessed by methods of historical construction. Stein reads the autobiographical malaise as reflective of Gil's melancholia regarding his place in the present, which is only made more acute as he develops a romance with Adriana in the past. Unrequited love feeds perfectly into the romantic yet tragic sensibility of nostalgic longing.

Midnight in Paris crystallizes the maxim that the past is irrevocably structured through the present, mirroring the sense that the conditions of postmodernism are rooted within modernism. For Gil, the initial romanticism of his time traveling gives way to a confrontation with the reality of eternal present-ness, which undermines his nostalgic vision. Gil and Adriana jump further back in time to her idealized past: Paris of La Belle Époque (1871–1914). There they meet Toulouse-Lautrec, Gauguin and Daguerre, who all suggest how *they* are living in an "empty generation" with "no imagination" and how it would be better to have lived in the renaissance. The dénouement is Gil's realization that the very notion of a golden age does not exist and his nostalgia is an endless deferral that provides a temporary and illusory escape from the dissatisfaction of the now.

Gil returns to the present to reject Inez and her parents, and instead begin a potential romance with Gabrielle, a French girl he met at an antique store who shares his love of Cole Porter. However, the film ends on an irrevocable contradiction. As he and Gabrielle disappear together into the Paris rain with the sound of a '20s jazz clarinet serenading them, the play of nostalgia is reiterated once again, but this time with a knowingly bittersweet tinge. Allen has exposed the existential impasse and naiveté of wishing to cross a bridge of historicity to a past that only exists in one's nostalgic imaginary. But he (and we?) cannot let go of the fantasy. It suggests that, despite time travel offering a glimpse behind the "past-ness" that he has created, a glimpse of self-reflexivity that could and perhaps should mitigate a feeling of reification from the present, the pleasures of nostalgia are still almost impossible to resist.

Conclusion

Viewing Allen's films as part of a commodificatory culture of nostalgia, that is at best superficial and inauthentic but at worst epitomizes an unrecoverable historical defamiliarization, fundamentally misunderstands both their cinematic and conceptual sophistication. They are critical, experimental mediations on the mechanics of cinema and its propensity to create a phantasmagoric window into the past. *Sleeper* and *Midnight in Paris* are two examples of the director using a temporal journey in order to interrogate the relationship between cinematic form and historical context. In moving between temporal points, both Miles and Gil bridge the aesthetic, social and cultural differences between "now" and "then." For Jameson, the vacuousness of the nostalgia film dislocates the historical territorialization of the past, and along with it the ability of the subject to cognitively position the self within a temporal totality. Woody Allen, however, is able to command the aesthetics of utopian pastness in a form that retains and asserts a political edge. As Angela McRobbie's critique of Jameson points out:

> There is no recognition that those elements contained within his diagnosis of postmodernism—including pastiche, the ransacking and recycling of culture, the direct to other texts and other images—can create a vibrant critique rather than an inward-looking, second hand aesthetic [McRobbie 1996, 391].

Allen's films are exemplary of the vibrant critique that McRobbie speaks of here. The dichotomy between the pleasures of the past offered by nostalgic cinema and the knowing sense of their illusory and superficial nature is a calculatingly pointed comment on the uncertain relationship between the temporal and the existential. Allen, through satirical humor and aesthetic indulgence, provokes a contestation of cinematic time and space as a mechanism of historical articulation. The accusation of indulging in consumerist pastiche, which one might make of postmodern cinema, cannot be aimed at films that appropriate parody and nostalgia as magnifying tools that bring into sharp focus the flaws of historical coherence.

Appendices

Appendix 1: Timeline of Literature

There is so much time travel literary fiction that the list below can only represent what we consider to be some of the most influential stories that moved the time travel concept along or that influenced its representations in other media. The list is presented below as a timeline in the hope that this will highlight the development of the genre from its early years to the present day.

Date of publication	Author	Country	Title
1770	Mercier, Louis Sébastien	UK	*The Year 2440*
1773	Madden, Samuel	Ireland	*Memoirs of the Twentieth Century*
1843	Dickens, Charles	UK	*A Christmas Carol*
1881	Mitchell, Edward Page	USA	"The Clock that Went Backwards"
1887	Rimbau, Enrique Gaspary	Spain	*El Anacronopete*
1888	Bellamy, Edward	USA	*Looking Backward: 2000–1888*
1888	Morris, William	UK	*A Dream of John Ball*
1888	Wells, H. G.	UK	*The Chronic Argonauts*
1888	Bellamy, Edward	USA	*Looking Backward: 2000–1887*
1889	Twain, Mark	USA	*A Connecticut Yankee in King Arthur's Court*
1889	Carroll, Lewis	UK	*Sylvie and Bruno*
1891	Gutherie, Thomas Anstey	UK	*Tourmalin's Time Cheques*
1895	Wells, H. G.	UK	*The Time Machine*
1941	Heinlein, Robert A.	USA	*By His Bootstraps*
1943	Barjavel, René	France	*Le Voyageur Imprudent*
1952	Bradbury, Ray	USA	"A Sound of Thunder"
1953	Moore, Ward	USA	*Bring the Jubilee*
1955	Asimov, Isaac	USA	*The End of Eternity*
1957	Lem, Stanislaw	Poland	"The Seventh Voyage"
1958	Pearce, Philippa	UK	*Tom's Midnight Garden*
1959	Heinlein, Robert A.	USA	"–All You Zombies–"
1968	Silverberg, Robert	USA	*Hawksbill Station*
1969	Vonnegut, Kurt	USA	*Slaughterhouse-Five*
1970	Finney, Jack	USA	*Time and Again*
1975	Matheson, Richard	USA	*Bid Time Return*

Date of publication	Author	Country	Title
1979	Alexander, Karl	USA	*Time After Time*
1980	Adams, Douglas	UK	*The Restaurant at the End of the Universe*
1980	Benford, Gregory	USA	*Timescape*
1981	Moorcock, Michael	UK	*The Dancers at the End of Time*
1985	Rau, Satyajit	India	*Professor Rondi's Time Machine*
1990	King, Stephen	USA	"The Langoliers"
1995	Egan, Greg	Australia	"The Hundred-Light-Year-Diary"
1999	Rowling, J. K.	UK	*Harry Potter and the Prisoner of Azkaban*
2002	Fforde, Jasper	UK	*The Eyre Affair*
2003	Niffenger, Audrey	USA	*The Time Traveler's Wife*
2011	King, Stephen	USA	*11/22/63*

Appendix 2: Asian Time Travel Films and Television Series by Country

As with the other lists provided in these appendices, this is not intended as a definitive guide, but rather as a suggestion of where an interested reader may begin their exploration.

Time Travel Films

INDIA

Bollywood and Indian films have become increasingly fascinated by time travel in the last twenty years. Many of these films involve time travel facilitated by reincarnation (see Introduction) and they also tend to revolve around romance and comedy.

Action Replayy (Vipul Shah, 2010).
Adhisaya Ulagam (Shakthi Scott, 2012).
Aditya 369 (Singeetam Srinivasa Rao, 1991).
Dangerous Love / Dangerous Ishhq (Vikram Bhatt, 2012).
Fun 2shh: Dudes in the 10th Century (Imtiaz Punjabi, 2003).
Love Story 2050 (Harry Baweja, 2008).
Our Story / Teri Meri Kahaani (Kunal Kohli, 2012).

TAIWAN

Secret / Bùnéng shuō de mìmì (Jay Chou, 2007).

SOUTH KOREA

2009 Lost Memories / 2009 Loseutumemorijeu (Lee Si-myung, 2002).

Japan

A Boy and His Samurai / Chonmage Purin (Yoshihiro Nakamura, 2010).

Bubble Fiction: Boom or Bust / Baburu e go!! Taimu mashin wa doramushiki (Yasuo Baba, 2007).

My Girlfriend Is a Cyborg / Boku no Kanojo wa Saibōgu (Kwak Jae-yong, 2008).

Summer Time Machine Blues / Samâ taimumashin burûsu (Katsuyuki Motohiro, 2005).

Time Travel Television Series

South Korea

The popularity of time travel stories on South Korean television is an interesting phenomenon and worthy of greater scrutiny.

Dr. Jin / Dakteo Jin. Originally aired 26 May 2012–12 August 2012. Munhwa Broadcasting Corporation.

God's Gift—14 Days / Sinui Sunmul—14il. Originally aired 3 March 2014–22 April 2014. Seoul Broadcasting System.

The Great Doctor / Faith. Originally aired 13 August 2012–30 October 2012. Seoul Broadcasting System.

Gu Family Book / Guga-ui Seo. Originally aired 8 April 2013–25 June 2013. MBC.

Marry Him If You Dare / Miraeui Seontaek. Originally aired 14 October 2013–3 December 2013. KBS.

Nine: Nine Time Travels / Na-in: Ahop Beon-ui Sigan-yeohaeng. Originally aired 11 March 2013–14 May 2013. tvN.

Operation Proposal / Pereopyojeu Daejakjeon. Originally aired 8 February 2012–29 March 2012. TV Chosun.

Thousand Years of Love / Cheonnyeon Ji-ae. Originally aired 22 March 2003–25 May 2003. Seoul Broadcasting System.

China

According to reports in Western newspapers and magazines, including *The New York Times* and *Time*, on 31 March 2011 the Chinese State Administration for Radio, Film and Television released a statement condemning time travel stories on film and television, claiming that such productions "casually make up myths, have monstrous and weird plots, use absurd tactics, and even promote feudalism, superstition, fatalism and reincarnation." This was often discussed as a ban, though in reality it fell short of such a move. Despite this proclamation, several popular time travel series have aired in China since 2011, so it is possible that foreign media misinterpreted the initial statement, which might simply have been aimed at discouraging inaccurate depictions of historical characters and events. The facts in this story remain unclear and further research would be welcome.

Palace: The Locked Heart Jade / Gong, Gong Suo Xin Yu. Originally aired 31 January 2011–19 February 2011. HBS.

Startling by Each Step / Bu Bu Jing Xin. Originally aired 10 September 2011–29 September 2011. HBS.

JAPAN

A Chef from Nobunaga / Nobunaga no Chef. Originally aired 11 January 2013–15 March 2013. TV Asahi.

Jin. Originally aired 11 October 2009–26 June 2011. TBS.

Appendix 3: Graphic Novels, Comics, Manga and Animé

Some of the areas that the essays of this collection have not covered include comics, graphic novels, manga and animé. Our intention had been to include at least one essay on these media, but such submissions were not forthcoming. While we acknowledge that this is problematic, below we provide an overview of the rich array of stories in this area. The following lists cover material from a range of countries, but are by no means definitive as the choice is vast. Nearly every superhero has, at one point, traveled through time, so we have selected a few titles that can be accessed as a starting point should readers wish to explore this area further.

Graphic Novels and Comics

Aronofsky, Darren, and Kent Williams. 2005. *The Fountain*. New York: Vertigo Comics.

Binder, Otto, Edmond Hamilton, Jerry Siegel and Jim Shooter. 2008. *Showcase Presents Legion of Super-heroes, Volume 2*. New York: DC Comics.

Burns, John M. 1970. "Glory Knight—Time Travel Courier." *June and Schoolfriend*.

Christin, Pierre, and Jean-Claude Mezieres. 2010. *The City of Shifting Waters: Valerian Volume 1*. Canterbury: Cinebook, The 9th Art Publisher.

Claremont, Chris, and John Byrne. January–February 1981. "Days of Future Past." *The Uncanny X-Men*. Issues 141–142. Marvel Comics.

Dowling, Steve, Gordon Boshell, et al. July 1943–March 1997. "Garth." *Daily Mirror*.

Jason. 2007. *I Killed Adolf Hitler*. Seattle: Fantagraphics.

Jones, Bruce, and Richard Corben. 1976. "Within You, Without You." *Eerie Comics*. Issues 77, 79 and 87. Warren Publishing.

Kerr, Tom. 1970–1976. "Adam Eterno." *Thunder* 1970–71: IPC; 1971–74, *Lion*; 1974–76: *Valiant*.

Lee, Stan, Mark Waid (writers), and Chad Hardin (artist). 2010–2011. *The Traveler*. Los Angeles: Boom! Studios.

Lemire, Jeff. 2014. *Trillium*. New York: DC Comics.

Maddocks, Peter. 1954–1964. "4D Jones." *Daily Express*.

Mathieu, Marc-Antoine. 2004. *Julius Corentin Acquefacques, prisonnier des rêves, Tome 1: L'Origine*. Paris: Guy Delcourt Productions.

Miller, Jack, Alex Toth and various. 2012. *Showcase Presents Rip Hunter Time Master, Volume 1*. New York: DC Comics.

Moore, Alan, and Dave Gibbons. 1987. *Watchmen*. New York: DC Comics.

Morrison, Grant. 2011. *Batman: The Return of Bruce Wayne*. New York: DC Comics.

Oesterheld, Héctor Germán. 1995. *El Eternauta*. Barcelona: Norma Editorial S.A.

Palmiotti, Jimmy, Justin Gray and Paul Gulacy. 2011. *Time Bomb*. Los Angeles: Radical Publishing.

Shaw, Malcolm, and Mario Capaldi. 4 February 1978–22 March 1978. "The Sentinels." *Misty*. Issues 1–12. London: Fleetway.

Smith, John, and Chris Weston. 1991. "Indigo Prime: Killing Time." *2000AD*. Issues 735–744. London: Fleetway.

Stern, Roger, and Mark Waid, et al. *Captain America: Road to Reborn*. 2010. New York: Marvel Comics.

Wagner, John, Alan Grant, Steve Dillon, Ian Gibson, Ron Smith, and Kim Raymond. 1984–1985. "The City of the Damned." *2000AD*. Issues 393–406, London: Fleetway.

Manga

Eiji, Otsuka, Kubuta Hiroyasu, and Tomozo Kaoru (artist). 2007–present. *Reversed Girl—Summer Vacation that Does Not End / Gyakusou Shoujo*. Tokyo: Media-Works.

Himekawa, Akira. 2013. "Hero of Time." *The Legend of Zelda*. San Francisco: Viz Media.

Iwashiro, Toshiaki. 2007–2010. *Shonen Jump / Psyren*. Originally published Tokyo: Shueisha. English publication San Francisco: Viz Media.

Mi-young, Noh. 2004–2007. *Threads of Time* Soeul: Daewon C.I.

Morimi, Tomihiko. 2004–2008. *Tatami Galaxy*. Tokyo: Kadokawa Shoten.

Morito, Mario, and Yuusuke Wakabayashi. 2012. *About How I Die If I Lose My Virginity / Ore ga doutei o sutetara shinu ken ni tsuite*. Tokyo: Holp Shuppan.

Murakami, Motoka. Apr. 2000–Nov. 2010. *Jin*. Tokyo: Shueisha. (Adapted into two live action television series by the Tokyo Broadcasting System in 2009 and 2011, and a South Korean television series, *Dr. Jin*, by the Munwha Broadcasting Corporation in 2012.)

Tanamura, Arina. 2008 (2000–2001). *Time Stranger Kyoko / Jikuu ihoujin Kyoko*. San Francisco: Viz Media.

Tanigawa, Nagaru (trans. Chris Pai). 2010. *The Disappearance of Suzumiya Haruhi.* New York: Hachette.

Taniguchi, Jiro. 2009. *A Distant Neighborhood / Harukana machi-e.* Wisbech, England: Fanfare. (Adapted as live action film in 2010.)

Tsutsui, Yasutaka, and Gaku Tsugano. 2004. *The Girl Who Runs Through Time.* Tokyo Kadokawa Shoten. (Adaptation of Tsutsui, Yasutaka. 1967. *The Girl Who Leapt Through Time.* Tokyo: Kadokawa Shoten.)

Yamazaki, Mari. 2012. *Thermae Romae.* New York: Yen Press.

Many of these texts can be accessed online at *Dynasty Reader* (http:www.dynasty-scans.com).

Animé

Bakemonogatari. Originally aired 3 July 2009–25 September 2009. Shaft.

The Girl Who Leapt Through Time / Toki o Kakeru Shōjo (Mamoru Hosoda, 2006).

InuYasha. Originally aired 16 October 2000–13 September 2004. Sunrise.

Kirara (Kiyoshi Murayama, 2000).

Legend of the Millennium Dragon / Onigamiden (Hirotsugu Kawasaki, 2011).

Popotan. Originally aired 17 July 2003–2 October 2003. Shaft.

Stein's Gate. Originally aired 6 April 2011–14 September 2011. White Fox.

Thermae romae. Originally aired 12 January 2012–26 January 2012. DLE.

Time Quest / Taimu Toraburu Tondekeman / Time Travel Tondekeman. Originally aired 19 October 1989–26 August 1990. Ashi Productions / Tatsunoko Production.

Appendix 4: Video Games

The following list represents a range of video games that deal with time travel. They are useful entry points for an exploration of the genre, though many other interesting time travel games exist besides these.

BioShock Infinite (Irrational Games, 2013).
Braid (Number None, 2008).
Chrono Trigger (Square, 1995).
Command and Conquer: Red Alert (Westwood, 1996).
Crash Bandicoot: Warped (Naughty Dog, 1998).
Day of the Tentacle (LucasArts, 1993).
Ecco the Dolphin: Defender of the Future (Appaloosa Interactive, 2000).
Escape from Monkey Island (LucasArts, 2000).
Eternal Darkness: Sanity's Requiem (Silicon Knights, 2002).
Fez (Polytron Corporation, 2012).
Final Fantasy (Square, 1987).
God of War II (SCE Santa Monica Studio, 2007).
InFAMOUS (Sucker Punch Productions, 2009).
The Journeyman Project (Presto Studios, 1993).
The Legend of Zelda: Majora's Mask (Nintendo, 2000).
The Legend of Zelda: Ocarina of Time (Nintendo, 1998).
Mario and Luigi: Partners in Time (AlphaDream, 2005).
Onimusha 3: Demon Siege (Capcom, 2004).
Prince of Persia: The Sands of Time (Ubisoft Montreal, 2003).
Professor Layton and the Unwound Future (Level-5, 2008).
Ratchet and Clank Future: A Crack in Time (Insomniac Games, 2009).
The Silent Age (House on Fire, 2012).
Sonic Generations (Sonic Team, 2011).
Time Commando (Adeline Software International, 1996).
Timequest (Legend Entertainment, 1991).
TimeSplitters (Free Radical Design, 2000).
Where in Time Is Carmen Sandiago? (Brøderbund, 1989).

Appendix 5: A Selected Webography of Sites Dedicated to Time Travel

Theory and Philosophy

Hunter, Joel. 2004. "Time Travel." *Internet Encyclopedia of Philosophy*. http://www.iep.utm.edu/timetrav/. Accessed 15 July 2014. A summary of philosophical approaches to time travel.

Miller, Paul D. 2001. "Material Memories: Time and the Cinematic Image." *Ctheory.net*. http://www.ctheory.net/articles.aspx?id=135. Accessed 14 July 2014. A discussion of the relationship between time and the cinematic image.

Smith, Nicholas J. J. 2013. "Time Travel." *Stanford Encyclopedia of Philosophy*. http://plato.stanford.edu/entries/time-travel/. Accessed 14 July 2014. A thorough analysis of time travel philosophy.

Review Sites

Chronos. *Ultimate Time Travel*. http://www.ultimatetimetravel.com/?page_id=668. Accessed 14 July 2014. A site that aims to "review every single book, movie or television show" that deals with time travel. It classifies texts by subgenres that the author has defined.

Information

AsianWiki. Category: Time Travel Films. http://asianwiki.com/Category:Time_Travel_films Accessed 24 September 2014.

"List of Games Containing Time Travel." Various contributors. *Wikipedia*. http://en.wikipedia.org/wiki/List_of_games_containing_time_travel. Accessed 14 July 2014.

Main, Michael. "Time Travel Fiction." *Storypilot*. http://www.storypilot.com/time-travel-fiction.html. Accessed 14 July 2014. An extensive list of historical time travel fiction, including an anonymous short story in *The Dublin University Magazine* from June 1838.

Main, Michael. "Time Travel in U.S. Comic Books through 1969." *Storypilot*. http:// www.storypilot.com/time-travel-comics.html. Accessed 10 July 2014.

Manui, Barbara, Chris Adams and Dave Fooden. "Timelinks: The Big List." *Aetherco*. http://www.aetherco.com/timelinks/. Accessed 14 July 2014. A list of over 800 time travel films, television episodes and videos with brief explanations. Includes links to video content.

Time Travel Asian Dramas and Movies. http://hkctvdramas.tumblr.com/post/ 51832709194/time-traveling-asian-dramas-movies. Accessed 24 September 2014.

"Time Travel in Comics." Various contributors. *Wikipedia*. http://en.wikipedia. org/wiki/Category:Time_travel_comics. Accessed 14 July 2014.

"Time Travel Strips in Girls' Comics." Various contributors. *Comics UK*. http:// comicsuk.co.uk/forum/viewtopic.php?f=140&t=5627&view=previous. Accessed 14 July 2014. A discussion about time travel stories in UK comics targeted at young female readers.

Classification Sites

These sites use different foundations of knowledge for their classifications of time travel media texts.

"Our Time Travel is Different." Various contributors. *TV Tropes*. http://tvtropes. org/pmwiki/pmwiki.php/Main/OurTimeTravelIsDifferent. Accessed 14 July 2014. Classifies time travel into four types: unseen, instantaneous, wormhole and videocassette.

"Time Travel Films." Various contributors. *Wikipedia*. http://en.wikipedia.org/ wiki/Category:Time_travel_films. Accessed 14 July 2014. A list of time travel films that includes anime and European films. Subcategories of films are organized by media franchise.

Travers, Olivier, and Sophie Bellais. Scifan "Themes: Time Travel—Time Control— Time Warp." *Scifan*. http://www.scifan.com/themes/themes.asp?TH_themeid= 4&Items=. Accessed 14 July 2014. This list is based on literature rather than media texts, but is certainly informative.

Bibliography

Aarseth, Espen. 1997. *Cybertext: Perspectives on Ergodic Literature*. Baltimore: Johns Hopkins University Press.

Aarseth, Espen. 2004. "Genre Trouble: Narrativism and the Art of Simulation." In Noah Wardrip-Fruin and Pat Harrigan, eds., *First Person: New Media as Story, Performance, and Game*. Cambridge: MIT Press. 45–55.

Abbruzzese, John. 2001. "On Using the Multiverse to Avoid the Paradoxes of Time Travel." *Analysis* 61. 36–38.

"Al. B." 24 December 1983. "Questo Fantozzi è una boiata pazzesca." *L'Unità*. 17.

Alexander, Edward P., and Mary Alexander. 2008. *Museums in Motion: An Introduction to the History and Functions of Museums*, 2d ed. Plymouth: AltaMira Press.

Alkon, Paul K. 1987. *Origins of Futuristic Fiction*. Athens: University of Georgia Press.

Altman, Rick. 1984. "A Semantic/Syntactic Approach to Film Genre." *Cinema Journal* 23 (3). 6–18.

Altman, Rick. 1999. *Film/Genre*. London: BFI.

Anders, Charlie Jane. 2012. "Why Time Travel Stories Should Be Messy." *IO9*. http://io9.com/5945991/why-time-travel-stories-should-be-messy. Accessed 10 August 2013.

The Ape News. 1968. New York: Harry K. McWilliams Associates.

Armitt, Lucie. 2005. *Fantasy Fiction: An Introduction*. New York: Continuum.

Arnott, Luke. 2012. "Unraveling *Braid*: Puzzle Games and Storytelling in the Imperative Mode." *Bulletin of Science, Technology, and Society* 32 (6). 433–440.

Bailey, Kenneth Vye. 1990. "H. G. Wells and C.S. Lewis: Two Sides of a Visionary Coin." In Patrick Parrinder, ed., *H. G. Wells Under Revision*. Cranbury, NJ: Associated University Press. 226–232.

Balló, Jordi, and Xavier Perez. 2005. *Yo Ya He Estado Aquí: Ficciones de la Repetición*. Madrid: Anagrama.

Barjavel, René. 1943. *Le Voyageur imprudent*. Paris: Les Éditions Denoël.

Barnett, Kyle, Hector Amaya, Sarah Lynne Bowman, and Avi Santo. 2003. "An Interview with Rick Altman." *The Velvet Light Trap* 51. 67–72.

Barthes, Roland. 1977. *Image-Music-Text*. Trans. Stephen Heath. New York: Hill and Wang.

Baudrillard, Jean. 1981. "Simulacra and Simulations." In Mark Poster, ed., 2001. *Jean Baudrillard: Selected Writings*, 2d ed. Cambridge: Polity Press. 169–187.

Baudrillard, Jean. 1994. *Simulacra and Simulation*. Ann Arbor: University of Michigan Press.

Baudry, Jean-Louis. 1986. "The Apparatus: Metaphysical Approaches to Ideology." In P. Rosen, ed., *Narrative, Apparatus, Ideology*. New York: Columbia University Press. 299–318.

Baxter, Stephen. 1995. *The Time Ships*. London: HarperCollins.

Bazin, André. 1997. *What is Cinema? Volume I*. Ed. and trans. Hugh Gray. Berkeley: University of California Press.

Belau, Linda. 2002. "Trauma, Repetition, and the Hermeneutics of Psychoanalysis." In Linda Belau and Petar Ramadanovic, eds., *Topologies of Trauma: Essays on the Limit of Knowledge and Memory*. New York: Other Press. 151–75.

Bellamy, Edward, 1967 (1888). *Looking Backward: 2000–1887*. Cambridge: Belknap Press of Harvard University Press.

Benedict, Steven. 2013. "Inception." *Stephen Benedict*. http://www.stevenbenedict.ie/2013/02/analysis-of-inception/. Accessed 6 October 2014.

Benjamin, Walter. 1936. "The Work of Art

in the Age of Mechanical Reproduction." In Leo Braudy and Marshall Cohen, eds., 2004. *Film Theory and Criticism*. Oxford: Oxford University Press. 791–811.

Bergson, Henri. 1910. *Time and Free Will: An Essay on the Immediate Data of Consciousness*. London: George Allen and Unwin.

Bergson, Henri. 1991. *Matter and Memory*. Trans. Nancy Margaret Paul and W. Scott Palmer. New York: Zone Books.

Bergson, Henri. 2002. *Matter and Memory*. Trans. Nancy Margaret Paul and W. Scott Palmer. New York: Zone Books.

Berman, Emanuel. 1997. "Hitchcock's *Vertigo*: The Collapse of a Rescue Fantasy." *International Journal of Psycho-Analysis* 78 (5). 975–996.

Bettelheim, Bruno. 1991. *The Uses of Enchantment: The Meaning and Importance of Fairy Tales*. Harmondsworth: Penguin.

Bignell, Jonathan. 2004. "Another Time, Another Space: Modernity, Subjectivity and *The Time Machine*." In Sean Redmond, ed., *Liquid Metal: The Science Fiction Film Reader*. London: Wallflower Press. 136–144.

Birchard, Robert S. 2004. *Cecil B. DeMille's Hollywood*. Lexington: University Press of Kentucky.

Blandin, Patrick. 2001. "The Grande Galerie de l'Evolution." In Barry Lord and Gail Dexter Lord, eds., *Manual of Museum Exhibitions*. Walnut Creek, CA: AltaMira Press. 479–481.

Bolter, Jay David, and Richard Grusin. 2000. *Remediation*. Cambridge: MIT Press.

Booth, Paul. 2010. *Digital Fandom: New Media Studies*. New York: Peter Lang.

Booth, Paul. 2012. *Time on TV: Temporal Displacement and Mashup Television*. New York: Peter Lang.

Bordwell, David. 1985. *Narration in the Fiction Film*. Madison: University of Wisconsin Press.

Borges, Jorge Luis. 2000. *Other Inquisitions 1937–1952*. Austin: University of Texas Press.

Botting, Fred. 1999. *Sex, Machines and Navels: Fiction, Fantasy and History in the Future Present*. Manchester: Manchester University Press.

Bould, Mark. 2012. *Science Fiction*. London: Routledge.

Bourdaa, Mélanie. 2013. "'Following the Pattern': The Creation of an Encyclopaedic Universe with Transmedia Storytelling." *Adaptation* 6 (2). 202–214.

Boussenard, Louis Henri. 1890. *Dix mille ans dans un bloc de glace*. Paris: E. Flammarion.

Boym, Svetlana. 2001. *The Future of Nostalgia*. New York: Basic.

Bradbury, Ray. 28 June 1952. "A Sound of Thunder." *Collier's*.

Braun, Beth. 2000. "*The X-Files* and *Buffy the Vampire Slayer*: The Ambiguity of Evil in Supernatural Representations." *Journal of Popular Film and Television* 28 (2). 88–94.

Brockmeier, Jens. 2002. "Remembering and Forgetting: Narrative as Cultural Memory." *Culture and Psychology* 8 (1). 15–43.

Brooker, M. Keith. 2002. *Strange TV: Innovative Television Series from The Twilight Zone to The X-Files*. Westport, CT: Greenwood Press.

Brooker, Will. 2012. *Hunting the Dark Knight: Twenty-First Century Batman*. London: I.B. Tauris.

Brooks, Ann. 1997. *Postfeminisms: Feminism, Cultural Theory and Cultural Forms*. London: Routledge.

Brown, William. 2013. *Supercinema: Film-Philosophy for the Digital Age*. New York: Berghahn Books.

Brunetta, Gian Piero. 2004. *Cent'anni di cinema italiano 2: Dal 1945 ai giorni nostri*. Bari: Laterza.

Buchanan, Ian. 2000. *Deleuzism: A Metacommentary*. Edinburgh: Edinburgh University Press.

Buckingham, David, Hannah Davies, Ken Jones, and Peter Kelley. 1999. *Children's Television in Britain: History, Discourse and Policy*. London: BFI.

Buckland, Warren, ed. 2009. *Puzzle Films: Complex Storytelling in Contemporary Cinema*. Oxford: Blackwell.

Butler, David. 2007. *Time and Relative Dissertations in Space: Critical Perspectives on Doctor Who*. Manchester: Manchester University Press.

Byrne, Dennis. 28 October 1998. "Not a Very Pleasant Place to Visit." *Chicago Sun-Times*. 145.

Camus, Albert. 1942. *Le Mythe de Sisyphe*. Paris: Gallimard.

Caruth, Cathy. 1996. *Unclaimed Experience: Trauma, Narrative, and History*. Baltimore: Johns Hopkins University Press.

Cecil B. DeMille Archives. Harold B. Lee Library. Brigham Young University, Provo, Utah.

Chien, Irene. 2007/2008. "Playing Undead." *Film Quarterly* 61 (2). 64–66.

Clarke, Arthur C., and Stephen Baxter. 2000. *The Light of Other Days*. London: HarperCollins.

Coates, Paul. 1987. "Chris Marker and the Cinema as Time Machine." *Science Fiction Studies* 14 (3). 307–315.

Colebrook, Claire. 2002. *Gilles Deleuze*. Oxford: Routledge.

Collins, Jim. 1993. "Genericity in the Nineties: Eclectic Irony and the New Sincerity." In Jim Collins, Hilary Radner, and Ava Preacher Collins, eds., *Film Theory Goes to the Movies*. New York: Routledge. 242–263.

Conway, Gerry, and Doug Moench. August 1974. "Editorial." *Planet of the Apes Magazine* 1. Magazine Management Co.

Conway, Martin A., and David C. Rubin. 1993. "The Structure of Autobiographical Memory." In Alan F. Collins, Susan E. Gathercole, Martin A. Conway and Peter E. Morris, eds., *Theories of Memory*, vol. 1. Hove: Lawrence Erlbaum Associates. 103–137.

Cook, Daniel. 2007. "The Chemistry of Game Design." *Gamasutra*. http://www.gamasutra.com/view/feature/129948/the_chemistry_of_game_design.php. Accessed 6 October 2014.

Cooke, Lez. 2003. *British Television Drama: A History*. London: BFI.

Cooke, Pam. 1990. *Back to the Future*. London: Unwin Hyman.

Cosslett, Tess. 2002. "'History from Below': Time-Slip Narratives and National Identity." *The Lion and the Unicorn* 26 (2). 243–253.

Coveney, Peter, and Roger Highfield. 1991. *The Arrow of Time: The Quest to Solve Science's Greatest Mystery*. London: Flamingo.

Cowie, Elizabeth. 1984. "Fantasia." *m/f*. 9. 70–105.

Crane, Susan. 2000. "Introduction: Of Museums and Memory." In Susan Crane, ed., *Museums and Memory*. Redwood City, CA: Stanford University Press. 1–14.

Crossley, Robert. 1991. "In the Palace of Green Porcelain: Artefacts from the Museums of Science Fiction." In Tom

Shippey, ed., *Fictional Space: Essays on Contemporary Science Fiction*. Oxford: Basil Blackwell. 76–103.

Davis, Fred. 1979. *Yearning for Yesterday: A Sociology of Nostalgia*. New York: Free Press.

Decker, Kevin S. 2013. *Who Is Who? The Philosophy of Doctor Who*. London: I.B. Tauris.

DeLanda, Manuel. 2006. *A New Philosophy of Society: Assemblage Theory and Social Complexity*. New York: Continuum.

DeLanda, Manuel. 2011. *Philosophy and Simulation: The Emergence of Synthetic Reason*. New York: Continuum.

Deleuze, Gilles. 1986. *Cinema 1: The Movement-Image*. Minneapolis: University of Minnesota Press.

Deleuze, Gilles. 1988. *Foucault*. Minneapolis: University of Minnesota Press.

Deleuze, Gilles. 1989. *Cinema 2: The Time Image*. London: Athlone Press.

Deleuze, Gilles. 1994. *Difference and Repetition*. New York: Continuum.

Deleuze, Gilles. 1995. *Negotiations 1972–1990*. New York: Columbia University Press.

Deleuze, Gilles. 2001a. *Cinema 2: The Time-image*. Trans. Hugh Tomlinson and Robert Galeta. Minneapolis: University of Minnesota Press.

Deleuze, Gilles. 2001b. *Pure Imminence: Essays on Life*. Cambridge: MIT Press.

Deleuze, Gilles. 2002. *Cinema 1: The Movement-image*. Trans. Hugh Tomlinson and Barbara Habberjam. London: The Athlone Press.

Deleuze, Gilles. 2004a. *Difference and Repetition*. London: Continuum.

Deleuze, Gilles. 2004b. *Logic of Sense*. Trans. Mark Lester with Charles Stivale. London: Continuum.

Deleuze, Gilles, and Félix Guattari. 1994. *What Is Philosophy?* London: Verso.

Deleuze, Gilles, and Félix Guattari. 2003. *Anti-Oedipus: Capitalism and Schizophrenia*. Trans. Robert Hurley, Mark Seem, and Helen R. Lane. London: Continuum.

Deleuze, Gilles, and Félix Guattari. 2004a. *Anti-Oedipus*. London: Continuum.

Deleuze, Gilles, and Félix Guattari. 2004b. *A Thousand Plateaus: Capitalism and Schizophrenia*. London: Continuum.

Deleuze, Gilles, and Claire Parnet. 2007. *Dialogues II*. New York: Columbia Press.

De Quincey, Thomas. 1821. "Confessions of an English Opium-Eater." *London Magazine* 4 (21), 293–312; 4 (22), 358–379.

De Souza e Silva, Adriana, and Daniel M. Sutko. 2011. "Placing Location-aware Media in a History of the Virtual." In David W. Park, Nicholas W. Jankowski and Steve Jones, eds., *The Long History of New Media*. New York: Peter Lang. 299–316.

Deutsch, David. 1991. "Quantum Mechanics Near Closed Timelike Lines." *Physical Review D* 44. 3197–217.

Deutsch, David. 1997. *The Fabric of Reality*. London: Allen Lane.

Deutsch, David, and Michael Lockwood. March 1994. "The Quantum Physics of Time Travel." *Scientific American* 270. 68–74.

Devlin, William J. 2008. "Some Paradoxes of Time-Travel in *The Terminator* and *12 Monkeys*." In Steven M. Sanders, ed., *The Philosophy of Science Fiction Film*. Lexington: University Press of Kentucky. 103–118.

Dickens, Charles. 1843. *A Christmas Carol*. London: Chapman and Hall.

Dika, Vera. 2003. *Recycled Culture in Contemporary Art and Film*. Cambridge: Cambridge University Press.

Dimitrakaki, Andrea, and Tsiantis Miltos. 2002. "Terminators, Monkeys and Mass Culture: The Carnival of Time in Science Fiction Films." *Time and Society* 11 (2/3). 209–231.

Doane, Mary Anne. 2002. *The Emergence of Cinematic Time: Modernity, Contingency, the Archive*. Cambridge: Harvard University Press.

Donaldson, Lucy Fife. 2010. "'There is something very familiar about all this': Generic Play and Performance in the *Back to the Future* Trilogy." In Sorcha Ní Fhlainn, ed., *The Worlds of Back to the Future: Critical Essays on the Films*. Jefferson, NC: McFarland. 73–90.

Edgerton, Gary R. 2001. "Introduction: Television as Historian: A Different Kind of History All Together." In Gary R. Edgerton and Peter C. Rollins, eds., *Television Histories: Shaping Collective Memory in the Media Age*. Lexington: University of Kentucky Press. 1–18.

Effingham, Nikk. 2012. "An Unwelcome Consequence of the Multiverse Thesis." *Synthese* 184. 375–86.

Effingham, Nikk, and Jon Robson. 2007. "A Mereological Challenge to Endurantism." *Australasian Journal of Philosophy* 85. 633–40.

Eisner, Will. 2008. *Comics and Sequential Art: Principles and Practices from the Legendary Cartoonist*. New York: W. W. Norton.

Eliade, Mircea. 1971. *The Myth of the Eternal Return, or, Cosmos and History*. Princeton: Princeton University Press.

Elsaesser, Thomas. 2009. "The Mind-Game Film." In Warren Buckland, ed., *Puzzle Films: Complex Storytelling in Contemporary Cinema*. Oxford: Blackwell. 13–41.

Elsaesser, Thomas. 2013. "Los Actos Tienen Consecuencias: Lógicas del Mind-Game Film en la Trilogía de Los Ángeles de David Lynch." *L'Atalante, Revista de Estudios Cinematográficos* 15. 7–18.

Erisman, Fred. 1992. "The Night Christopher Lloyd Danced with Mary Steenburgen." *Journal of Popular Film and Television* 20 (1). 29–33.

Errando, Jose Antonio Palao. 2004. *La Profecía de la Imagen-mundo: Para una Genealogía del Paradigma Informativo*. Valencia: IVAC.

Exshaw, John. 2010. "Bury My Heart in Hill Valley, or, The Kid Who KO'd Liberty Valance." In Sorcha Ní Fhlainn, ed., *The Worlds of Back to the Future: Critical Essays on the Films*. Jefferson, NC: McFarland. 91–111.

Fancy, David. 2010. "Difference, Bodies, Desire: The Collaborative Thought of Gilles Deleuze and Félix Guattari." *Science Fiction Film and Television* 3 (1). 93–106.

Findlen, Paula. 1994. *Possessing Nature: Museums, Collecting, and Scientific Culture in Early Modern Italy*. Berkeley: University of California Press.

Firchow, Peter. 1976. "Wells and Lawrence in Huxley's *Brave New World*." *Journal of Modern Literature* 5 (2). 260–278.

Forrest, Peter. 2010. "Van Inwagen's Irresponsible Time-travelers." *Oxford Studies in Metaphysics* 5. 29–39.

Frasca, Gonzalo. 1999. "Ludology Meets Narratology: Similitude and Differences Between (Video) Games and Narrative." *Parnasso* 3. www.ludology.org/articles/

ludology.htm. 365–371. Accessed 6 June 2013.

Frasca, Gonzalo. 2003a. "Ludologists Love Stories, Too: Notes from a Debate that Never Took Place." *Digital Games Research Conference 2003 Proceedings.* http://www.ludology.org/articles/frasca_levelup2003.pdf. Accessed 5 June 2013.

Frasca, Gonzalo. 2003b. "Simulation Versus Narrative: Introduction to Ludology." In Mark J.P. Wolf and Bernard Perron, eds., *The Video Game Theory Reader.* London: Routledge. 221–236.

Freedman, Carl. 2000. "Science Fiction and Utopia: A Historico-philosophical Overview." In Patrick Parrinder, ed., *Learning from Other Worlds: Estrangement, Cognition, and the Politics of Science Fiction and Utopia.* Liverpool: University of Liverpool Press. 72–97.

French, Sean. 1996. *The Terminator.* London: BFI.

Freud, Sigmund. 1991. *The Interpretation of Dreams.* The Penguin Freud Library. Vol. 4. Angela Richards, ed., Trans. James Strachey. London: Penguin.

Freud, Sigmund. 2003a. *The Uncanny.* Trans. David McLintock. London: Penguin Classics.

Freud, Sigmund. 2003b. *Tótem y Tabú.* Madrid: Alianza Editorial.

Freud, Sigmund. 2006. "Remembering, Repeating, and Working Through." In Adam Phillips, ed., *The Penguin Freud Reader.* Trans. John Reddick. New York: Penguin. 391–401.

Freud, Sigmund. 2011. *Beyond the Pleasure Principle.* Todd Dufresne, ed., Trans. Gregory C. Richter. Peterborough, ON: Broadview Editions.

Friedberg, Anne. 1993. *Window Shopping: Cinema and the Postmodern.* Berkeley: University of California Press.

Fromm, Erich. 1960. "Foreword." In Edward Bellamy. *Looking Backward 2000–1887.* New York: Signet.

Furby, Jacqueline. 2013. "The Fissure King." In Jeff Birkenstein, Anna Froula, and Karen Randell, eds., *The Cinema of Terry Gilliam: It's a Mad World.* Chichester: Wallflower Press. 79–91.

Furby, Jacqueline. 2014. "Mad as a Hamster." *Deletion: The Open Access Forum in Science Fiction Studies.* Episode 3. February.

http://www.deletionscifi.org/episodes/mad-as-a-hamster/. Accessed 28 May 2014.

García-Catalán, Shaila. 2012. "El Delorean Extraviado: Usos Confusos del *Flashback* Postclásico (y Otros Viajes Temporales)." *Revista Comunicación* 10 (1). 1103–1115.

Garland-Thompson, Rosemarie. "Integrating Disability, Transforming Feminist Theory." In Lennard J. Davis, ed., *The Disability Studies Reader.* London: Routledge. 333–54.

Garritano, Brian. 2010. "Video Gaming: A New Form of Story Telling." In Rachel Rigolino, Joann K. Deiudicibus and James R. Sherwood, eds., *New Voices, New Visions.* http://www.newpaltz.edu/english/composition/nvnv2010.pdf. 109–114. Accessed 12 August 2013.

Geach, Peter. 1977. *Providence and Evil.* Cambridge: Cambridge University Press.

Gee, James Paul. 2007. *What Video Games Have to Teach Us About Learning and Literacy,* 2d ed. New York: Palgrave Macmillan.

Gemlis, Joseph. February 1968. "Planet of the Apes." *Newsday.*

Geraghty, Lincoln. 2010. "The *Star Trek* Franchise." In Stacey Abbott, ed., *The Cult TV Book.* London: I.B. Tauris. 131–134.

Gerrold, David. 1973. *The Man Who Folded Himself.* New York: Random House.

Giacovelli, Enrico. 1992. *Breve storia del cinema comico italiano.* Turin: Lindau.

Gill, Pat. 1997. "Technostalgia: Making the Future Past Perfect." *Camera Obscura* 14 (1–2 40–41). 161–79.

Gillan, Jennifer. 2010. *Television and New Media: Must Click TV.* New York: Routledge.

Gleick, James. 1988. *Chaos: Making a New Science.* London: Penguin.

Goddu, G.C. 2003. "Time Travel and Changing the Past (or How to Kill Yourself and Live to Tell the Tale)." *Ratio* 16. 16–32.

Goff, Philip. 2010. "Could the Daleks Stop the Pyramids Being Built?" In Courtland Lewis and Paula Smithka, eds., *Doctor Who and Philosophy.* Chicago: Open Court. 67–74.

Golding, Jonathan M., and Colin M. Macleod, eds., 1998. *Intentional Forgetting: Interdisciplinary Approaches.* Mahwah, NJ: Lawrence Erlbaum Associates.

Goodman, David A. 2013. *Federation: The First 150 Years.* London: Titan Books.

Gordon, Andrew. 1987. "*Back to the Future*: Oedipus as Time Traveler." *Science Fiction Studies* 14 (3). 372–385.

Gordon, Andrew. 2004. "*Back to the Future*: Oedipus as Time Traveler." In Sean Redmond, ed., *Liquid Metal: The Science Fiction Film Reader*. London: Wallflower Press. 116–125.

Grainge, Paul. 2000. "Nostalgia and Style in Retro America: Moods, Modes, and Media Recycling." *Journal of American Culture* 23 (1). 27–34.

Grey, William. 1999. "Troubles with Time Travel." *Philosophy* 74 (287). 55–70.

Grieco, David. 23 November 1974. "Le catastrofi di Fantozzi sullo schermo." *L'Unità*. 9.

Groensteen, Thierry. 2007. *The System of Comics*. Trans. Bart Beaty and Nick Nguyen. Jackson: University Press of Mississippi.

Grosz, Elizabeth. 2004. *The Nick of Time: Politics, Evolution, and the Untimely*. Durham: Duke University Press.

Grosz, Elizabeth. 2005. *Time Travels: Feminism, Nature, Power*. Durham: Duke University Press.

Hall, Linda. 1998. "Aristocratic Houses and Radical Politics: Historical Fiction and the Time-Slip Story in E. Nesbit's The House of Arden." *Children's Literature in Education* 29 (1). 51–58.

Hall, Linda. 2003. "Ancestral Voices—'Since Time Everlasting Beyond': Kipling and the Invention of the Time-Slip Story." *Children's Literature in Education* 34 (4). 305–321.

Handley, Rich. 2008. *Timeline of the Planet of the Apes: The Definitive Chronology*. New York: Hasslein.

Harbord, Janet. 2009. *Chris Marker, La jetée*. London: Afterall Books.

Hardt, Michael, and Antonio Negri. 2000. *Empire*. Cambridge: Harvard University Press.

Hark, Ina Rae. 2008. *Star Trek*. London: Palgrave Macmillan.

Harwich, Paul. 1987. *Asymmetries in Time: Problems in the Philosophy of Science*. Cambridge: MIT Press.

Harwood-Smith, Jennifer, and Francis Ludlow. 2010. "'Doing it in style': The Narrative Rules of Time Travel in the *Back to the Future* Trilogy." In Sorcha Ní Fhlainn, ed., *The Worlds of Back to the Future: Crit-ical Essays on the Film*. Jefferson, NC: McFarland. 232–254.

Hawking, Stephen. 1990. *A Brief History of Time: From the Big Bang to Black Holes*. London: Guild Publishing.

Hawking, Stephen. 2001. *The Universe in a Nutshell*. London: Bantam Press.

Hayles, N. Katherine. 1999. *How We Became Posthuman: Virtual Bodies in Cybernetics, Literature, and Informatics*. Chicago: University of Chicago Press.

Hayne, Donald, ed., 1959. *The Autobiography of Cecil B. DeMille*. Englewood Cliffs, NJ: Prentice-Hall.

Hein, George E. 1999. "Is Meaning Making Constructivism? Is Constructivism Meaning Making?" *The Exhibitionist* 18 (2). 15–18.

Heinlein, Robert A. 1959. "–All You Zombies–." In Orson Scott Card, ed., *Masterpieces: The Best Science Fiction of the Twentieth Century*. New York: Ace. 36–46.

Henderson, Brian. 2004. "Toward a Non-Bourgeois Camera Style." In Leo Braudy and Marshall Cohen, eds., *Film Theory and Criticism: Introductory Readings*, 6th ed. New York: Oxford University Press. 54–64.

Herman, David. 2002. *Story Logic: Problems and Possibilities of Narrative*. Lincoln: University of Nebraska Press.

Hersey, Eleanor. 1998. "Word-Healers and Code-Talkers: Native Americans in *The X-Files*." *Journal of Popular Film and Television* 26 (3). 108–119.

Herzog, Amy. 2012. "Fictions of the Imagination: Habit, Genre and Powers of the False." In David Martin-Jones and William Brown. *Deleuze and Film*. Edinburgh: Edinburgh University Press. 137–154.

Hewett, LD. 1994. "Letters to the Editor." *Scientific American* 271. 5.

Hijiya, James A. 2011. "The *Gita* of Robert Oppenheimer." *Proceedings of the American Philosophical Society* 2. 123–167.

Hills, Matt. 2002. *Fan Cultures*. London: Routledge.

Hooper-Greenhill, Eilean. 1994. *Museums and Their Visitors*. London: Routledge.

Hooper-Greenhill, Eilean. 2000. "Changing Values in the Art Museum: Rethinking Communication and Learning." *International Journal of Heritage Studies* 6 (1). 9–31.

Horwich, Paul. 1975. "On Some Alleged Paradoxes of Time Travel." *Journal of Philosophy* 72. 432–44.

Howells, Sacha A. 2002. "Watching a Game, Playing a Movie: When Media Collide." In Geoff King and Tanya Kryzwinska, eds., *Screenplay: Cinema/Videogames/Interfaces*. London: Wallflower Press. 110–121.

Hudson, Hud, and Ryan Wasserman. 2010. "Van Inwagen on Time Travel and Changing the Past." *Oxford Studies in Metaphysics* 5. 41–49.

Hunt, Peter. 1987. "Landscapes and Journeys, Metaphors and Maps: The Distinctive Feature of English Fantasy." *Children's Literature Association Quarterly* 12 (1). 11–14.

Husbands, Chris, Alison Kitson, and Anna Pendry. 2003. *Understanding History Teaching: Teaching and Learning about the Past in Secondary Schools*. Maidenhead: Open University Press.

Hutcheon, Linda. 1989. *The Politics of Postmodernism*. London: Routledge.

Hutcheon, Linda. 2002. *The Politics of Postmodernism*. London: Routledge.

Huxley, Aldous. 1932. *Brave New World*. London: Chatto and Windus.

Huxley, Aldous. 2007. *Brave New World*. London: Vintage.

Inglis, Fred. 2000. *The Delicious History of the Holiday*. London: Routledge.

Jackson, Rosemary. 1981. *Fantasy: The Literature of Subversion*. London: Routledge.

Jameson, Frederic. 1989. "Nostalgia for the Present." In Jane Gaines, ed., *Classical Hollywood Narrative: The Paradigm Wars*. Durham: Duke University Press. 253–75.

Jameson, Fredric. 1991. *Postmodernism, or, The Cultural Logic of Late Capitalism*. Durham: Duke University Press.

Jameson, Fredric. 1992. *Signatures of the Visible*. London: Routledge.

Jameson, Fredric. 1998. "Postmodernism and Consumer Society." In Hal Foster, ed., *The Anti-Aesthetic: Essays on Postmodern Culture*. New York: The New Press. 111–125.

Jameson, Fredric. 2001. "Postmodernism, or the Cultural Logic of Late Capitalism." In Meenakshi Gigi Durham and Douglas M. Kellner, eds., *Media and Cultural Studies: Key Works*. Malden, MA: Blackwell. 482–519.

Jameson, Frederic. 2002. "Postmodernism and the Consumer Society." In Hal Foster, ed., *The Anti-Aesthetic: Essays on Postmodern Culture*. New York: New Press. 111–125.

Jenkins, Henry. 2003. "Transmedia Storytelling. Moving Characters from Books to Films to Video Games Can Make Them Stronger and More Compelling." *Technology Review*. http://www.technologyreview.com/news/401760/transmedia-storytelling/. Accessed 31 August 2013.

Jenkins, Henry. 2004. "Game Design as Narrative Architecture." In Noah Wardrip-Fruin and Pat Harrigan, eds., *First Person: New Media as Story, Performance and Game*. Cambridge: MIT Press. 118–130.

Jenkins, Henry. 2006. *Convergence Culture: Where Old and New Media Collide*. New York: New York University Press.

Jenkins, Robert, and Susan Jenkins. 1998. *Life Signs: The Biology of Star Trek*. London: HarperCollins.

Jennings, Michael, ed., 2006. *The Writer of Modern Life: Essays on Charles Baudelaire by Walter Benjamin*. Cambridge: Belknap Press of Harvard University Press.

Jindra, Michael. 1999. "'*Star Trek* to Me is a Way of Life': Fan Expressions of *Star Trek* Philosophy." In Jennifer E. Porter and Darcee L. McLaren, eds., *Star Trek and Sacred Ground: Explorations of Star Trek, Religion, and American Culture*. New York: State University of New York Press. 217–230.

Johnson, Catherine. 2005. *Telefantasy*. London: BFI.

Johnson-Smith, Jan. 2005. *American Science Fiction TV: Star Trek, Stargate and Beyond*. London: I. B. Tauris.

Jones, Sara Gwenllian. 2002. "The Sex Lives of Cult Television Characters." *Screen* 43 (1). 79–90.

Jordanova, Ludmilla. 1989. "Objects of Knowledge: A Historical Perspective on Museums." In Peter Vergo, ed., *The New Museology*. London: Reaktion Books. 22–40.

Juul, Jesper. 2004. "Introduction to Game Time." In Noah Wardrip-Fruinm and Pat Harrigan, eds., *First Person: New Media as Story, Performance, and Game*. Cambridge: MIT Press. 131–142.

Juul, Jesper. 2013. *The Art of Failure: An Essay on the Pain of Playing Videogames*. Cambridge: MIT Press.

Kawin, Bruce. 1982. "Time and Stasis in *La Jetée.*" *Film Quarterly* 36 (1). 15–20.

Kellner, Douglas. 2011. "Frederic Jameson." *Illuminations.* http://www.uta.edu/huma/illuminations/kell19.htm. Accessed 11 May 2005.

Kitses, Jim. 1969. *Horizons West: Anthony Mann, Budd Boetticher, Sam Peckinpah: Studies of Authorship within the Western.* London: BFI/Thames and Hudson.

Kitses, Jim. 1998. "Introduction: Postmodernism and The Western." In Jim Kitses and Gregg Rickman, eds., *The Western Reader.* New York: Limelight Editions. 15–31.

Klastrup, Lisbeth. 2007. "Why Death Matters: Understanding Gameworld Experience." *Journal of Virtual Reality and Broadcasting* 4 (3). http://www.jvrb.org/past-issues/4.2007/1022. Accessed 17 July 2014.

Kompare, Derek. 2006. "Publishing Flow: DVD Box Sets and the Reconception of Television." *Television and New Media* 7 (4). 335–360.

Kowalski, Dean A., ed., 2007. *The Philosophy of the X-Files.* Lexington: University Press of Kentucky.

Krämer, Peter. 2005. "Big Pictures: Studying Contemporary Hollywood Cinema Through its Greatest Hits." In Jacqueline Furby and Karen Randell, eds., *Screen Methods: Comparative Readings in Film Studies.* London: Wallflower Press. 124–132.

Krauss, Lawrence. 1995. *The Physics of Star Trek.* New York: Basic Books.

Krondorfer, Björn. 2008. "Is Forgetting Reprehensible? Holocaust Remembrance and the Tack of Oblivion." *Journal of Religious Ethics* 36 (2). 233–267.

Kuhn, Annette. 1990. *Alien Zone.* London: Verso.

Kujundzic, Dragan. 2003. "After 'After': The 'Arkive' Fever of Alexander Sokurov." *Quarterly Review of Film and Video* 21 (3). 219–239.

Lacan, Jacques. 1977. *Écrits. A Selection.* Trans. Alan Sheridan. London: Tavistock Publications.

Landsberg, Alison. 1995. "Prosthetic Memory: *Total Recall* and *Blade Runner.*" In Mike Featherstone and Roger Burrows, eds., *Cyberspace/Cyberbodies/Cyberpunk.* London: Sage. 175–189.

Langshaw, Mark. 2010. "Retro Corner: 'Day of the Tentacle.'" *Digital Spy: Level Up.* http://www.digitalspy.com/gaming/levelup/a245962/retro-corner-day-of-the-tentacle-pc.html#ixzz2blfNxt8D. Accessed 12 August 2013.

Layton, David. 2012. *The Humanism of Doctor Who: A Critical Study in Science Fiction and Philosophy.* Jefferson, NC: McFarland.

Leftow, Brian. 2004. "A Latin Trinity." *Faith and Philosophy* 21. 304–33.

Le Poidevin, Robin. 2005. "The Cheshire Cat Problem and Other Spatial Obstacles to Backwards Time Travel." *The Monist* 88. 336–52.

Levinson, Paul. September 1995. "The Chronology Protection Case." *Analog.*

Lewis, C. S. 1986. *That Hideous Strength.* New York: Scribner Paperbacks.

Lewis, Courtland, and Paula Smithka. 2010. *Doctor Who and Philosophy: Bigger on the Inside.* Chicago: Open Court.

Lewis, David. 1976a. "The Paradoxes of Time Travel." *American Philosophical Quarterly* 13 (2). 145–152.

Lewis, David. 1976b. "The Paradoxes of Time Travel." In Susan Schneider, ed., 2009. *Science Fiction and Philosophy: From Time Travel to Superintelligence.* Malden, MA: Blackwell. 310–321.

Livingstone, Sonia. 1998. *Making Sense of Television: The Psychology of Audience Interpretation,* 2d ed. London: Routledge.

Louvish, Simon. 2007. *Cecil B. DeMille: A Life in Art.* New York: St. Martin's Press.

"L.P." 21 November 1980. "La riscossa di Fantozzi." *L'Unità.* 9.

Lupoff, Richard A. December 1973. "12:01 PM." *The Magazine of Fantasy and Science Fiction.*

Lyotard, Jean-François. 1984. *The Postmodern Condition: A Report on Knowledge.* Trans. Geoffrey Bennington and Brian Massumi. Minneapolis: University of Minnesota Press.

MacKinnon, Dolly. 2011. "'That Brave Company of Shadows': Gender, National Identity, and the Formation of Children's British History in Alison Uttley's *A Traveler in Time.*" *Women's History Review* 20 (5). 809–827.

Marcus, Daniel. 1997. "NBC's 'Project XX': Television and American History at the End of Ideology." *Historical Journal of Film, Radio and Television* 17 (3). 347–367.

Martin-Jones, David. 2011. *Deleuze and World Cinemas*. London: Continuum.

McArthur, Colin. 1980. *BFI Television Monograph 8: Television and History*. London: BFI.

McCarthy, Elizabeth. 2010. "Back to the Fifties! Fixing the Future." In Sorcha Ní Fhlainn, ed., *The Worlds of Back to the Future: Critical Essays on the Films*. Jefferson, NC: McFarland. 133–156.

McCloud, Scott. 1994. *Understanding Comics*. New York: Harper Perennial.

McGowan, Todd. 2011. *Out of Time: Desire in Atemporal Cinema*. Minneapolis: University of Minnesota Press.

McMahon, Allison. 2003. "Immersion, Engagement, and Presence: A Method for Analyzing 3-D Video Games." In Mark J.P. Wolf and Bernard Perron, eds., *The Video Game Theory Reader*. New York: Routledge. 67–86.

McManus, Paulette M. 1989. "Oh, Yes, They Do: How Museum Visitors Read Labels and Interact with Exhibit Texts." *Curator: The Museum Journal* 32 (3). 174–189.

McRobbie, Angela. 1996. "Postmodernism and Popular Culture." In Paul Marris and Sue Thornham, eds., *Media Studies: A Reader*. Edinburgh: Edinburgh University Press. 350–361.

McRuer, Robert. 2006. *Crip Theory: Cultural Signs of Queerness and Disability*. New York: New York University Press.

Meiland, Jack. 1974. "A Two-Dimensional Passage Model of Time for Time Travel." *Philosophical Studies* 26. 153–73.

Meisler, Andy. 1998. *I Want to Believe: The Official Guide to The X-Files*. Vol. 3. New York: HarperCollins.

Meisler, Andy. 2000. *The End of the Beginning: The Official Guide to The X-Files*. Vol. 5. New York: HarperCollins.

Metz, Christian. 1974. *Film Language: A Semiotics of the Cinema*. Chicago: University of Chicago Press.

Metz, Christian. 1983. *Psychoanalysis and Cinema: The Imaginary Signifier*. London: Macmillan.

Middleton, Peter, and Tim Woods. 2000. *Literatures of Memory: History, Time and Space in Postwar Writing*. Manchester: Manchester University Press.

Mitchell, David, and Sharon Snyder. "Narrative Prosthesis." In Lennard J. Davis, ed., *The Disability Studies Reader*. London: Routledge. 222–36.

Mitchell, Edward Page. 1881. "The Clock that Went Backward." In Ann and Jeff Vandemeer, eds., 2013. *The Time Traveler's Almanac: The Ultimate Treasury of Time Travel Stories*. London: Head of Zeus. 450–459.

Mitry, Jean. 1998. *The Aesthetics and Psychology of the Cinema*. Trans. Christopher King. London: The Athlone Press.

Mittell, Jason. 2011. *Complex TV: The Poetics of Contemporary Television Storytelling*. http://mediacommons.futureofthebook.org/mcpress/complextelevision/transmedia-storytelling/. Accessed 4 September 2012.

Moench, Doug, and Alfredo Alcala. June 1975. "Kingdom on an Island of the Apes." *Planet of the Apes Magazine* 9. Magazine Management Co.

Moorcock, Michael. 1969. *Behold the Man*. London: Allison and Busby.

Moorcock, Michael. 1993. *Dancers at the End of Time*. London: Orion.

Moore, Alan, and David Gibbons. 1987. *Watchmen*. New York: DC Comics.

Morgan, David L. 2013. "We Came From Your Future." In John Huss, ed., *Planet of the Apes and Philosophy*. Chicago: Open Court. 99–110.

Morrison, Grant. 2010. *The Return of Bruce Wayne*. New York: DC Comics.

Moses, Michael Valdez. 2008. "Kingdom of Darkness: Autonomy and Conspiracy in *The X-Files* and *Millennium*." In Steven M. Sanders and Aeon J. Skoble, eds., *The Philosophy of TV Noir*. Lexington: University Press of Kentucky. 203–227.

Mulvey, Laura. 1975. "Visual Pleasure and Narrative Cinema." *Screen* 16 (3). 6–18.

Mulvey, Laura. 2000. "The Index and the Uncanny." In Carolyn Bailey Gill, ed., *Time and the Image*. Manchester: Manchester University Press. 139–148.

Nahin, Paul J. 1993. *Time Machines: Time Travel in Physics, Metaphysics, and Science Fiction*. Woodbury, NY: American Institute of Physics.

Nahin, Paul J. 1999. *Time Machines: Time Travel in Physics, Metaphysics, and Science Fiction*. New York: Springer.

Nahin, Paul J. 2003. *Time Machines: Time Travel in Physics, Metaphysics, and Science*

Fiction. New York: American Institute of Physics.

Nahin, Paul J. 2011. *Time Travel: A Writer's Guide to the Real Science of Plausible Time Travel*, 2d ed. Baltimore: Johns Hopkins University Press.

Navarro-Remesal, Víctor. 2013. *Libertad Dirigida: Análisis Formal del Videojuego Como Sistema, Su Estructura y Su Avataridad*. PhD dissertation. http://hdl.handle.net/10803/111168. Accessed 16 May 2013.

Neale, Steve. 1985. *Cinema and Technology: Image, Sound, Color*. London: Macmillan/BFI.

Newman, James. 2002. "The Myth of the Ergodic Videogame. Some Thoughts on Player–Character Relationships in Videogames." *Game Studies* 2 (1). http://www.gamestudies.org/0102/newman/. Accessed 17 July 2014.

Newman, Kim. 2005. *Doctor Who*. London: BFI.

Ní Fhlainn, Sorcha. 2010. *The Worlds of Back to the Future*. Jefferson, NC: McFarland.

Nodelman, Perry. 1985. "Interpretation and the Apparent Sameness of Children's Novels." *Studies in the Literary Imagination* 18 (2). 5–20.

Noonan, Harold. 2005. *Personal Identity*, 2d ed. London: Routledge.

Novick, Peter. 1988. *That Noble Dream: The "Objectivity Questions" and the American Historical Profession*. New York: Cambridge University Press.

Okuda, Michael, and Denise Okuda. 1993. *Star Trek Chronology: The History of the Future*. New York: Pocket Books.

Okuda, Michael, Denise Okuda, and Debbie Mirek. 2011. *The Star Trek Encyclopedia: A Reference Guide to the Future. Updated and Expanded Edition*. New York: Simon & Schuster.

Orr, Jon. 2009. "Hitch as Matrix Figure: Hitchcock and Twentieth Century Cinema." In Marshall Deutelbaum and Leland Poague, eds., *A Hitchcock Reader*. Chichester: Blackwell. 47–67.

Orwell, George. 1949. *Nineteen Eighty-Four*. London: Secker and Warburg.

Orwell, George. 1970. *Wells, Hitler and the World State*. London: Penguin.

Ovid. 1955. *Metamorphoses*. Trans. Mary M. Innes. London: Penguin.

Papacharissi, Zizi. 2013. "A Networked Self: Identity Performance and Sociability on Social Network Sites." In Francis L.F. Lee, Louis Leung, Jack Linchuan Qiu, Donna S.C. Chu, eds., *Frontiers in New Media Research*. New York: Routledge. 207–221.

Parrinder, Patrick. 1995. *Shadows of the Future: H.G. Wells, Science Fiction, and Prophecy*. Syracuse: Syracuse University Press.

Pearce, Celia. 2004. "Towards a Game Theory of Game." In Noah Wardrip-Fruin and Pat Harrigan, eds., *First Person: New Media as Story, Performance and Game*. Cambridge: MIT Press. 143–153.

Penley, Constance. 1986. "Time Travel, Primal Scene and the Critical Dystopia." *Camera Obscura* 5 (3 15). 66–85.

Penley, Constance. 1990. "Time Travel, Primal Scene and the Critical Dystopia." In Annette Kuhn, ed., *Alien Zone: Cultural Theory and Contemporary Science Fiction Cinema*. London: Verso. 116–127.

Penley, Constance. 1991. *Close Encounters*. Minneapolis: University of Minnesota Press.

Pennebaker, James W., and Becky L. Banasik. 1997. "On the Creation and Maintenance of Collective Memories: History as Social Psychology." In James W. Pennebaker, Bernard Rime, and Dario Paez, eds., *Collective Memory of Political Events: Social Psychological Perspectives*. Mahwah, NJ: Lawrence Erlbaum Associates. 3–20.

Pinsky, Michael. 2003. *Future Present: Ethics and/as Science Fiction*. Carnbury, NJ: Associated University Press.

Pratt, George C. 1989. "Forty-Five Years of Picture Making: An Interview with Cecil B. DeMille." *Film History* 3. 133–145.

Priest, Graham, and Francesco Berto. 2013. "Dialetheism." *Stanford Encyclopedia of Philosophy*. Edward N. Zalta, ed. http://plato.stanford.edu/entries/dialetheism/. Accessed 17 September 2014.

Prigogine, Ilya, and Isabelle Stengers. *Order Out of Chaos: Man's New Dialogue with Nature*. London: Heinemann, 1984.

Ragland, Ellie. 2002. "The Psychical Nature of Trauma: Freud's Dora, the Young Homosexual Woman, and the *Fort! Da!* Paradigm." In Linda Belau and Petar Ramadanovic, eds., *Topologies of Trauma: Essays on the Limit of Knowledge and Memory*. New York: Other Press. 75–100.

Rapp, Bernhard. 2007. "Self-Reflexivity in Computer Games: Analyzes of Selected Examples." In Winfried Nöth and Nina Bishara, eds., *Self-reference in the Media*. Berlin: Walter de Greyter. 253–268.

Rascaroli, Laura. 2001. "Scopic Drive, Time Travel and Film Spectatorship in Gilliam's *Twelve Monkeys* and Bigelow's *Strange Days*." *Kinema: A Journal for Film and Audiovisual Media* 29. 29–41.

Ravetto-Biagioli, Kriss. 2005. "Floating on the Borders of Europe: Sokurov's *Russian Ark*." *Film Quarterly* 59 (1). 18–26.

Rayment-Pickard, Hugh. 2004. *Myths of Time: From Saint Augustine to American Beauty*. London: Darton, Longman and Todd.

Redmond, Sean, ed., 2004. *Liquid Metal*. London: Wallflower Press.

Renzi, Thomas C. 2004. *Six Scientific Romances Adapted for Film*. Lanham, MD: Scarecrow Press.

Reynolds, Richard. 1992. *Superheroes: A Modern Mythology*. Jackson: University Press of Mississippi.

Richmond, Alasdair. 2003. "Recent Work: Time Travel." *Philosophical Books* 44. 297–309.

Rickman, Gregg. 2004. *The Science Fiction Film Reader*. New York: Limelight Editions.

Ricoeur, Paul. 2004. *Memory, History, Forgetting*. Trans. Kathleen Blamey and David Pellauer. Chicago: Chicago University Press.

Rieder, John. 2010. "On Defining SF, or Not: Genre Theory, SF, and History." *Science Fiction Studies* 37 (2). 191–209.

Rodowick, David N. 1997. *Gilles Deleuze's Time Machine*. Durham: Duke University Press.

Rodowick, David N. 2000. "Unthinkable Sex: Conceptual Personae and the Time-Image." *Invisible Culture: An Electronic Journal for Visual Studies* 3. http://www.rochester.edu/in_visible_culture/issue3/rodowick.htm. Accessed October 2013.

Rodowick, David N. 2003. *Gilles Deleuze's Time Machine*. Durham: Duke University Press.

Rodowick, David N. 2007. *The Virtual Life of Film*. Cambridge: Harvard University Press.

Rosenstone, Robert A. 1995. *Visions of the Past: The Challenge of Film to Our Idea of History*. Cambridge: Harvard University Press.

Ryan, Marie-Laure. 2001. *Narrative as Virtual Reality*. Baltimore: Johns Hopkins University Press.

Ryan, Marie-Laure. 2004. *La Narración Como Realidad Virtual: La Inmersión y la Interactividad en la Literatura y en los Medios Electrónicos*. Barcelona: Paidós Comunicación.

Salen, Katie, and Eric Zimmerman. 2004. *Rules of Play: Game Design Fundamentals*. Cambridge: MIT Press.

Salinger, J. 1951. *Catcher in the Rye*. New York: Little, Brown.

Schneider, Susan. 2009. "Thought Experiments: Science Fiction as a Window into Philosophical Puzzles." In Susan Schneider, ed., *Science Fiction and Philosophy: From Time Travel to Superintelligence*. Chichester: Wiley-Blackwell. 1–14.

Schools History Project. 1976. *A New Look at History: Schools History 13–16 Project*. Edinburgh: Homes McDougall.

Scolari, Carlos A., Paolo Bertetti, and Matthew Freeman. 2014. *Transmedia Archaeology: Storytelling in the Borderlines of Science Fiction, Comics and Pulp Magazines*. London: Palgrave Pivot.

Shail, Andrew, and Robin Stoate. 2010. *Back to the Future*. London: BFI.

Shain, Ralph. 2013. "Escape from the Paradox of the Apes." In John Huss, ed., *Planet of the Apes and Philosophy*. Chicago: Open Court. 111–122.

Shary, Timothy. 1998. "Reification and Loss in Postmodern Puberty: The Cultural Logic of Fredric Jameson and American Youth Movies." In Cristina Degli-Esposti, ed., *Postmodernism in the Cinema*. New York: Berghahn Books. 73–89.

Shaviro, Steven. 2010. *Post-Cinematic Affect*. Winchester: Zero Books.

Sherlock, Lee. 2012. "Tres Días en Termina: Zelda y Esa Cosa Tan Rara Llamada Tiempo." In *Extra Life: 10 Juegos Que Han Revolucionado la Cultura Contemporánea*. Madrid: Errata Naturae.

Short, Sue. 2011. *Cult Telefantasy Series: A Critical Analysis of The Prisoner, Twin Peaks, The X-Files, Buffy the Vampire Slayer, Lost, Heroes, Doctor Who and Star Trek*. Jefferson, NC: McFarland.

Sider, Ted. 1997. "A New Grandfather Paradox?" *Philosophy and Phenomenological Research* 57. 139–44.

Siebers, Tobin. 2008. *Disability Theory*. Ann Arbor: University of Michigan Press.

Siebers, Tobin. 2010. *Disability Aesthetics*. Ann Arbor: University of Michigan Press.

Silverberg, Robert. 1968. *The Masks of Time*. New York: Ballantine.

Slusser, George. 1995. "Spacetime Geometries: Time Travel and the Modern Geometrical Narrative." *Science Fiction Studies* 22 (2). 161–186.

Slusser, George, Patrick Parrinder and Danièle Chatelain, eds. 2001. *H. G. Wells' Perennial Time Machine*. Athens: University of Georgia Press.

Smith, Nicholas. 2005. "Why Would Time Travelers Try to Kill Their Younger Selves?" *The Monist* 88. 388–95.

Sobchack, Vivian. 1987. *Screening Space: The American Science Fiction Film*. New York: Ungar.

Sorolla, Teresa, and Shaila García-Catalán. 2013. "El MacGuffin Es el Film: Destinos Carnavalescos de las Narrativas Complejas Hoy." *Archivos de la Filmoteca* 72. 105–117.

Spigel, Lynn. 2001. *Welcome to the Dreamhouse: Popular Media and Postwar Suburbs*. Durham: Duke University Press.

Stanfield, Peter. 1996. "Country Music and the 1939 Western: From Hillbillies to Cowboys." In Ian Cameron and Douglas Pye, eds., *The Movie Book of the Western*. London: Studio Vista. 22–33.

Stein, Ruthe. 1998. "Ross' Memories of the '50s Populate *Pleasantville*." *The San Francisco Chronicle*. 28 October. E1.

Stephen, Awoniyi. 2001. "The Contemporary Museum and Leisure: Recreation as a Museum Function." *Museum Management and Curatorship* 19 (3). 297–308.

Stewart, Garrett. 2007. *Framed Time: Toward a Postfilmic Cinema*. Chicago: University of Chicago Press.

Tannock, Stuart. 1995. "Nostalgia Critique." *Cultural Studies* 9 (3). 453–464.

Thomas, Sue. 2006. "The End of Cyberspace and Other Surprises." *Convergence: The International Journal of Research into New Media Technologies* 12 (4). 383–391.

Thompson, Anne. 1992. "Beyond-the-Pale Riders." *Film Comment* 28 (4). 52–54.

Todd, Patrick. 2011. "Geachianism." *Oxford Studies in Philosophy of Religion* 3. 222–51.

Todorov, Tzvetan. 1973. *The Fantastic: A Structural Approach to a Literary Genre*. Trans. Richard Howard. Cleveland: The Press of Case Western Reserve University.

Twain, Mark. 1884. *The Adventures of Huckleberry Finn*. London: Chatto and Windus.

Twain, Mark. 1889. *A Connecticut Yankee in King Arthur's Court*. New York: Marple and Brothers.

Twain, Mark. 1996. *The Personal Recollections of Joan of Arc*. New York: Oxford University Press.

Uttley, Alison. 1939. *A Traveler in Time*. London: Faber.

van Inwagen, Peter. 2010. "Changing the Past." *Oxford Studies in Metaphysics* 5. 3–28.

VanWinkle, Matthew. 2007. "Tennyson's 'Tithonus' and the Exhaustion of Survival in *The X-Files*." In Sharon R. Yang, ed., *The X-Files and Literature: Unweaving the Story, Unraveling the Lie to Find the Truth*. Newcastle: Cambridge Scholars. 298–311.

Variety Staff. 31 December 1970. "Review: *Escape from the Planet of the Apes*." *Variety*.

Vecchi, Bruno. 28 December 1996. "Vanzina e gli USA fanno il pienone." *L'Unità*. 27.

Wagar, W. Warren. 2004. *H. G. Wells: Traversing Time*. Middletown, CT: Wesleyan University Press.

Wallace, Elizabeth Kowaleski. 2006. *The British Slave Trade and Public Memory*. New York: Columbia University Press.

Wandtke, Terence, ed. 2007. *The Amazing Transforming Superhero! Essays on the Revision of Characters in Comic Books, Film and Television*. Jefferson, NC: McFarland.

Warf, Barney. 2002. "The Way It Wasn't: Alternative Histories, Contingent Geographies." In R. Kitchin and J. Kneale, eds., *Lost in Space: Geographies of Science Fiction*. London: Continuum. 17–38.

Watson, Ian. 1978. "The Very Slow Time Machine." In Christopher Priest, ed., *Anticipations*. New York: Charles Scribner's Sons.

Wattenberg, Daniel. 1998. "Unpleasantville: How the 1950s Looked in the 1960s." *The Weekly Standard*. 9 November. 38.

Weatherson, Brian. 2009. "David Lewis."

Stanford Encyclopedia of Philosophy, Summer 2010. Edward N. Zalta, ed. http://plato.stanford.edu/entries/david-lewis/. Accessed 17 September 2014.

Wells, H. G. 1888. "The Chronic Argonauts." http://www.colemanzone.com/Time_Machine_Project/chronic.htm. Accessed August 2012.

Wells, H. G. 1895. *The Time Machine*. London: Heinemann.

Wells, H. G. 1968. *The War of the Worlds*. London: Heinmann.

Wells, H. G. 1971. *The Time Machine*. Cambridge, MA: R. Bentley.

Wells, H. G. 1984. *An Experiment in Autobiography*. Boston: Little, Brown, 1984.

Wells, H. G. 2001. *The Time Machine*. London: Everyman.

Wheatley, Helen. 2012. "Uncanny Children, Haunted Houses, Hidden Rooms: Children's Gothic Television in the 1970s and '80s." *Visual Culture in Britain* 13 (3). 383–397.

White, Hayden. 1987. *The Content of the Form: National Discourse and Historical Representation*. Baltimore: Johns Hopkins University Press.

White, Hayden. 1990. *Tropics of Discourse: Essays in Cultural Criticism*. Baltimore: Johns Hopkins University Press.

White, Mimi. 1992. *Tele-Advising: Therapeutic Discourse in American Television*. Chapel Hill: University of North Carolina Press.

White, Susan. 1991. "Allegory and Referentiality: *Vertigo* and Feminist Criticism." *Modern Language Notes* 106 (5). 910–932.

Whitmore, Jim. August 1975. "Outlines of Tomorrow." *Planet of the Apes Magazine* 11. Magazine Management Co.

Williams, Keith. 2007. *H. G. Wells: Modernism and the Movies*. Liverpool: Liverpool University Press.

Williams, Keith. 2009. "Victorian Cinemacity and H. G. Wells's Early Scientific Romances." *Comparative Critical Studies* 6. 347–360.

Winogura, Dale. Summer 1972. "Apes, Apes, and More Apes." *Cinefantastique* 2 (2). 16–37.

Wittenberg, David. 2012. *Time Travel: The Popular Philosophy of Narrative*. New York: Fordham University Press.

Wittenberg, David. 2013. *Time Travel: The Popular Philosophy of Narrative*. New York: Fordham University Press.

Wittgenstein, Ludwig. 1953. *Philosophical Investigations*. Trans. G.E.M. Anscombe. Oxford: Basil Blackwell.

Wolf, Mark J.P. 2003. "Abstraction in the Video Game." In Mark J.P. Wolf and Bernard Perron, eds., *The Video Game Theory Reader*. New York: Routledge. 47–66.

Zagal, Jose, and Michael Mateas. 2010. "Time in Video Games: A Survey and Analysis." *Simulation and Gaming* 41 (6). 844–868.

Zagzebski, Linda. 2011. "Foreknowledge and Free Will." *Stanford Encyclopedia of Philosophy*, Fall 2011. Edward N. Zalta, ed., http://plato.stanford.edu/entries/free-will-foreknowledge/. Accessed 17 September 2014.

Zimmerman, Eric. 2004. "Narrative, Interactivity, Play, and Games: Four Naughty Concepts in Need of Discipline." In Noah Wardrip-Fruin and Pat Harrigan, eds., *First Person: New Media as Story, Performance and Game*. Cambridge: MIT Press. 154–164.

Filmography

Films

About Time (Richard Curtis, 2013).

Adam's Rib (Cecil B. DeMille, 1923).

The Amazing Spider-Man (Marc Webb, 2012).

Amici Miei (Mario Monicelli, 1975).

The Animatrix (Mahiro Maeda *et al.*, 2003)

Annie Hall (Woody Allen, 1977).

Back to the Future (Robert Zemeckis, 1985).

Back to the Future Part II (Robert Zemeckis, 1989).

Back to the Future Part III (Robert Zemeckis, 1990).

Batman Begins (Christopher Nolan, 2005).

Battle for Planet of the Apes (J. Lee Thompson, 1973).

Beneath the Planet of the Apes (Ted Post, 1970).

The Big Country (William Wyler, 1958).

Bill and Ted's Excellent Adventure (Stephen Hereck, 1989).

The Birth of a Nation (David W. Griffith, 1915).

Blade Runner (Ridley Scott, 1982).

The Blue Yonder (Mark Rosman, 1985).

The Butterfly Effect (Eric Bress and J. Mackye Gruber, 2004).

Carrie (Kimberly Peirce, 2013).

City Slickers (Ron Underwood, 1991).

Cloud Atlas (Tom Tykwer and Andy Wachowski, 2012).

A Connecticut Yankee (David Butler, 1931).

Connecticut Yankee in the Court of King Arthur (Emmett J. Flynn, 1921).

Connecticut Yankee in the Court of King Arthur (Tay Garnett, 1949).

Conquest of Planet of the Apes (J. Lee Thompson, 1972).

The Covered Wagon (James Cruze, 1923).

Dances with Wolves (Kevin Costner, 1990).

Dark City (Alex Proyas, 1998).

The Dark Knight (Christopher Nolan, 2008).

The Dark Knight Rises (Christopher Nolan, 2012).

The Day the Earth Stood Still (Scott Derrickson, 2008).

The Devil-Stone (Cecil B. DeMille, 1917).

Il Disco Volante (Tinto Brass, 1964).

Dodge City (Michael Curtiz, 1939).

Donnie Darko (Richard Kelly, 2001).

Dubarry Was a Lady (Roy Del Ruth, 1943).

Easy Rider (Dennis Hopper, 1969).

Edge of Tomorrow (Doug Liman, 2014).

The End of St. Petersburg / Konets Sankt-Peterburga (Vsevolod Pudovkin, 1927).

Enemy of the State (Tony Scott, 1998).

Escape from Planet of the Apes (Don Taylor, 1971).

Eternal Sunshine of the Spotless Mind (Michel Gondry, 2004).

The Evil Dead (Fede Alvarez, 2013).

Fantozzi (Luciano Salce, 1975).

Fantozzi Contro Tutti (Neri Parenti, 1980).

Feet of Clay (Cecil B. DeMille, 1924).

The Final Cut (Omar Naïm, 2004).

The Fisher King (Terry Gilliam, 1991).

A Fistful of Dollars (Sergio Leone, 1964).

For Better For Worse (Cecil B. DeMille, 1919).

Frequency (Gregory Hoblit, 2000).

The Good, the Bad and the Ugly (Sergio Leone, 1966).

La Grande Guerra (Mario Monicelli, 1959).

Groundhog Day (Harold Ramis, 1993).

Hells Angels (Lee Maddon, 1969).

Hot Tub Time Machine (Steve Pink, 2010).

The Hunchback of Notre Dame (Wallace Worsley, 1923).

Inception (Christopher Nolan, 2010).

Intolerance: Love's Struggle through the Ages (D. W. Griffith, 1916).

Joan the Woman (Cecil B. DeMille, 1917).

Jesse James (Henry King, 1939).

La Jetée (Chris Marker, 1962).

Last Year in Marienbad (Alain Resnais, 1961).

L'Ombrellone (Dino Risi, 1966).

Looper (Rian Johnson, 2012).

Male and Female (Cecil B. DeMille, 1919).

Man of Steel (Zack Snyder, 2013).

The Man Who Shot Liberty Valance (John Ford, 1962).

I Marziani Hanno 12 Mani (Franco Castellano and Giuseppe Moccia, 1964).

The Matrix (Andy Wachowski and Lana Wachowski, 1999).

The Matrix Reloaded (Andy Wachowski and Lana Wachowski, 2003).

Metropolis (Fritz Lang, 1927).

Midnight in Paris (Woody Allen, 2011).

Minority Report (Steven Spielberg, 2002).

Moulin Rouge (Baz Luhrmann, 2001).

Momento (Christopher Nolan, 2000).

My Darling Clementine (John Ford, 1946).

Non Ci Resta Che Piangere (Roberto Benigni and Massimo Troisi, 1984).

October / Oktyabr (Grigori Aleksandrov and Sergei Eisenstein, 1927).

Omicron (Ugo Gregoretti, 1963).

Once Upon a Time in the West (Sergio Leone, 1968).

Open Your Eyes/ Abre los Ojos (Alejandro Amenábar, 1997).

Peggy Sue Got Married (Francis Ford Coppola, 1986).

Planet of the Apes (Franklin J. Schaffner, 1968).

Play It Again, Sam (Woody Allen, 1972).

Pleasantville (Gary Ross, 1998).

Portrait of Jennie (William Dieterle, 1948).

Primer (Shane Carruth, 2004).

Prometheus (Ridley Scott, 2012).

The Purple Rose of Cairo (Woody Allen, 1985).

The Road to Yesterday (Cecil B. DeMille, 1925).

Robocop (José Padilha, 2014).

Rope (Alfred Hitchcock, 1948).

Russian Ark / Russkiy Kovcheg (Alexander Sokurov, 2002).

Safety Not Guaranteed (Colin Trevorrow, 2012).

Sapore di Mare (Carlo Vanzina, 1983).

Il Secondo Tragico Fantozzi (Luciano Salce, 1976).

Shadows and Fog (Woody Allen, 1991).

Shutter Island (Martin Scorsese, 2010).

Sleeper (Woody Allen, 1973).

Something to Think About (Cecil B. DeMille, 1920).

Somewhere in Time (Jeannot Szwarc, 1980).

Il Sorpasso (Dino Risi, 1962).

Source Code (Duncan Jones, 2011).

A Spasso nel Tempo (Carlo Vanzina, 1996).

A Spasso nel Tempo 2: L'Avventura Continua (Carlo Vanzina, 1997).

Stagecoach (John Ford, 1939).

Stardust Memories (Woody Allen, 1980).

Star Trek (J. J. Abrams, 2009).

Star Trek II: The Wrath of Khan (Nicholas Meyer, 1982).

Star Trek into Darkness (J. J. Abrams, 2012).

Star Trek IV: The Voyage Home (Leonard Nimoy, 1986).

Superfantozzi (Neri Parenti, 1986).

Superman (Ricghard Donner, 1978).

The Ten Commandments (Cecil B. DeMille, 1923).

The Terminator (James Cameron, 1984).

Terminator 2: Judgment Day (James Cameron, 1991).

Terminator 3: Rise of the Machines (Jonathan Mostow, 2003).

Terminator Salvation (McG, 2009).

THX 1138 (George Lucas, 1971).

Time After Time (Nicholas Meyer, 1979).

Time Bandits (Terry Gilliam, 1989).

Timecop (Peter Hyams, 1994).

Timecrimes / Los Cronocrímenes (Nacho Vigalondo, 2007).

The Time Machine (George Pal, 1960).

The Time Machine (Simon Wells, 2002).

Timescape (David Twohy, 1991).

The Time Traveler's Wife (Robert Schwentke, 2009).

Total Recall (Paul Verhoeven, 1990).

Totò, Peppino e la Malafemmina (Camillo Mastrocinque, 1956).

Triangle (Christopher Smith, 2009).

Twelve Monkeys (Terry Gilliam, 1995).

12.01 (Jack Sholder, 1993).

2001: A Space Odyssey (Kubrick, Stanley, 1968).

Unforgiven (Clint Eastwood, 1992).

Vacanze di Natale (Carlo Vanzina, 1983).

Vertigo (Alfred Hitchcock, 1958).

Virtual Nightmare (Michael Pattinson, 2000).

Les Visiteurs (Jean-Marie Poiré, 1993).

War of the Worlds (Steven Spielberg, 2005).

Westworld (Michael Crichton, 1973).

The Wild One (László Benedek, 1953).

The Wizard of Oz (Victor Fleming, 1939).

X-Men: Days of Future Past (Bryan Singer, 2014).

Zelig (Woody Allen, 1983).

Television Series/Episodes

"All Good Things ... Parts I and II." *Star Trek: The Next Generation.* Originally aired 23 May 1994. CBS.

"The Angels Take Manhattan." *Doctor Who.* Originally aired 29 September 2012. BBC.

"The Big Bang." *Doctor Who.* Originally aired 26 June 2010. BBC.

The Black and White Minstrel Show. Originally aired 14 June 1958–21 July 1978. BBC.

"City on the Edge of Forever." *Star Trek.* Originally aired 6 April 1967. NBC.

"Clyde Bruckman's Final Repose." *The X-Files.* Originally aired 13 October 1995. Fox.

"The Day of the Doctor." *Doctor Who.* Originally aired 23 November 2013. BBC.

Doctor Who. Originally aired 23 November 1963–6 December 1989, 12 May 1996 and 26 March 2005–present. BBC.

Edward the Seventh. Originally aired 1 April 1975–1 July 1975. ITV/ATV.

"Endgame." *Star Trek: Voyager.* Originally aired 23 May 2001. Paramount.

"Escape from Ape City." *Return to the Planet of the Apes.* Originally aired 13 September 1975. NBC.

Father Knows Best. Originally aired 3 October 1954–17 September 1960. CBS and NBC.

"The Fires of Pompeii." *Doctor Who.* Originally aired 12 April 2008. BBC.

The Flintstones. Originally aired 30 September 1960–1 April 1966. ABC.

Futurama. Originally aired 28 March 1999–10 August 2003 and 23 March 2008–4 September 2013. Fox.

The Georgian House. Originally aired 2 January 1976–13 February 1976. HTV West.

Goodnight Sweetheart. Originally aired 18 November–28 June 1999. BBC.

It Ain't Half Hot, Mum. Originally aired 3 January 1974–3 September 1981. BBC.

Leave It to Beaver. Originally aired 7 October 1957–20 June 1963. CBS.

Lost. Originally aired 22 September 2004–23 May 2010. ABC.

Love Thy Neighbor. Originally aired 13 April 1972–22 January 1976. ITV.

"Max." *The X-Files.* Originally aired 23 March 1997. Fox

"Monday." *The X-Files.* Originally aired 28 February 1999. Fox.

"The Myth Makers." *Doctor Who.* Originally aired 16 October–6 November 1965. BBC.

"Operation—Annihilate!." *Star Trek.* Originally aired 13 April 1967. NBC.

Poldark. Originally aired 5 October 1975–4 December 1977. BBC.

Puck of Pook's Hill. Originally aired 25 September 1951. BBC.

Quantum Leap. Originally aired 26 March 1989–5 May 1993. NBC.

Red Dwarf. Originally aired 15 February 1988–5 April 1999, 10 April 2009–12 April 2009 and 4 October 2012–present. BBC and Dave.

Return to the Planet of the Apes. Originally aired 6 September 1975–4 September 1976. 20th Century–Fox Television.

"Shadow Play." *The Twilight-Zone.* Originally aired 5 May 1961. CBS.

The Simpsons. Originally aired 17 October 1989–present. Fox.

"Space Seed." *Star Trek.* Originally aired 16 February 1967. NBC.

"The Space Museum." *Doctor Who.* Originally aired 24 April–15 May 1965. BBC.

Star Trek: Enterprise. Originally aired 26 September 2001–13 May 2005. CBS.

Star Trek: The Next Generation. Originally aired 28 September 1987–23 May 1994. CBS.

"Synchrony." *The X-Files.* Originally aired 13 April 1997. Fox.

"Tempus Fugit." *The X-Files.* Originally aired 16 March 1997. Fox.

"Tempus Fugitive." *Lois and Clark: The New Adventures of Superman.* Originally aired 26 March 1995. ABC.

"Timelash" *Doctor Who.* Originally aired 9 March–16 March 1985. BBC.

"The Time of Angels." *Doctor Who.* Originally aired 24 April 2010. BBC.

The Time Tunnel. Originally aired 9 September 1966–7 April 1967. ABC.

"Tithonus." *The X-Files.* Originally aired 24 January 1999. Fox.

Torchwood. Originally aired 22 October 2006–9 September 2011. BBC and Starz.

A Traveler in Time. Originally aired 4 January 1978–1 February 1978. BBC.

"Trials and Tribble-ations." *Star Trek: Deep Space Nine.* Originally aired 4 November 1996. Paramount.

"Triangle." *The X-Files*. Originally aired 22 November 1998. Fox.

"Unification I." *Star Trek: The Next Generation*. Originally aired 4 November 1991. CBS.

Upstairs, Downstairs. Originally aired 10 October 1971–21 December 1975. ITV/ LWT.

Warehouse 13. Originally aired 7 July 2009– 19 May 2014. Syfy.

"The Wedding of River Song." *Doctor Who*. Originally aired 1 October 2011. BBC.

"The Wheel." *Mad Men*. Originally aired 18 October 2007. AMC.

"Where No Man Has Gone Before." *Star Trek*. Originally aired 22 September 1966. NBC.

The X-Files. Originally aired 10 September 1993–19 May 2002. Twentieth Century– Fox Television.

Comics, Games, Other Works

Comics

Conway, Jerry, and Doug Moench. *Planet of the Apes Magazine*. New York: Marvel Comics. August 1974–February 1977.

Conway, Jerry, and Doug Moench. "Future History Chronicles." *Planet of the Apes Magazine*. Issues 12, 15, 17, 29. New York: Marvel Comics, 1975–1977.

Conway, Jerry, and Doug Moench. "Kingdom on an Island of Apes." *Planet of the Apes Magazine*. Issues 9–10. New York: Marvel Comics, 1975.

Moore, Alan, and Dave Gibbons. *Watchmen*. New York: DC Comics, 1986.

Morrison, Grant. *Batman: The Return of Bruce Wayne*. New York: DC Comics, 2010.

Video Games

Animal Crossing (Nintendo, 2001).
Braid (Number None, 2008).
Catherine (Atlus Persona Team, 2011).
Day of the Tentacle (LucasArts, 1993).
Enter the Matrix (Shiny Entertainment, 2003).
Eternal Darkness: Sanity's Requiem (Silicon Knights, 2002).
The Legend of Zelda: Majora's Mask (Nintendo, 2000).
Maniac Mansion (LucasArts, 1987).
Mortal Kombat (NetherRealm Studios, 2011).
Pac-Man: Adventures in Time (Creative Asylum, 2000).
Prince of Persia (Brøderbund, 1989).
Prince of Persia: The Sands of Time (Ubisoft Montreal, 2003).
Save the Date (Chris Cornell, 2013).
Superhot (SUPERHOT Team, 2013).
Super Mario Bros. (Nintendo, 1985).
Teenage Mutant Ninja Turtles: Turtles in Time (Konami, 1991).
Wild Gunman (Nintendo, 1984).

Digital Narratives

Norris, Andrew. "Solar Pons's War of the Worlds." *The Solar Pons Gazette*. 2008. http://www.solarpons.com/Annual_2008_1.pdf. Accessed 18 September 2014.

Music Videos

"Closing Time." Semisonic. Dir. Chris Applebaum. MCA. 1998.

Web Serials

Cataclysmo and the Battle for Earth. Originally released 4 April 2008. New Renaissance Pictures. https://www.youtube.com/playlist?list=PL1D6380E63915DBEF. Accessed 18 September 2014.

About the Contributors

David **Blanke** is a professor of history at Texas A&M University—Corpus Christi. He is the author of *Sowing the American Dream: How Consumer Culture Took Root in the Rural Midwest* (2000), *The 1910s* (2002), and *Hell on Wheels: The Promise and Peril of America's Car Culture, 1900–1940* (2007).

Giacomo **Boitani** earned a Ph.D. in film studies from the National University of Ireland, Galway. His articles and reviews have appeared in journals such as *Senses of Cinema, Alphaville, Kinema, Status Quaestionis, Slovo*, and in the edited collection *The Great War in Italy—Representation and Interpretation* (2013).

Paul **Booth** is an associate professor of media and cinema studies at DePaul University in Chicago. He is the editor of *Fan Phenomena: Doctor Who* (2013), and the author of *Game Play: Paratextuality in Contemporary Board Games* (2015), *Time on TV: Temporal Displacement and Mashup Television* (2012) and *Digital Fandom: New Media Studies* (2010).

Charles **Burnetts** teaches film in the Department of Philosophy and Religious Studies at Kings University College, the University of Western Ontario. He wrote *Improving Passions: Sentimental Aesthetics and American Film* (forthcoming 2015). He has published articles in *Scope* and *The New Review of Film and Television Studies*.

Victoria **Byard** is a Ph.D. candidate at the University of Leicester. Her research is part of the AHRC-funded Spaces of Television project at the Universities of Reading, South Wales, and Leicester, and examines children's television fantasy drama, 1955–1994. She has published on *The Sarah Jane Adventures* and 1950s children's drama.

David **Deamer** lectures on cinema at Manchester Metropolitan University and is co-founder of *A/V*. He is the author of *Deleuze, Japanese Cinema and the Atom Bomb* (2014), and has been published in *Deleuze and Film* (2012) and the *Deleuze Studies* journal. His research interests includes Nietzsche and Hollywood sci-fi.

Jason N. **Dittmer** is a reader in human geography at University College London and is the author of *Captain America and the Nationalist Superhero* (2013).

Eleanor **Dobson** is a Ph.D. candidate at the University of Birmingham researching ancient Egypt in late Victorian fiction. She is also interested in the supernatural, the Gothic and science fiction from the nineteenth century to the present day.

Nikk **Effingham** is a senior lecturer at the University of Birmingham. His research interests include the philosophy of time, ontology, and the philosophy of religion.

He is the author of *An Introduction to Ontology* (2013). Other research interests include the philosophy of time travel.

Pete **Falconer** is a lecturer in film at the University of Bristol. He has published work on the forms and genres of popular cinema (particularly Westerns) and on other aspects of popular culture (including music).

Matthew **Freeman** is a visiting lecturer in media and communication at Birmingham City University, and holds a Ph.D. from the University of Nottingham. His research interests include transmedia, convergence, branding and promotion, and media-industry research. He is the author (with Carlos Scolari and Paolo Bertetti) of *Transmedia Archaeology: Storytelling in the Borderlines of Science Fiction, Comics and Pulp Magazines* (2014).

Jacqueline **Furby** is a senior lecturer and the course leader of film at Southampton Solent University. She has published on time in *American Beauty* and in the TV show *24* and on Terry Gilliam's films. She is a co-author of the Routledge guide to fantasy film (2011).

Rosalind **Fursland** is completing an Ph.D. in English literature at the University of Birmingham. While primarily focussing on modernist New York writers, she also has an interest in science-fiction in literature, film and television.

Shaila **García-Catalán** is a researcher in communication at the Universitat Jaime I of Castellón, Spain. Her Ph.D. dissertation deals with science fiction, neuroscience and hypertexts. She teaches visual culture and mass media in a game design degree and is interested in complex contemporary narratives.

Owen R. **Horton** is a Ph.D. candidate at the University of Kentucky, where he specializes in film, masculinity and cultural criticism. He has a forthcoming article on comic book films in *Critical Insights: The Comic Book*.

Matthew **Jones** is a lecturer in cinema and television history at De Montfort University. He specializes in audiences, memory and genre. He has published work on *Doctor Who* and *Battlestar Galactica*. Other research interests include the reception of 1950s science fiction cinema in Britain.

Dolly **Jørgensen**, an environmental historian at Umeå University, Sweden, has written on medieval forestry and urban sanitation, the modern practice of converting offshore oil structures into artificial reefs, and environmentalism in science fiction. She also studies animal reintroduction and ideas of belonging in Scandinavia.

Matthew **Kimberley** is a Ph.D. student at University College London, studying the imagined geographies of the Marvel universe across a range of media. His research work spans linguistics, textual studies, social and cultural history, film and visual arts, and human geography.

Dario **Llinares** is a senior lecturer in film at Falmouth University. His research on masculinities include *The Astronaut: Cultural Mythology and Idealised Masculinity* (2011) and he has co-edited journals on austerity culture and networked knowledge.

He also leads "Interactive Spectatorships," a project investigating new forms of cinematic spectatorship in the digital age.

Travis L. **Martin** teaches at the University of Kentucky and studies war literature, sci-fi films, and psychoanalytic trauma theory. His forthcoming dissertation examines veterans' writing/arts communities, including Military Experience & the Arts, a non-profit he founded after designing America's first minor in "Veterans Studies" at Eastern Kentucky University.

Víctor **Navarro-Remesal** is a researcher in video game design theory. His Ph.D. dissertation presents "directed freedom" as the basis of the relationship between player and discourse. He teaches video games at CESAG, in Palma de Mallorca (Spain), and his interests are player representation, agency, freedom and game structure.

Elissa **Nelson** teaches in the Film and Media Studies Department at Purchase College, State University of New York. She has published work on 1980s Hollywood and on film industry strategies. She also studies media industries, genre studies, and representations of youth.

Joan **Ormrod** is a senior lecturer in the Department of Media at Manchester Metropolitan University. Her research interests include science fiction and fantasy in the media. She edits Routledge's *Journal of Graphic Novels and Comics* and is part of the committee organizing the International Graphic Novel and Comics Conference. Her latest publication is the co-edited *Superheroes and Identities* (2014).

Sofia **Pantouvaki** is a scenographer and professor of costume design at Aalto University, Finland. Her design credits include over sixty theater, opera and dance productions. She is the co-author of *History of Dress: The Western World and Greece* (2010) and co-editor of *Presence and Absence: The Performing Body* (2014).

Michael **Starr** lectures in film and screen studies at the University of Northampton. His research interests concern philosophical conceptions of science fiction media; recent publications include a co-edited journal collection on the works of Alan Moore and book articles on Joss Whedon and the TV series *Dollhouse*.

Elena **Trencheva** is a post-doctoral researcher in costume design at Aalto University, Finland, and an active costume and production designer. She is the author of *From Metropolis to the Matrix: Semiotics of Costume in Science Fiction Film* (2009) and a number of articles on film costume.

Index